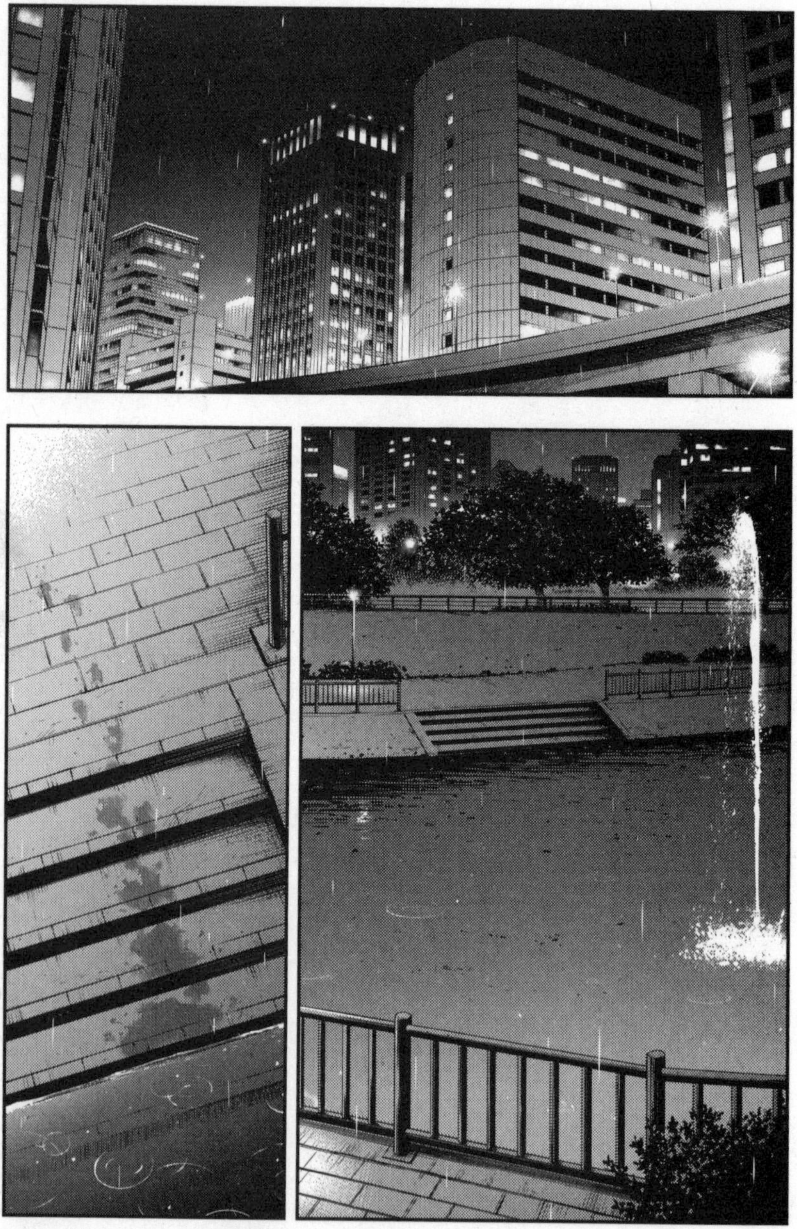

#104 INTRUDER ①

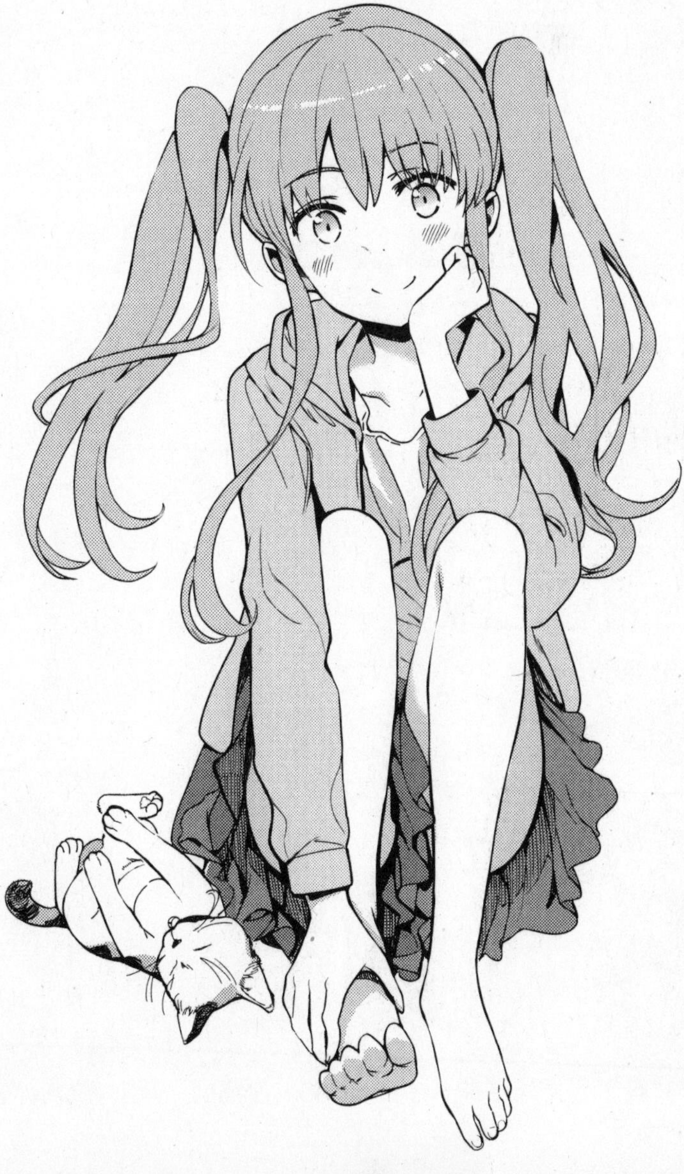

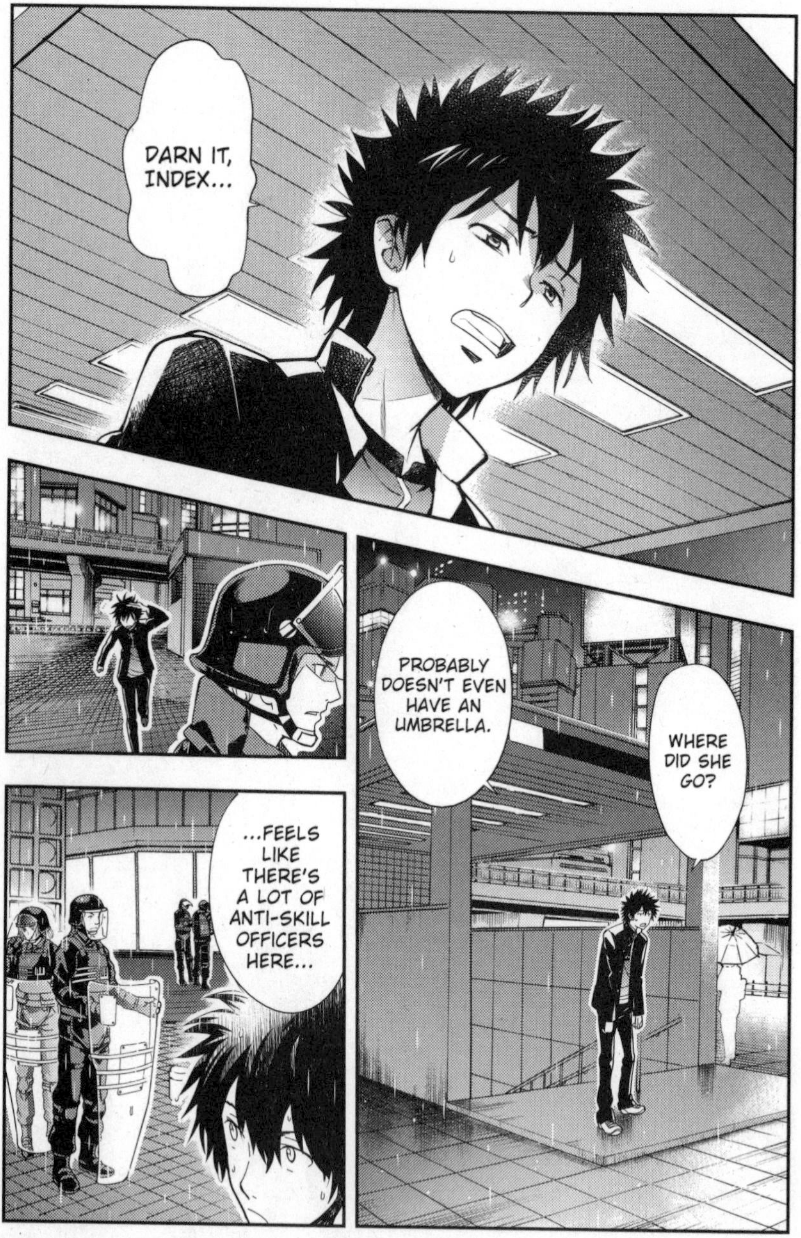
DARN IT, INDEX...
WHERE DID SHE GO?
PROBABLY DOESN'T EVEN HAVE AN UMBRELLA.
...FEELS LIKE THERE'S A LOT OF ANTI-SKILL OFFICERS HERE...

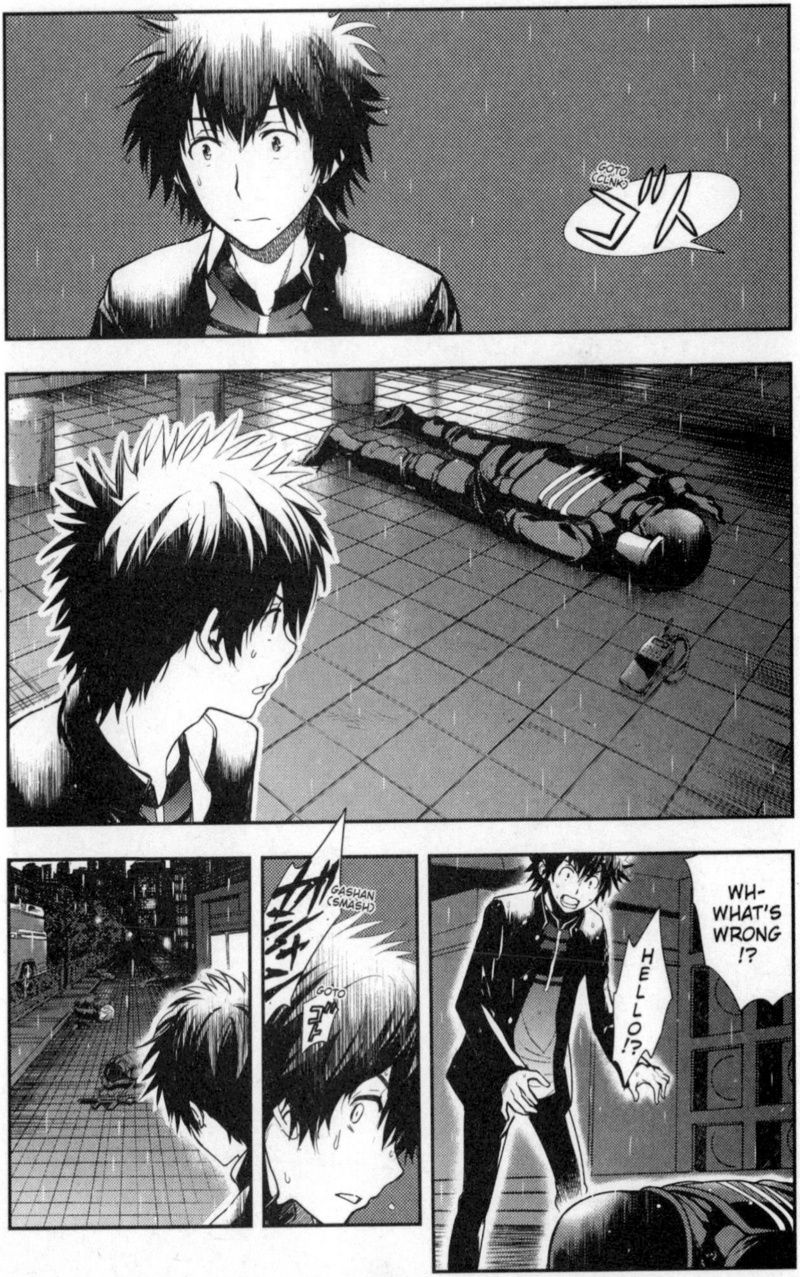
GOTO (CLNK)
WH-WHAT'S WRONG!?
HELLO!?
GASHAN (SMASH)
GOTO

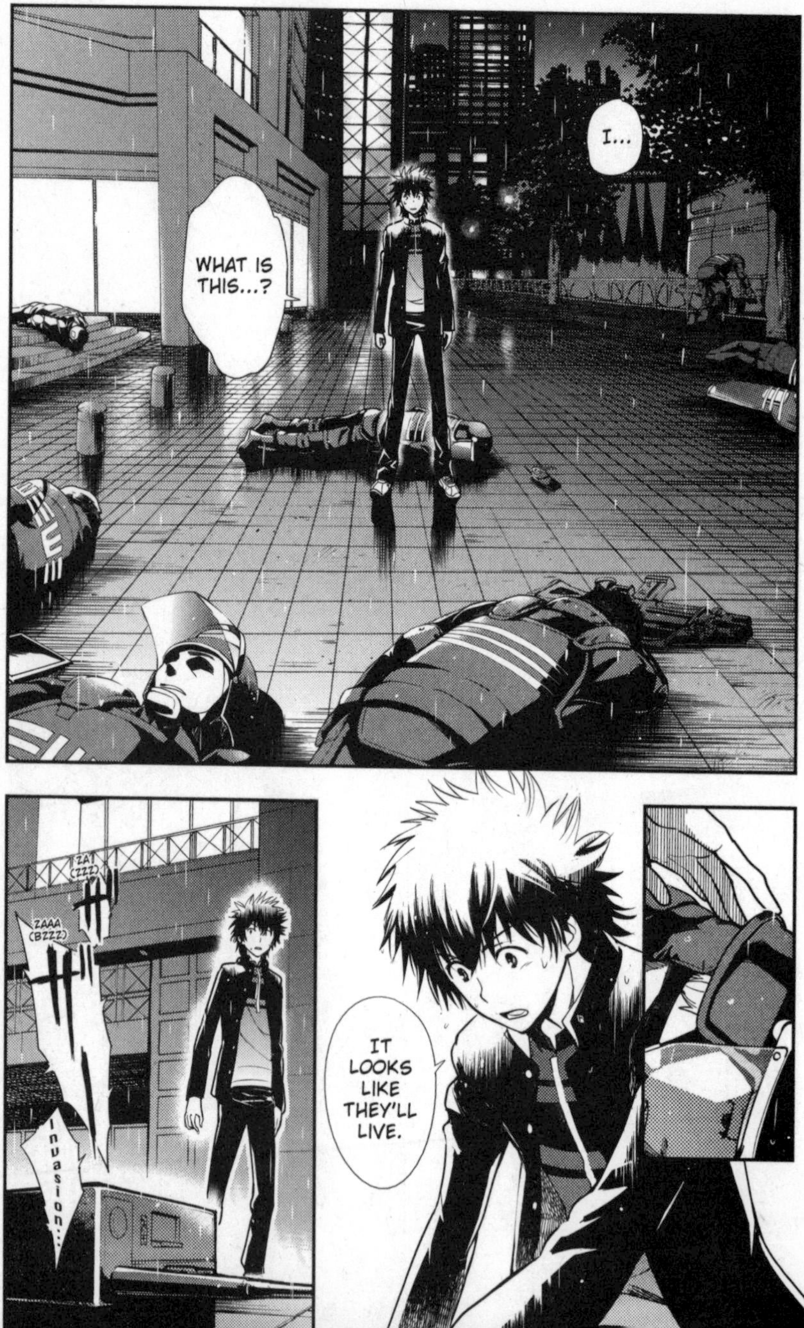

I...
WHAT IS THIS...?
IT LOOKS LIKE THEY'LL LIVE.
ZAT (ZZZZ)
ZAAA (BZZZ)
Invasion...

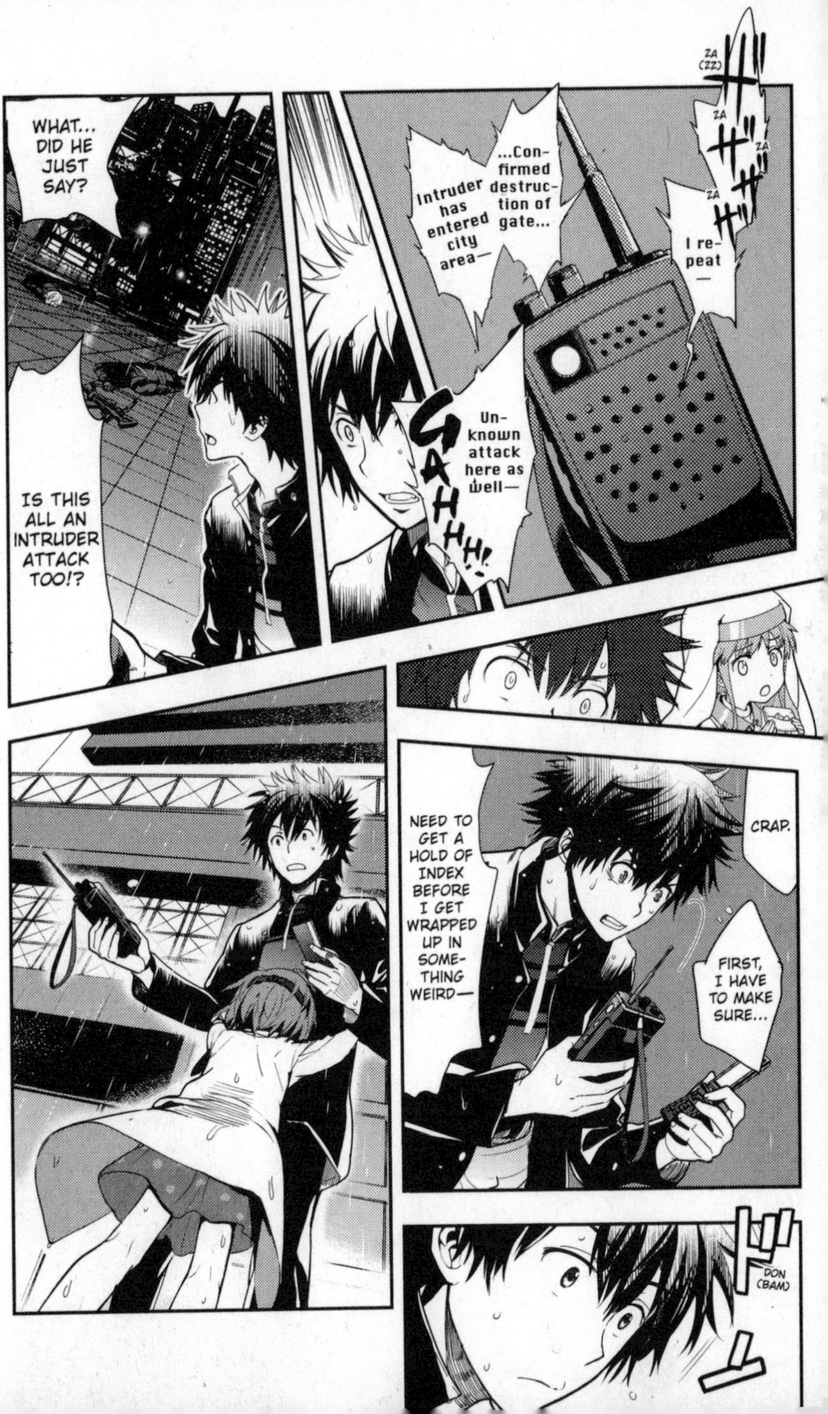
ZA (ZZ)
ZA
ZA
ZA
I re-peat—
...Con-firmed destruc-tion of gate...
Intruder has entered city area—
Un-known attack here as well—
GAHHH!!
WHAT... DID HE JUST SAY?
IS THIS ALL AN INTRUDER ATTACK TOO!?
CRAP.
FIRST, I HAVE TO MAKE SURE...
NEED TO GET A HOLD OF INDEX BEFORE I GET WRAPPED UP IN SOME-THING WEIRD—
DON (BAM)

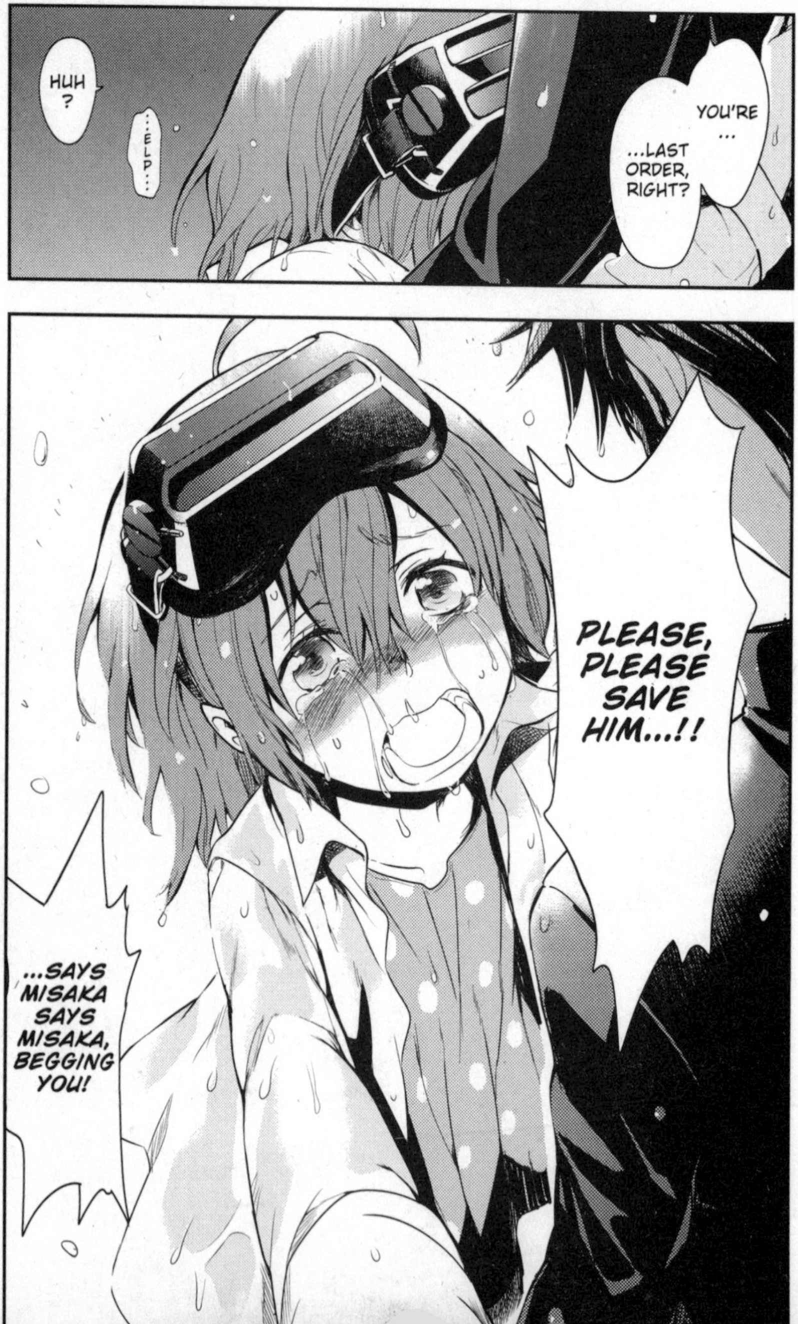
YOU'RE ... ...LAST ORDER, RIGHT?
...ELP...
HUH ?
PLEASE, PLEASE SAVE HIM...!!
...SAYS MISAKA SAYS MISAKA, BEGGING YOU!

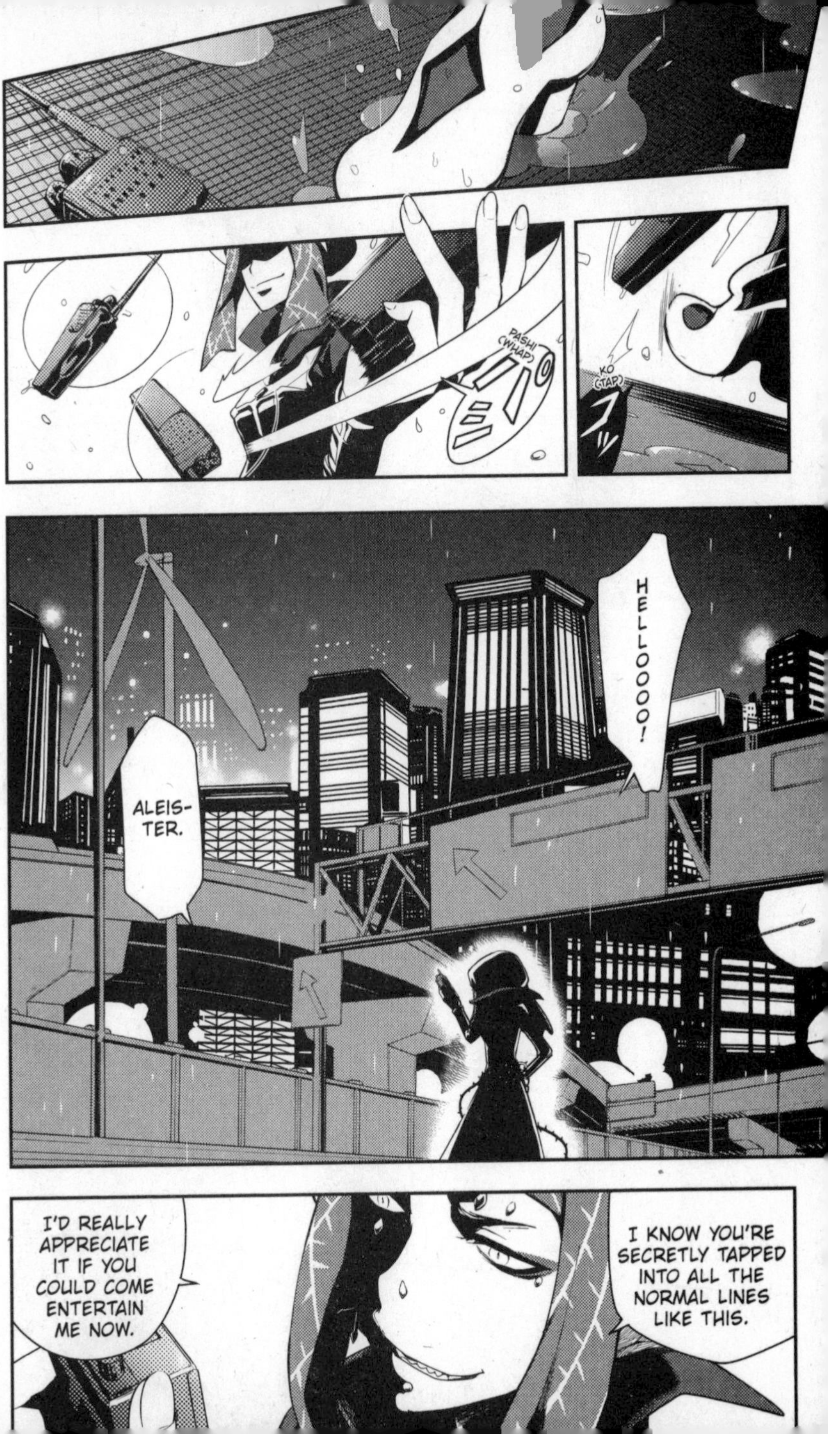
KO (TAP)
PASHI (WHAP)
HELLOOOO!
ALEISTER.
I KNOW YOU'RE SECRETLY TAPPED INTO ALL THE NORMAL LINES LIKE THIS.
I'D REALLY APPRECIATE IT IF YOU COULD COME ENTERTAIN ME NOW.

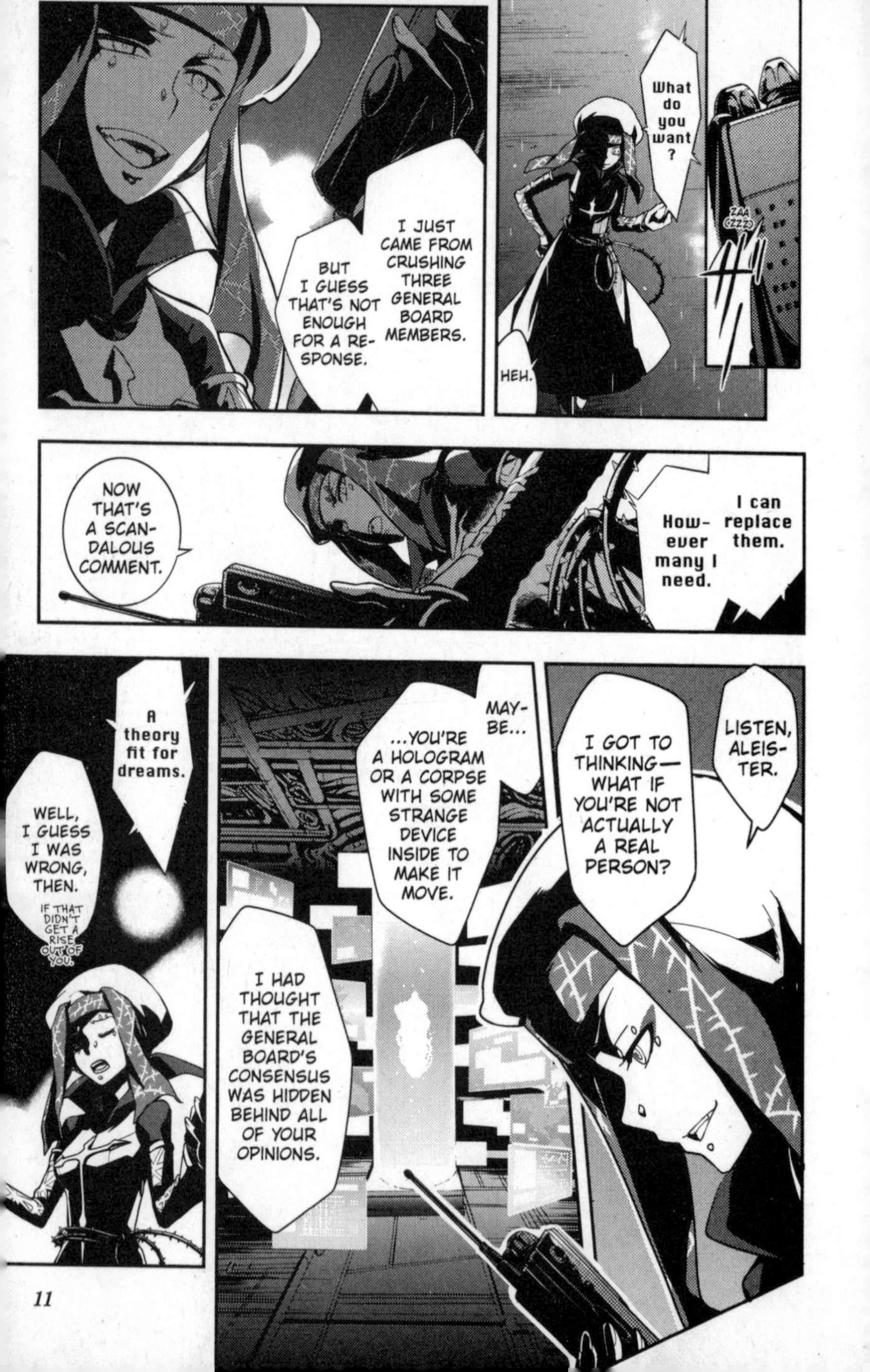
What do you want?
HEH.
ZAA (ZZZ)
I JUST CAME FROM CRUSHING THREE GENERAL BOARD MEMBERS.
BUT I GUESS THAT'S NOT ENOUGH FOR A RE-SPONSE.
I can replace them.
How-ever many I need.
NOW THAT'S A SCAN-DALOUS COMMENT.
LISTEN, ALEIS-TER.
I GOT TO THINKING— WHAT IF YOU'RE NOT ACTUALLY A REAL PERSON?
MAY-BE...
...YOU'RE A HOLOGRAM OR A CORPSE WITH SOME STRANGE DEVICE INSIDE TO MAKE IT MOVE.
I HAD THOUGHT THAT THE GENERAL BOARD'S CONSENSUS WAS HIDDEN BEHIND ALL OF YOUR OPINIONS.
A theory fit for dreams.
WELL, I GUESS I WAS WRONG, THEN.
IF THAT DIDN'T GET A RISE OUT OF YOU.

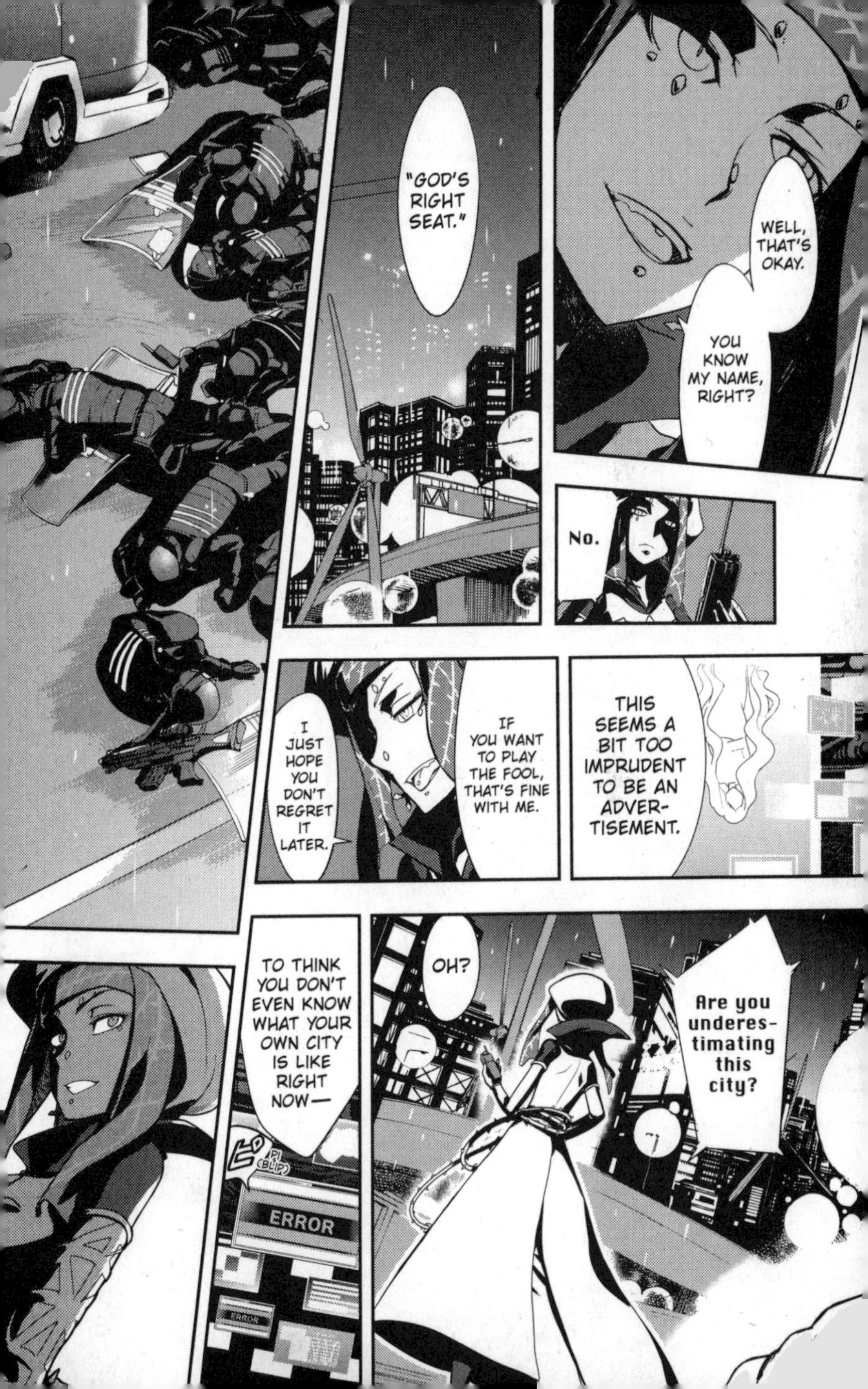
WELL, THAT'S OKAY.
YOU KNOW MY NAME, RIGHT?
No.
"GOD'S RIGHT SEAT."
THIS SEEMS A BIT TOO IMPRUDENT TO BE AN ADVERTISEMENT.
IF YOU WANT TO PLAY THE FOOL, THAT'S FINE WITH ME.
I JUST HOPE YOU DON'T REGRET IT LATER.
Are you underestimating this city?
OH?
TO THINK YOU DON'T EVEN KNOW WHAT YOUR OWN CITY IS LIKE RIGHT NOW—
PI (BLIP)
ERROR
ERROR

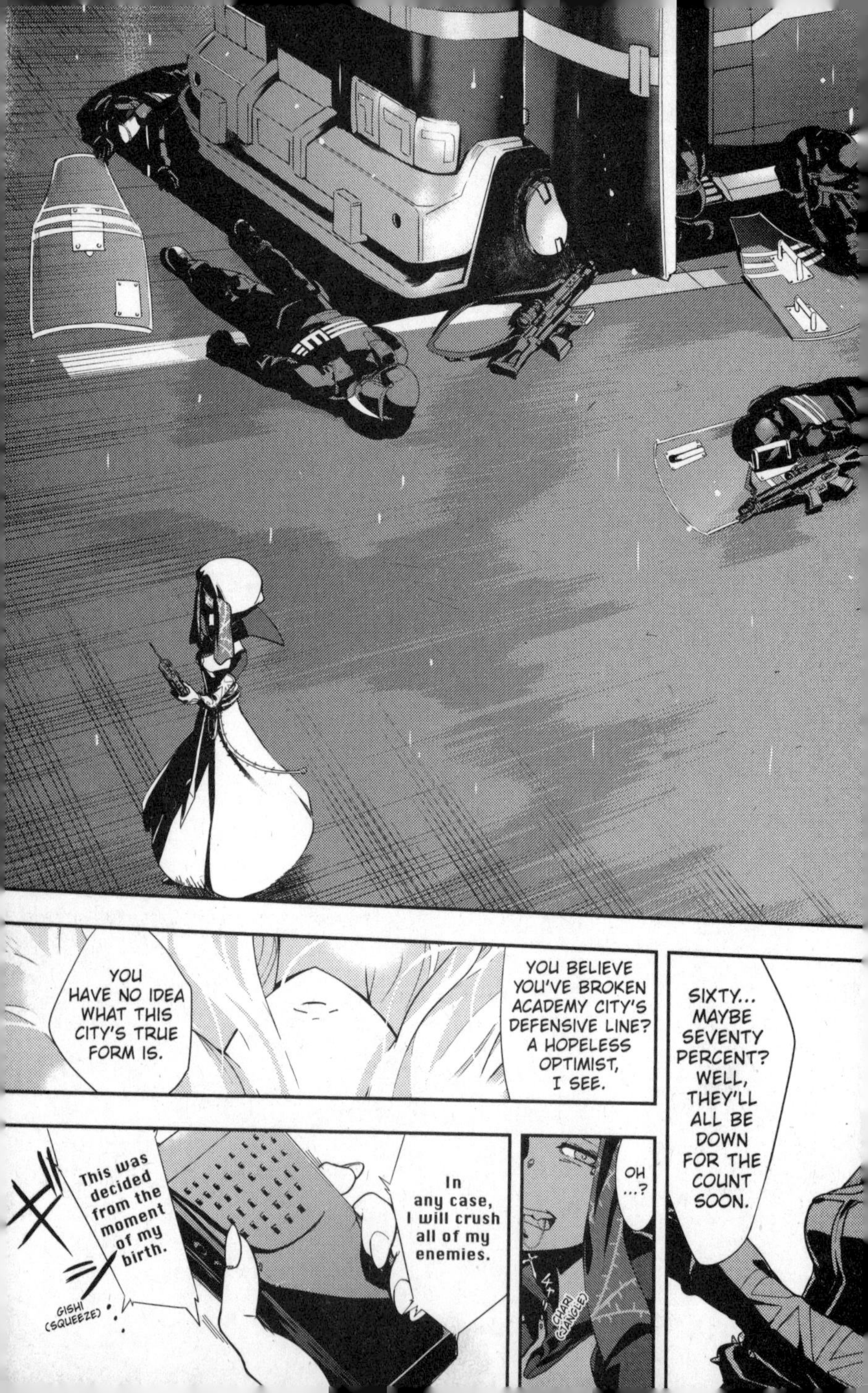
SIXTY... MAYBE SEVENTY PERCENT? WELL, THEY'LL ALL BE DOWN FOR THE COUNT SOON.
YOU BELIEVE YOU'VE BROKEN ACADEMY CITY'S DEFENSIVE LINE? A HOPELESS OPTIMIST, I SEE.
YOU HAVE NO IDEA WHAT THIS CITY'S TRUE FORM IS.
OH ...?
CHARI (JANGLE)
In any case, I will crush all of my enemies.
This was decided from the moment of my birth.
GISHI (SQUEEZE)

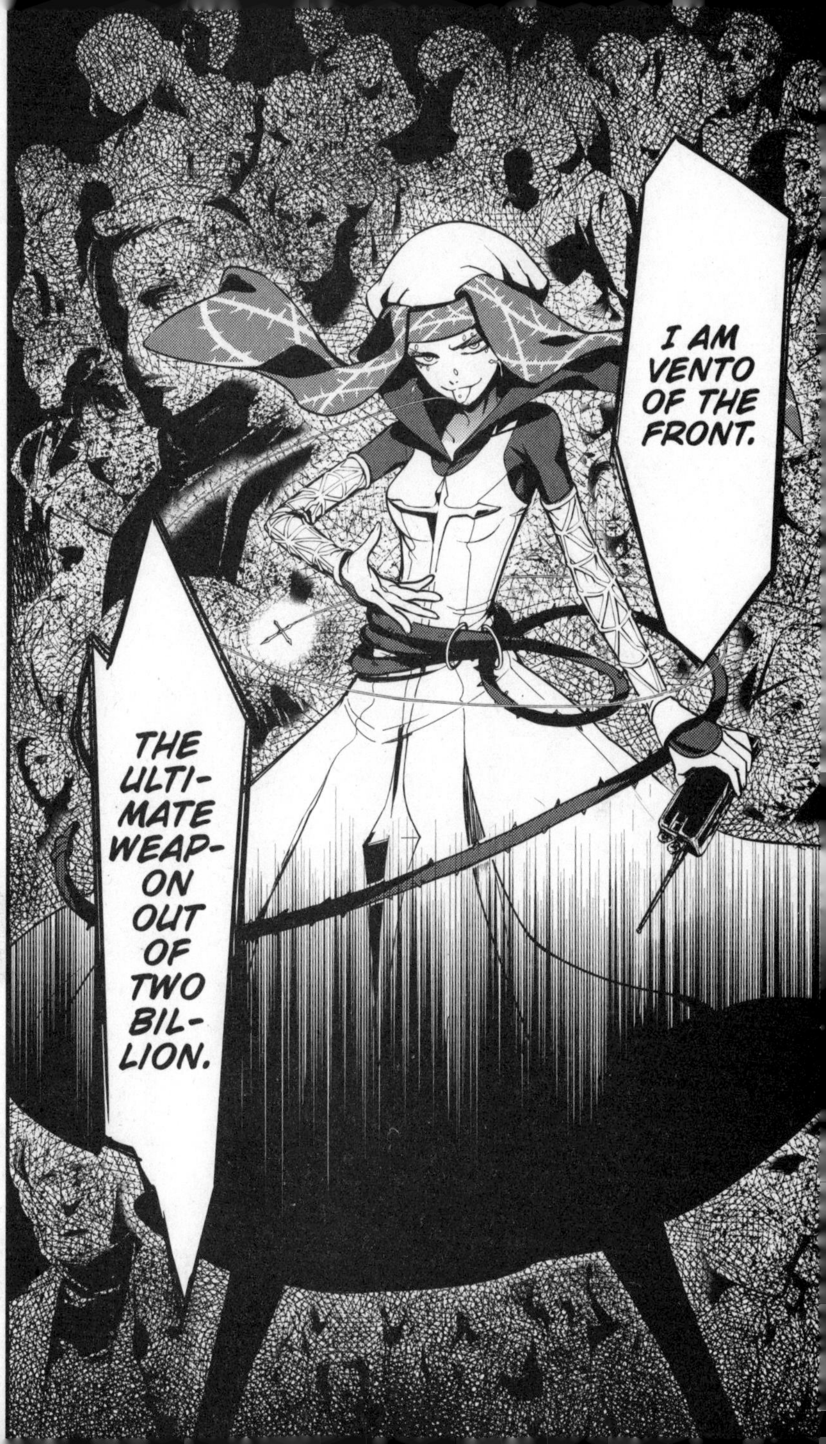
I AM VENTO OF THE FRONT.
THE ULTIMATE WEAPON OUT OF TWO BILLION.

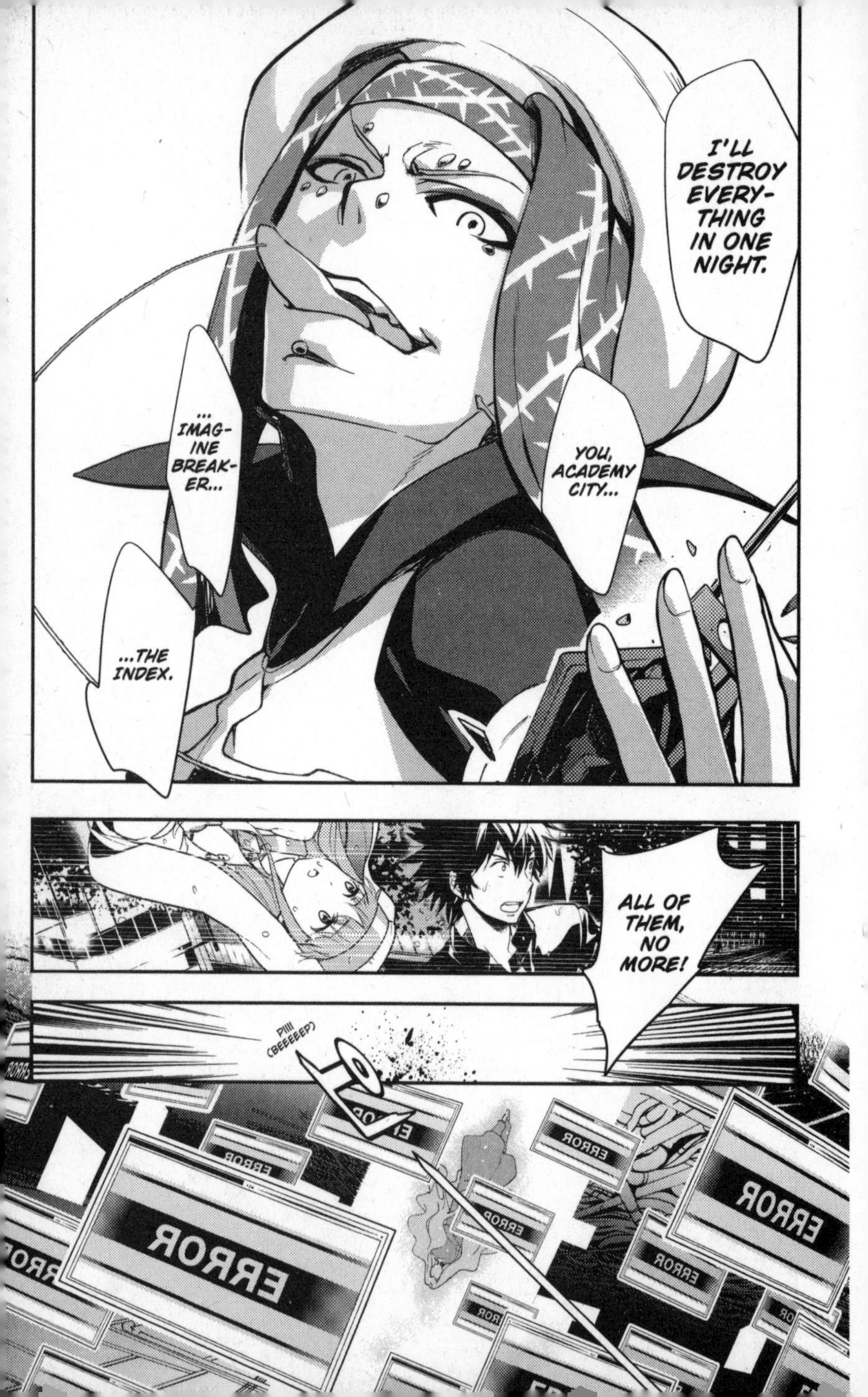
I'LL DESTROY EVERY-THING IN ONE NIGHT.
YOU, ACADEMY CITY...
... IMAG-INE BREAK-ER...
...THE INDEX.
ALL OF THEM, NO MORE!
PIIII (BEEEEEP)

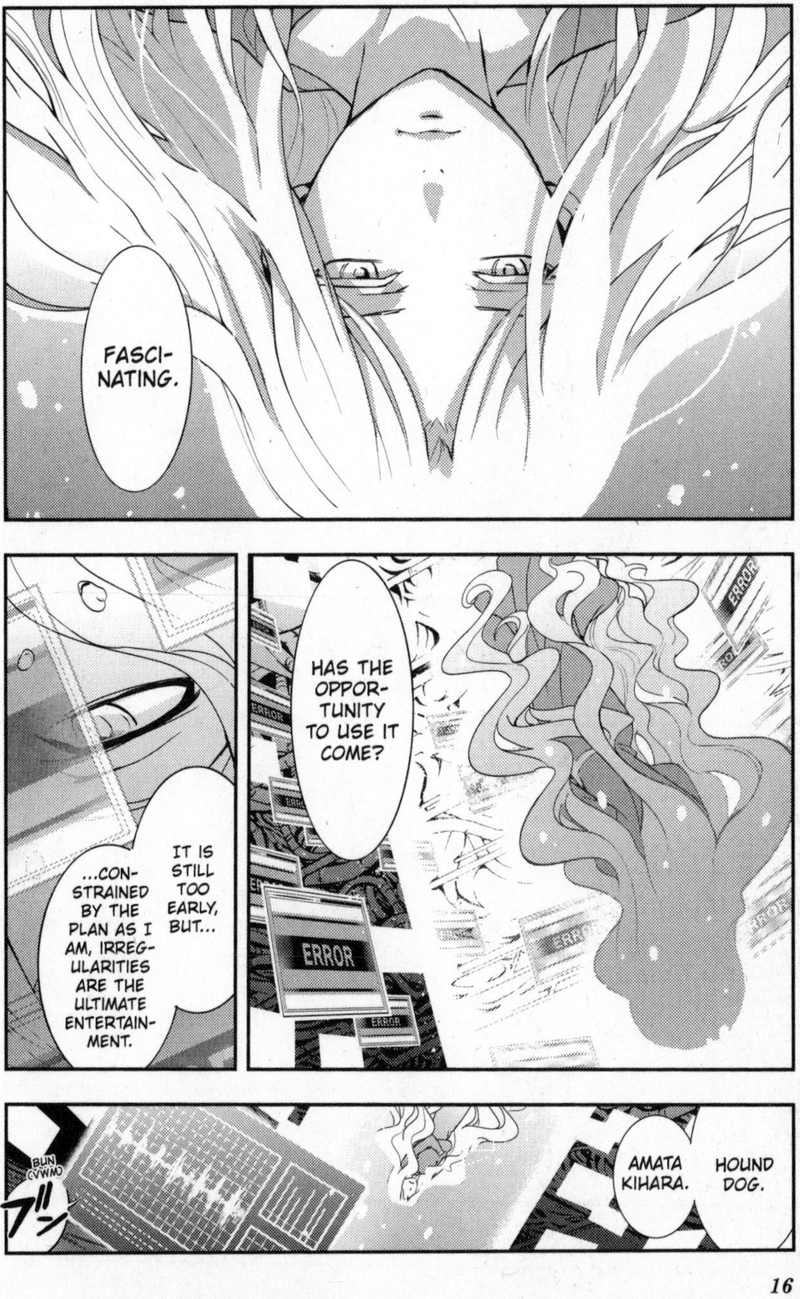
FASCINATING.
HAS THE OPPORTUNITY TO USE IT COME?
ERROR
IT IS STILL TOO EARLY, BUT...
...CONSTRAINED BY THE PLAN AS I AM, IRREGULARITIES ARE THE ULTIMATE ENTERTAINMENT.
HOUND DOG.
AMATA KIHARA.
BUN (VWM)

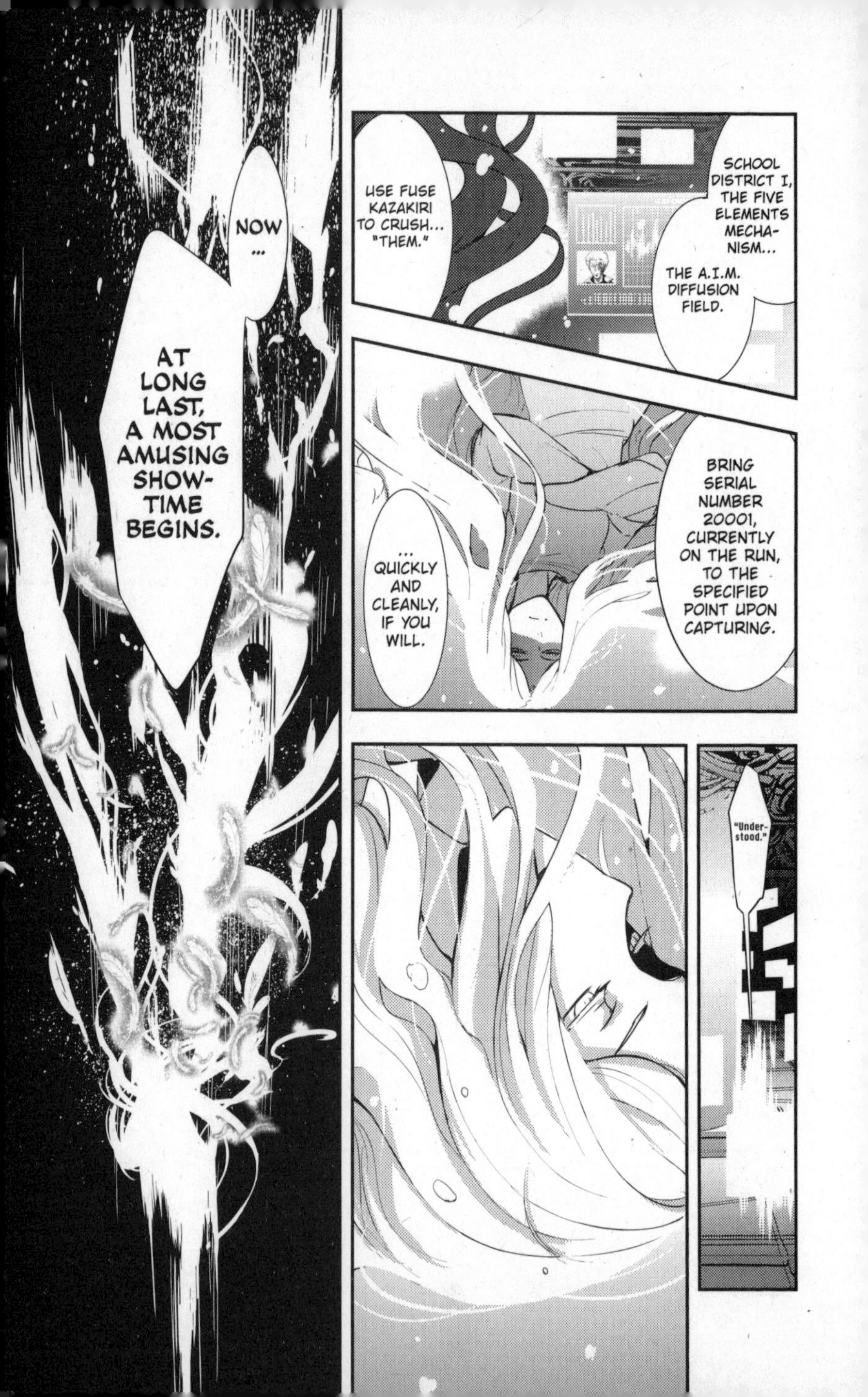
SCHOOL DISTRICT I, THE FIVE ELEMENTS MECHANISM...
THE A.I.M. DIFFUSION FIELD.
USE FUSE KAZAKIRI TO CRUSH... "THEM."
BRING SERIAL NUMBER 20001, CURRENTLY ON THE RUN, TO THE SPECIFIED POINT UPON CAPTURING.
...QUICKLY AND CLEANLY, IF YOU WILL.
"Understood."
NOW...
AT LONG LAST, A MOST AMUSING SHOWTIME BEGINS.

A Certain Magical Index

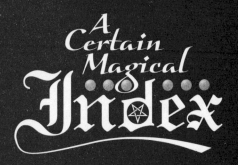

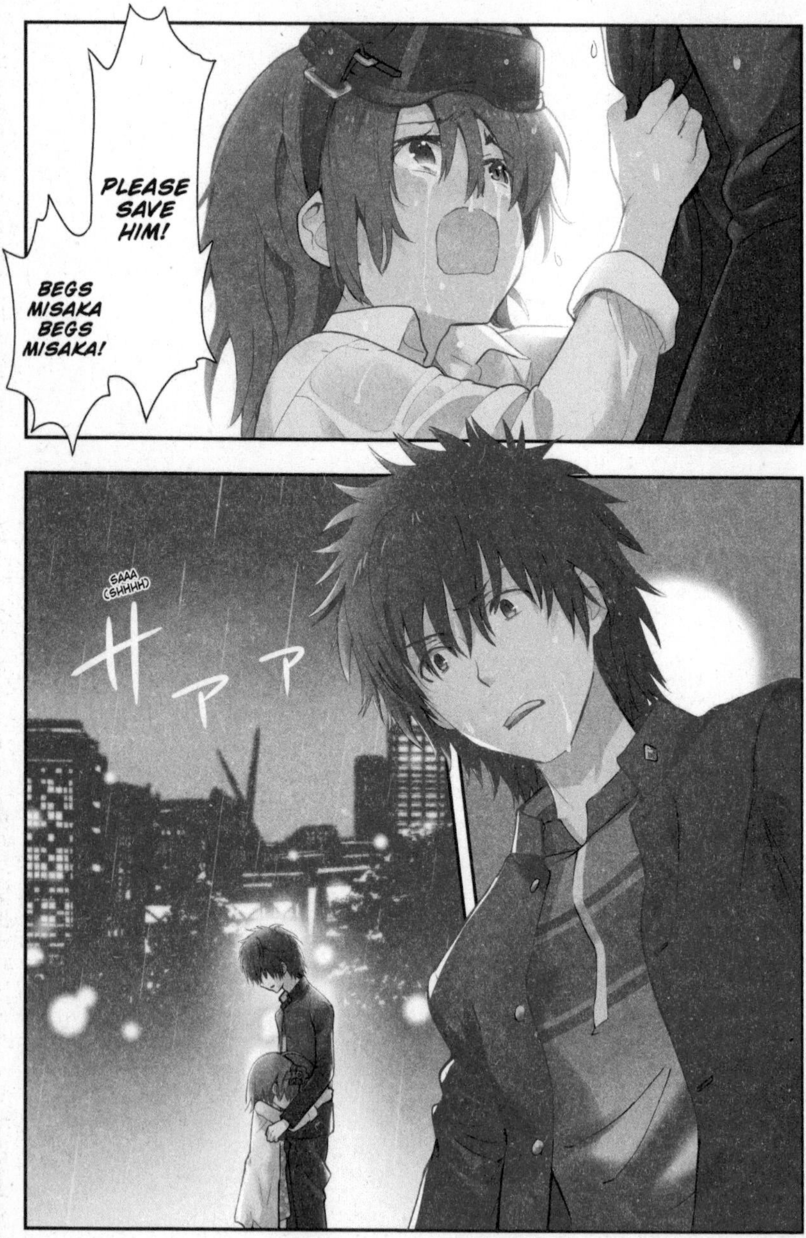
PLEASE SAVE HIM!
BEGS MISAKA BEGS MISAKA!
SAAA (SHHHH)
サァァ

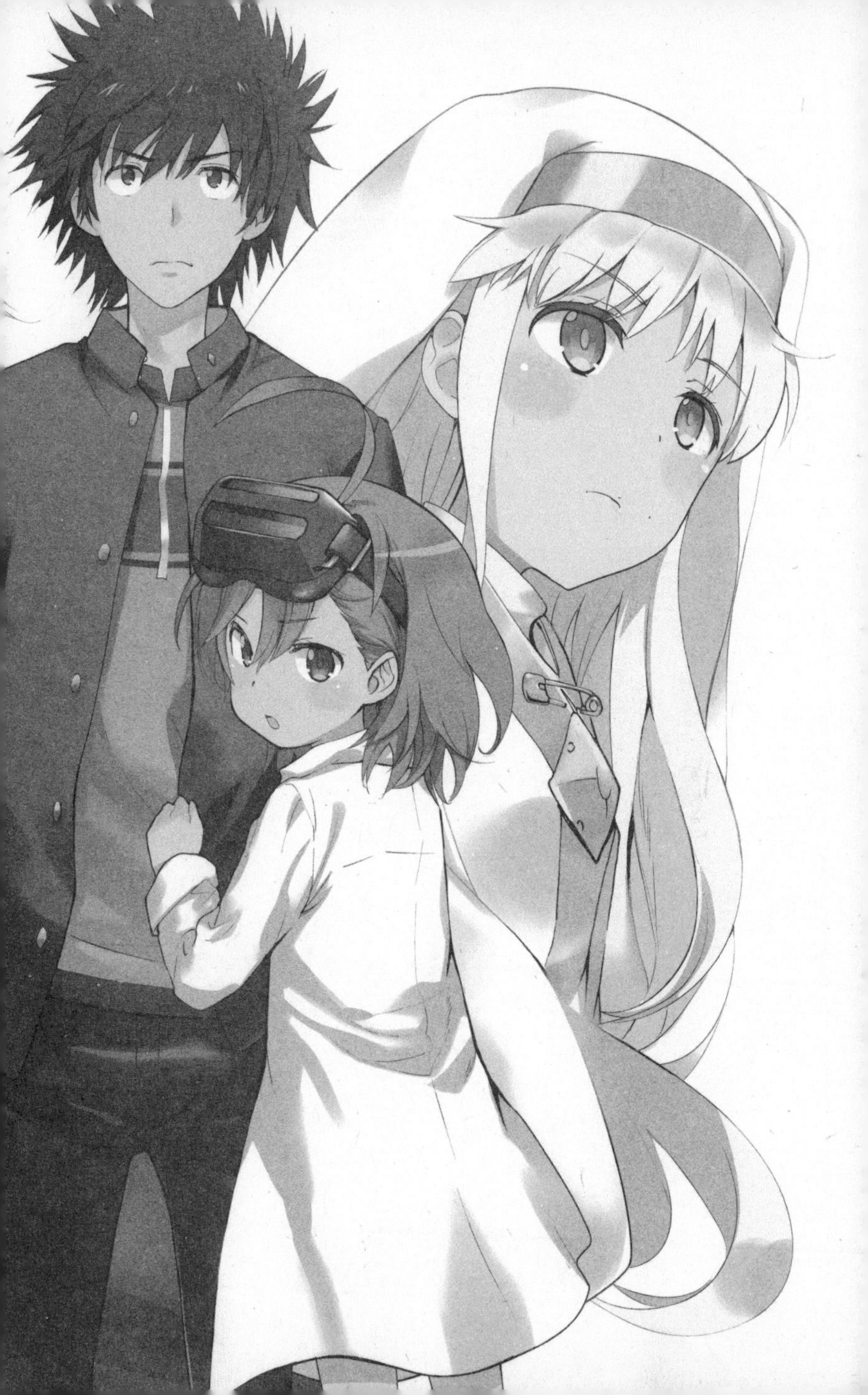

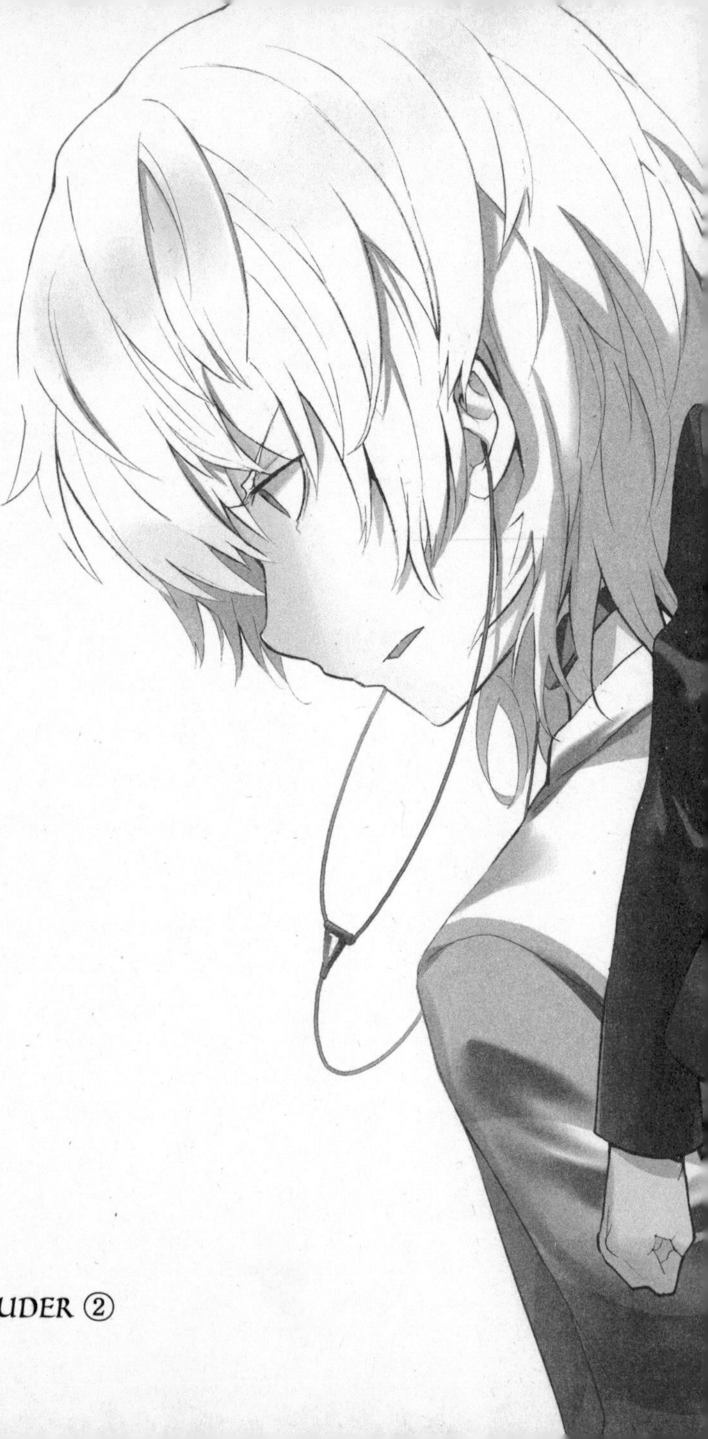

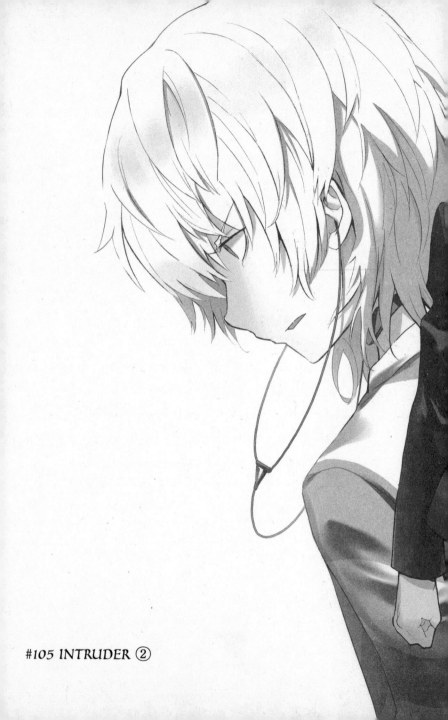

#105 INTRUDER ②

A Certain Magical Index

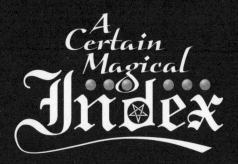

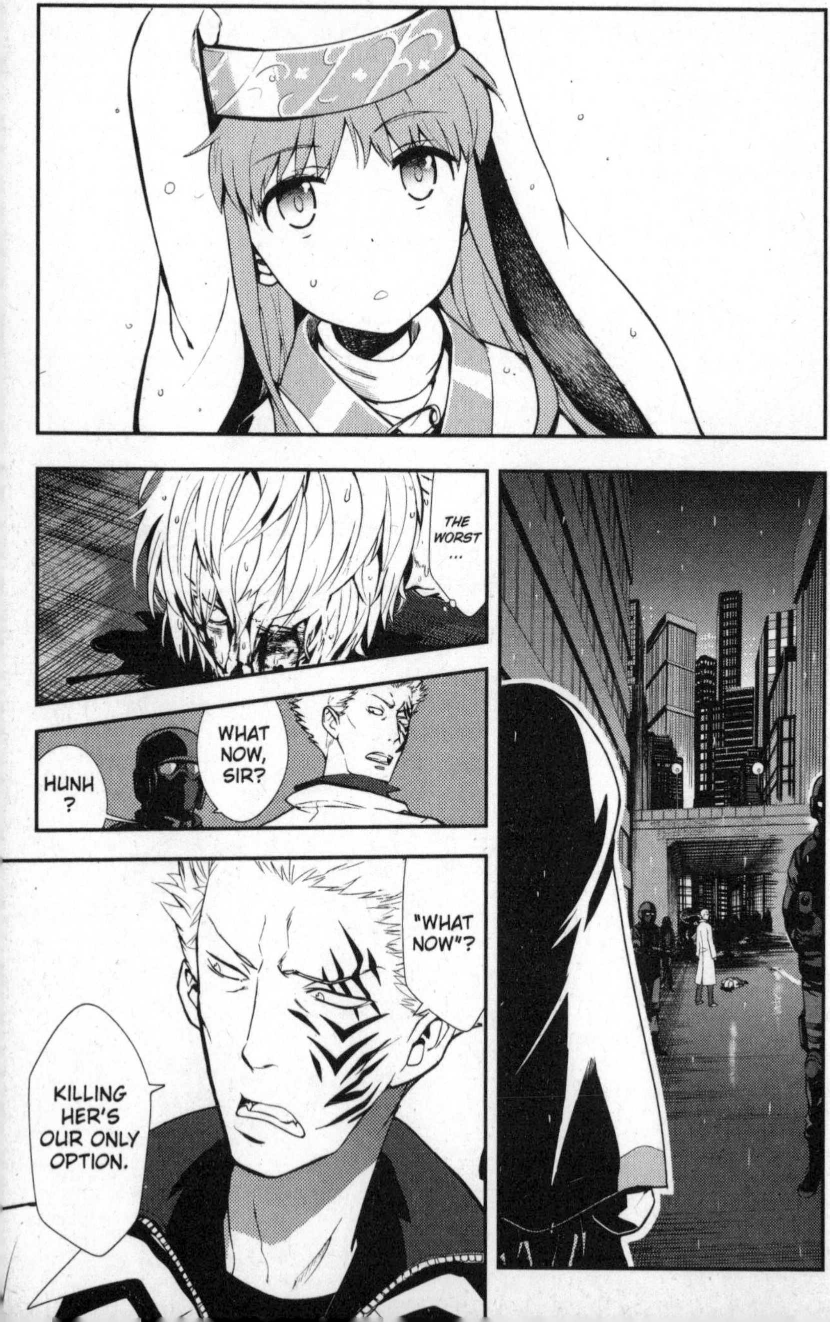
THE WORST ...
WHAT NOW, SIR?
HUNH ?
"WHAT NOW"?
KILLING HER'S OUR ONLY OPTION.

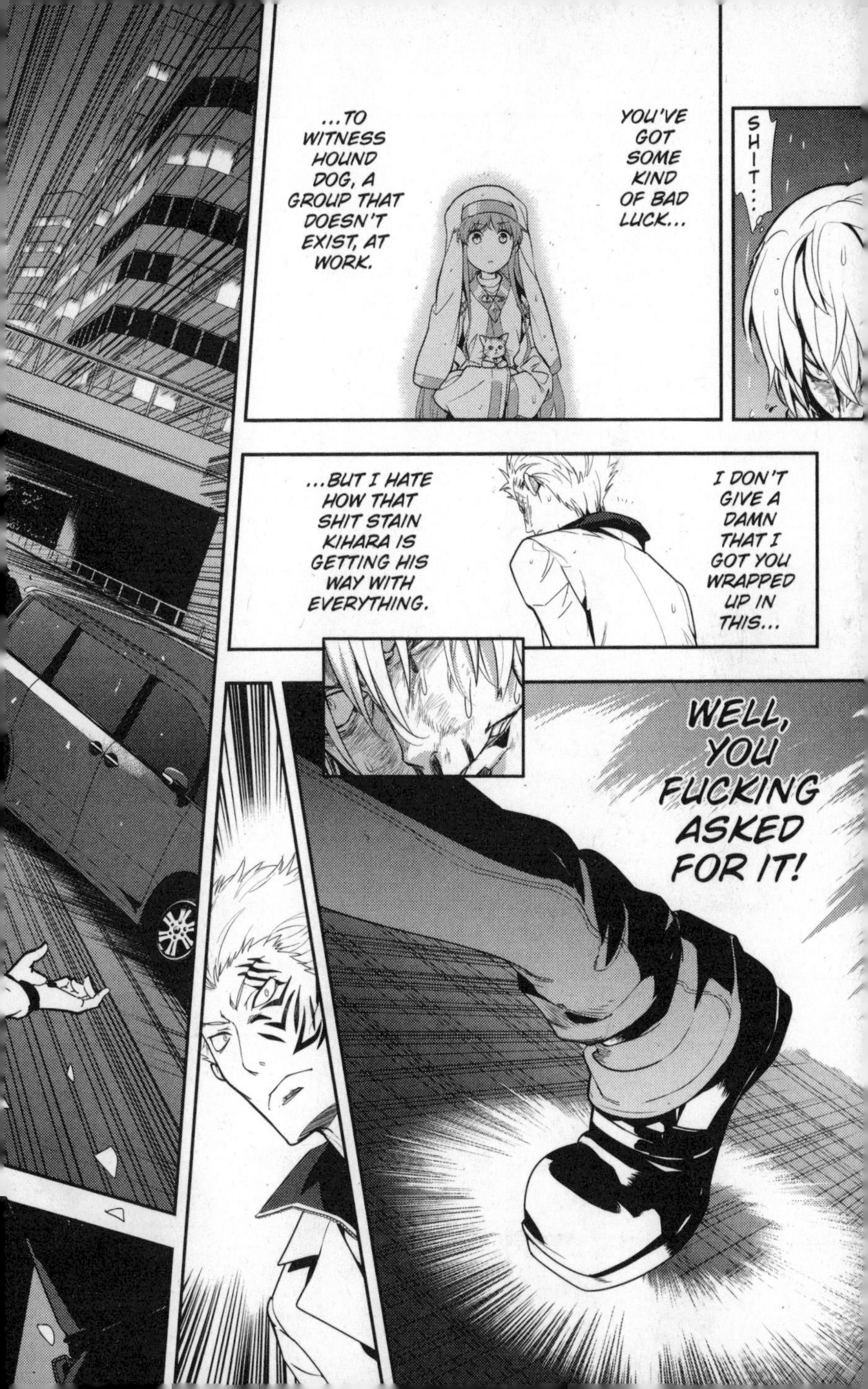
SHIT...
YOU'VE GOT SOME KIND OF BAD LUCK...
...TO WITNESS HOUND DOG, A GROUP THAT DOESN'T EXIST, AT WORK.
I DON'T GIVE A DAMN THAT I GOT YOU WRAPPED UP IN THIS...
...BUT I HATE HOW THAT SHIT STAIN KIHARA IS GETTING HIS WAY WITH EVERYTHING.
WELL, YOU FUCKING ASKED FOR IT!

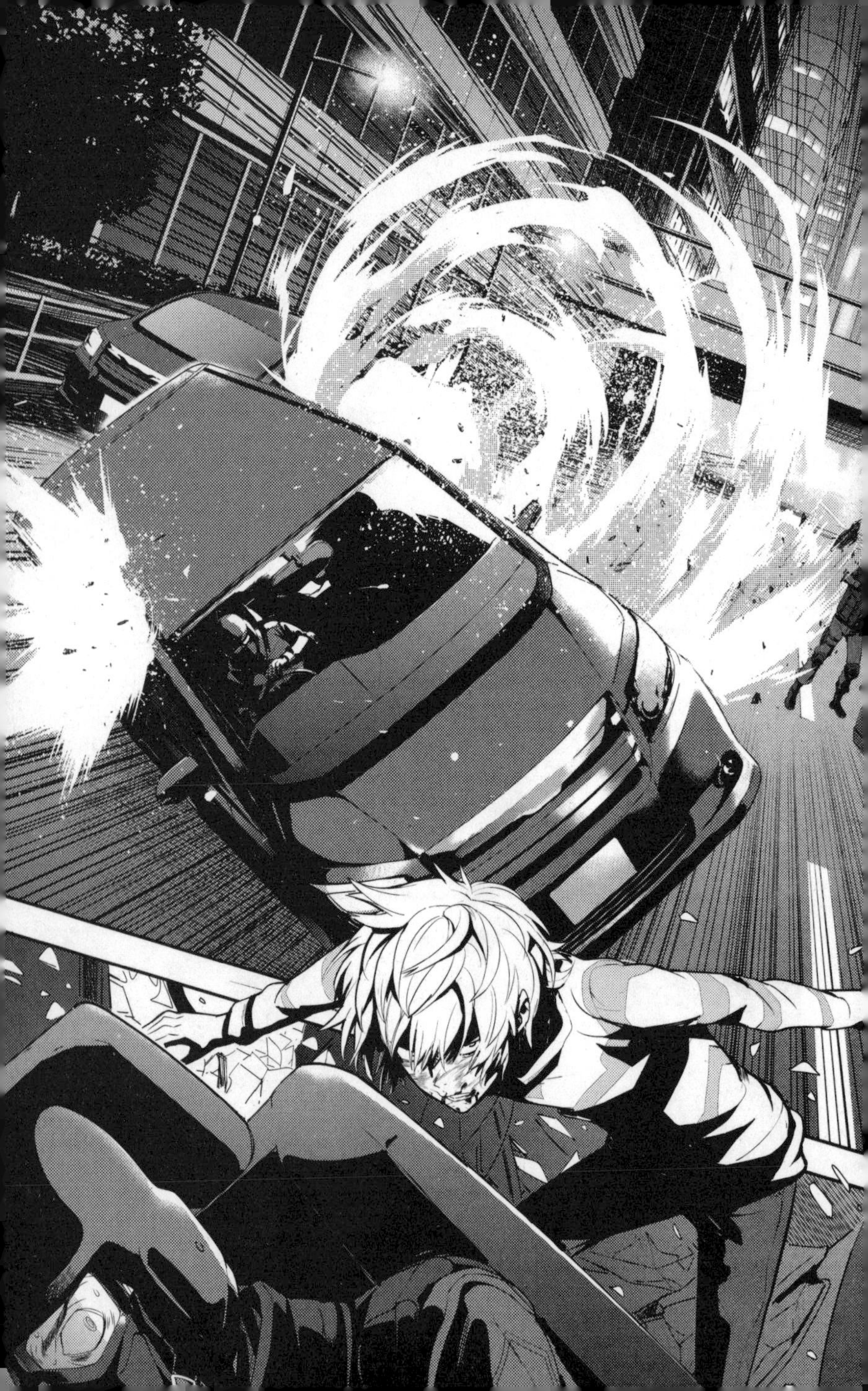

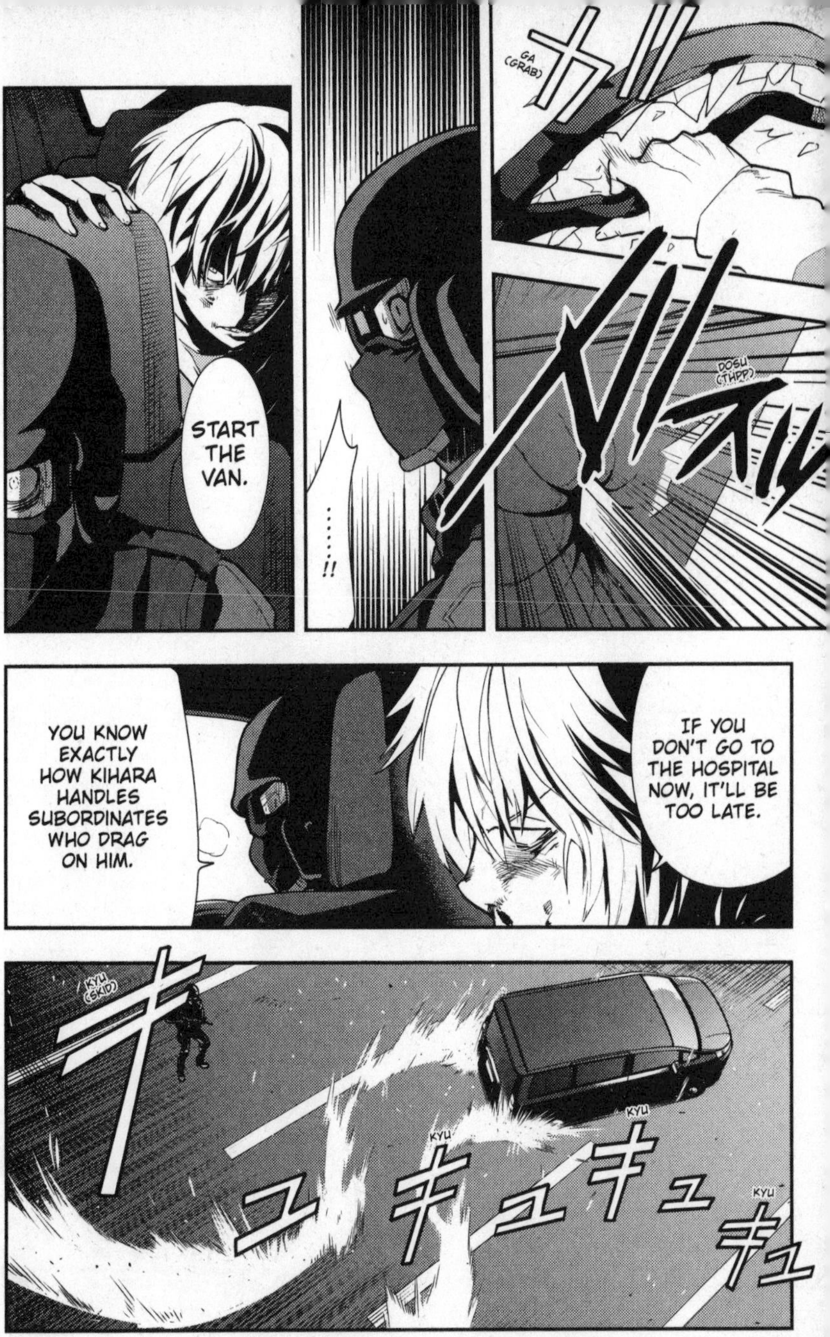
GA (GRAB)
DOSU (THPP)
......!!
START THE VAN.
IF YOU DON'T GO TO THE HOSPITAL NOW, IT'LL BE TOO LATE.
YOU KNOW EXACTLY HOW KIHARA HANDLES SUBORDINATES WHO DRAG ON HIM.
KYU (SKID)
KYU
KYU
KYU

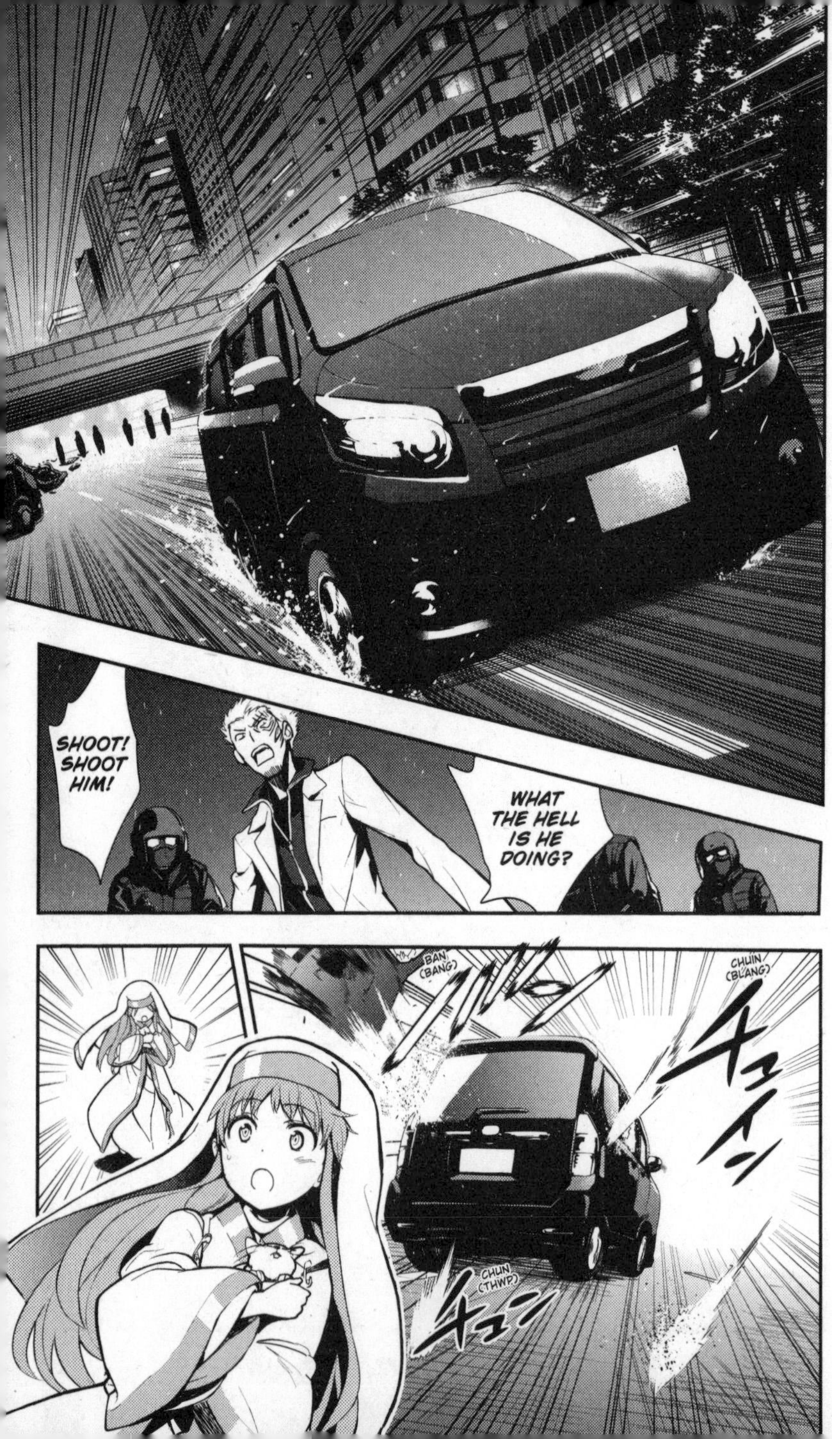
WHAT THE HELL IS HE DOING?
SHOOT! SHOOT HIM!
CHUIN (BLANG)
BAN (BANG)
CHUIN (THWP)

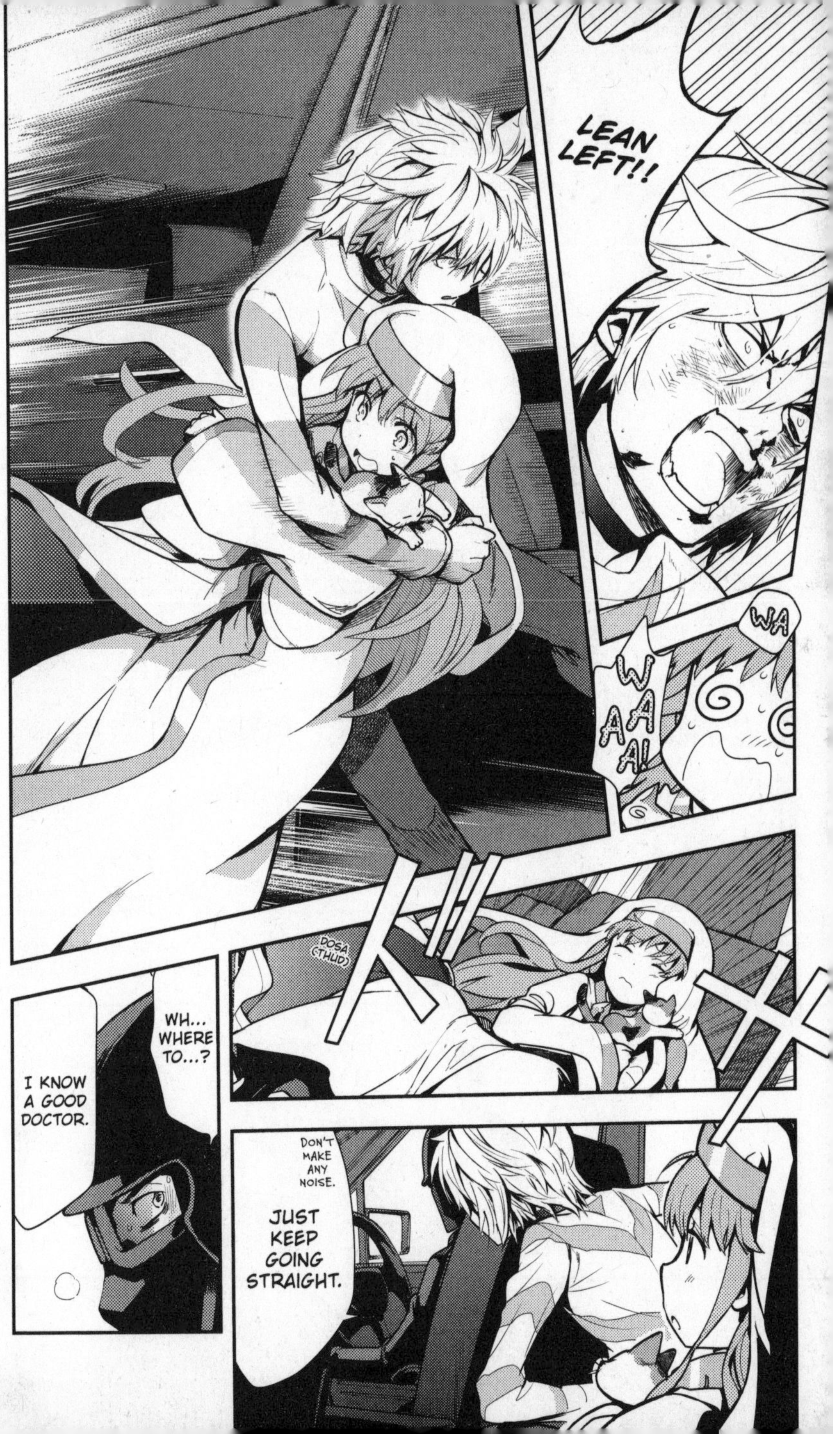
LEAN LEFT!!
WA
WAAAA!
DOSA (THUD)
WH... WHERE TO...?
I KNOW A GOOD DOCTOR.
DON'T MAKE ANY NOISE.
JUST KEEP GOING STRAIGHT.

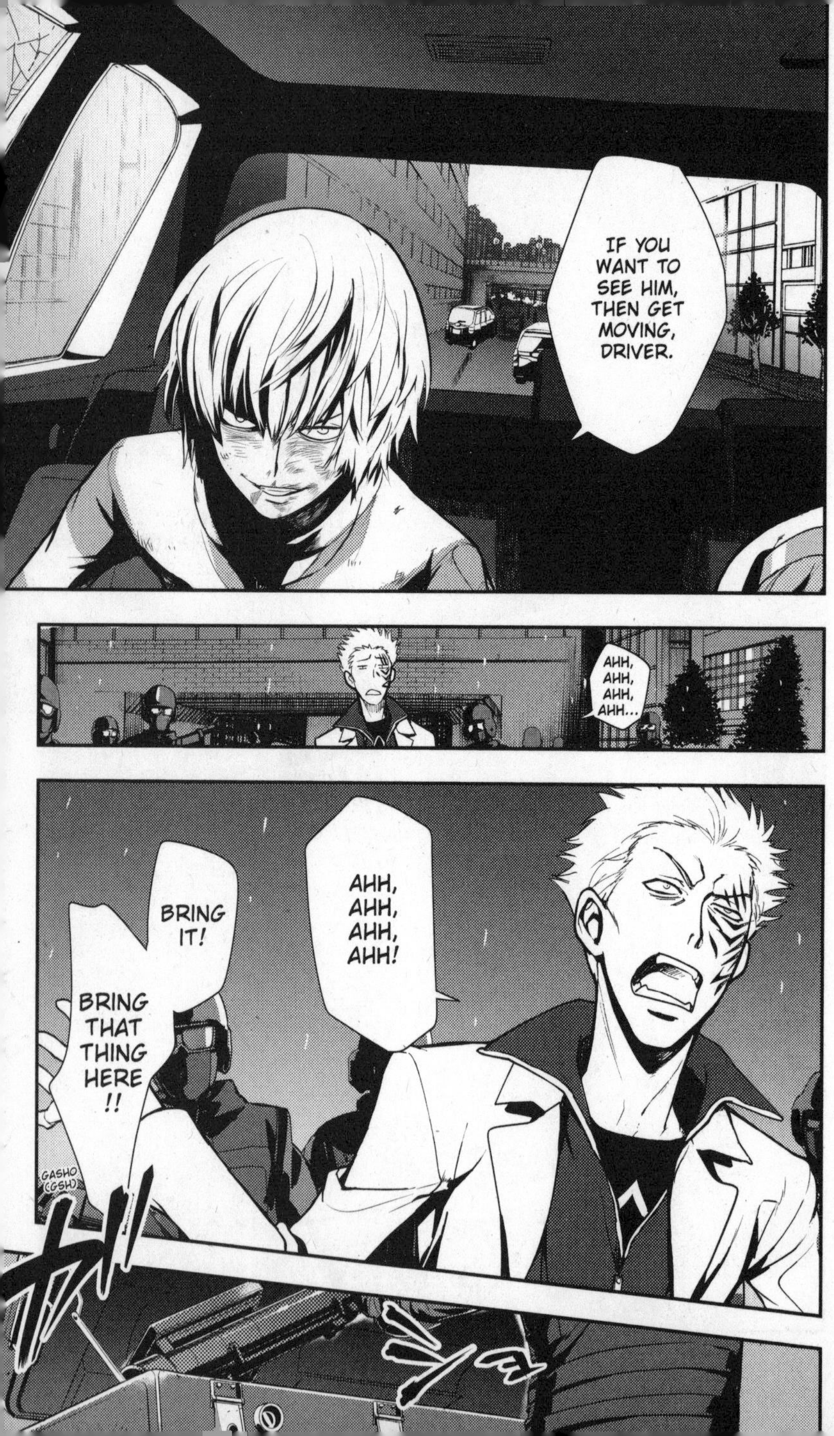
IF YOU WANT TO SEE HIM, THEN GET MOVING, DRIVER.
AHH, AHH, AHH, AHH...
AHH, AHH, AHH, AHH!
BRING IT!
BRING THAT THING HERE!!
GASHO (GSH)

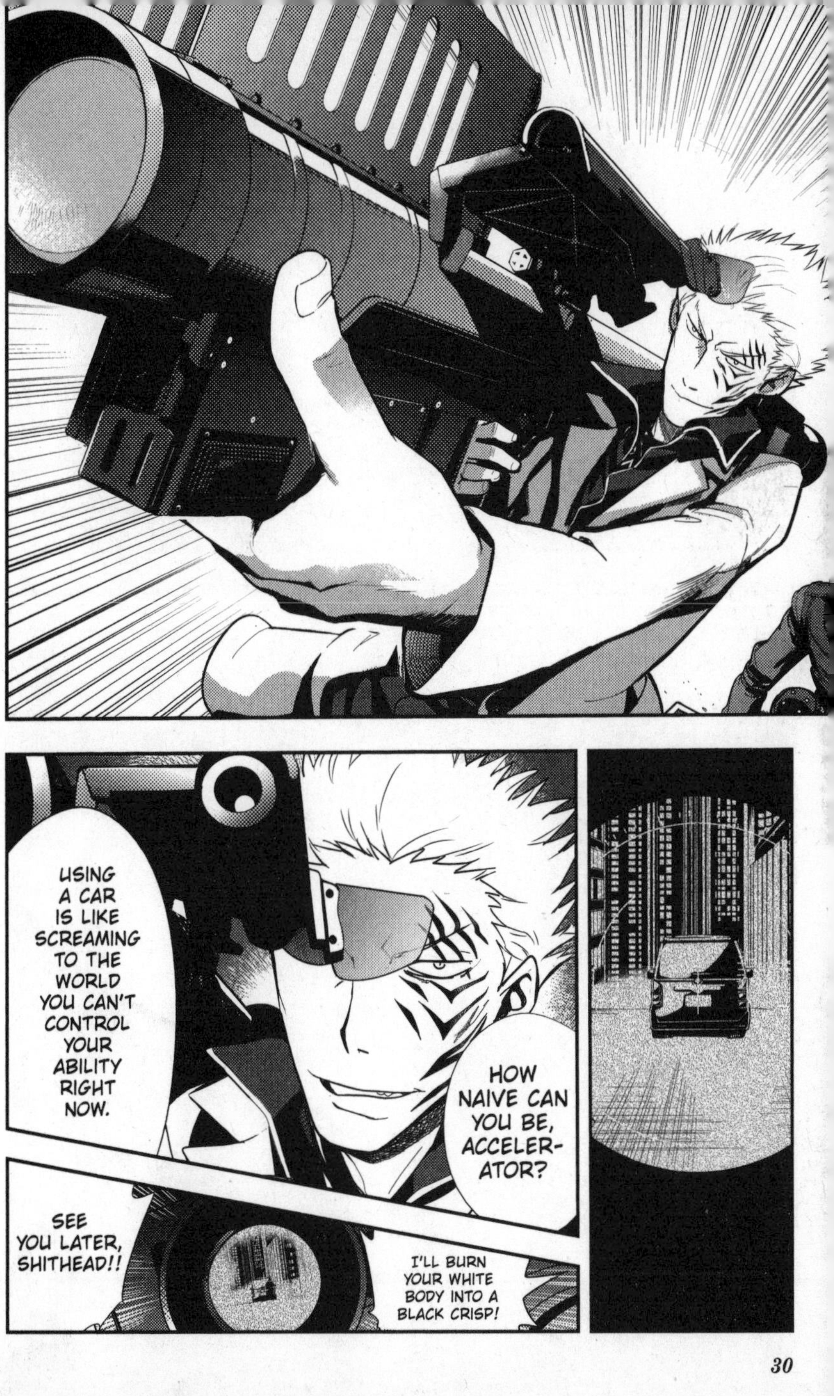
HOW NAIVE CAN YOU BE, ACCELER-ATOR?
USING A CAR IS LIKE SCREAMING TO THE WORLD YOU CAN'T CONTROL YOUR ABILITY RIGHT NOW.
I'LL BURN YOUR WHITE BODY INTO A BLACK CRISP!
SEE YOU LATER, SHITHEAD!!

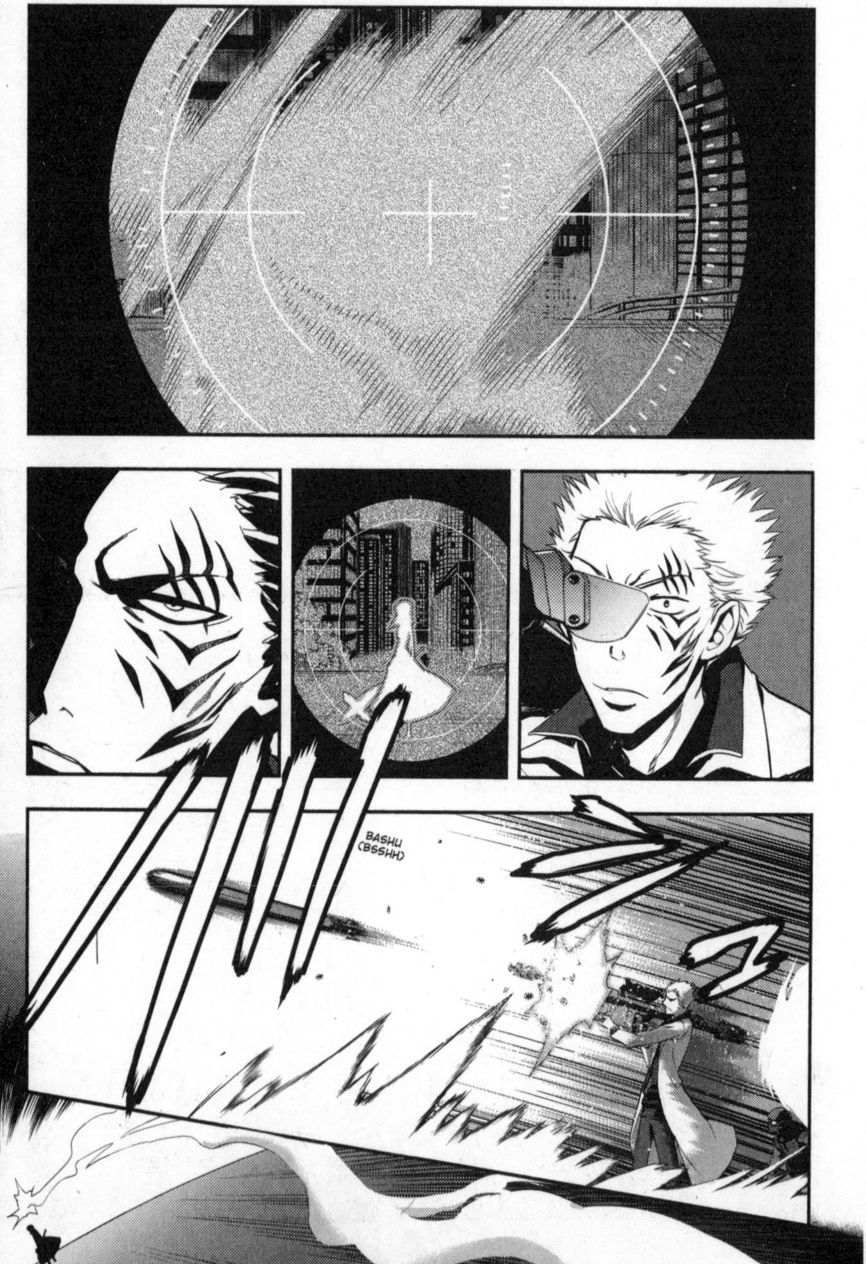
BASHU
(BSSHH)

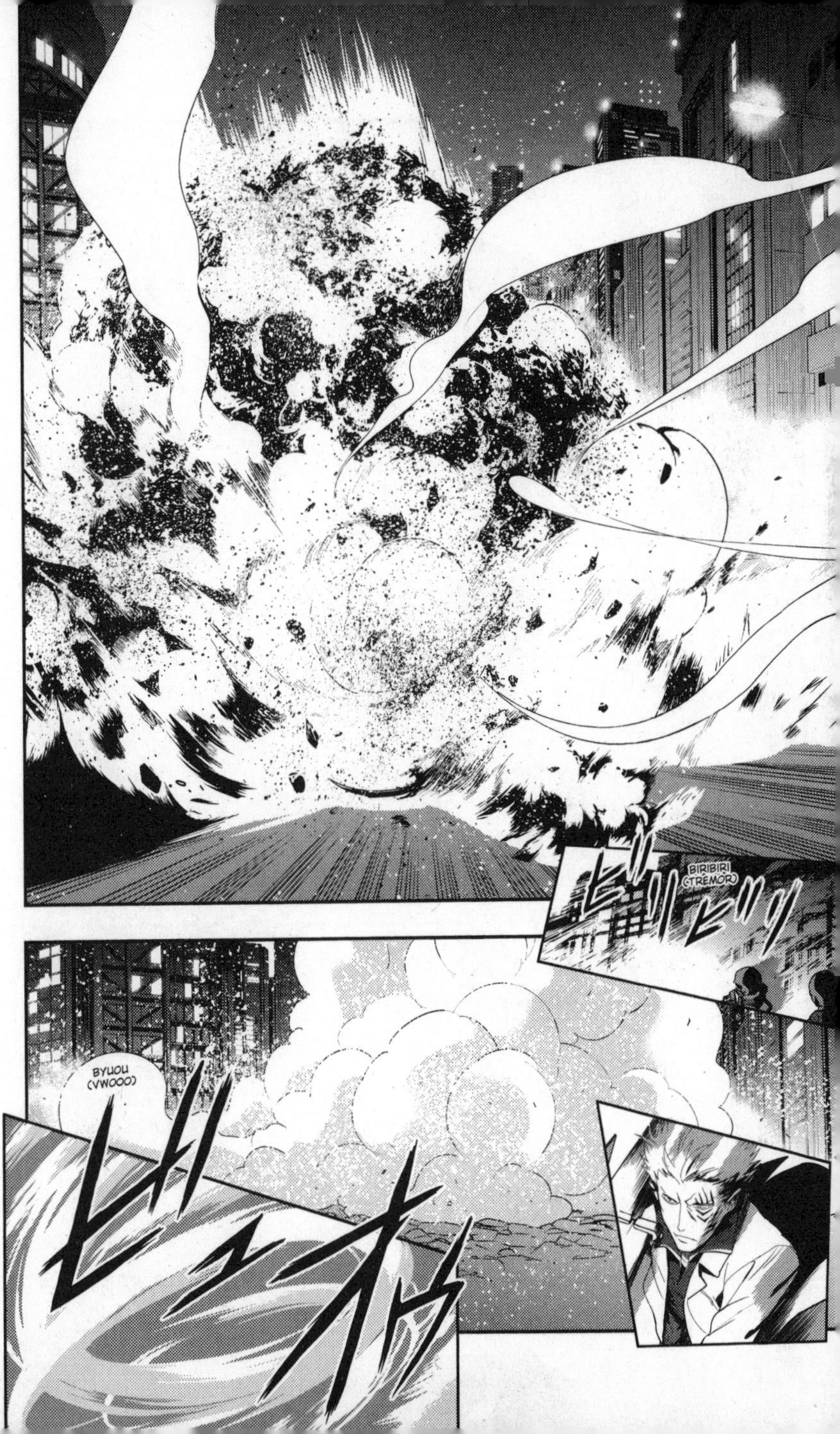
BIRIBIRI
(TREMOR)
BYUOU
(VWOOO)

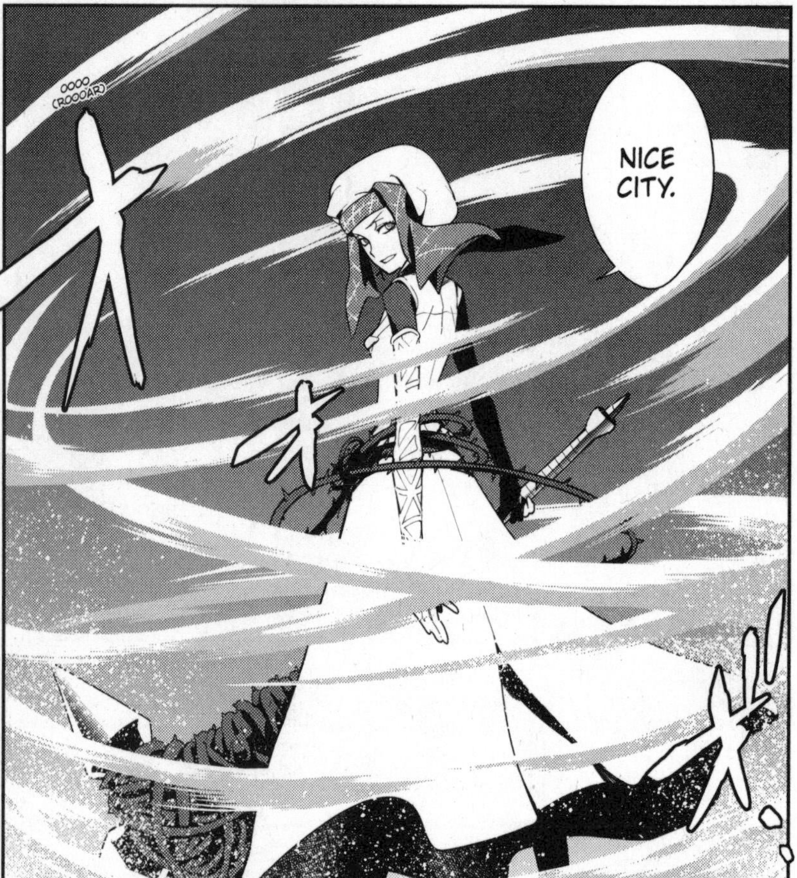
NICE CITY.
OOOO (ROOOAR)

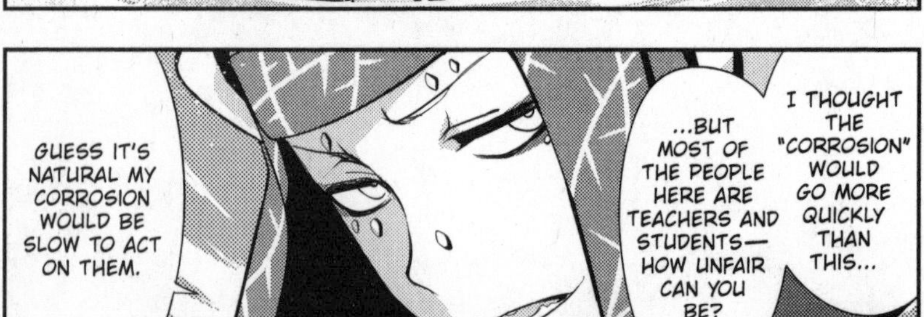
I THOUGHT THE "CORROSION" WOULD GO MORE QUICKLY THAN THIS...
...BUT MOST OF THE PEOPLE HERE ARE TEACHERS AND STUDENTS—HOW UNFAIR CAN YOU BE?
GUESS IT'S NATURAL MY CORROSION WOULD BE SLOW TO ACT ON THEM.

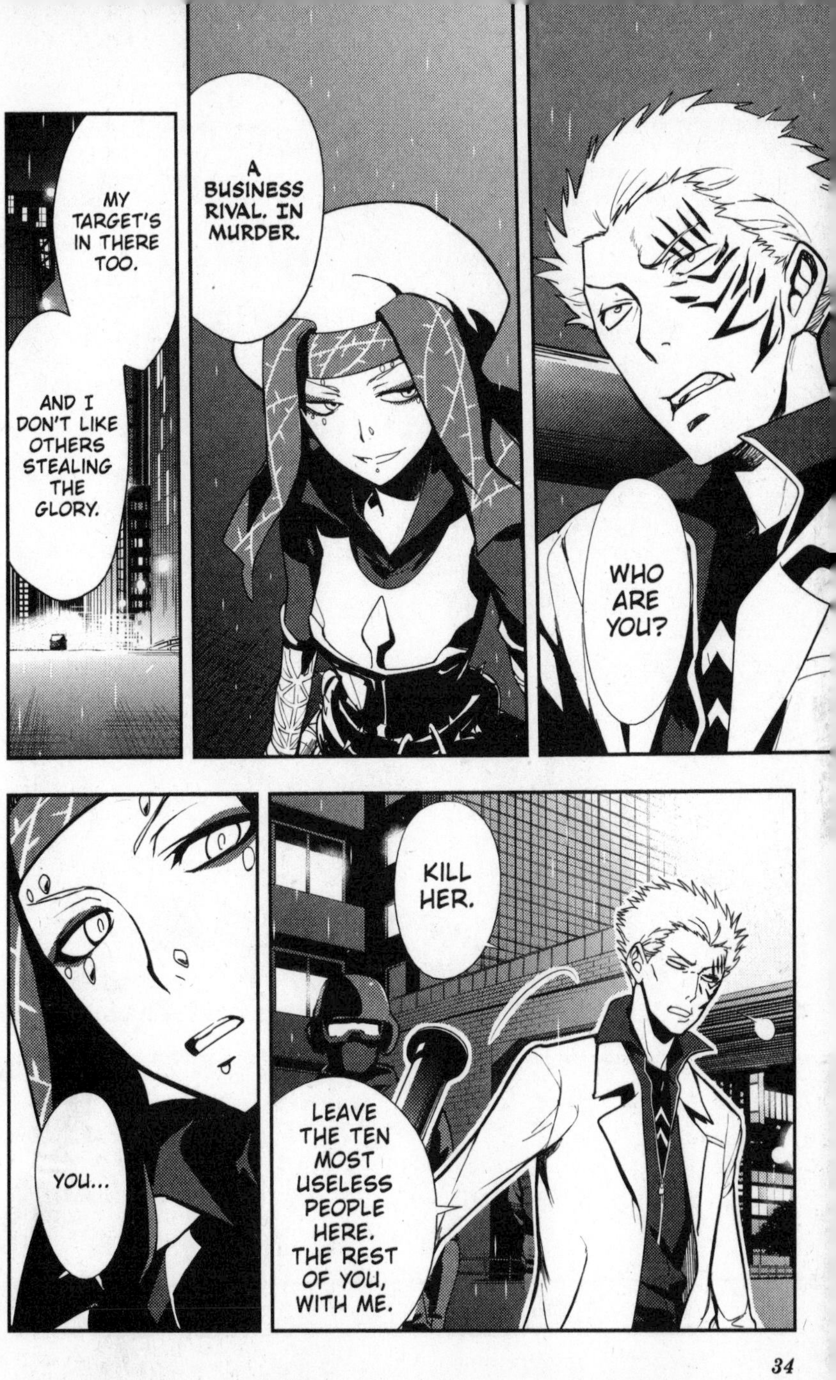
WHO ARE YOU?
A BUSINESS RIVAL. IN MURDER.
MY TARGET'S IN THERE TOO.
AND I DON'T LIKE OTHERS STEALING THE GLORY.
KILL HER.
LEAVE THE TEN MOST USELESS PEOPLE HERE. THE REST OF YOU, WITH ME.
YOU...

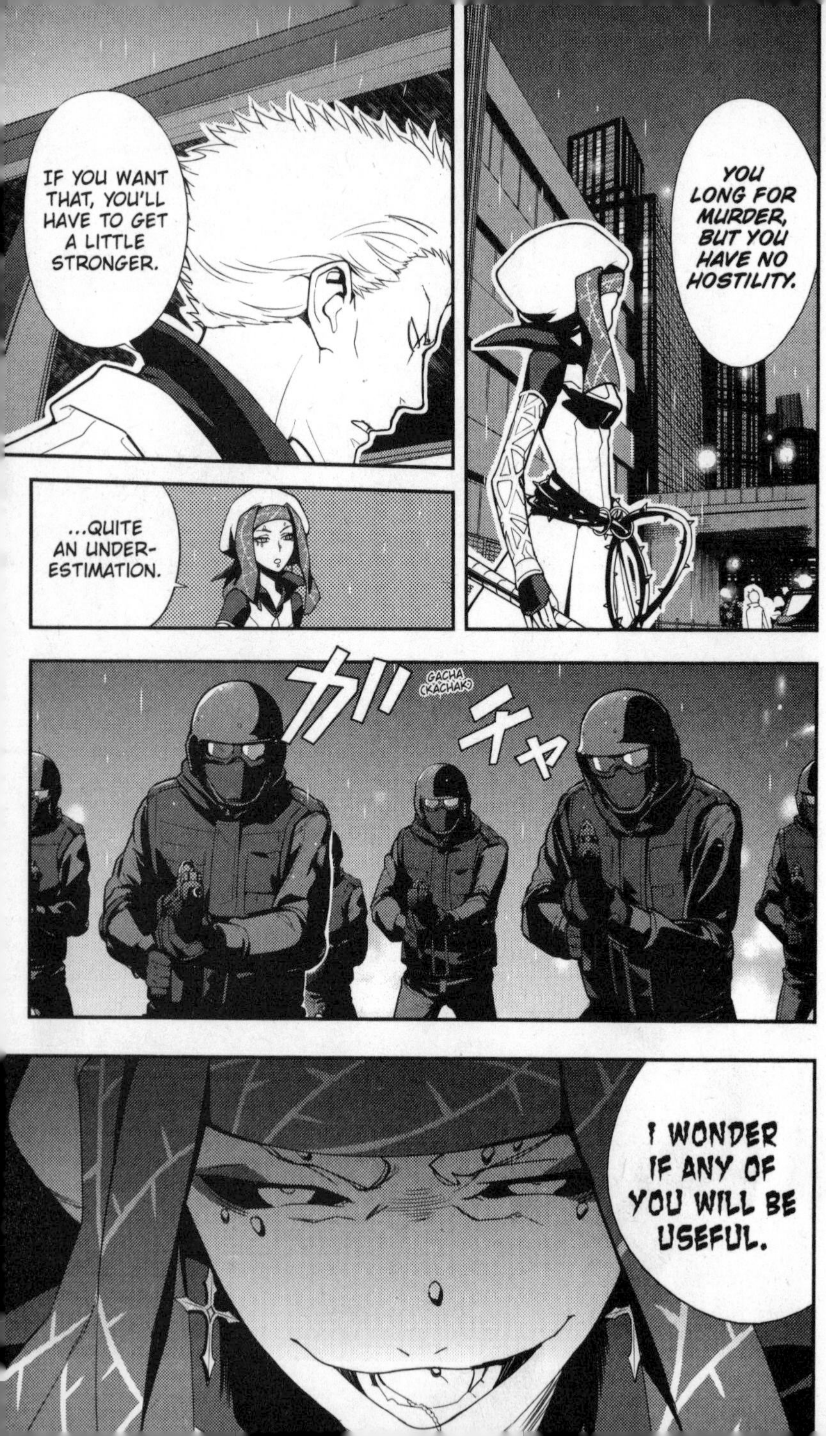
YOU LONG FOR MURDER, BUT YOU HAVE NO HOSTILITY.
IF YOU WANT THAT, YOU'LL HAVE TO GET A LITTLE STRONGER.
...QUITE AN UNDER-ESTIMATION.
GACHA (KACHAK)
I WONDER IF ANY OF YOU WILL BE USEFUL.

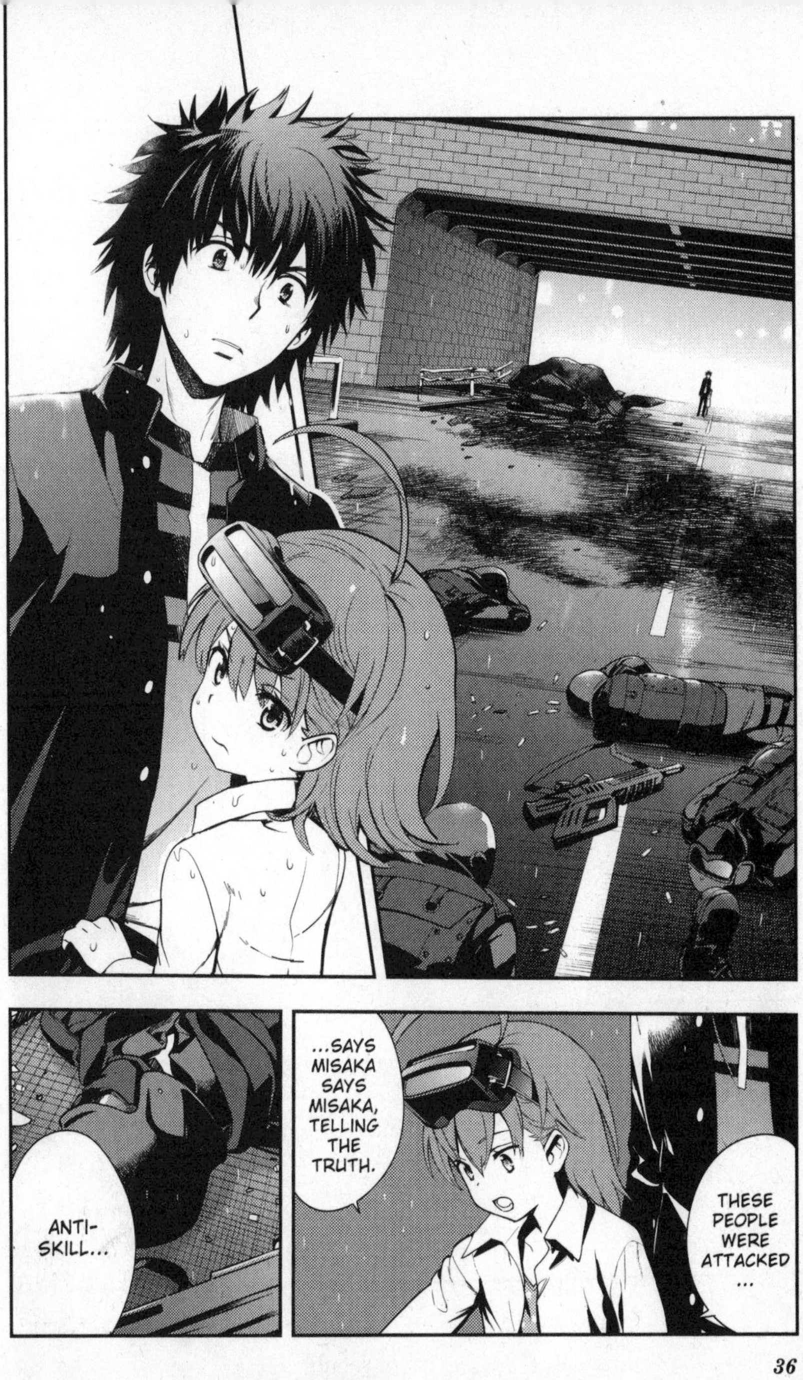
THESE PEOPLE WERE ATTACKED ...
...SAYS MISAKA SAYS MISAKA, TELLING THE TRUTH.
ANTI-SKILL...

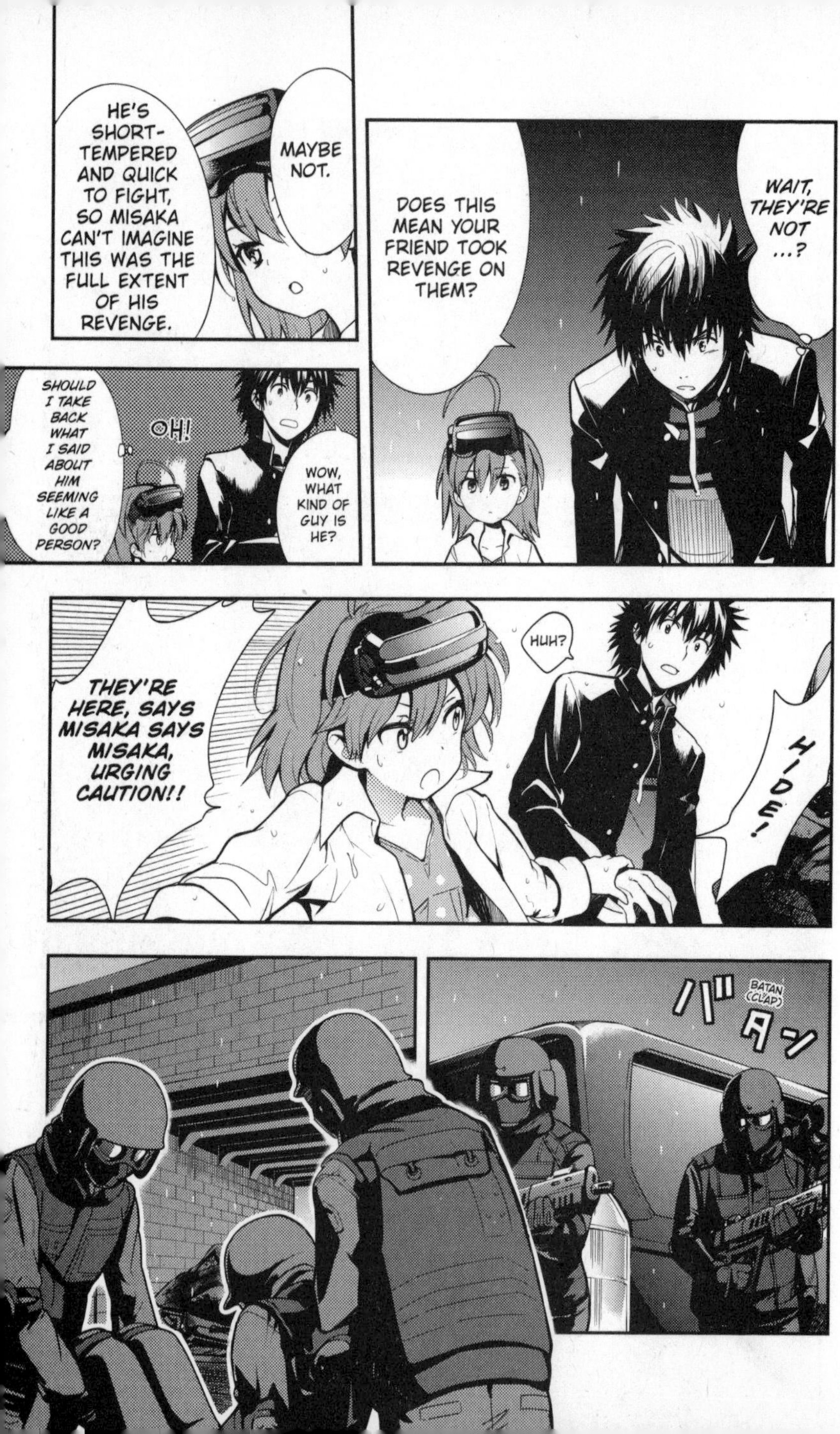
WAIT, THEY'RE NOT ...?
DOES THIS MEAN YOUR FRIEND TOOK REVENGE ON THEM?
MAYBE NOT.
HE'S SHORT-TEMPERED AND QUICK TO FIGHT, SO MISAKA CAN'T IMAGINE THIS WAS THE FULL EXTENT OF HIS REVENGE.
WOW, WHAT KIND OF GUY IS HE?
OH!
SHOULD I TAKE BACK WHAT I SAID ABOUT HIM SEEMING LIKE A GOOD PERSON?
HIDE!
HUH?
THEY'RE HERE, SAYS MISAKA SAYS MISAKA, URGING CAUTION!!
バタン
BATAN (CLAP)

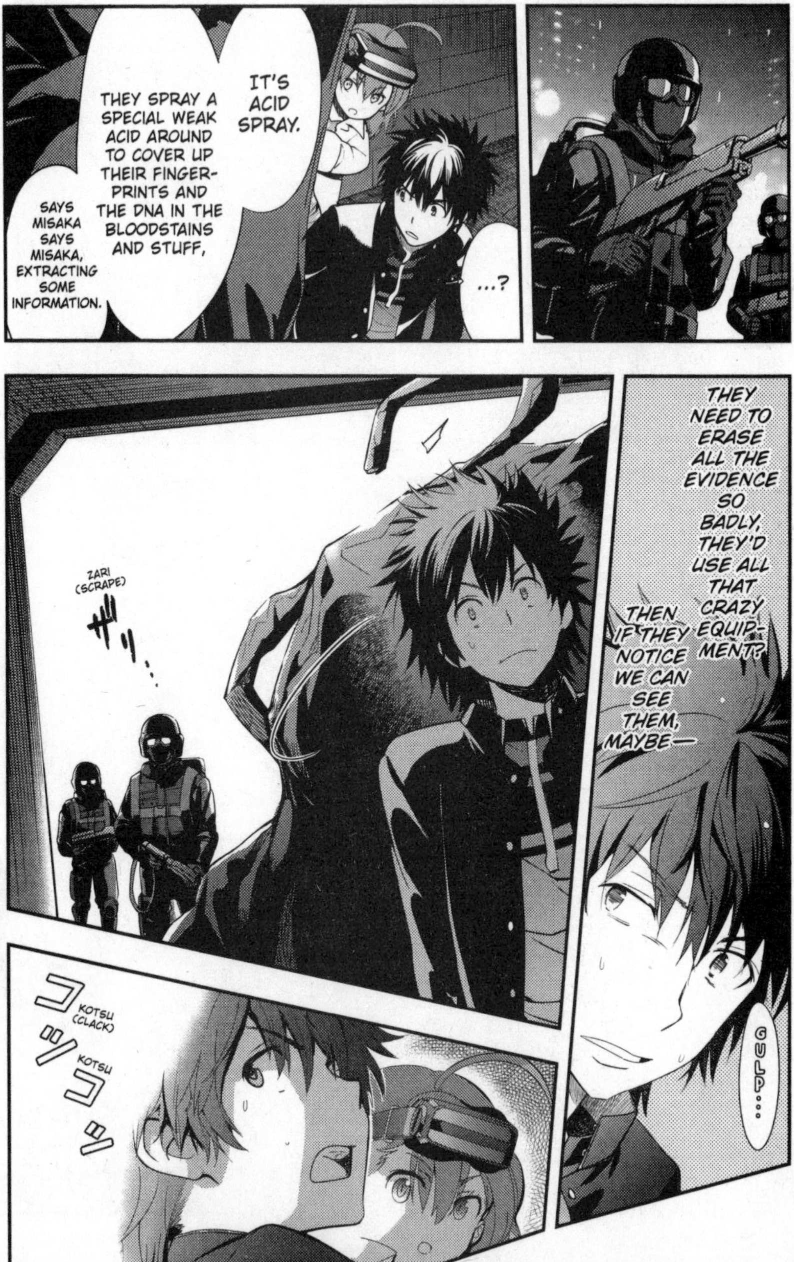
IT'S ACID SPRAY.
THEY SPRAY A SPECIAL WEAK ACID AROUND TO COVER UP THEIR FINGER-PRINTS AND THE DNA IN THE BLOODSTAINS AND STUFF,
SAYS MISAKA SAYS MISAKA, EXTRACTING SOME INFORMATION.
...?
THEY NEED TO ERASE ALL THE EVIDENCE SO BADLY, THEY'D USE ALL THAT CRAZY EQUIP-MENT?
THEN IF THEY NOTICE WE CAN SEE THEM, MAYBE—
GULP...
ZARI (SCRAPE)
KOTSU (CLACK)
KOTSU

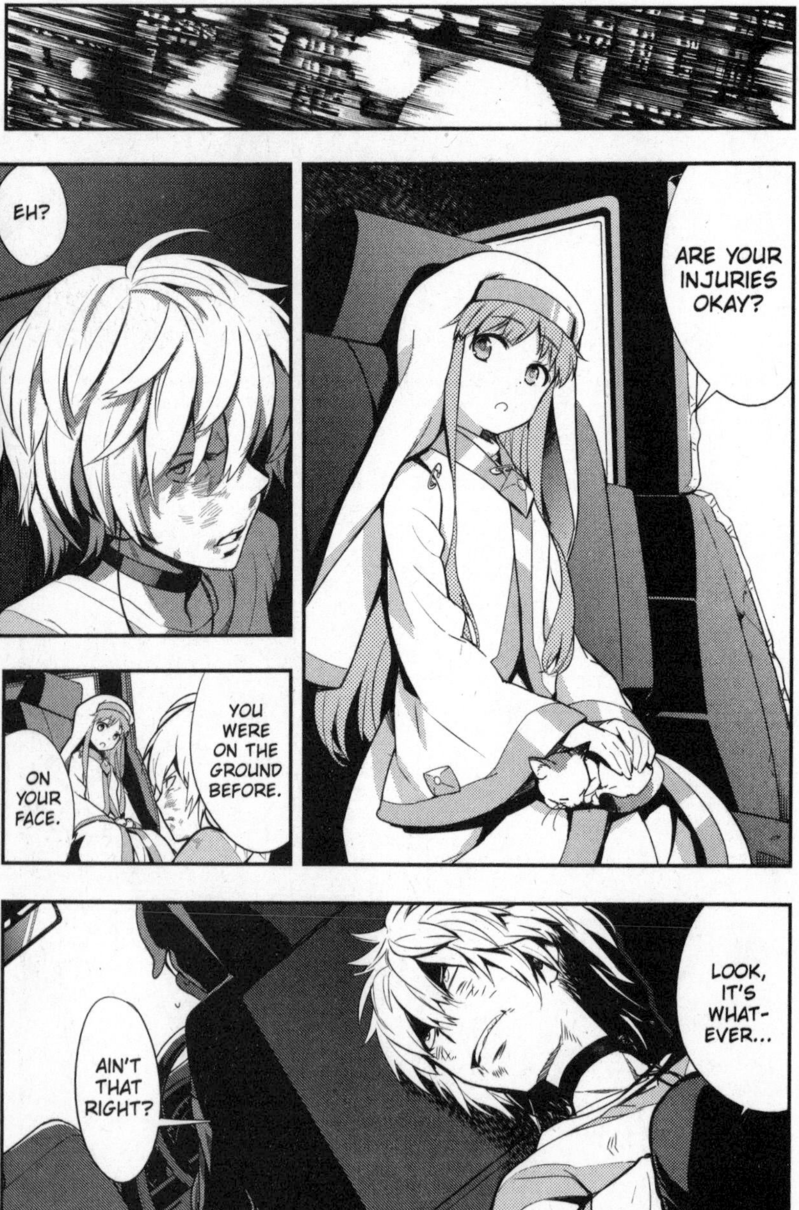
ARE YOUR INJURIES OKAY?
EH?
YOU WERE ON THE GROUND BEFORE.
ON YOUR FACE.
LOOK, IT'S WHAT-EVER...
AIN'T THAT RIGHT?

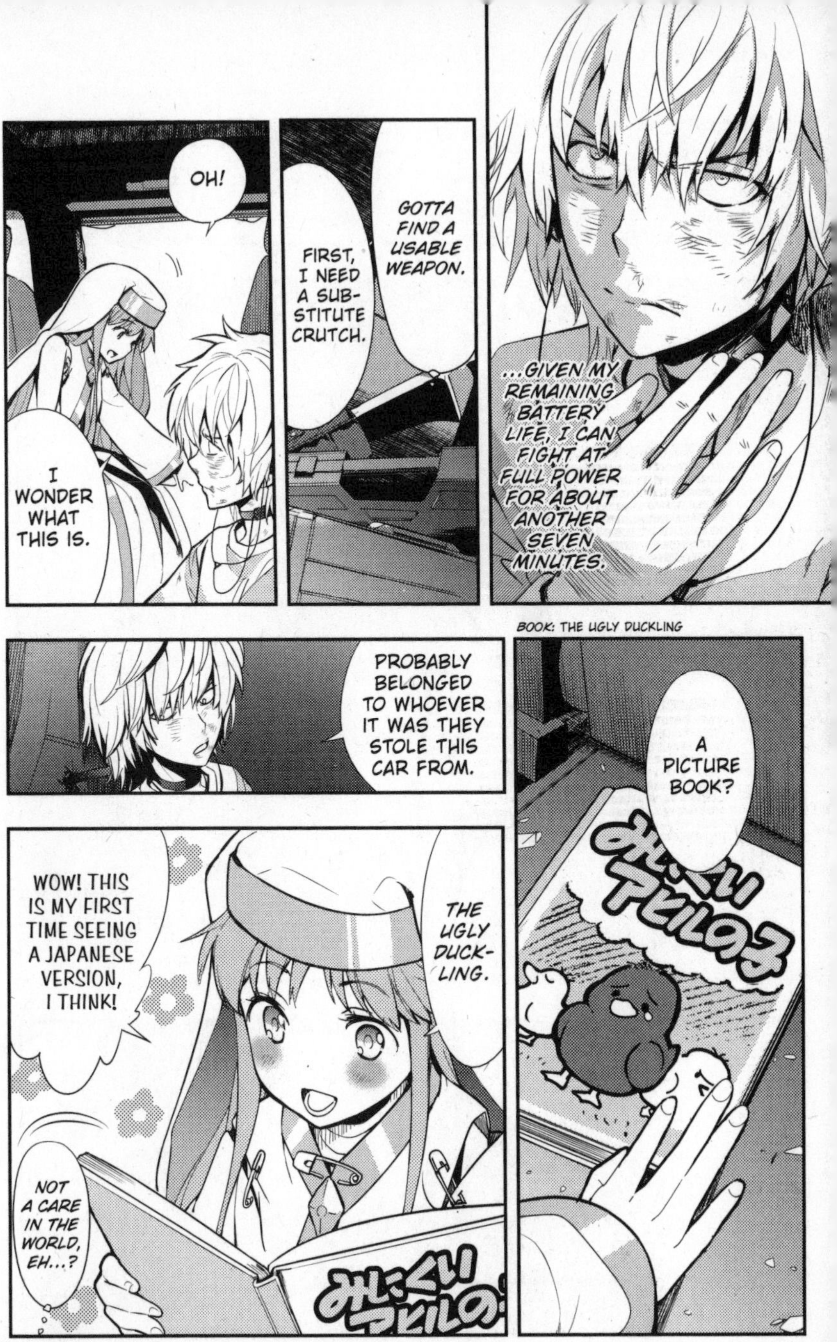
...GIVEN MY REMAINING BATTERY LIFE, I CAN FIGHT AT FULL POWER FOR ABOUT ANOTHER SEVEN MINUTES.
GOTTA FIND A USABLE WEAPON.
FIRST, I NEED A SUBSTITUTE CRUTCH.
OH!
I WONDER WHAT THIS IS.
BOOK: THE UGLY DUCKLING
A PICTURE BOOK?
PROBABLY BELONGED TO WHOEVER IT WAS THEY STOLE THIS CAR FROM.
THE UGLY DUCKLING.
WOW! THIS IS MY FIRST TIME SEEING A JAPANESE VERSION, I THINK!
NOT A CARE IN THE WORLD, EH...?

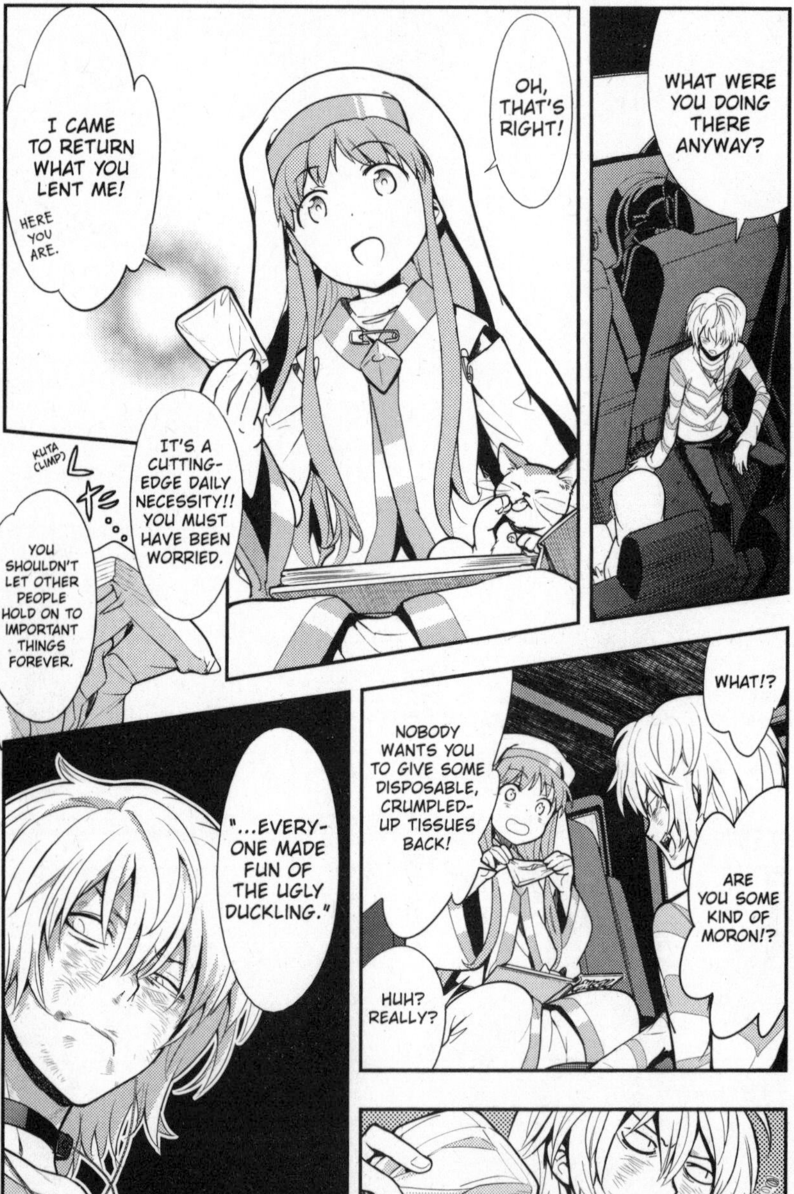
WHAT WERE YOU DOING THERE ANYWAY?
OH, THAT'S RIGHT!
I CAME TO RETURN WHAT YOU LENT ME!
HERE YOU ARE.
IT'S A CUTTING-EDGE DAILY NECESSITY!! YOU MUST HAVE BEEN WORRIED.
KUTA (LIMP)
YOU SHOULDN'T LET OTHER PEOPLE HOLD ON TO IMPORTANT THINGS FOREVER.
WHAT!?
NOBODY WANTS YOU TO GIVE SOME DISPOSABLE, CRUMPLED-UP TISSUES BACK!
ARE YOU SOME KIND OF MORON!?
HUH? REALLY?
"...EVERY-ONE MADE FUN OF THE UGLY DUCKLING."

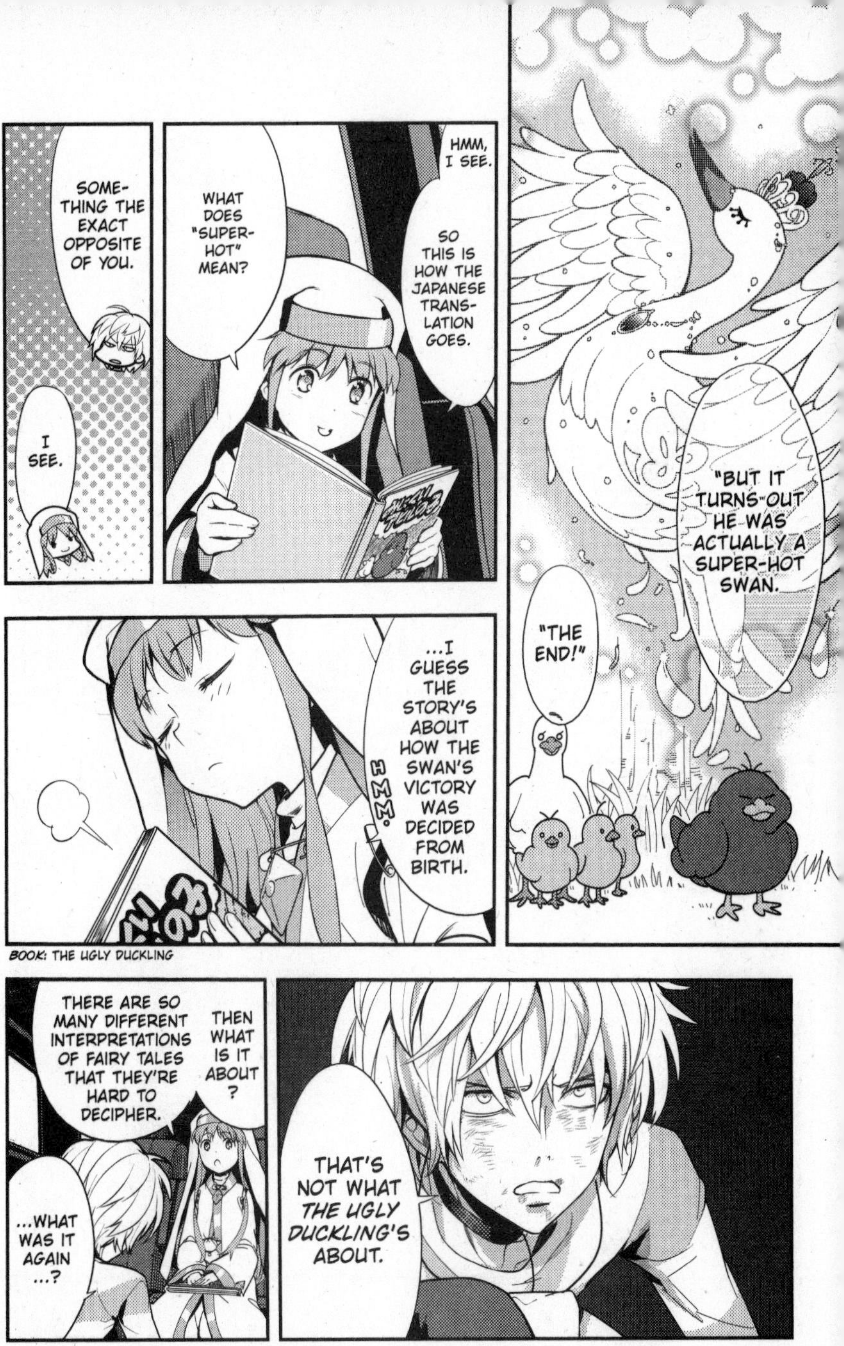
"BUT IT TURNS OUT HE WAS ACTUALLY A SUPER-HOT SWAN.
"THE END!"
HMM, I SEE.
SO THIS IS HOW THE JAPANESE TRANSLATION GOES.
WHAT DOES "SUPER-HOT" MEAN?
SOMETHING THE EXACT OPPOSITE OF YOU.
I SEE.
...I GUESS THE STORY'S ABOUT HOW THE SWAN'S VICTORY WAS DECIDED FROM BIRTH.
HMM.
BOOK: THE UGLY DUCKLING
THAT'S NOT WHAT *THE UGLY DUCKLING*'S ABOUT.
THEN WHAT IS IT ABOUT?
THERE ARE SO MANY DIFFERENT INTERPRETATIONS OF FAIRY TALES THAT THEY'RE HARD TO DECIPHER.
...WHAT WAS IT AGAIN ...?

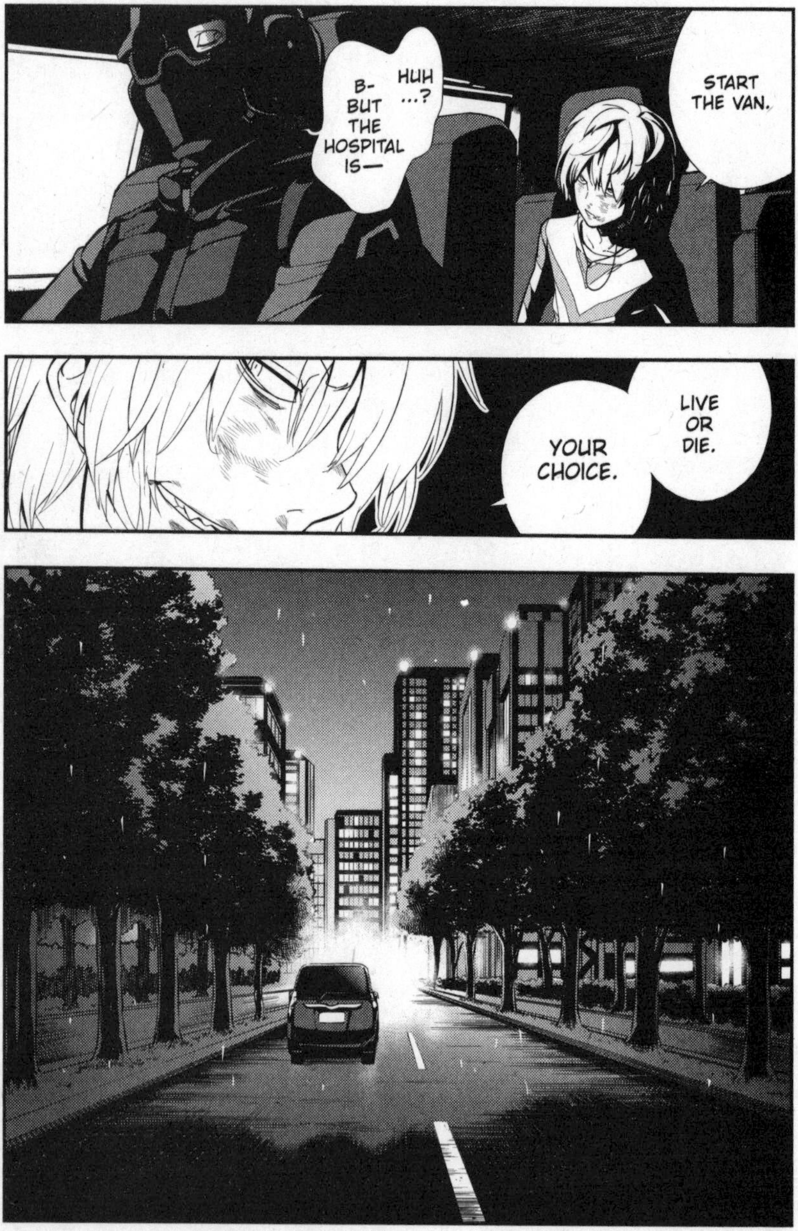
START THE VAN.
HUH ...? B-BUT THE HOSPITAL IS—
LIVE OR DIE.
YOUR CHOICE.

A Certain Magical Index

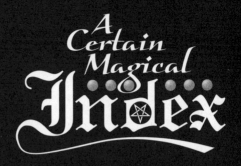

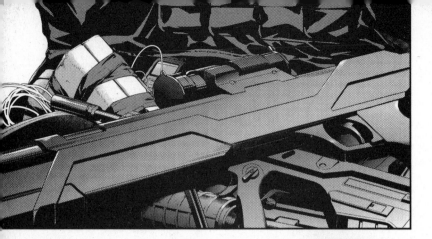

GUESS A SHOTGUN'S THE ONLY THING LONG ENOUGH TO BE A CRUTCH.

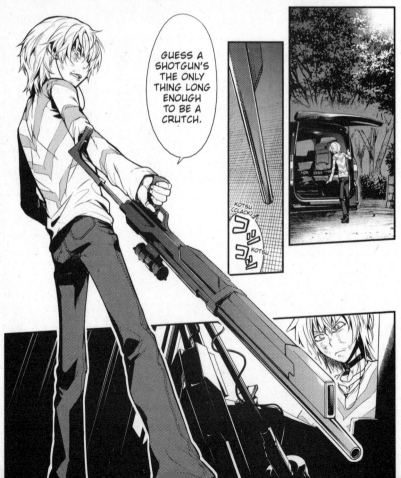

KOTSU
(CLACK)

KOTSU

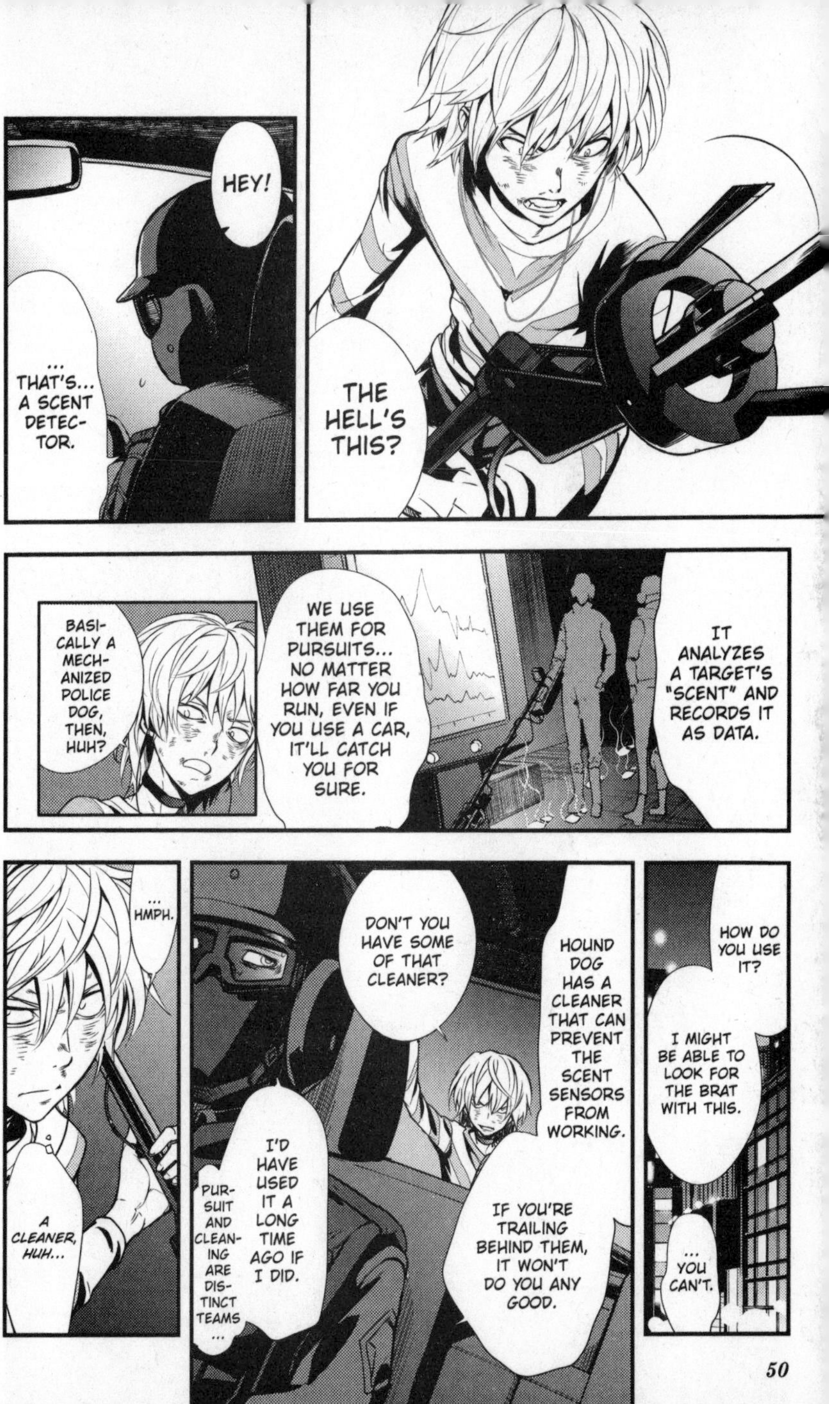
THE HELL'S THIS?
HEY!
...THAT'S... A SCENT DETECTOR.
IT ANALYZES A TARGET'S "SCENT" AND RECORDS IT AS DATA.
WE USE THEM FOR PURSUITS... NO MATTER HOW FAR YOU RUN, EVEN IF YOU USE A CAR, IT'LL CATCH YOU FOR SURE.
BASICALLY A MECHANIZED POLICE DOG, THEN, HUH?
HOW DO YOU USE IT?
I MIGHT BE ABLE TO LOOK FOR THE BRAT WITH THIS.
... YOU CAN'T.
HOUND DOG HAS A CLEANER THAT CAN PREVENT THE SCENT SENSORS FROM WORKING.
DON'T YOU HAVE SOME OF THAT CLEANER?
IF YOU'RE TRAILING BEHIND THEM, IT WON'T DO YOU ANY GOOD.
I'D HAVE USED IT A LONG TIME AGO IF I DID.
PURSUIT AND CLEANING ARE DISTINCT TEAMS...
... HMPH.
A CLEANER, HUH...

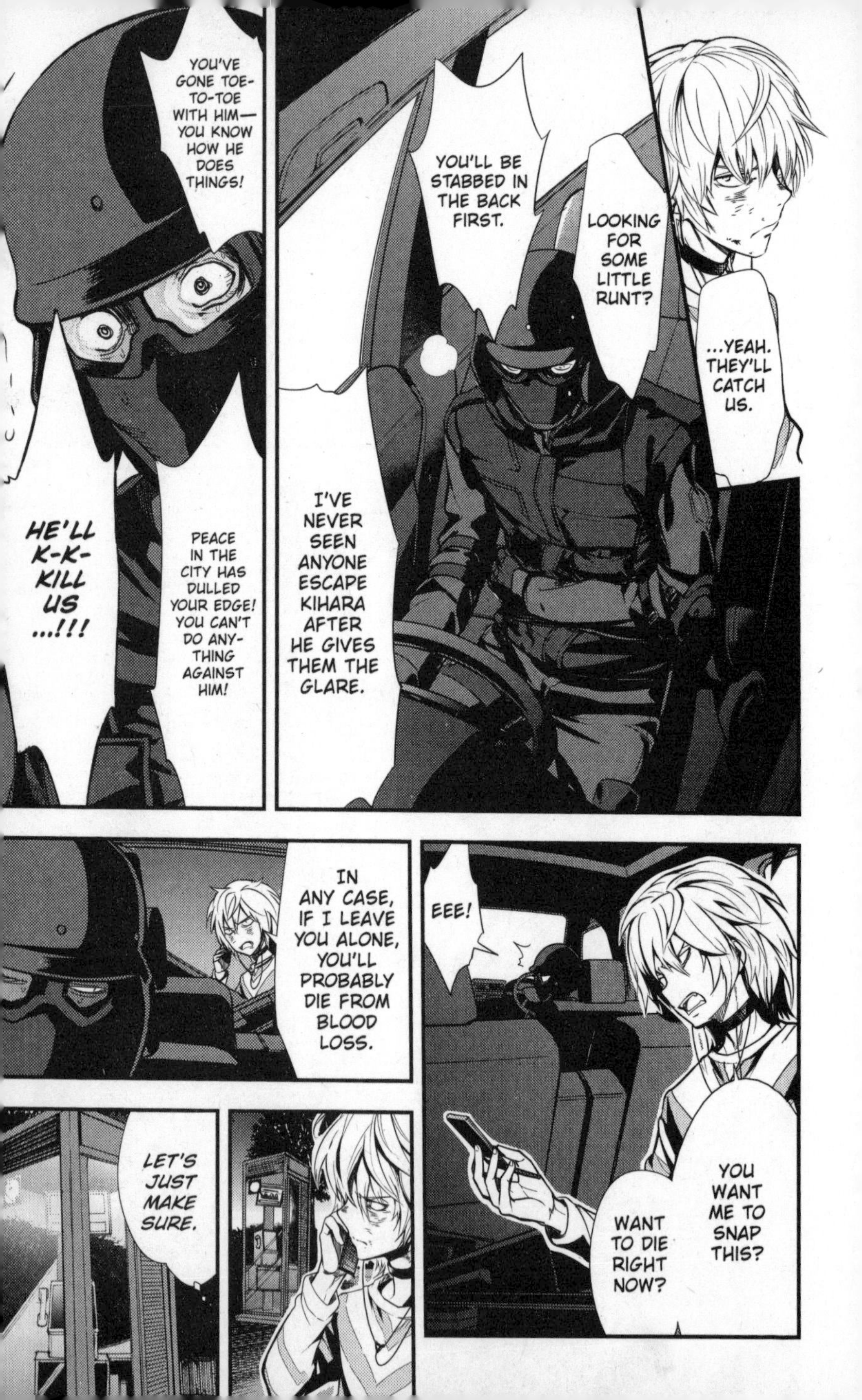
LOOKING FOR SOME LITTLE RUNT?
...YEAH. THEY'LL CATCH US.
YOU'LL BE STABBED IN THE BACK FIRST.
I'VE NEVER SEEN ANYONE ESCAPE KIHARA AFTER HE GIVES THEM THE GLARE.
YOU'VE GONE TOE-TO-TOE WITH HIM—YOU KNOW HOW HE DOES THINGS!
PEACE IN THE CITY HAS DULLED YOUR EDGE! YOU CAN'T DO ANYTHING AGAINST HIM!
HE'LL K-K-KILL US ...!!!
EEE!
YOU WANT ME TO SNAP THIS?
WANT TO DIE RIGHT NOW?
IN ANY CASE, IF I LEAVE YOU ALONE, YOU'LL PROBABLY DIE FROM BLOOD LOSS.
LET'S JUST MAKE SURE.

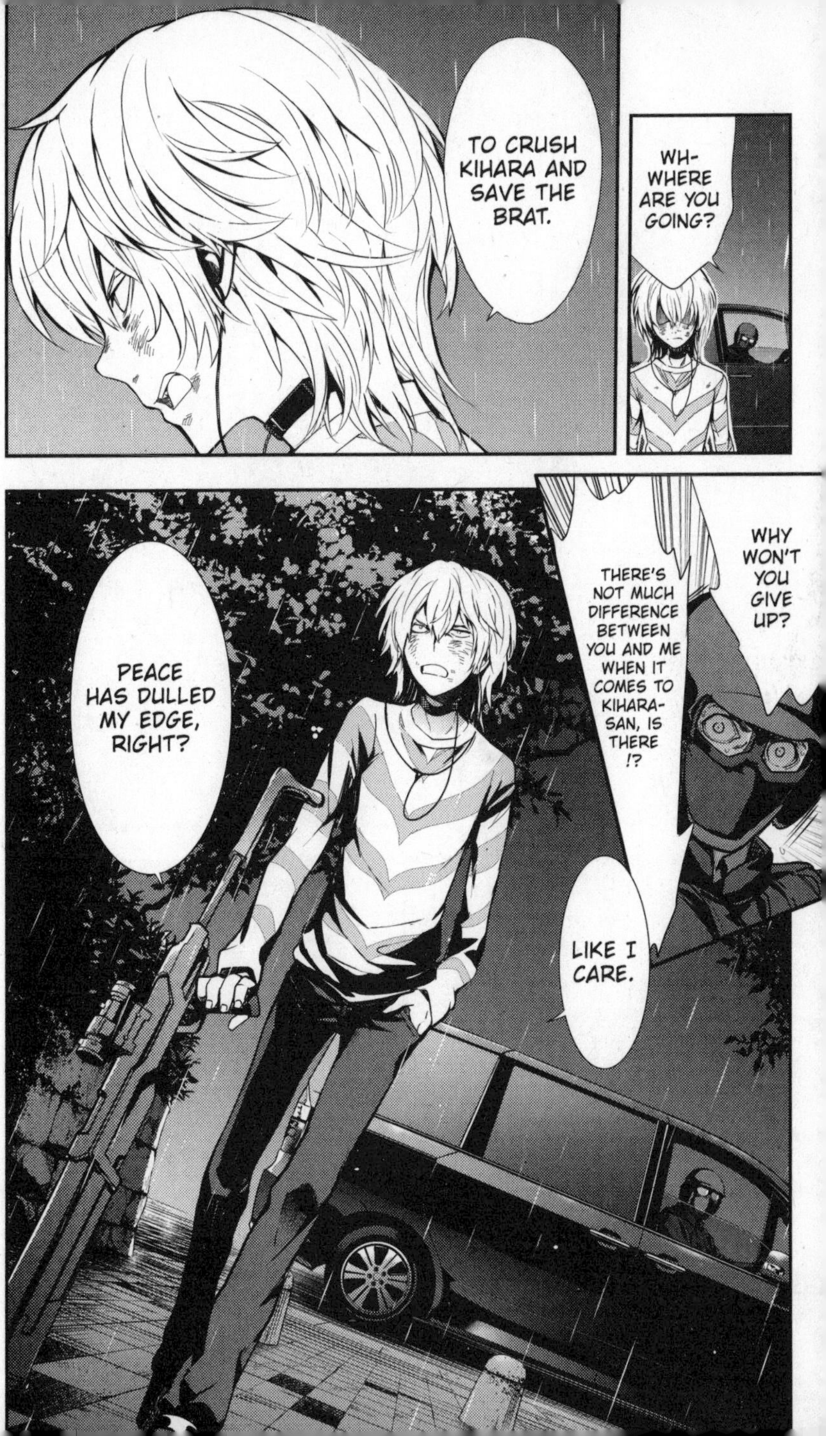
WH- WHERE ARE YOU GOING?
TO CRUSH KIHARA AND SAVE THE BRAT.
WHY WON'T YOU GIVE UP?
THERE'S NOT MUCH DIFFERENCE BETWEEN YOU AND ME WHEN IT COMES TO KIHARA-SAN, IS THERE !?
LIKE I CARE.
PEACE HAS DULLED MY EDGE, RIGHT?

#106 INTRUDER ③

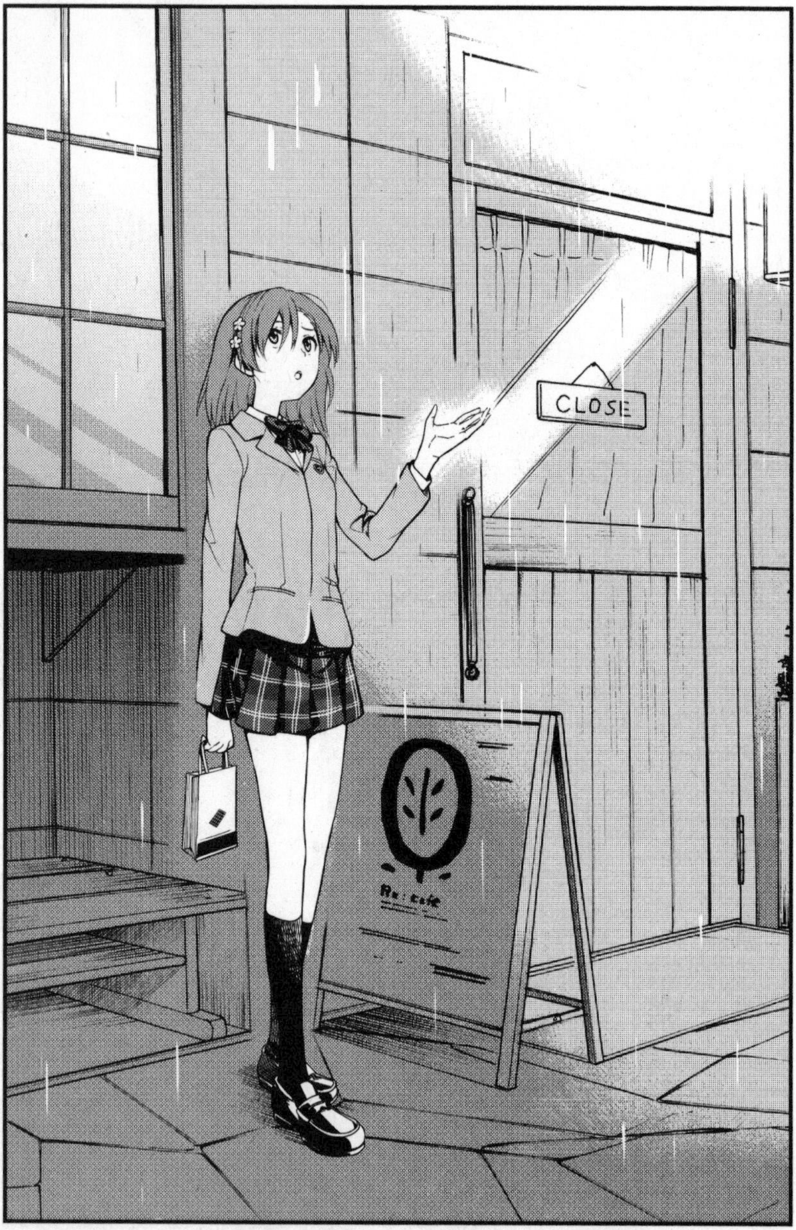
CLOSE

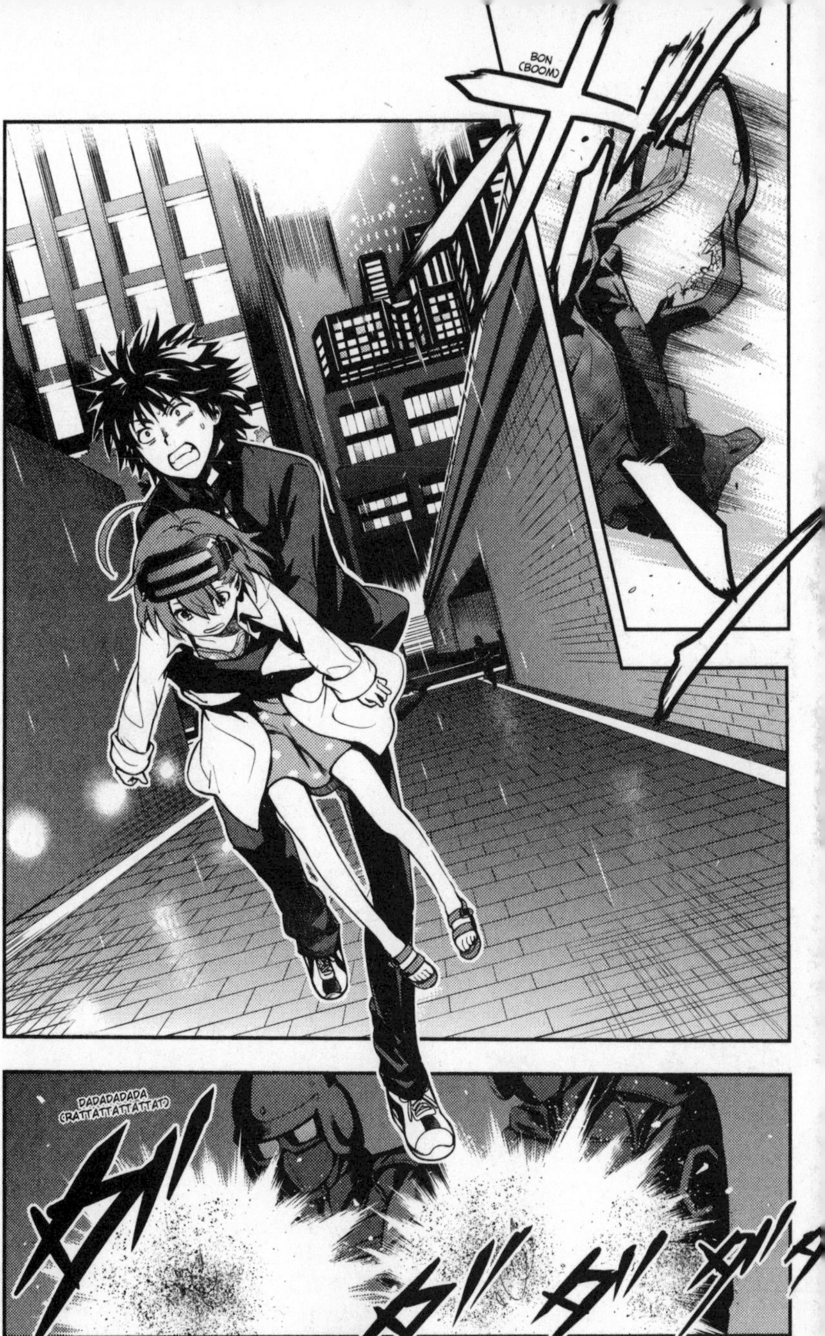
BON
(BOOM)
DADADADADA
(RATTATTATTATTAT)

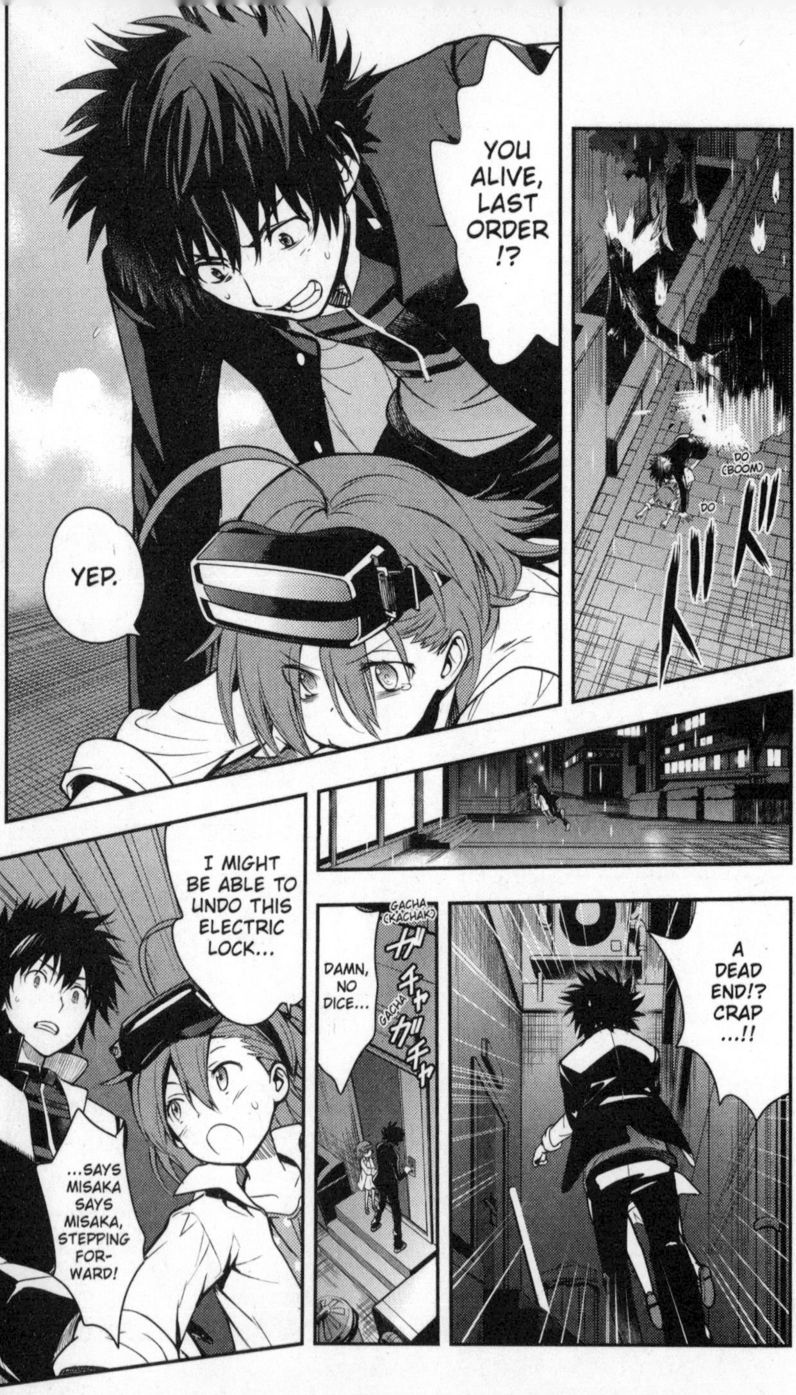

DO (BOOM)
DO
YOU ALIVE, LAST ORDER!?
YEP.
A DEAD END!? CRAP...!!
GACHA (KACHAK)
DAMN, NO DICE...
GACHA
I MIGHT BE ABLE TO UNDO THIS ELECTRIC LOCK...
...SAYS MISAKA SAYS MISAKA, STEPPING FOR-WARD!

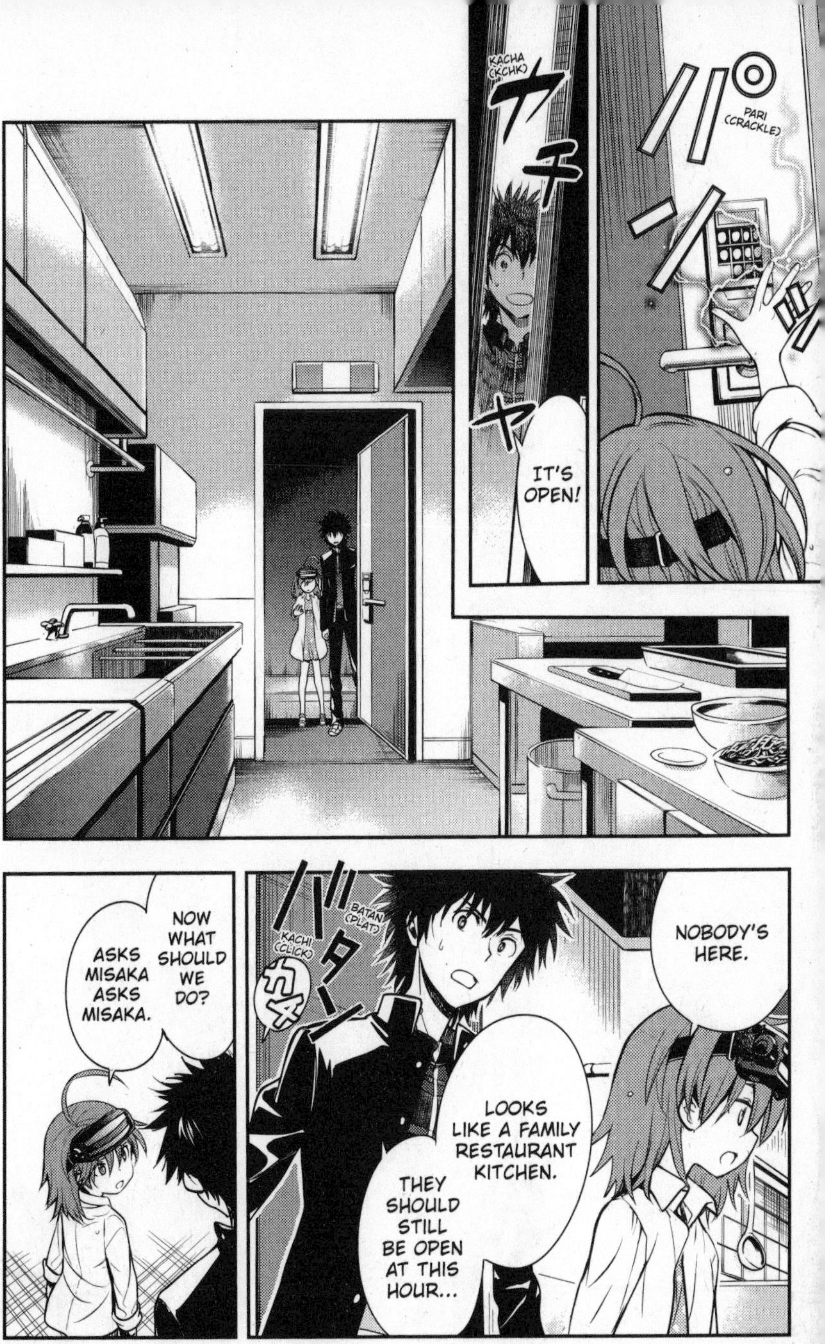
PARI (CRACKLE)
KACHA (KCHK)
IT'S OPEN!
NOBODY'S HERE.
BATAN (PLAT)
KACHI (CLICK)
LOOKS LIKE A FAMILY RESTAURANT KITCHEN.
THEY SHOULD STILL BE OPEN AT THIS HOUR...
NOW WHAT SHOULD WE DO?
ASKS MISAKA ASKS MISAKA.

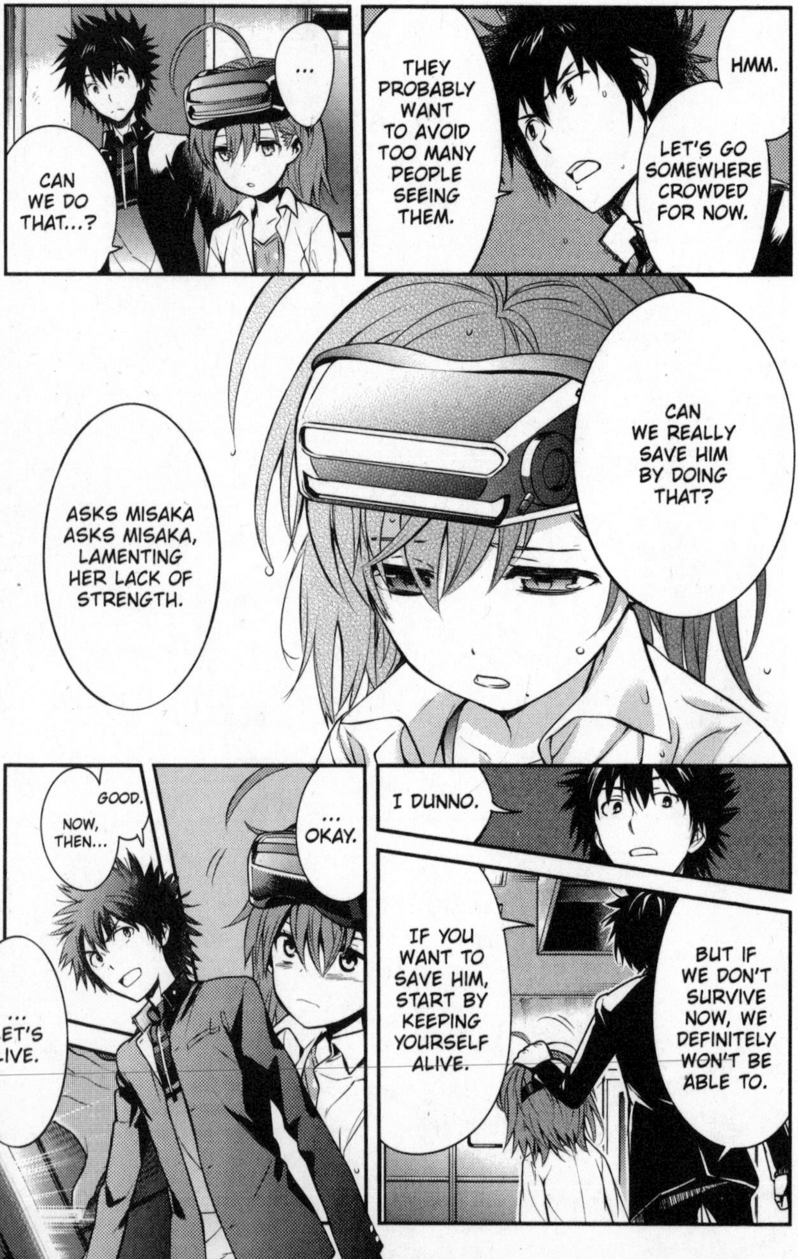
HMM.
LET'S GO SOMEWHERE CROWDED FOR NOW.
THEY PROBABLY WANT TO AVOID TOO MANY PEOPLE SEEING THEM.
...
CAN WE DO THAT...?
CAN WE REALLY SAVE HIM BY DOING THAT?
ASKS MISAKA ASKS MISAKA, LAMENTING HER LACK OF STRENGTH.
I DUNNO.
BUT IF WE DON'T SURVIVE NOW, WE DEFINITELY WON'T BE ABLE TO.
IF YOU WANT TO SAVE HIM, START BY KEEPING YOURSELF ALIVE.
... OKAY.
GOOD. NOW, THEN...
... LET'S LIVE.

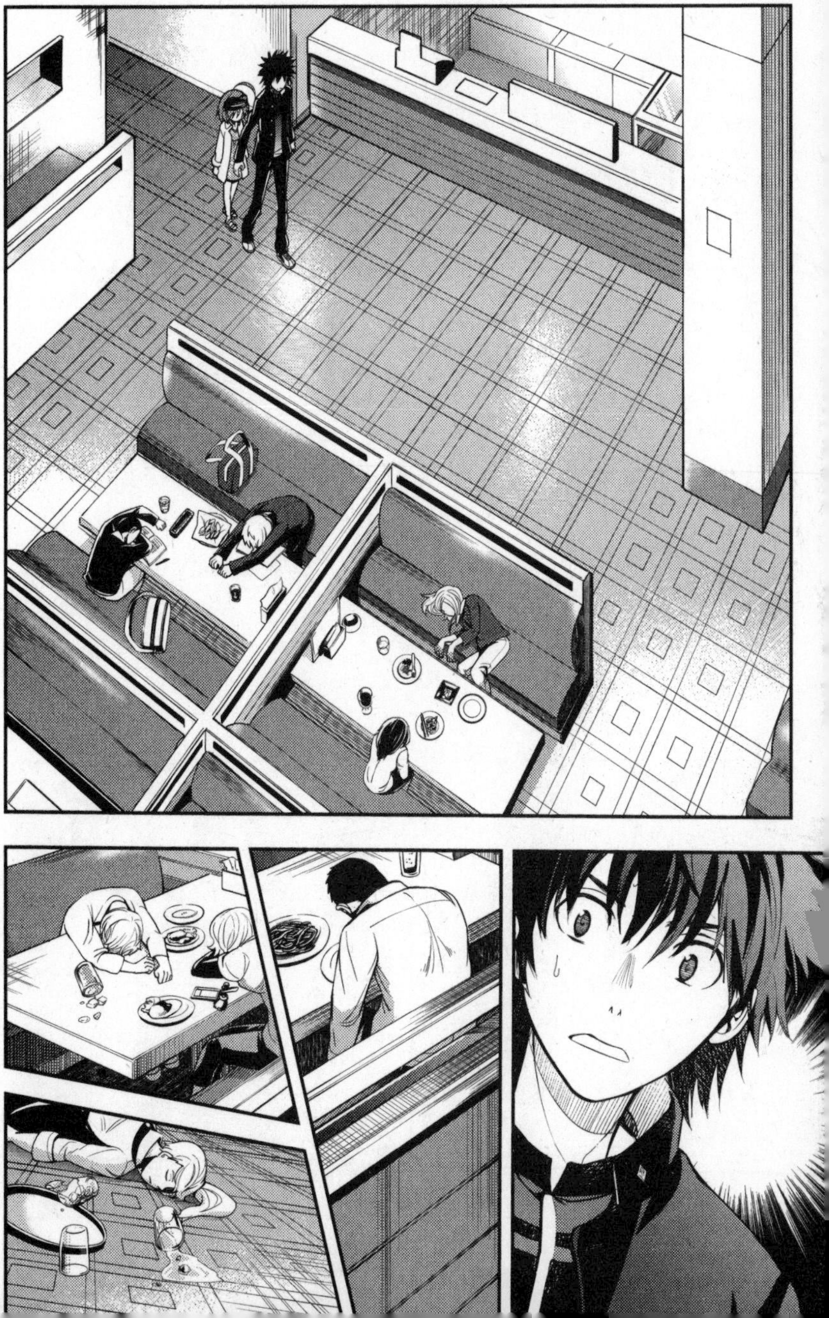

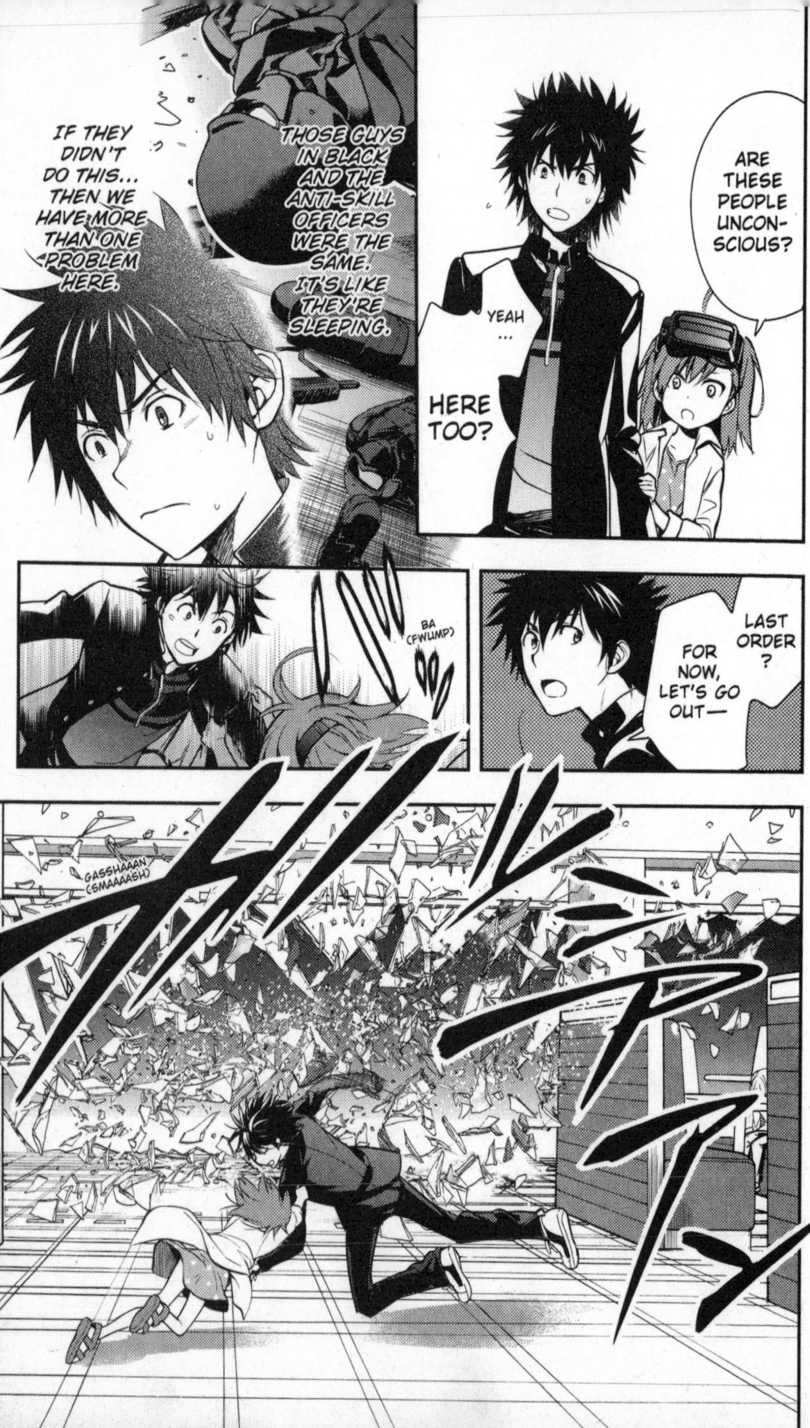
ARE THESE PEOPLE UNCON-SCIOUS?
YEAH ...
HERE TOO?
THOSE GUYS IN BLACK AND THE ANTI-SKILL OFFICERS WERE THE SAME. IT'S LIKE THEY'RE SLEEPING.
IF THEY DIDN'T DO THIS... THEN WE HAVE MORE THAN ONE PROBLEM HERE.
LAST ORDER ?
FOR NOW, LET'S GO OUT—
BA (FWUMP)
GASSHAAAN (SMAAAASH)

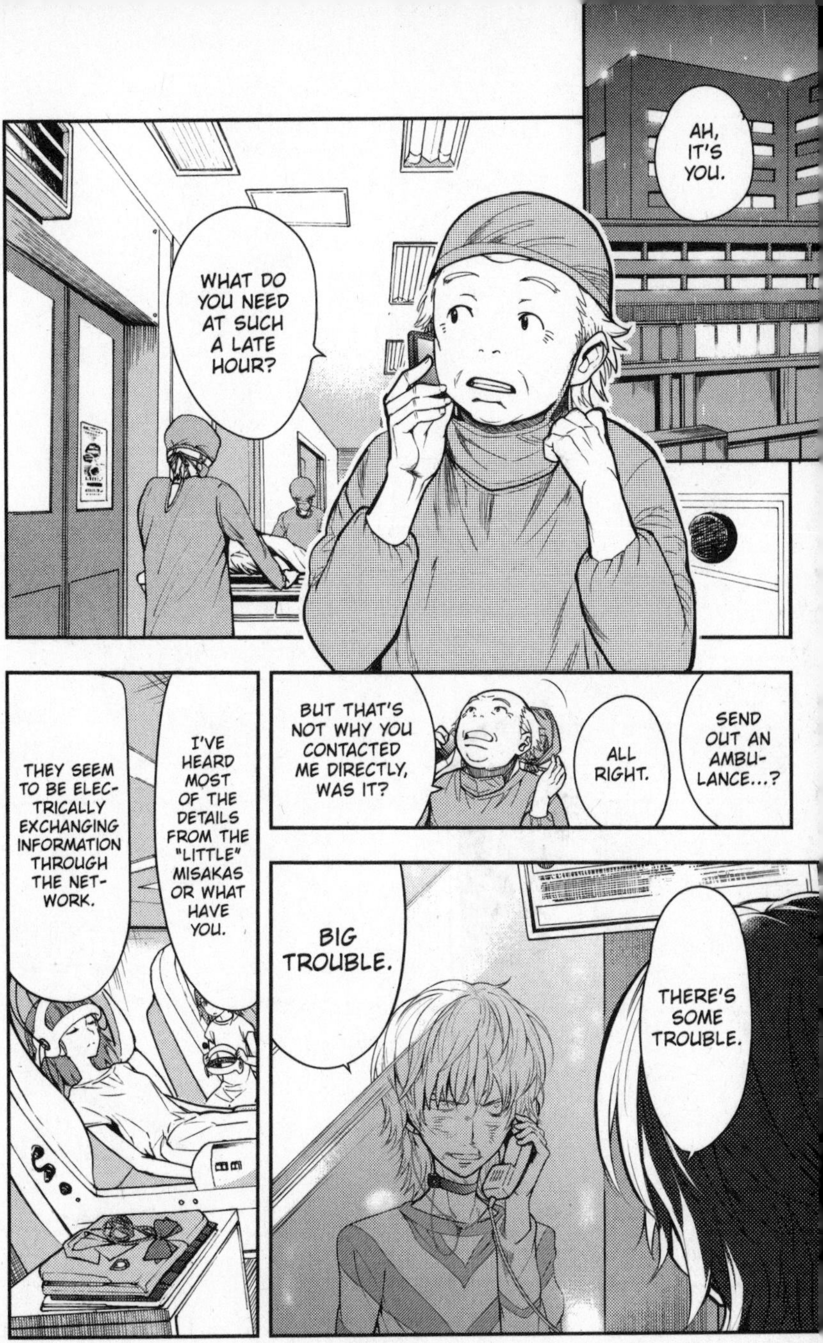
AH, IT'S YOU.
WHAT DO YOU NEED AT SUCH A LATE HOUR?
SEND OUT AN AMBULANCE...?
ALL RIGHT.
BUT THAT'S NOT WHY YOU CONTACTED ME DIRECTLY, WAS IT?
THERE'S SOME TROUBLE.
BIG TROUBLE.
I'VE HEARD MOST OF THE DETAILS FROM THE "LITTLE" MISAKAS OR WHAT HAVE YOU.
THEY SEEM TO BE ELECTRICALLY EXCHANGING INFORMATION THROUGH THE NETWORK.

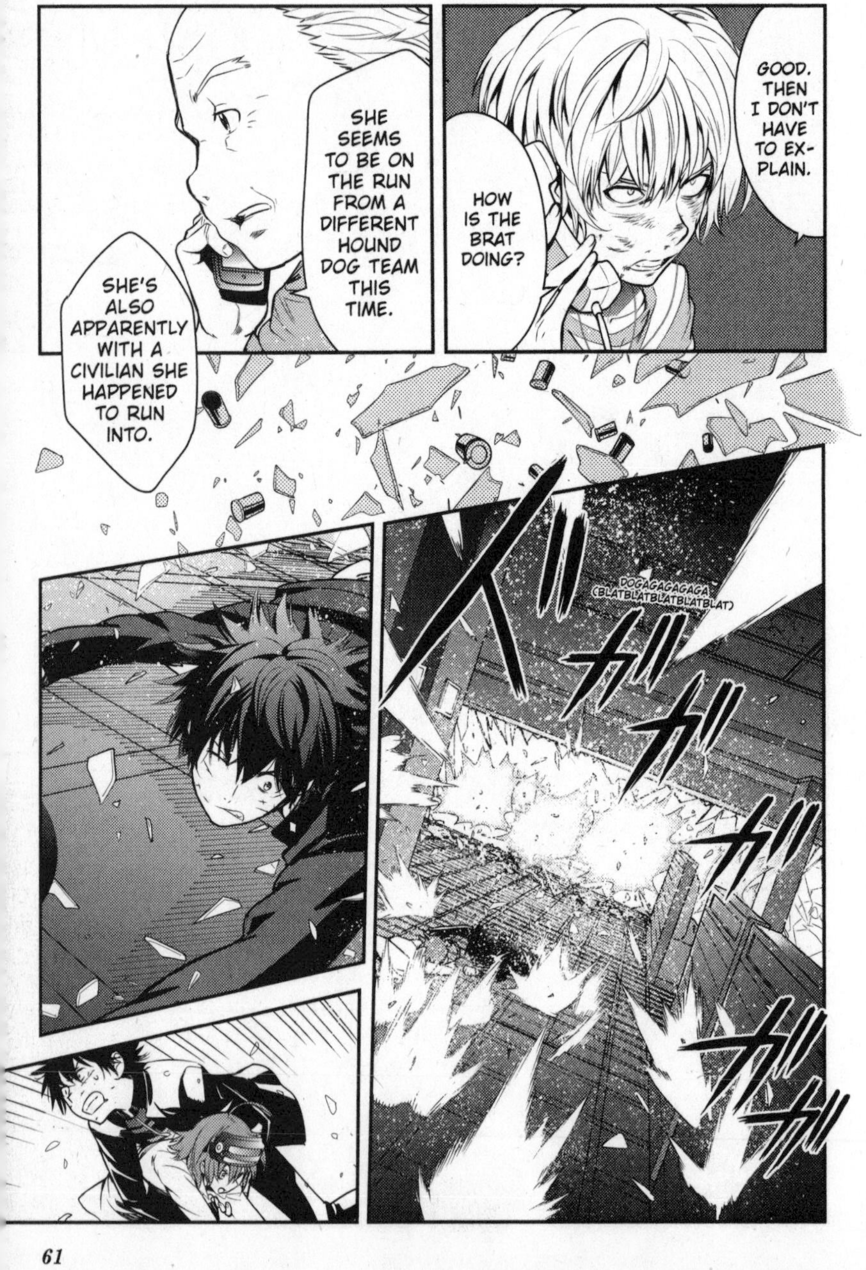
GOOD. THEN I DON'T HAVE TO EX-PLAIN.
HOW IS THE BRAT DOING?
SHE SEEMS TO BE ON THE RUN FROM A DIFFERENT HOUND DOG TEAM THIS TIME.
SHE'S ALSO APPARENTLY WITH A CIVILIAN SHE HAPPENED TO RUN INTO.
DOGAGAGAGAGA (BLATBLATBLATBLATBLAT)

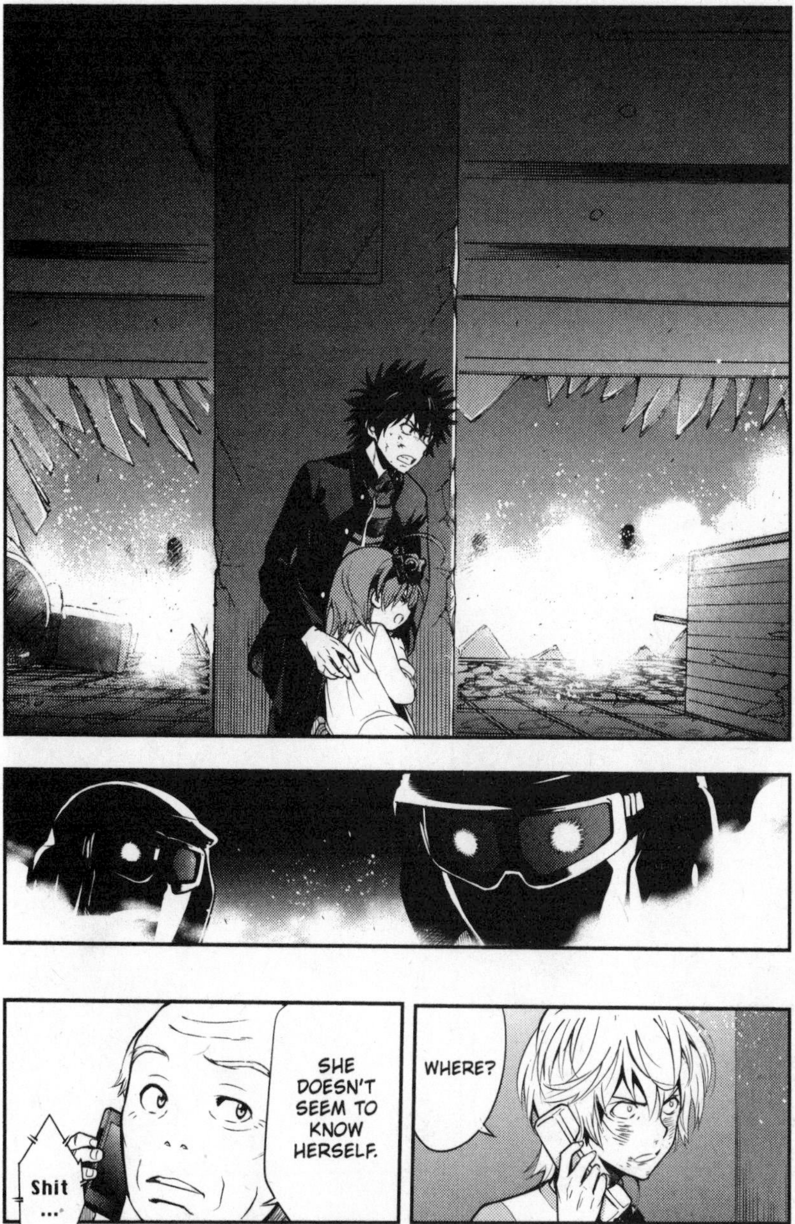
WHERE?
SHE DOESN'T SEEM TO KNOW HERSELF.
Shit ...

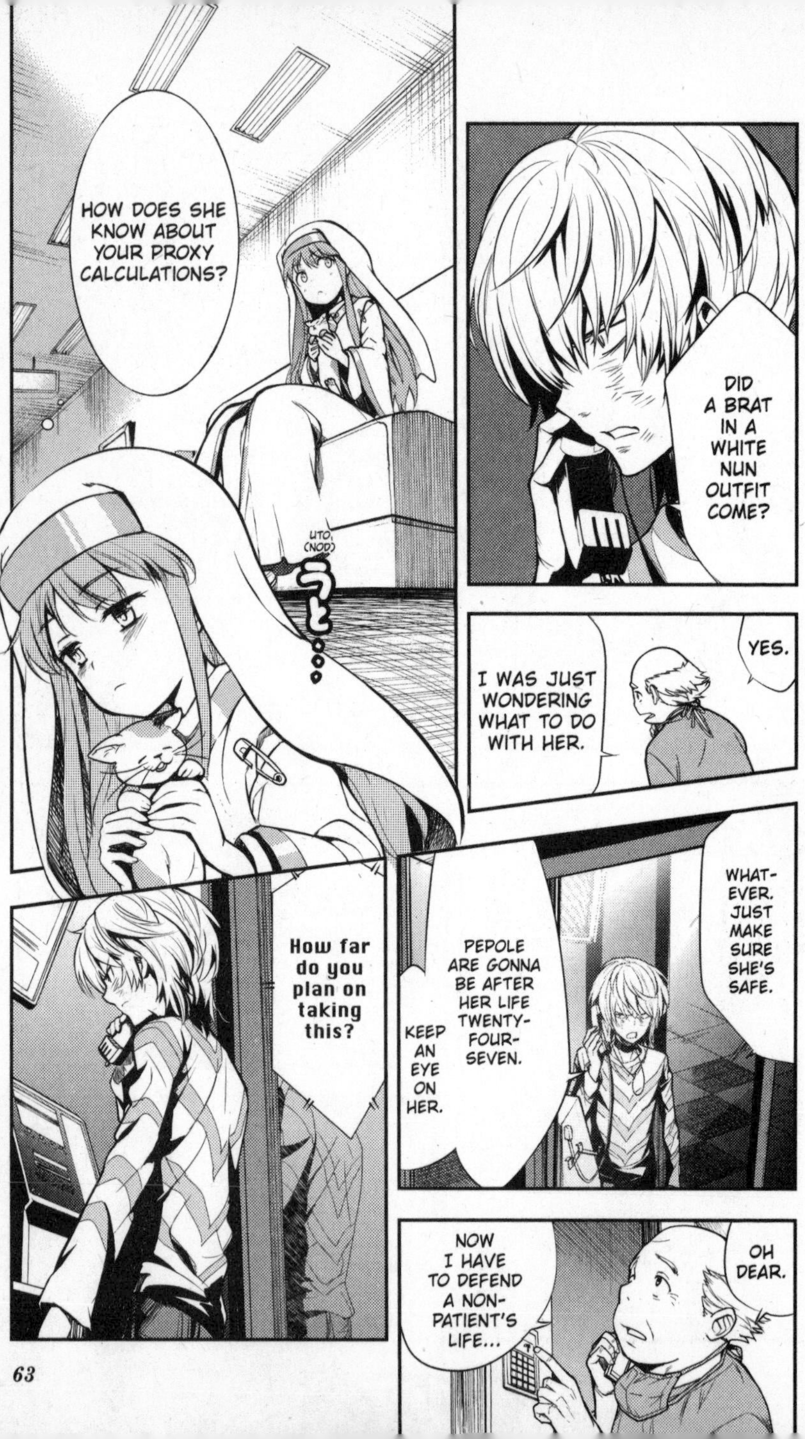
DID A BRAT IN A WHITE NUN OUTFIT COME?
YES.
I WAS JUST WONDERING WHAT TO DO WITH HER.
HOW DOES SHE KNOW ABOUT YOUR PROXY CALCULATIONS?
UTO (NOD)
うと…
WHAT-EVER. JUST MAKE SURE SHE'S SAFE.
PEPOLE ARE GONNA BE AFTER HER LIFE TWENTY-FOUR-SEVEN.
KEEP AN EYE ON HER.
How far do you plan on taking this?
OH DEAR.
NOW I HAVE TO DEFEND A NON-PATIENT'S LIFE...

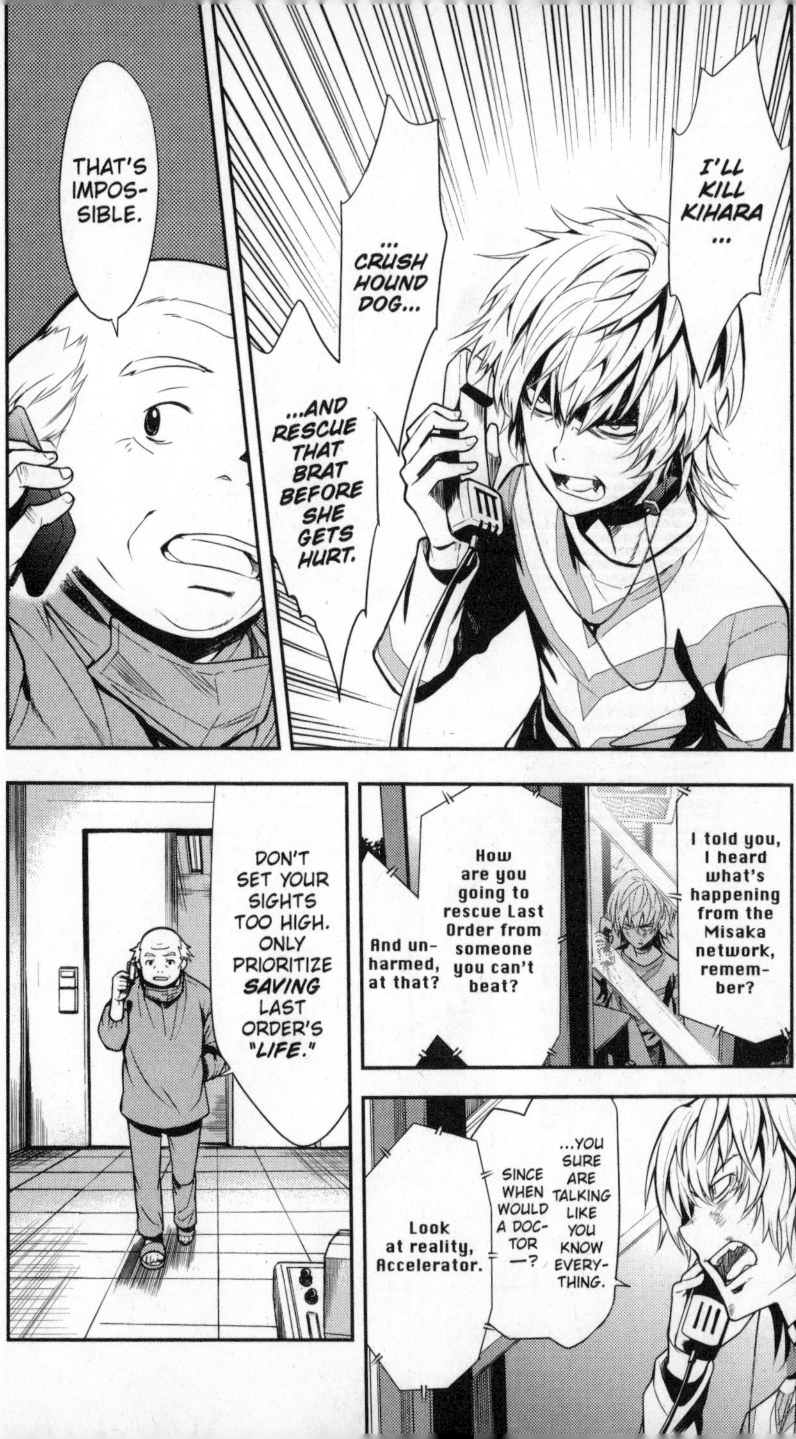
I'LL KILL KIHARA...
...CRUSH HOUND DOG...
...AND RESCUE THAT BRAT BEFORE SHE GETS HURT.
THAT'S IMPOS-SIBLE.
I told you, I heard what's happening from the Misaka network, remem-ber?
How are you going to rescue Last Order from someone you can't beat?
And un-harmed, at that?
...YOU SURE ARE TALKING LIKE YOU KNOW EVERY-THING.
SINCE WHEN WOULD A DOC-TOR —?
Look at reality, Accelerator.
DON'T SET YOUR SIGHTS TOO HIGH. ONLY PRIORITIZE *SAVING* LAST ORDER'S *"LIFE."*

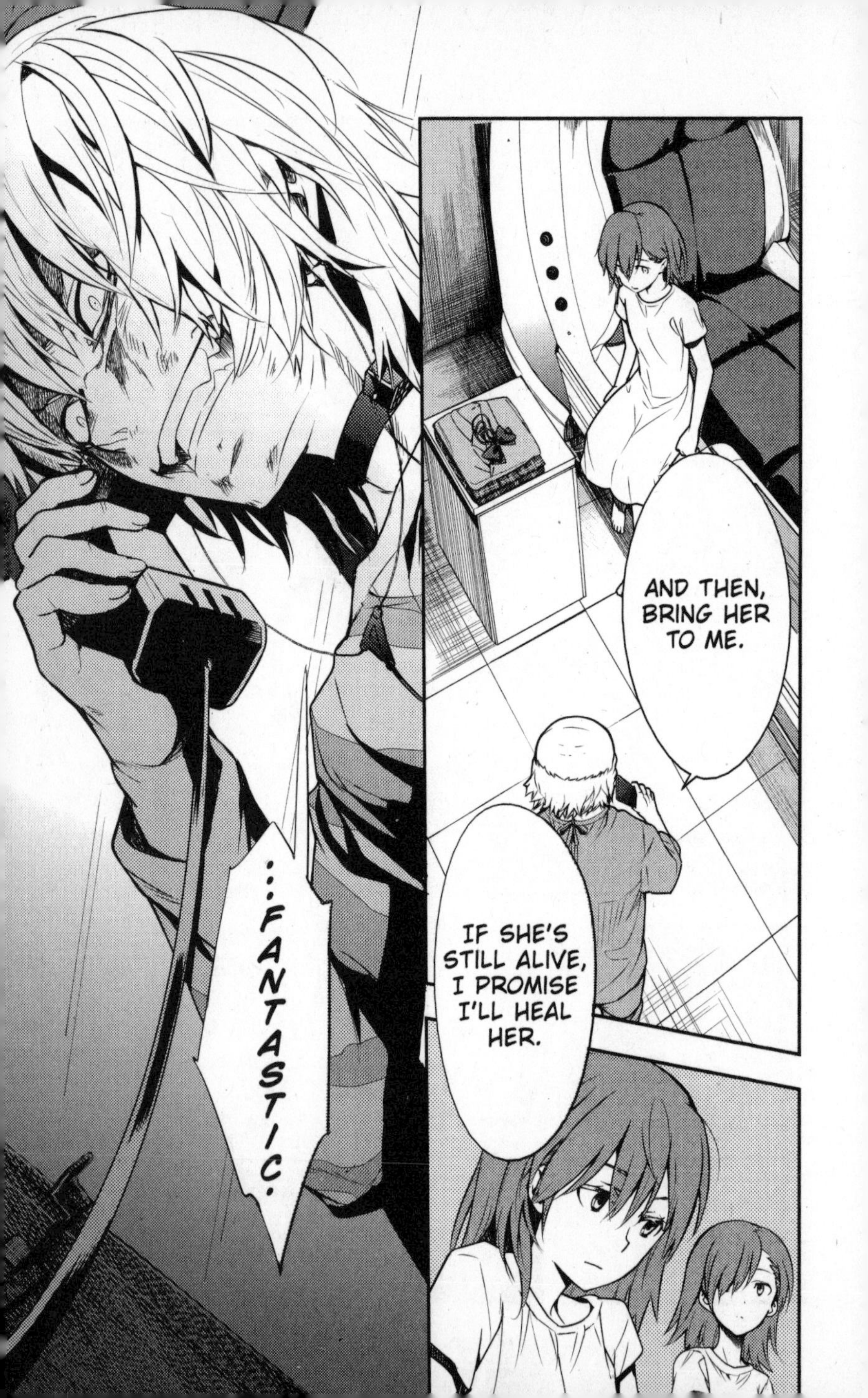
AND THEN, BRING HER TO ME.
IF SHE'S STILL ALIVE, I PROMISE I'LL HEAL HER.
...FANTASTIC.

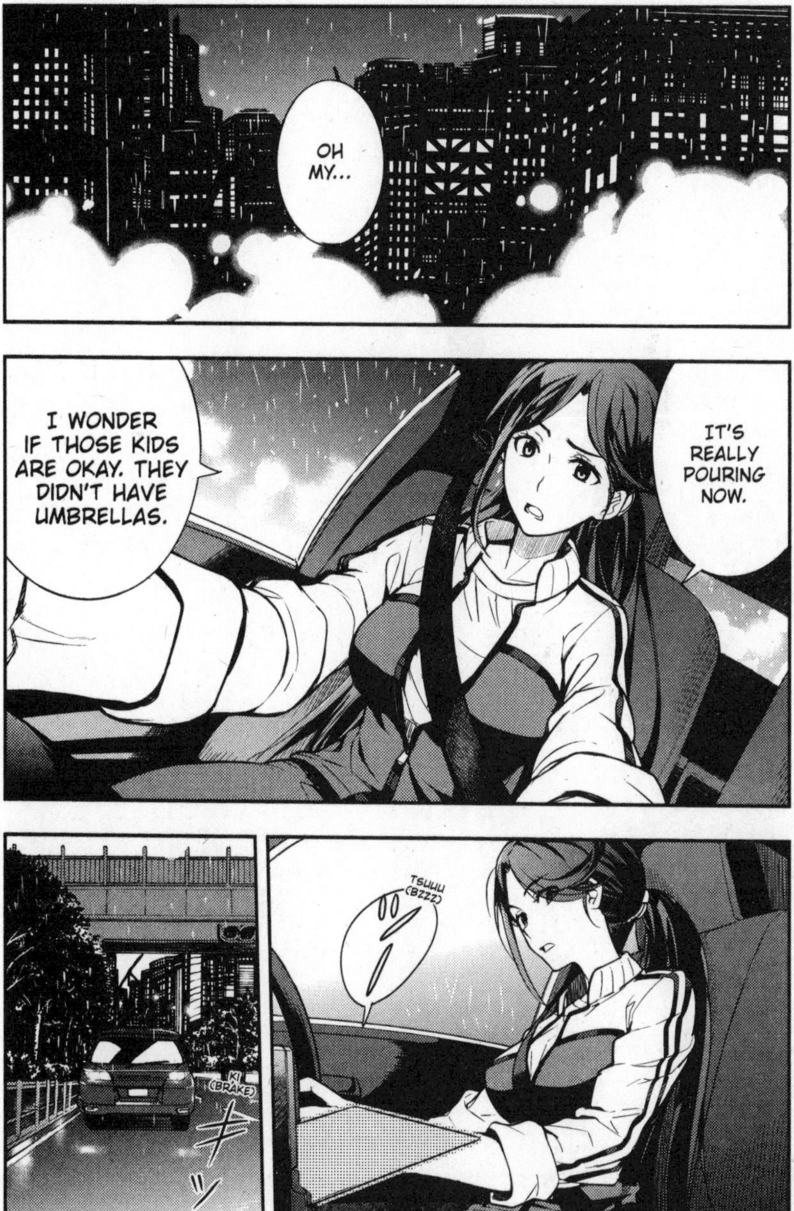
OH MY...
IT'S REALLY POURING NOW.
I WONDER IF THOSE KIDS ARE OKAY. THEY DIDN'T HAVE UMBRELLAS.
TSUUU (BZZZ)
KI (BRAKE)

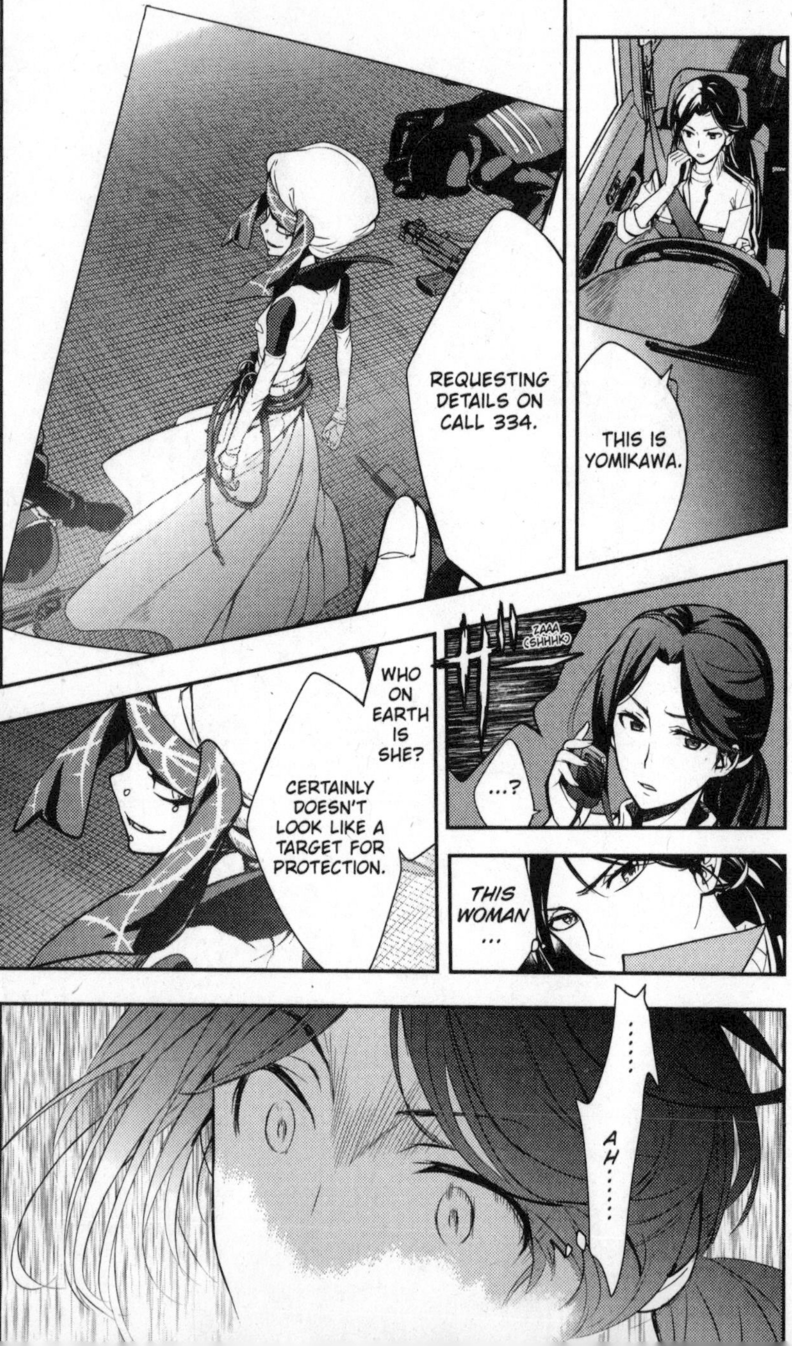
THIS IS YOMIKAWA.
REQUESTING DETAILS ON CALL 334.
ZAAA (SHHHK)
...?
THIS WOMAN ...
WHO ON EARTH IS SHE?
CERTAINLY DOESN'T LOOK LIKE A TARGET FOR PROTECTION.
......
AH......

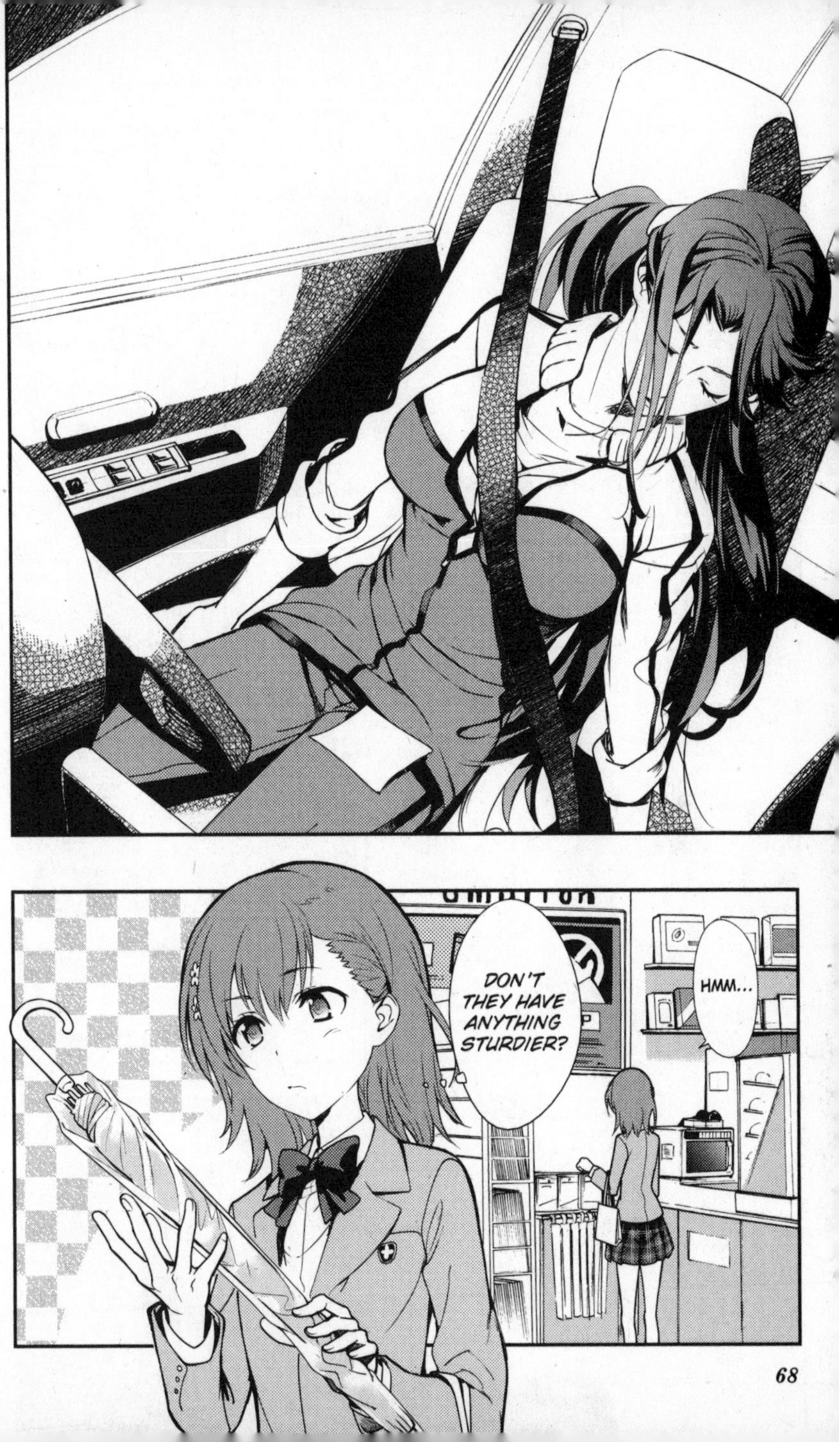
HMM...
DON'T THEY HAVE ANYTHING STURDIER?

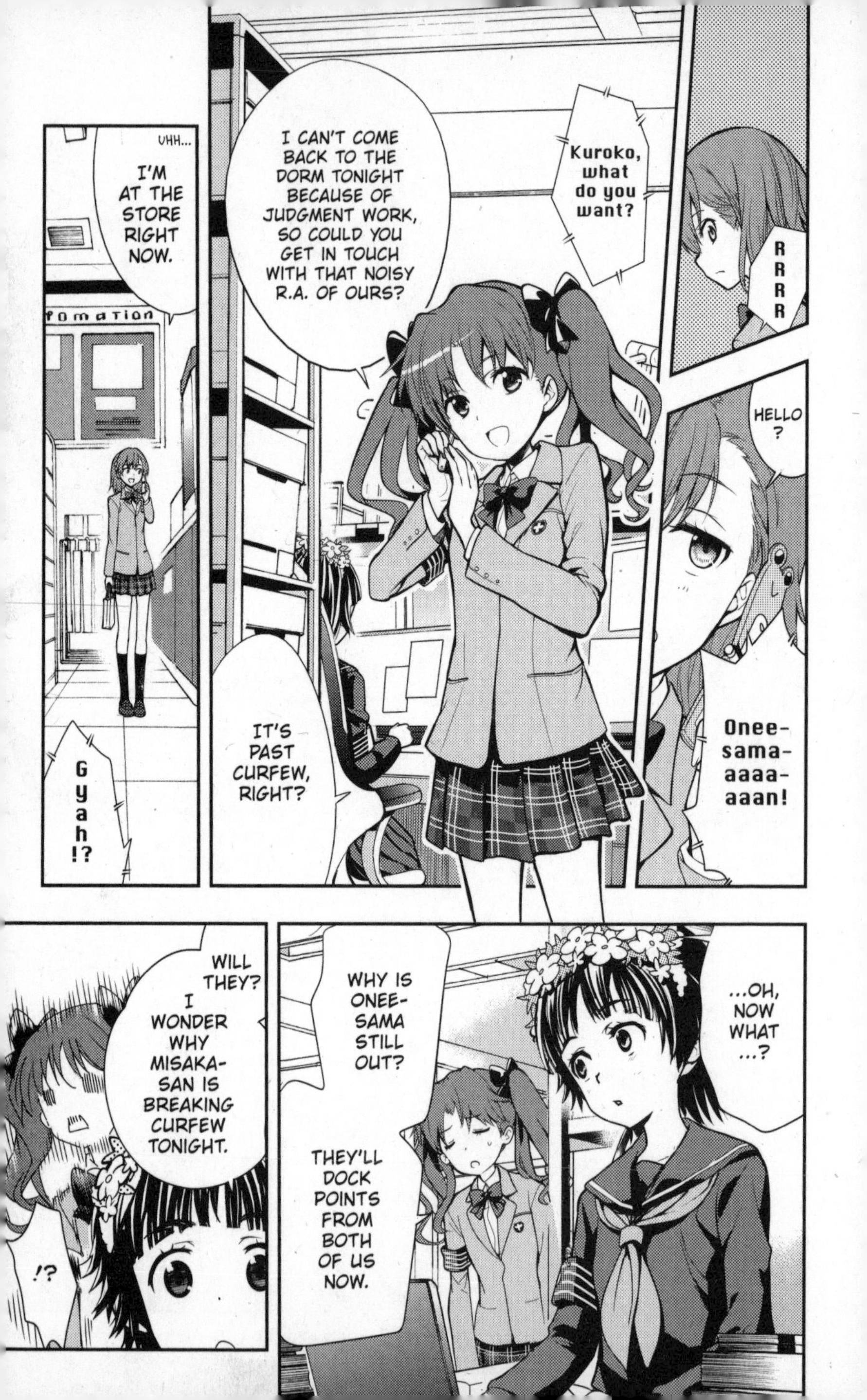
RRRR
Kuroko, what do you want?
HELLO?
Onee-sama-aaaa-aaan!
I CAN'T COME BACK TO THE DORM TONIGHT BECAUSE OF JUDGMENT WORK, SO COULD YOU GET IN TOUCH WITH THAT NOISY R.A. OF OURS?
IT'S PAST CURFEW, RIGHT?
UHH...
I'M AT THE STORE RIGHT NOW.
Gyah!?
...OH, NOW WHAT...?
WHY IS ONEE-SAMA STILL OUT?
THEY'LL DOCK POINTS FROM BOTH OF US NOW.
WILL THEY? I WONDER WHY MISAKA-SAN IS BREAKING CURFEW TONIGHT.
!?

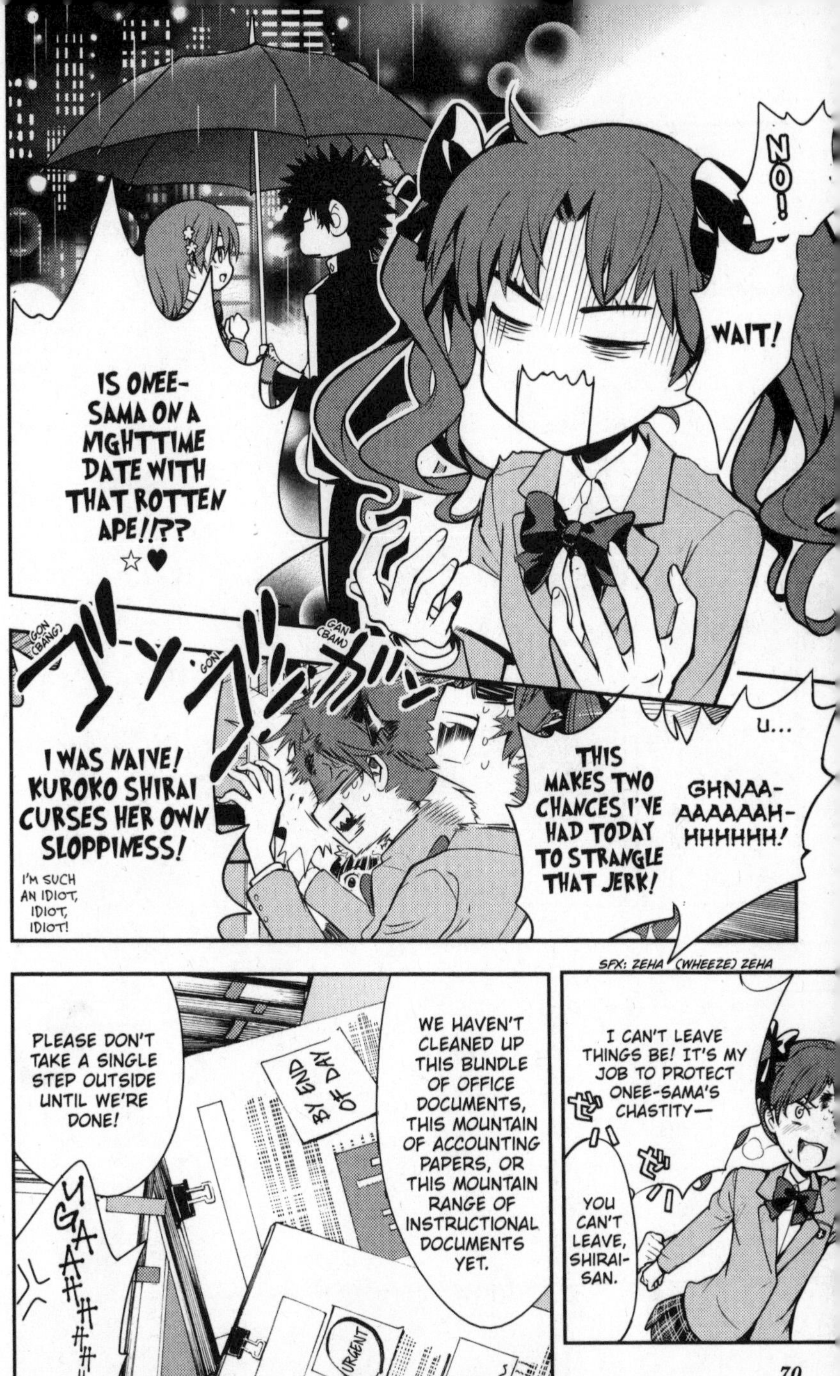
NO!
WAIT!
IS ONEE-SAMA ON A NIGHTTIME DATE WITH THAT ROTTEN APE!!?? ☆♥
GON (BANG) GON GAN (BAM)
U...
GHNAA-AAAAAAH-HHHHHH!
THIS MAKES TWO CHANCES I'VE HAD TODAY TO STRANGLE THAT JERK!
I WAS NAIVE! KUROKO SHIRAI CURSES HER OWN SLOPPINESS!
I'M SUCH AN IDIOT, IDIOT, IDIOT!
SFX: ZEHA (WHEEZE) ZEHA
I CAN'T LEAVE THINGS BE! IT'S MY JOB TO PROTECT ONEE-SAMA'S CHASTITY—
YOU CAN'T LEAVE, SHIRAI-SAN.
WE HAVEN'T CLEANED UP THIS BUNDLE OF OFFICE DOCUMENTS, THIS MOUNTAIN OF ACCOUNTING PAPERS, OR THIS MOUNTAIN RANGE OF INSTRUCTIONAL DOCUMENTS YET.
BY END OF DAY
PLEASE DON'T TAKE A SINGLE STEP OUTSIDE UNTIL WE'RE DONE!
URGENT
UGAH###!!

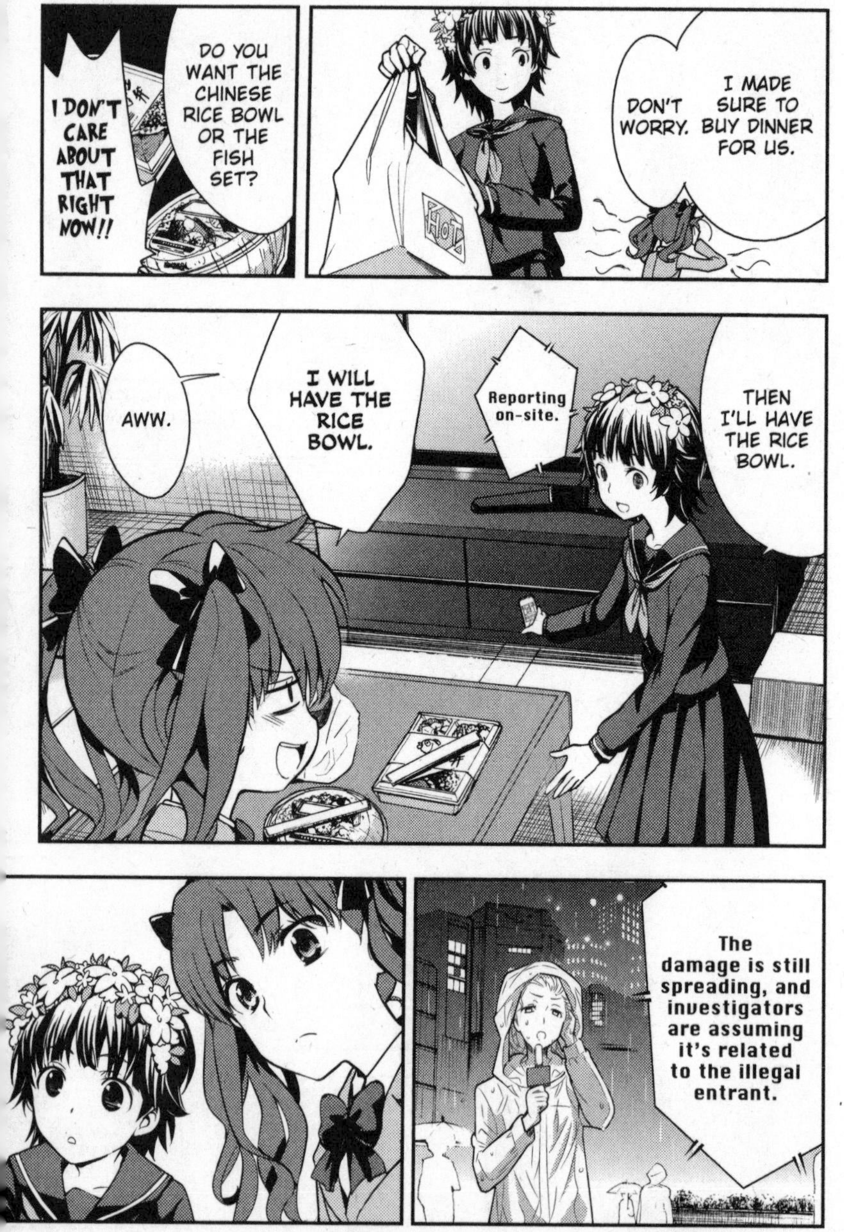
DON'T WORRY. I MADE SURE TO BUY DINNER FOR US.
DO YOU WANT THE CHINESE RICE BOWL OR THE FISH SET?
I DON'T CARE ABOUT THAT RIGHT NOW!!
THEN I'LL HAVE THE RICE BOWL.
Reporting on-site.
I WILL HAVE THE RICE BOWL.
AWW.
The damage is still spreading, and investigators are assuming it's related to the illegal entrant.

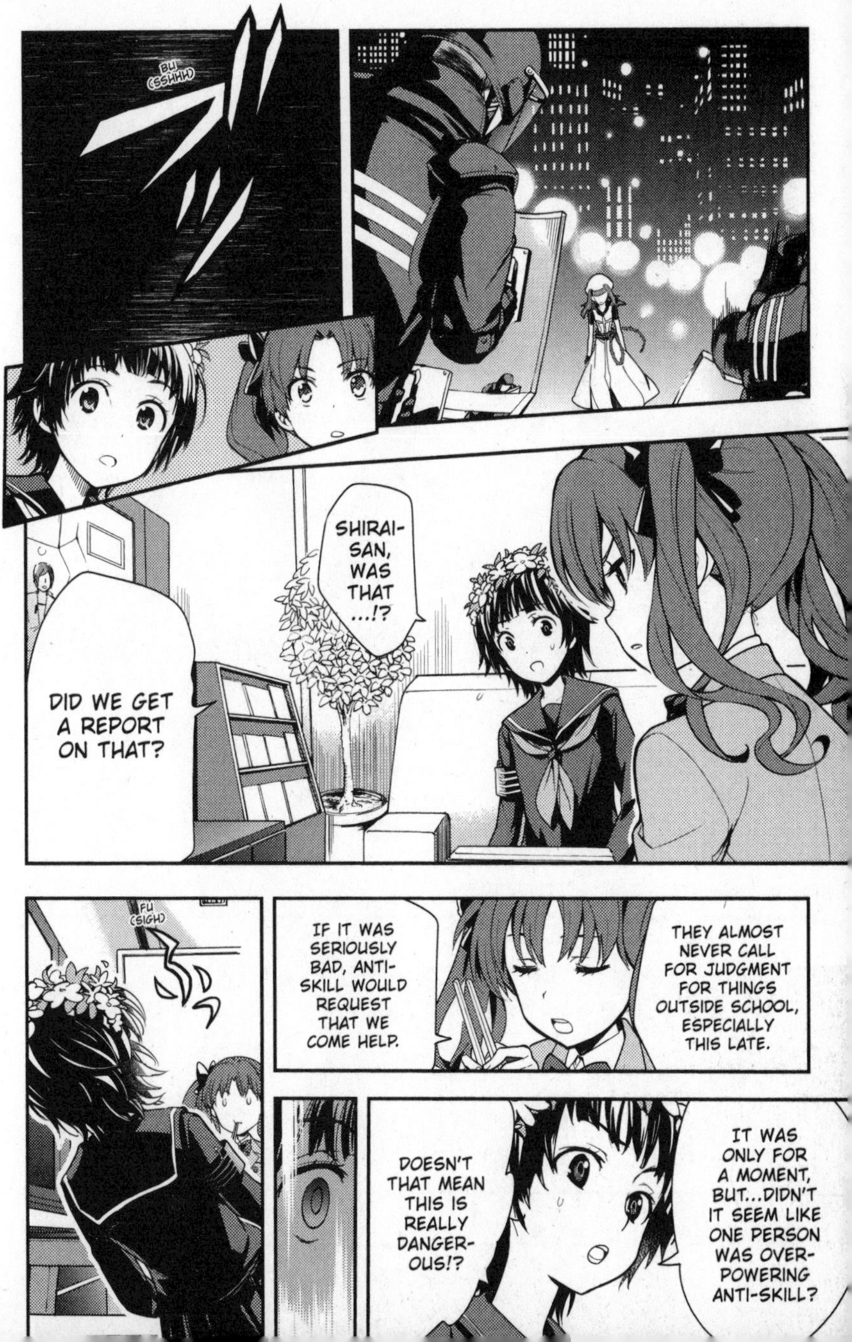
BU (SSHHH)
SHIRAI-SAN, WAS THAT ...!?
DID WE GET A REPORT ON THAT?
THEY ALMOST NEVER CALL FOR JUDGMENT FOR THINGS OUTSIDE SCHOOL, ESPECIALLY THIS LATE.
IF IT WAS SERIOUSLY BAD, ANTI-SKILL WOULD REQUEST THAT WE COME HELP.
IT WAS ONLY FOR A MOMENT, BUT...DIDN'T IT SEEM LIKE ONE PERSON WAS OVER-POWERING ANTI-SKILL?
DOESN'T THAT MEAN THIS IS REALLY DANGER-OUS!?
FU (SIGH)

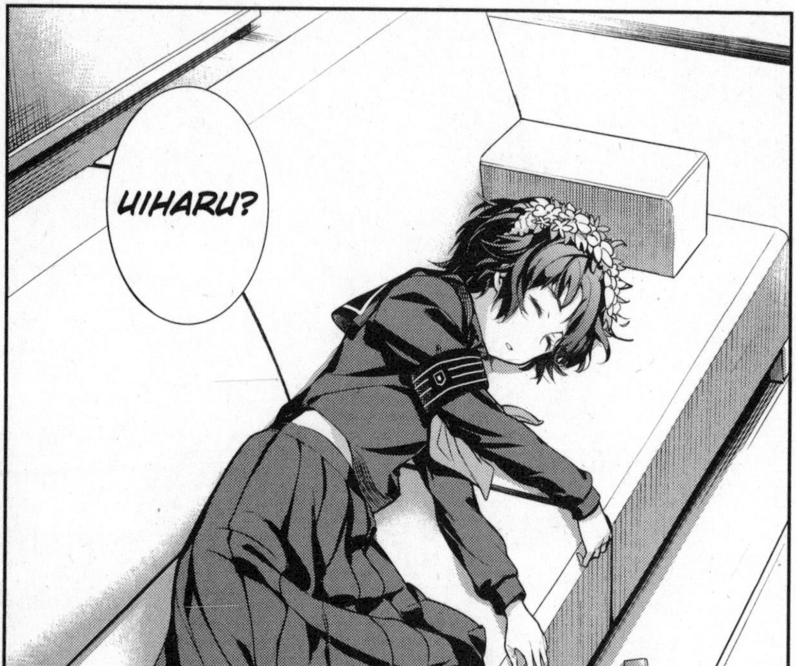
UIHARU?
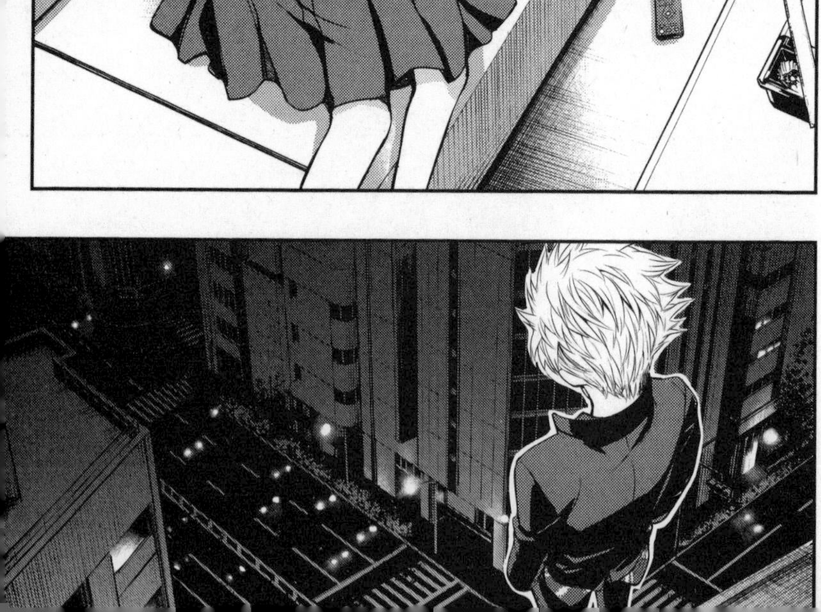

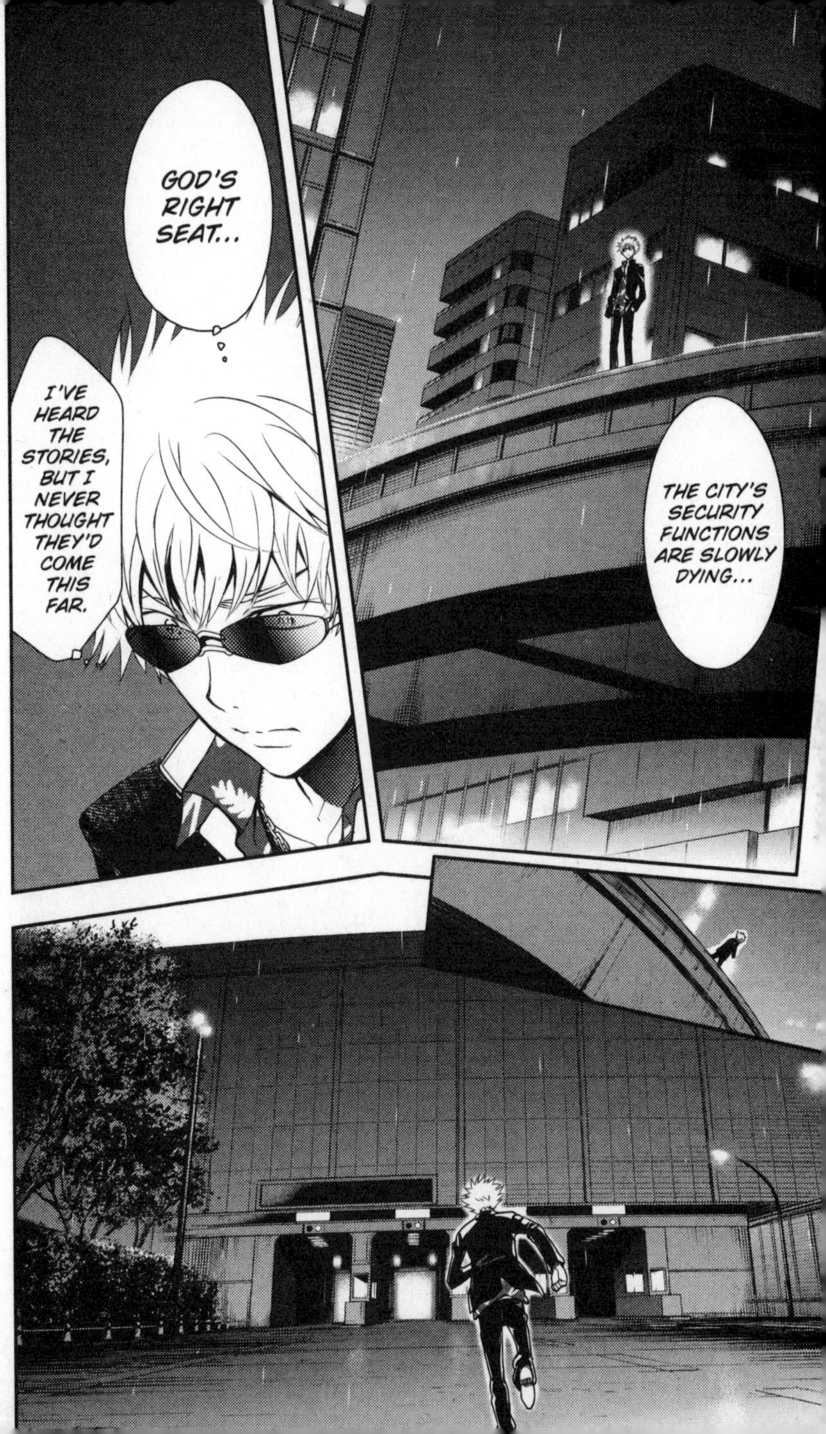
THE CITY'S SECURITY FUNCTIONS ARE SLOWLY DYING...
GOD'S RIGHT SEAT...
I'VE HEARD THE STORIES, BUT I NEVER THOUGHT THEY'D COME THIS FAR.

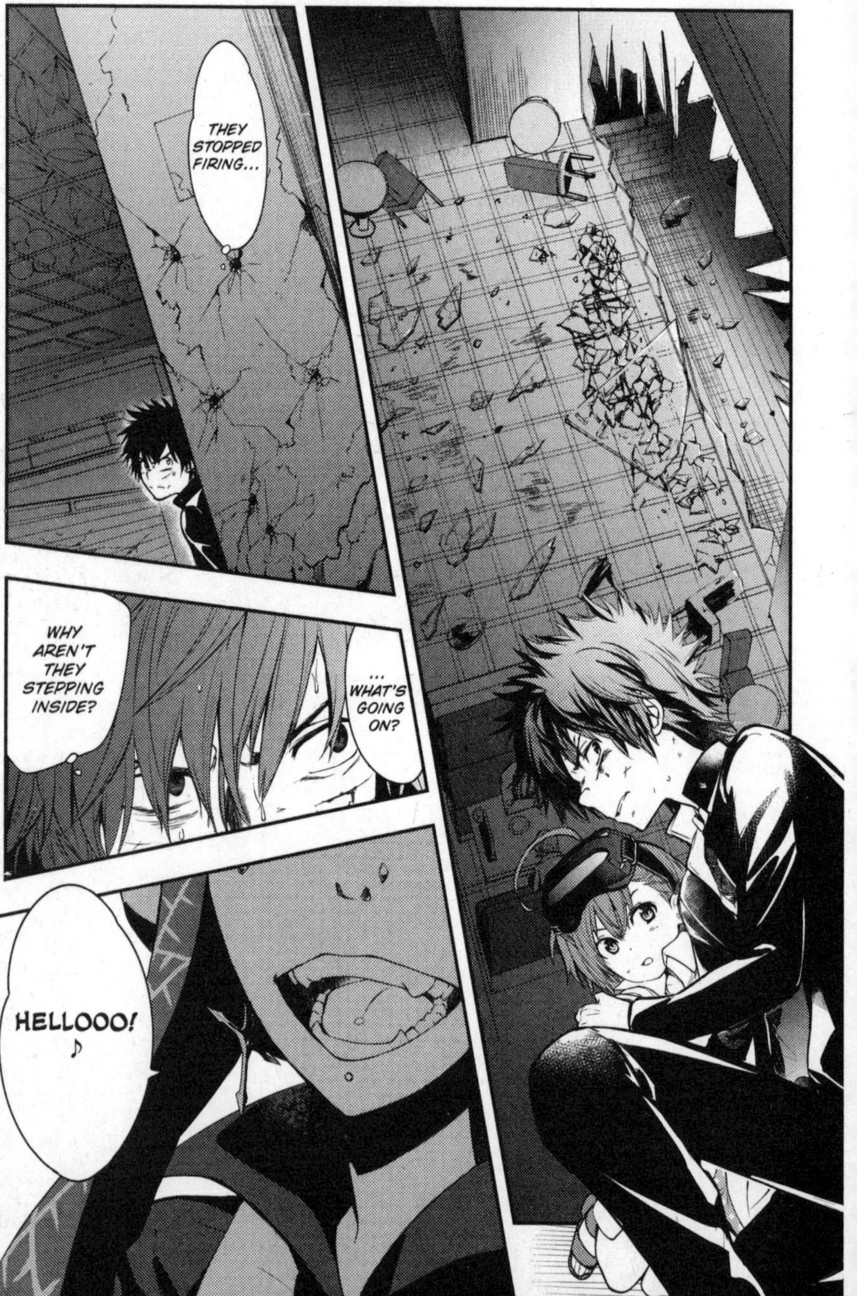
THEY STOPPED FIRING...
...WHAT'S GOING ON?
WHY AREN'T THEY STEPPING INSIDE?
HELLOOO! ♪

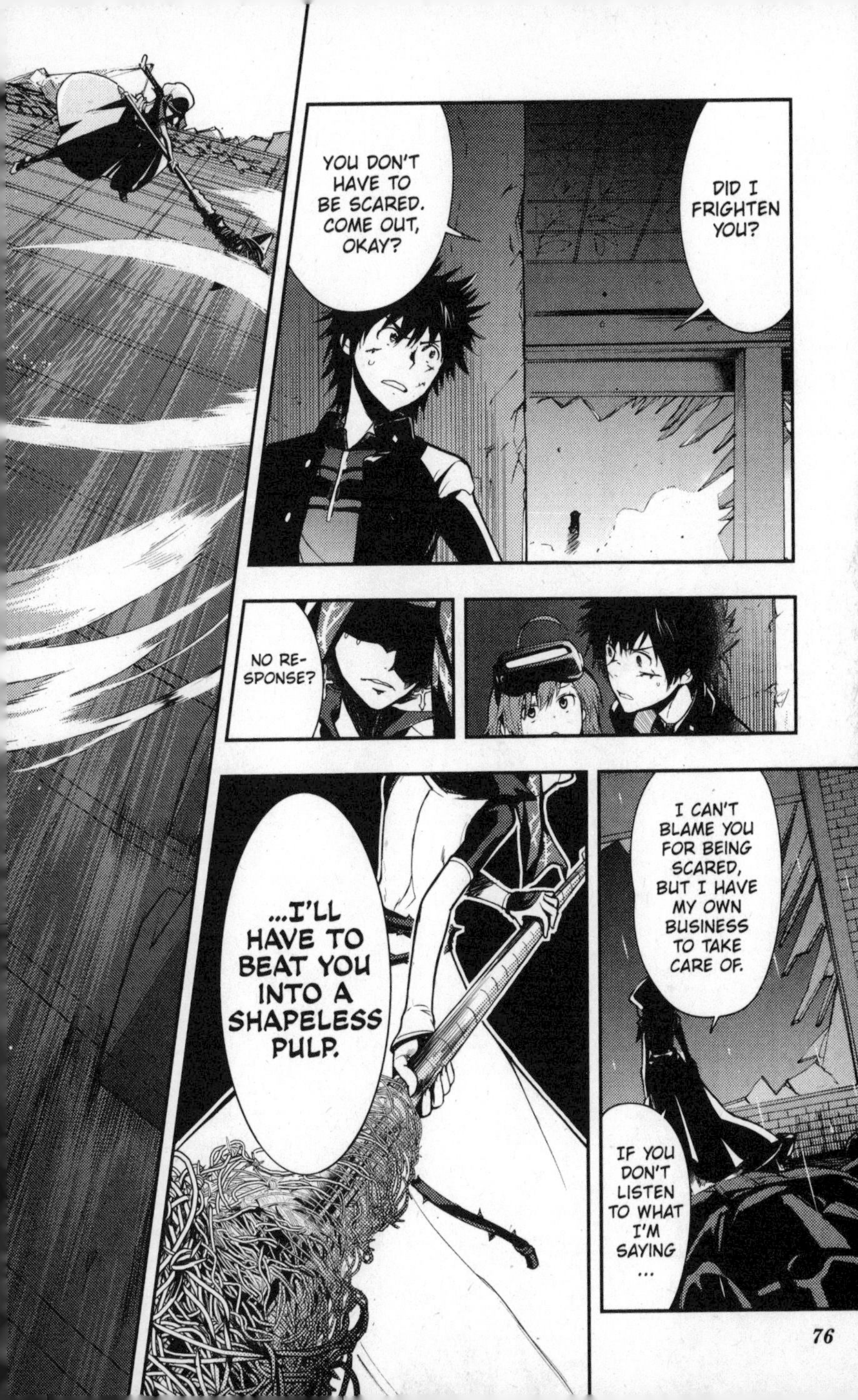
DID I FRIGHTEN YOU?
YOU DON'T HAVE TO BE SCARED. COME OUT, OKAY?
NO RE-SPONSE?
I CAN'T BLAME YOU FOR BEING SCARED, BUT I HAVE MY OWN BUSINESS TO TAKE CARE OF.
IF YOU DON'T LISTEN TO WHAT I'M SAYING ...
...I'LL HAVE TO BEAT YOU INTO A SHAPELESS PULP.

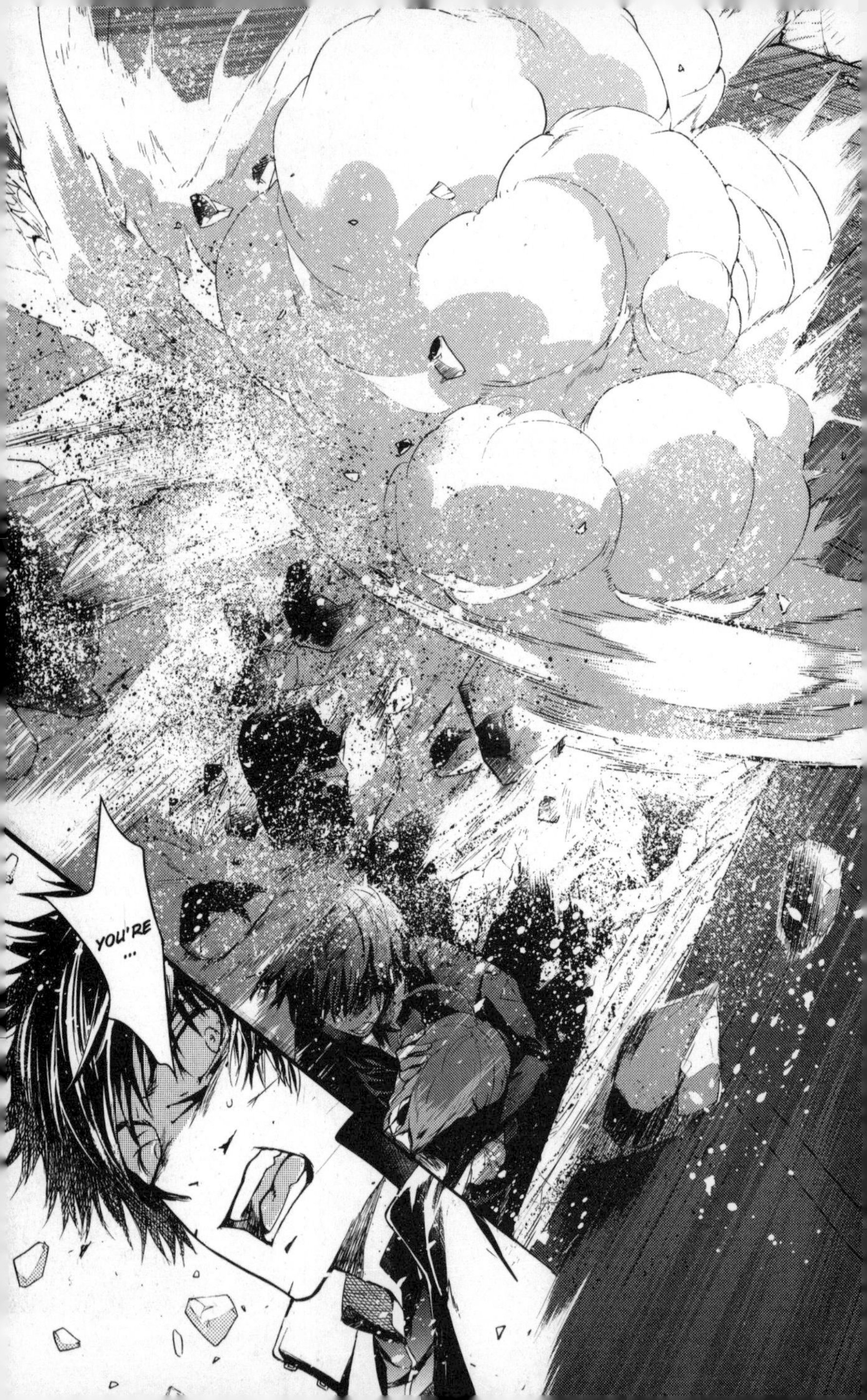
YOU'RE
...

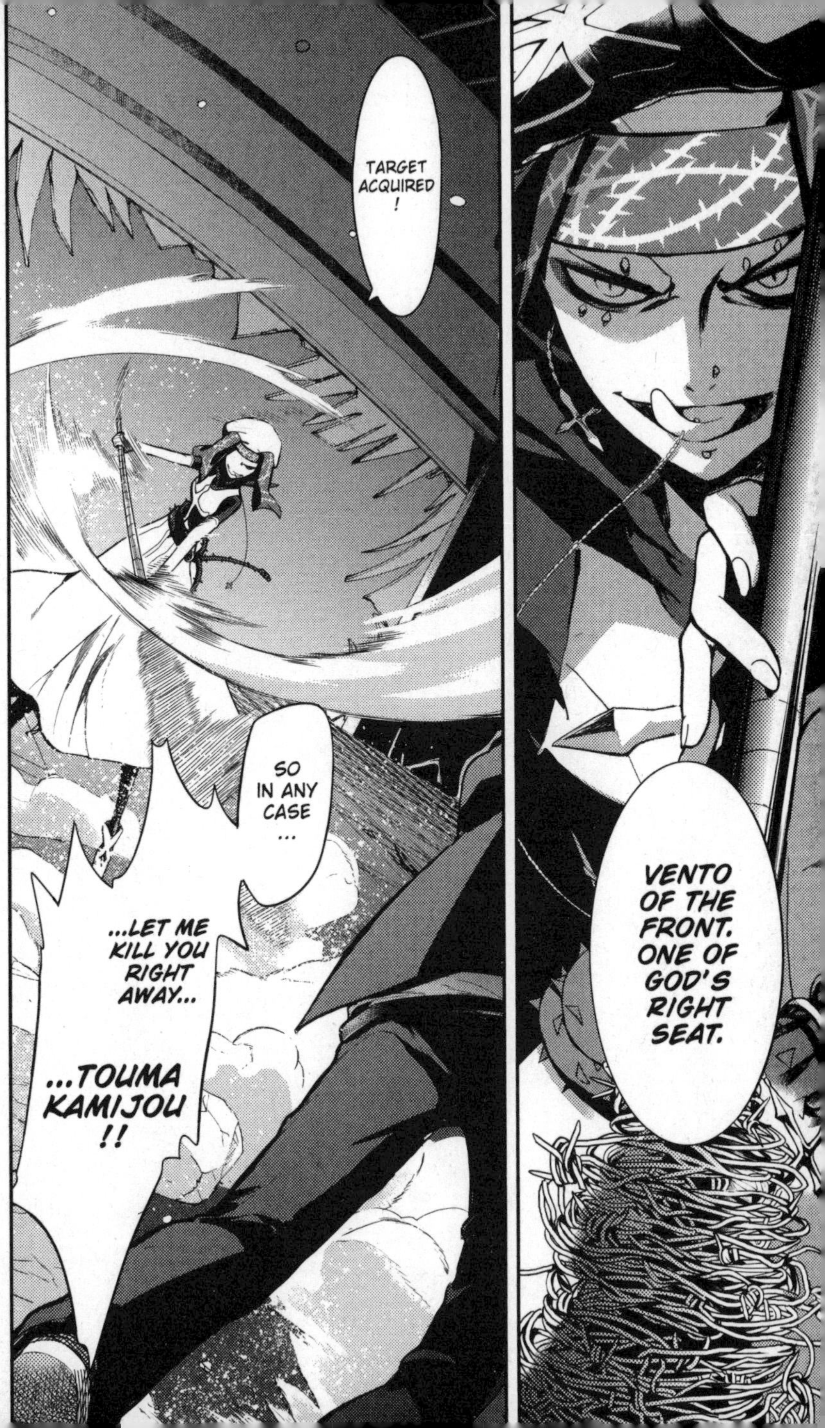
VENTO OF THE FRONT. ONE OF GOD'S RIGHT SEAT.
TARGET ACQUIRED!
SO IN ANY CASE...
...LET ME KILL YOU RIGHT AWAY...
...TOUMA KAMIJOU!!

A Certain Magical Index

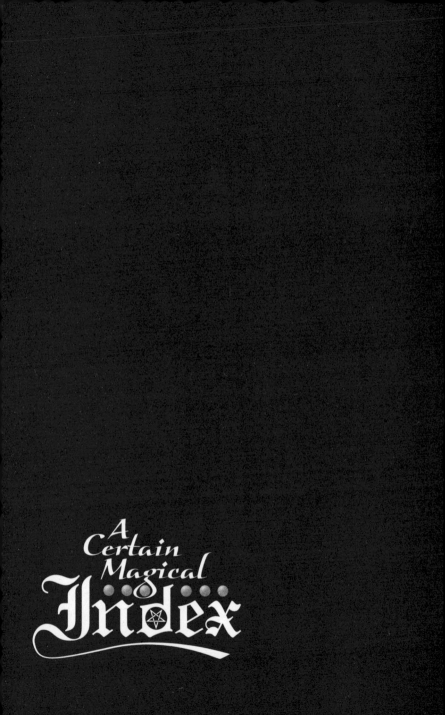

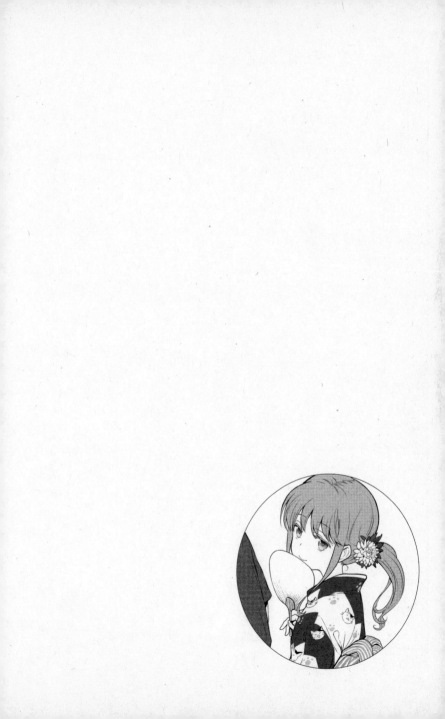

#107 INTRUDER ④

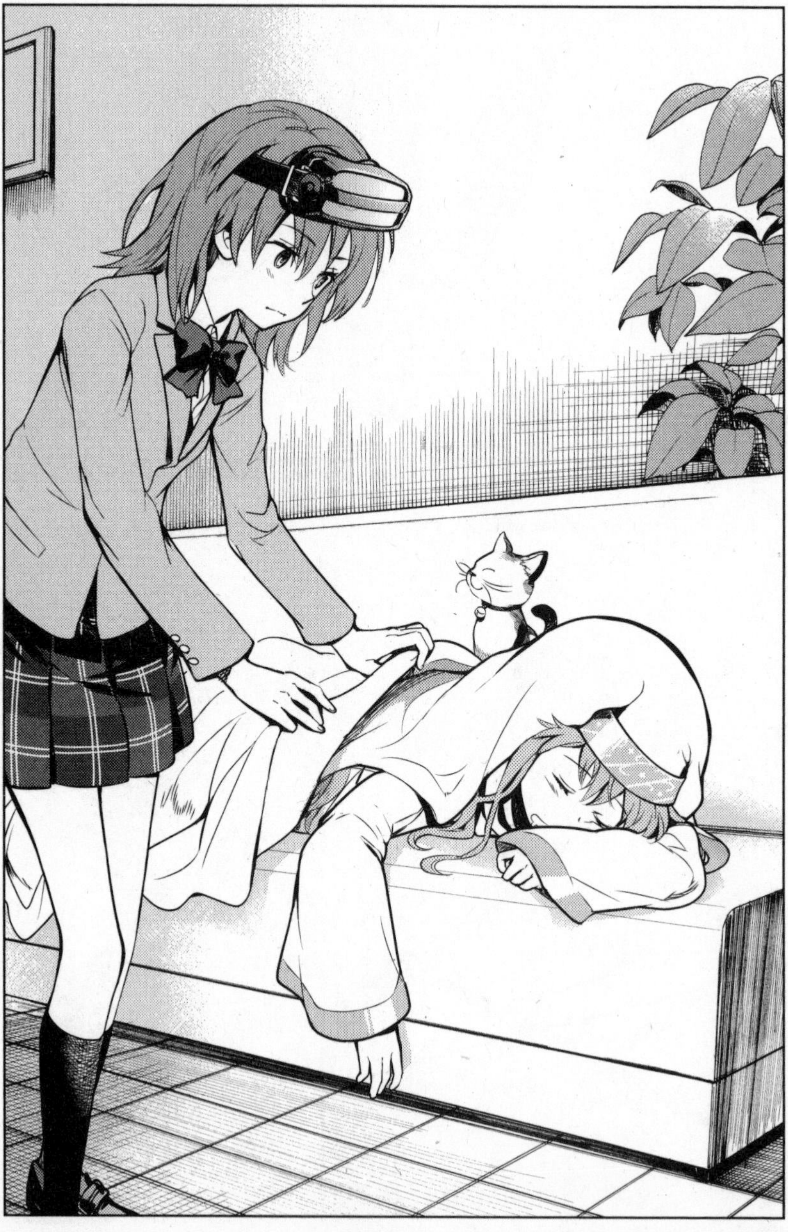

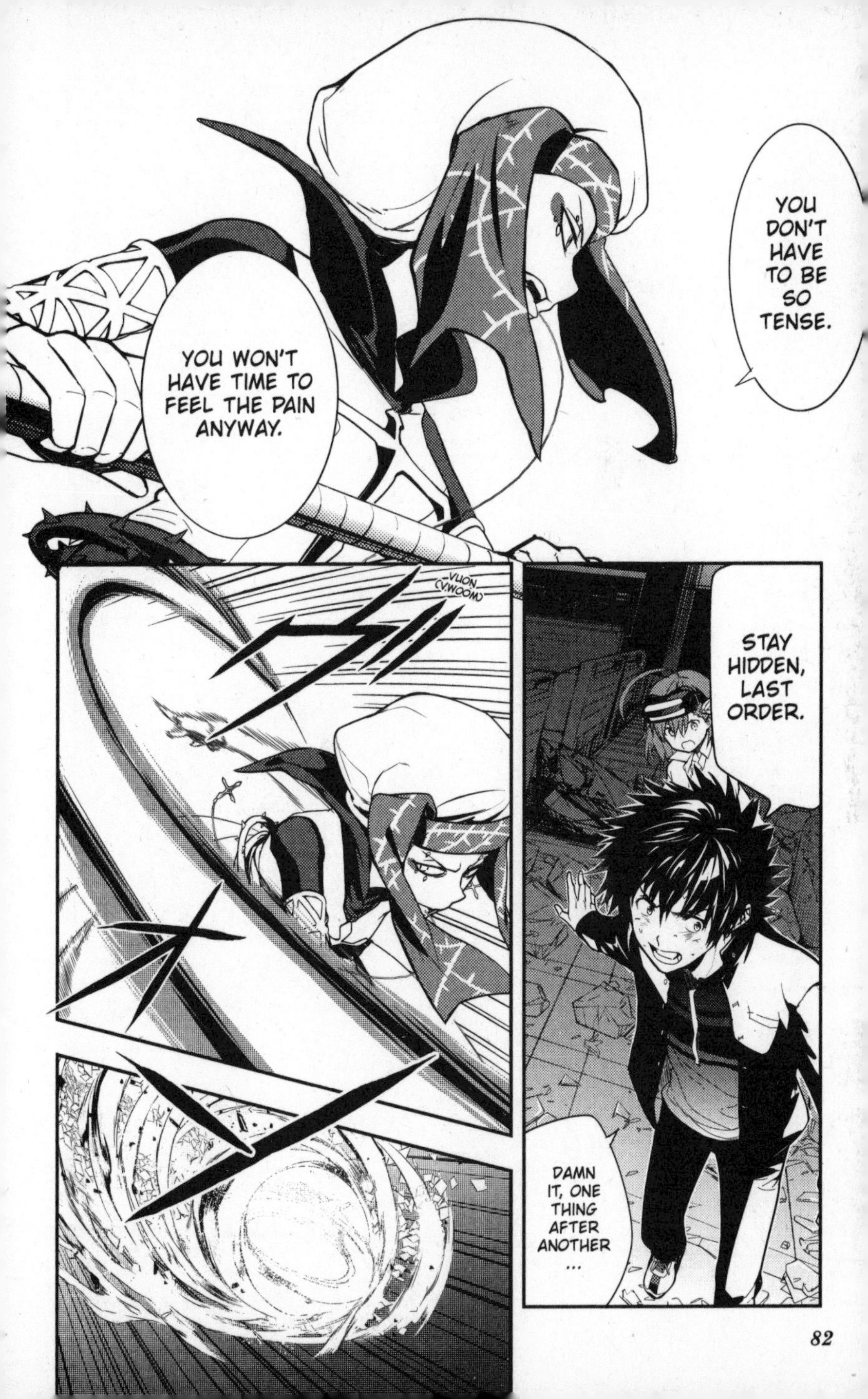
YOU DON'T HAVE TO BE SO TENSE.
YOU WON'T HAVE TIME TO FEEL THE PAIN ANYWAY.
STAY HIDDEN, LAST ORDER.
DAMN IT, ONE THING AFTER ANOTHER ...
VUON (VWOOM)

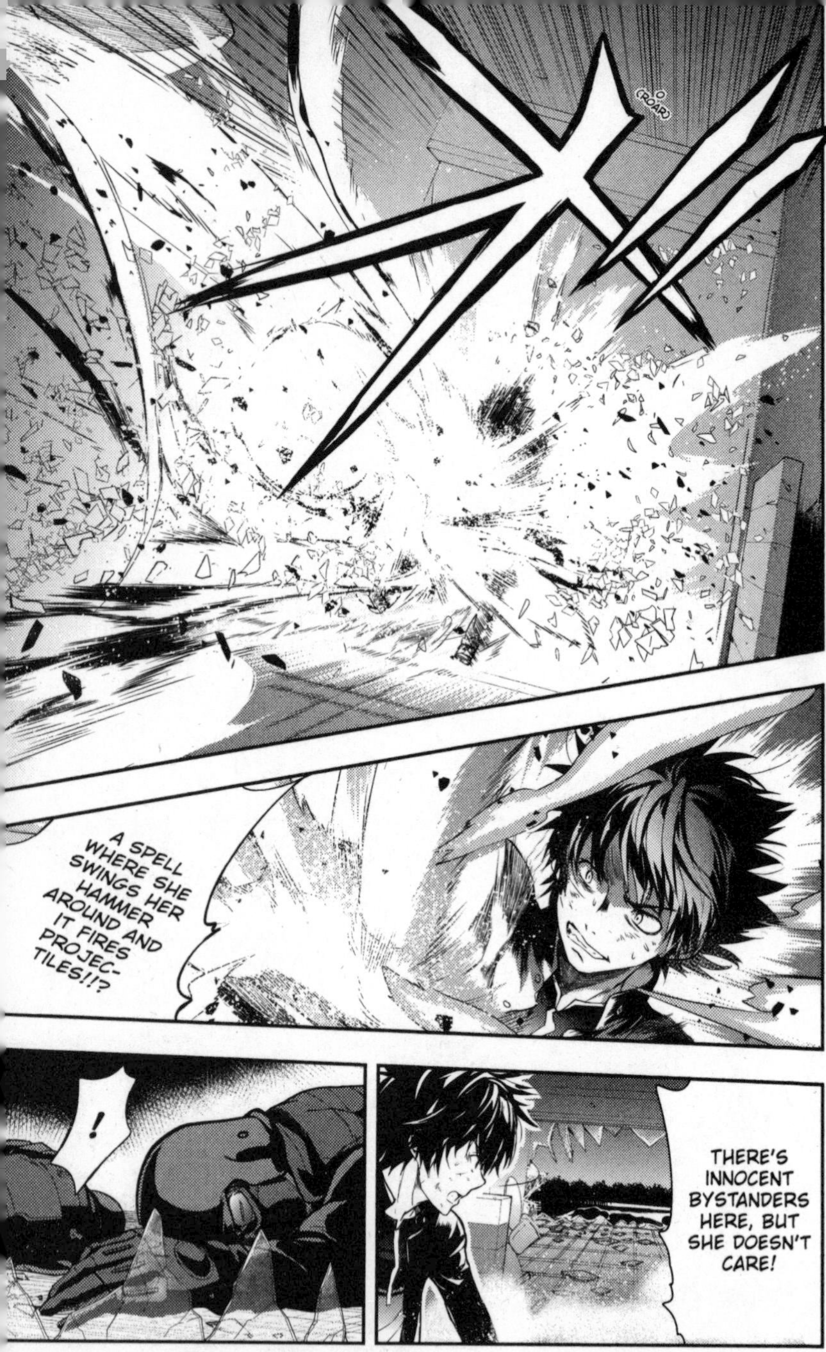
(ROAR)
A SPELL WHERE SHE SWINGS HER HAMMER AROUND AND IT FIRES PROJEC-TILES!!?
THERE'S INNOCENT BYSTANDERS HERE, BUT SHE DOESN'T CARE!
!

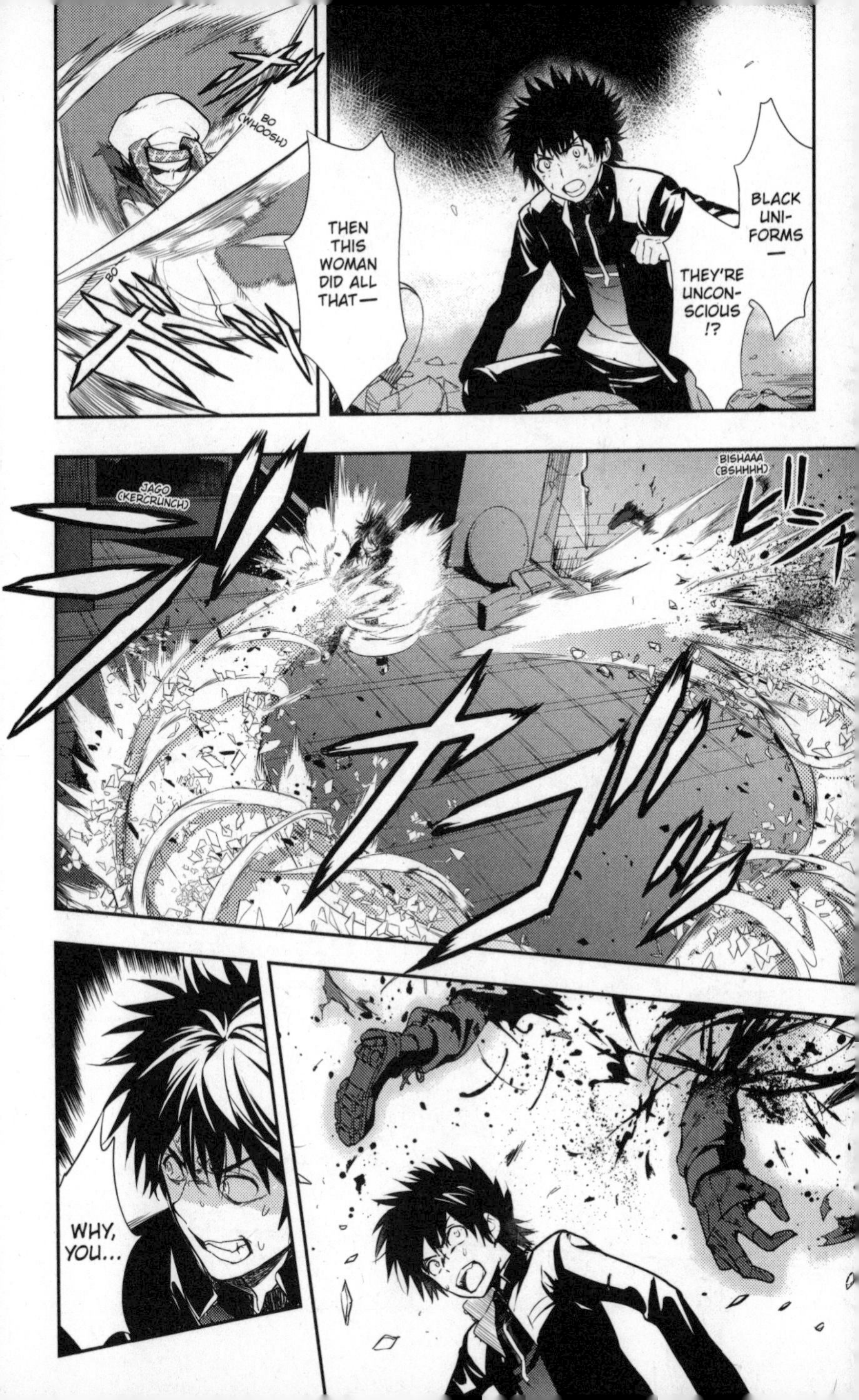
BLACK UNI-FORMS—
THEY'RE UNCON-SCIOUS!?
THEN THIS WOMAN DID ALL THAT—
BO (WHOOSH)
BO
BISHAAA (BSHHHH)
JAGO (KERCRUNCH)
WHY, YOU...

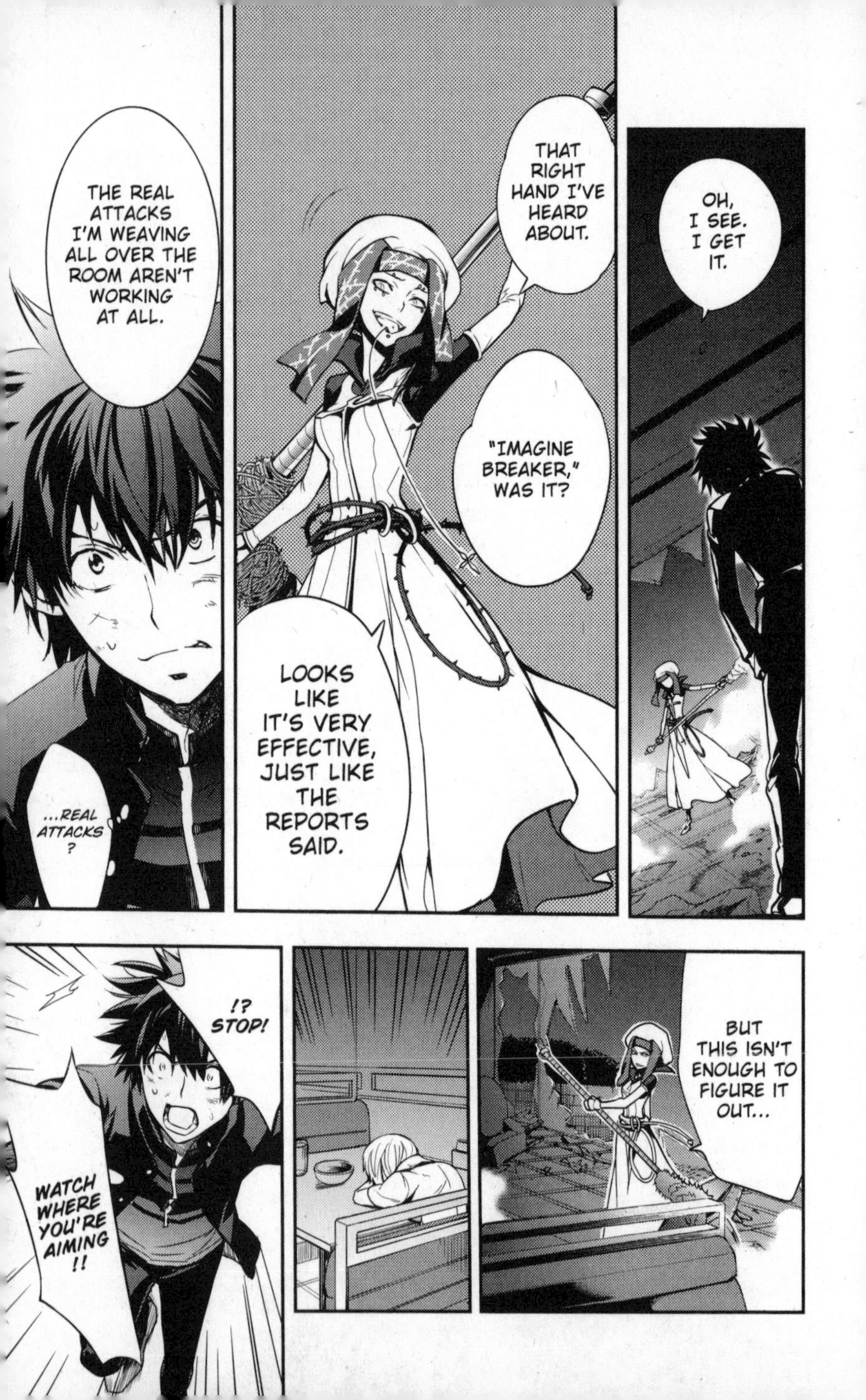
OH, I SEE. I GET IT.
THAT RIGHT HAND I'VE HEARD ABOUT.
"IMAGINE BREAKER," WAS IT?
LOOKS LIKE IT'S VERY EFFECTIVE, JUST LIKE THE REPORTS SAID.
THE REAL ATTACKS I'M WEAVING ALL OVER THE ROOM AREN'T WORKING AT ALL.
...REAL ATTACKS?
BUT THIS ISN'T ENOUGH TO FIGURE IT OUT...
!? STOP!
WATCH WHERE YOU'RE AIMING!!

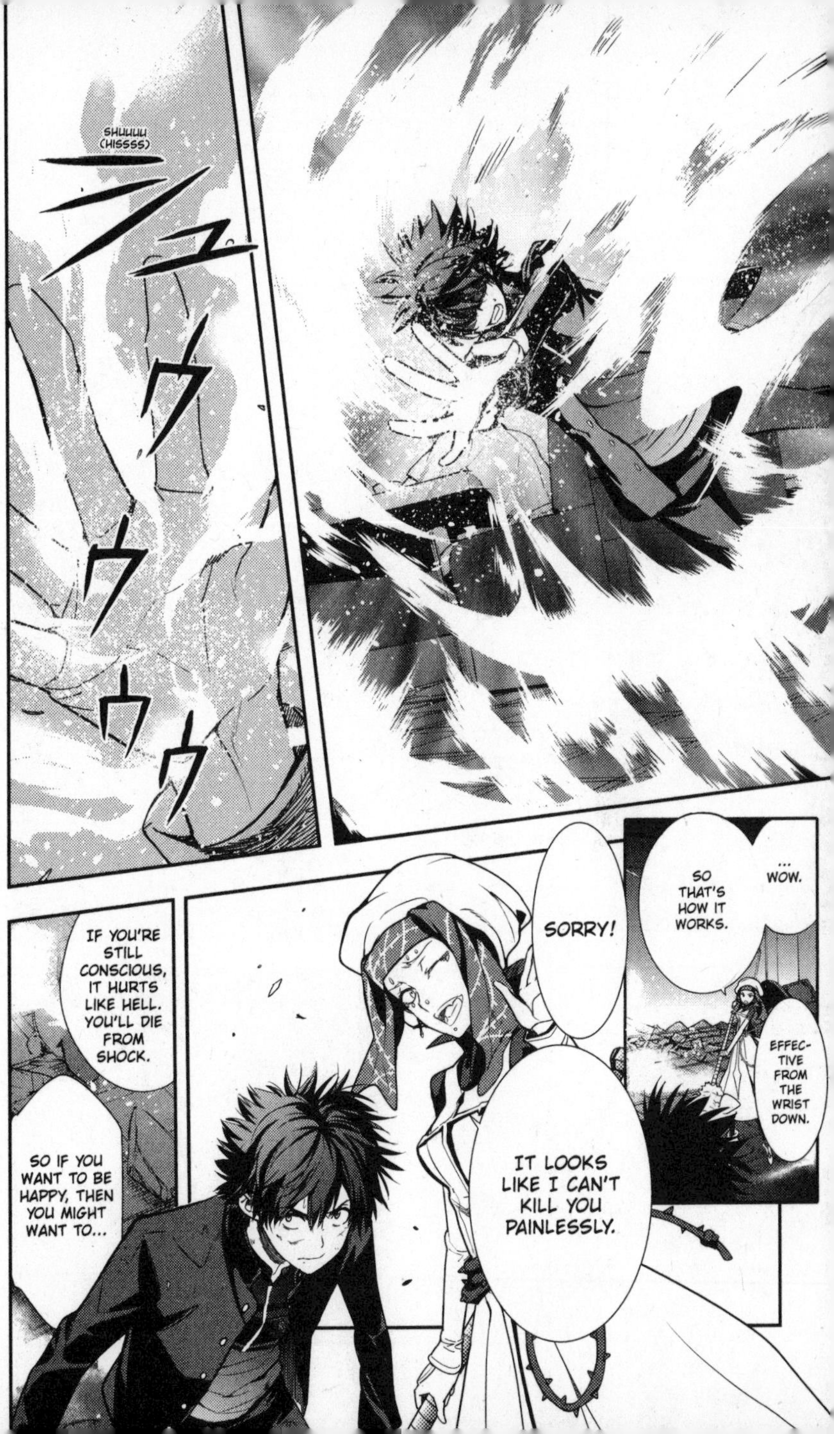
SHUUUU (HISSSS)
... WOW.
SO THAT'S HOW IT WORKS.
EFFECTIVE FROM THE WRIST DOWN.
SORRY!
IT LOOKS LIKE I CAN'T KILL YOU PAINLESSLY.
IF YOU'RE STILL CONSCIOUS, IT HURTS LIKE HELL. YOU'LL DIE FROM SHOCK.
SO IF YOU WANT TO BE HAPPY, THEN YOU MIGHT WANT TO...

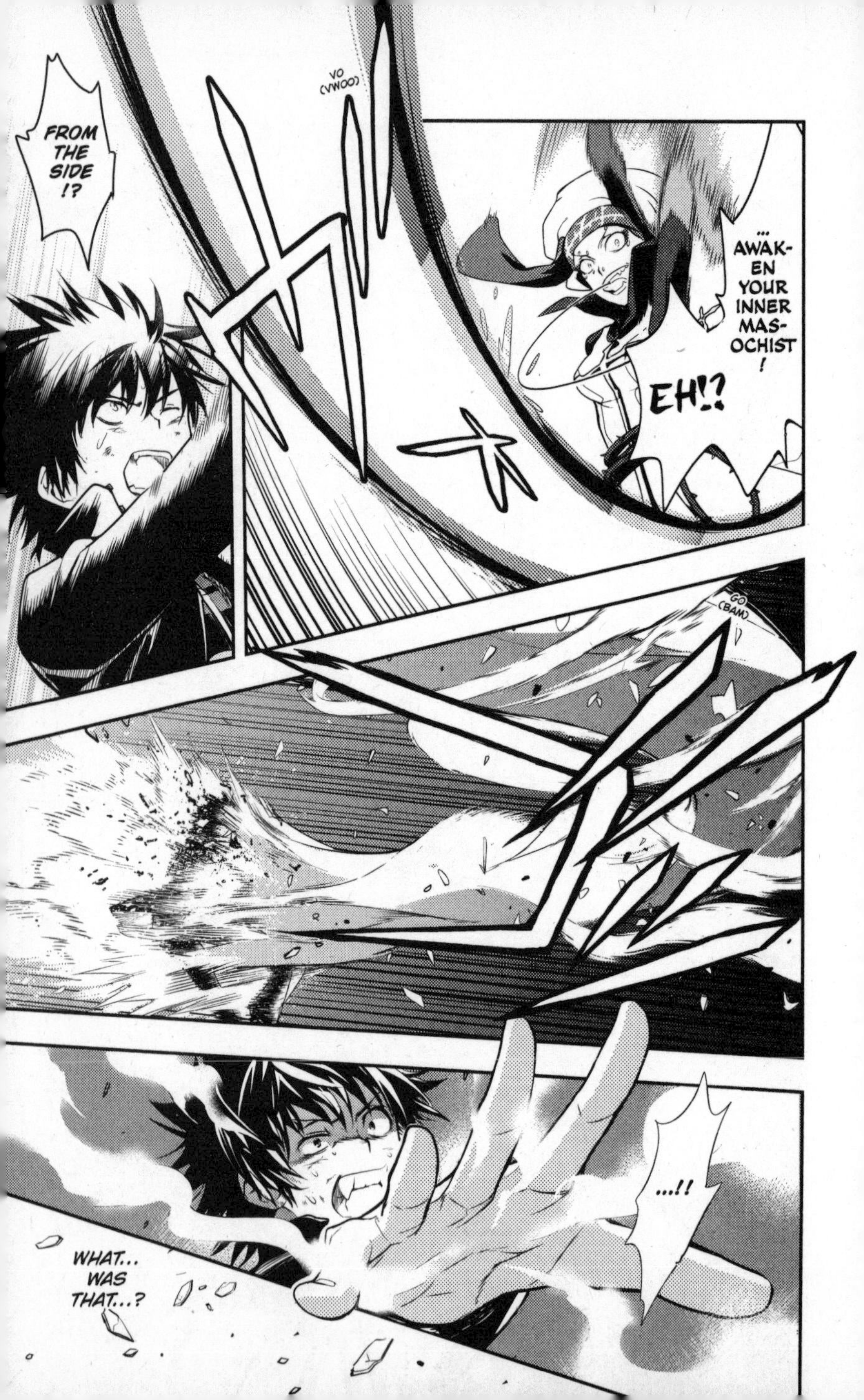

VO (VWOO)
...AWAK-EN YOUR INNER MAS-OCHIST!
EH!?
FROM THE SIDE!?
GO (BAM)
...!!
WHAT... WAS THAT...?

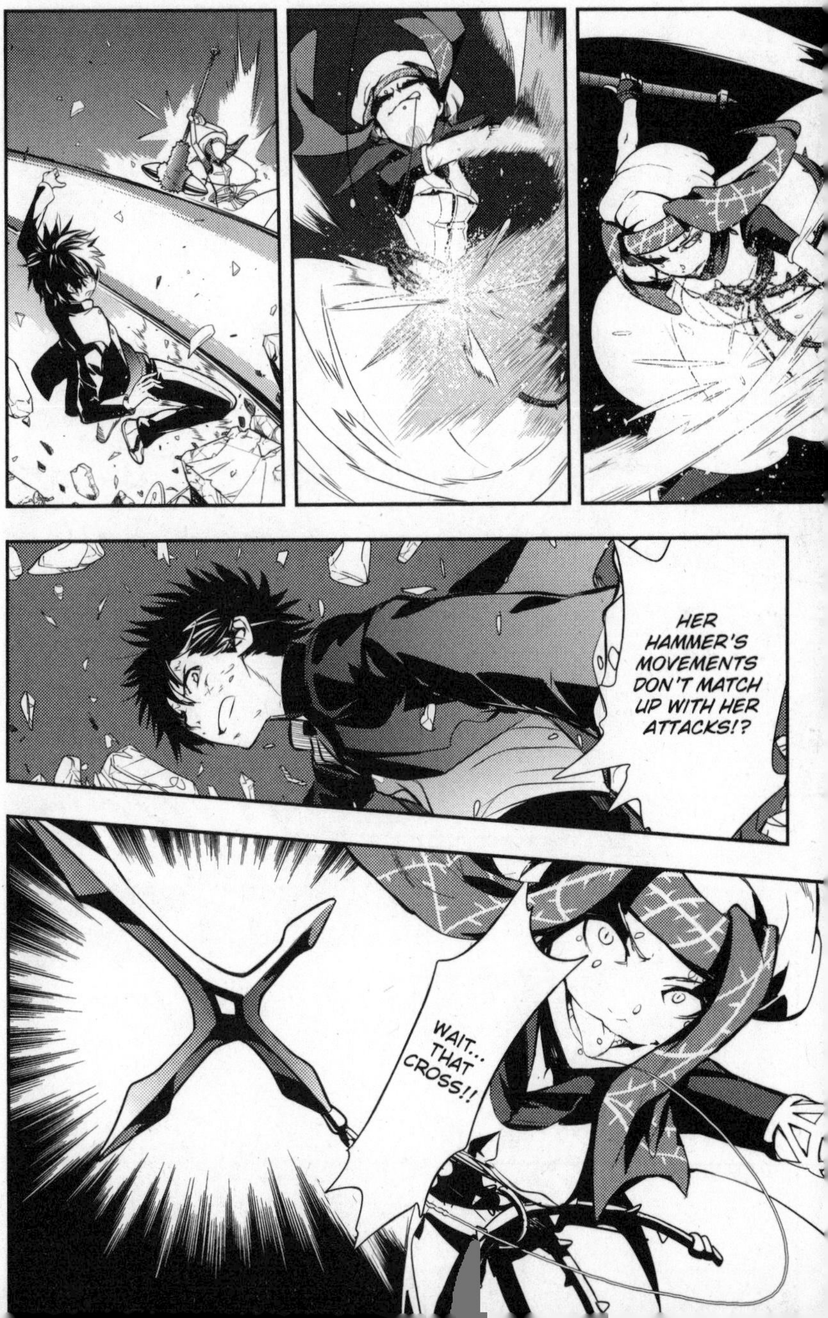
HER HAMMER'S MOVEMENTS DON'T MATCH UP WITH HER ATTACKS!?
WAIT... THAT CROSS!!

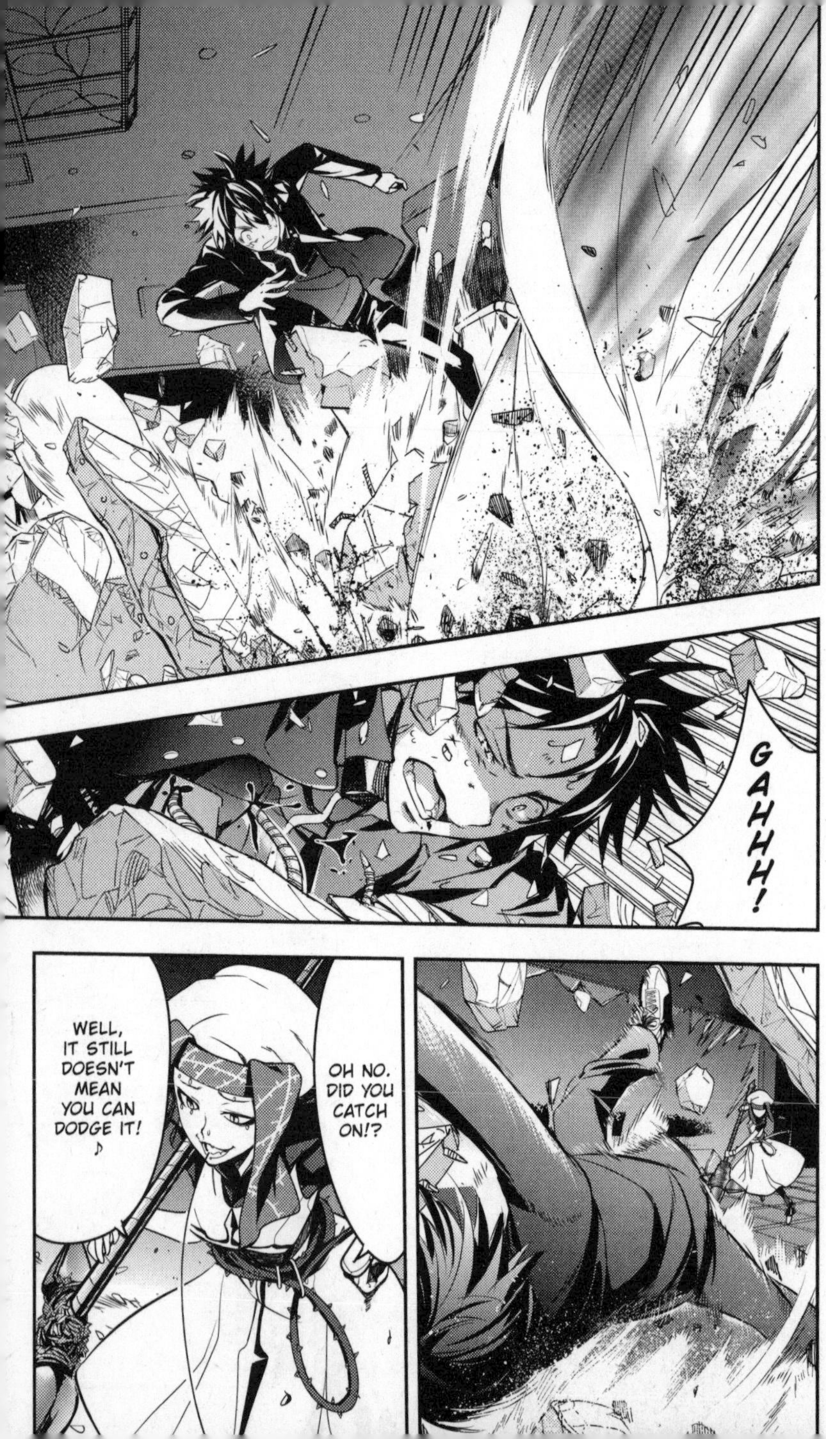
GAHHH!
OH NO. DID YOU CATCH ON!?
WELL, IT STILL DOESN'T MEAN YOU CAN DODGE IT! ♪

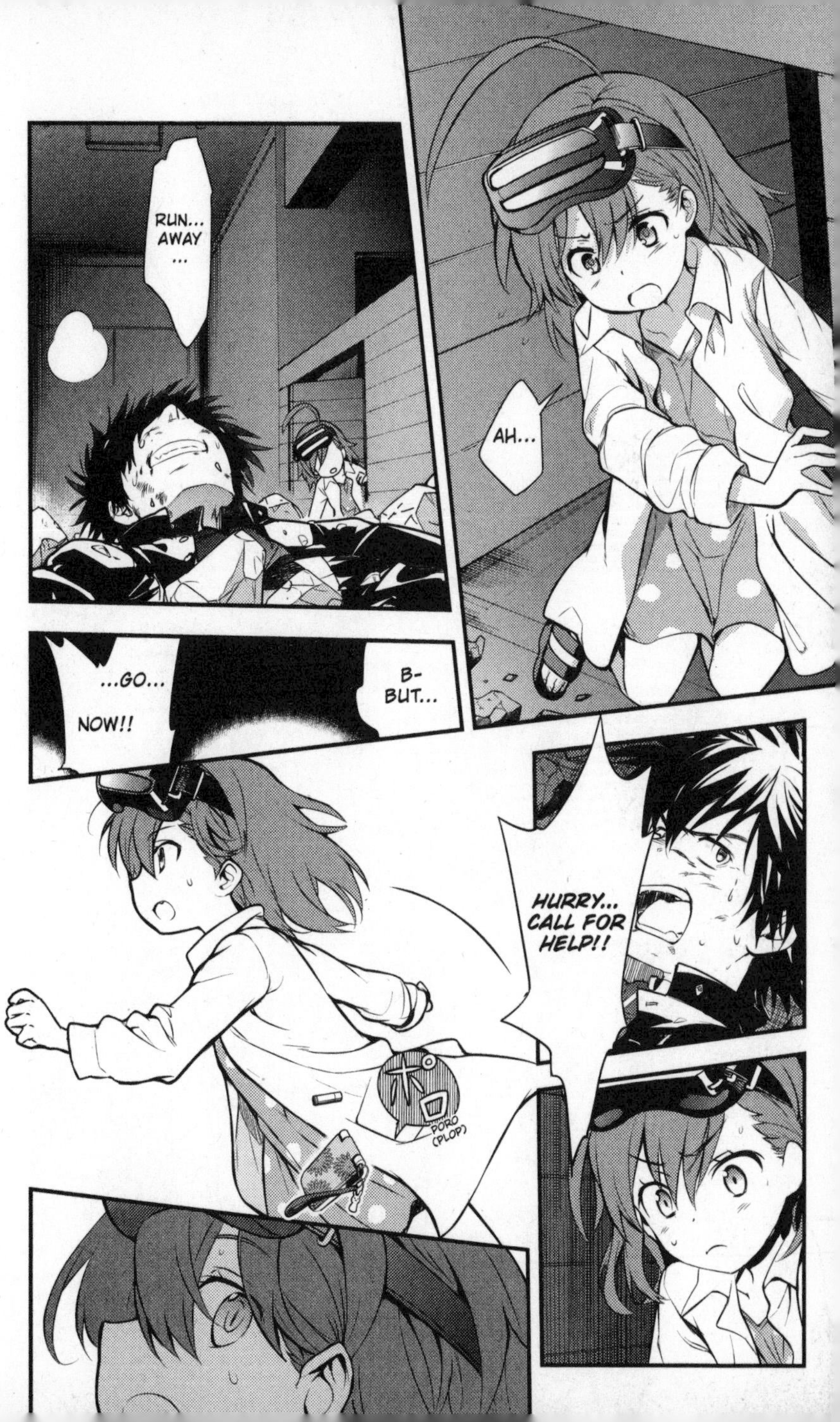
AH...
RUN... AWAY ...
B- BUT...
...GO... NOW!!
HURRY... CALL FOR HELP!!
PORO (PLOP)

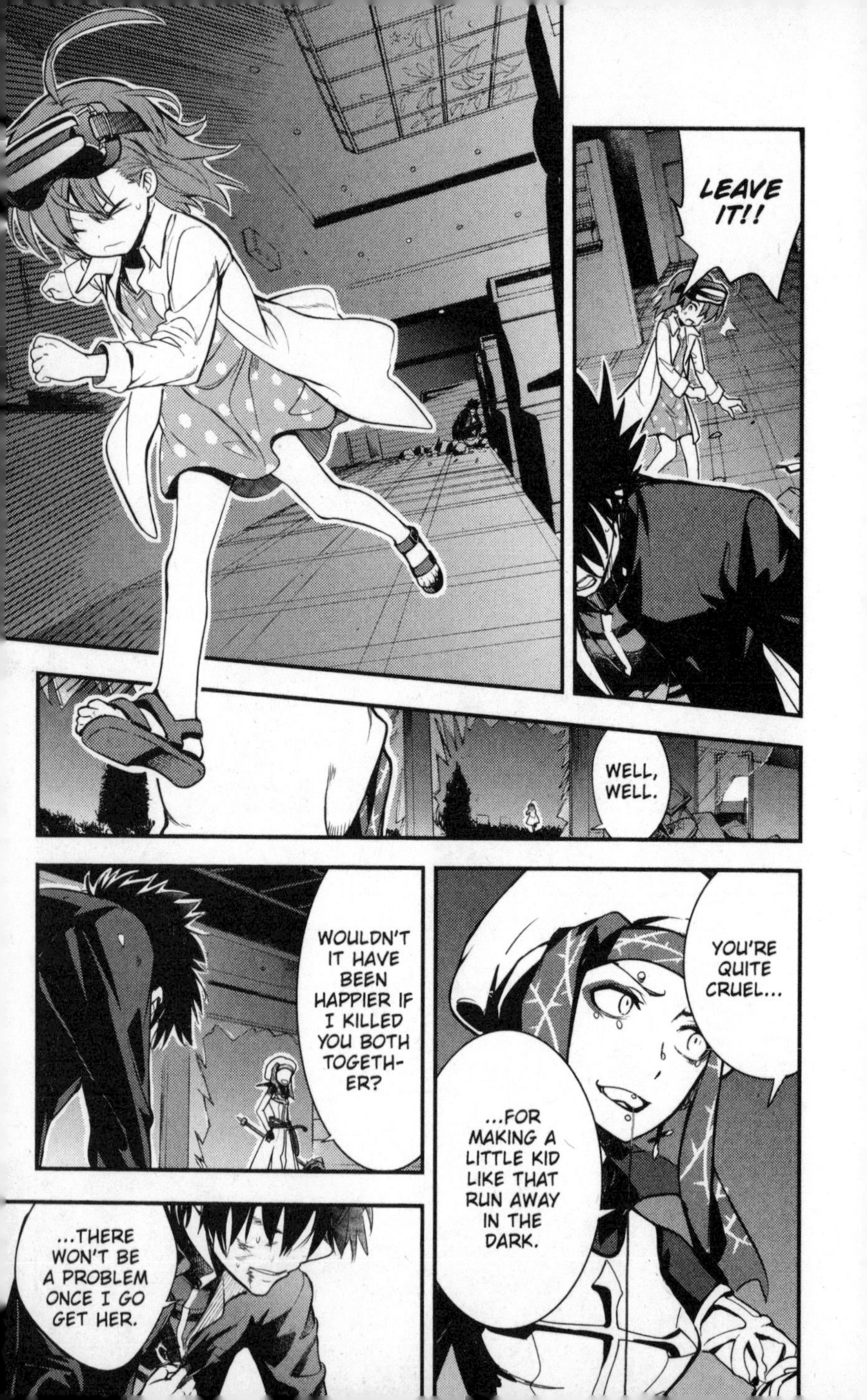
LEAVE IT!!
WELL, WELL.
YOU'RE QUITE CRUEL...
...FOR MAKING A LITTLE KID LIKE THAT RUN AWAY IN THE DARK.
WOULDN'T IT HAVE BEEN HAPPIER IF I KILLED YOU BOTH TOGETH-ER?
...THERE WON'T BE A PROBLEM ONCE I GO GET HER.

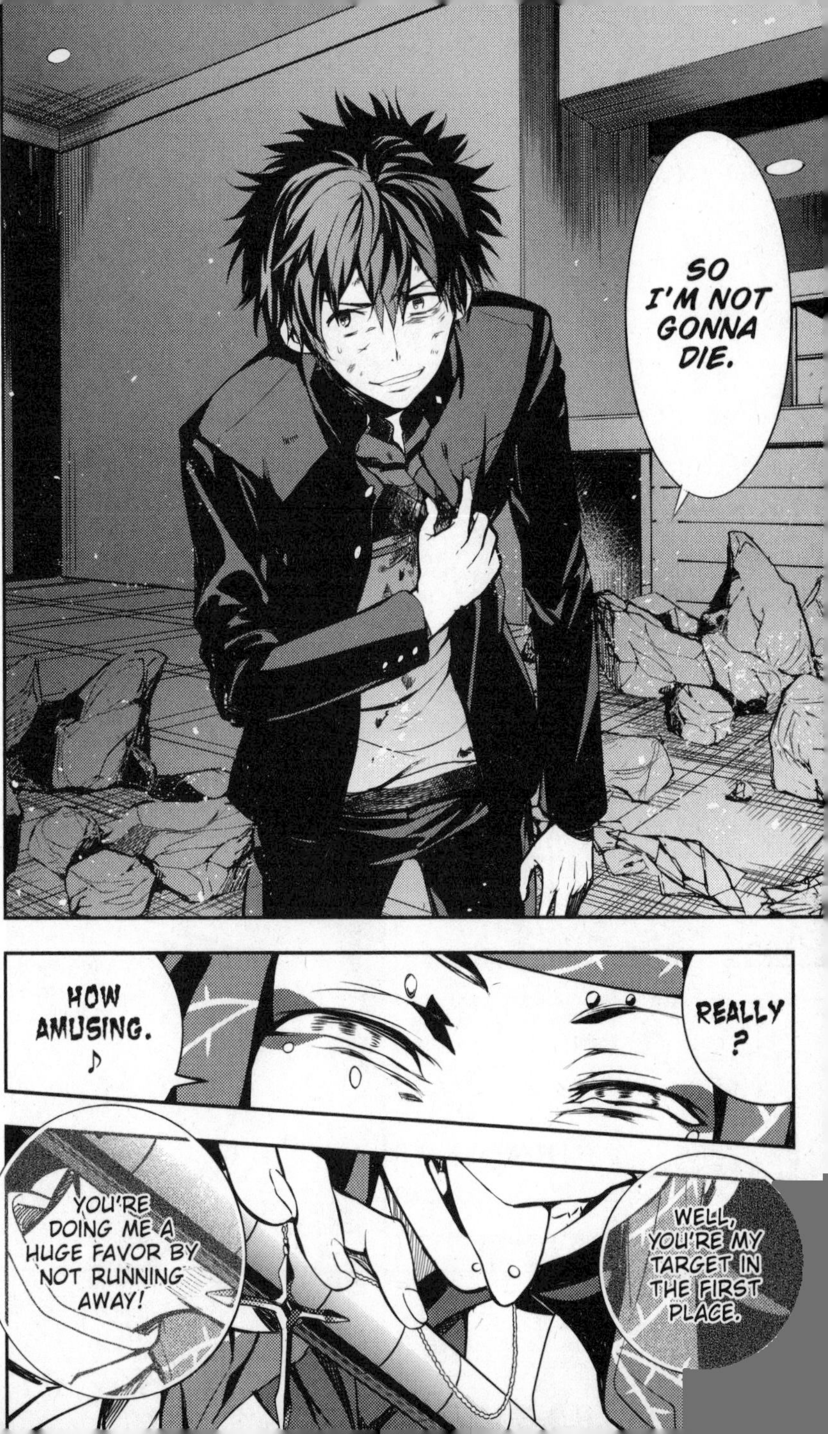
SO I'M NOT GONNA DIE.
REALLY?
HOW AMUSING. ♪
WELL, YOU'RE MY TARGET IN THE FIRST PLACE.
YOU'RE DOING ME A HUGE FAVOR BY NOT RUNNING AWAY!

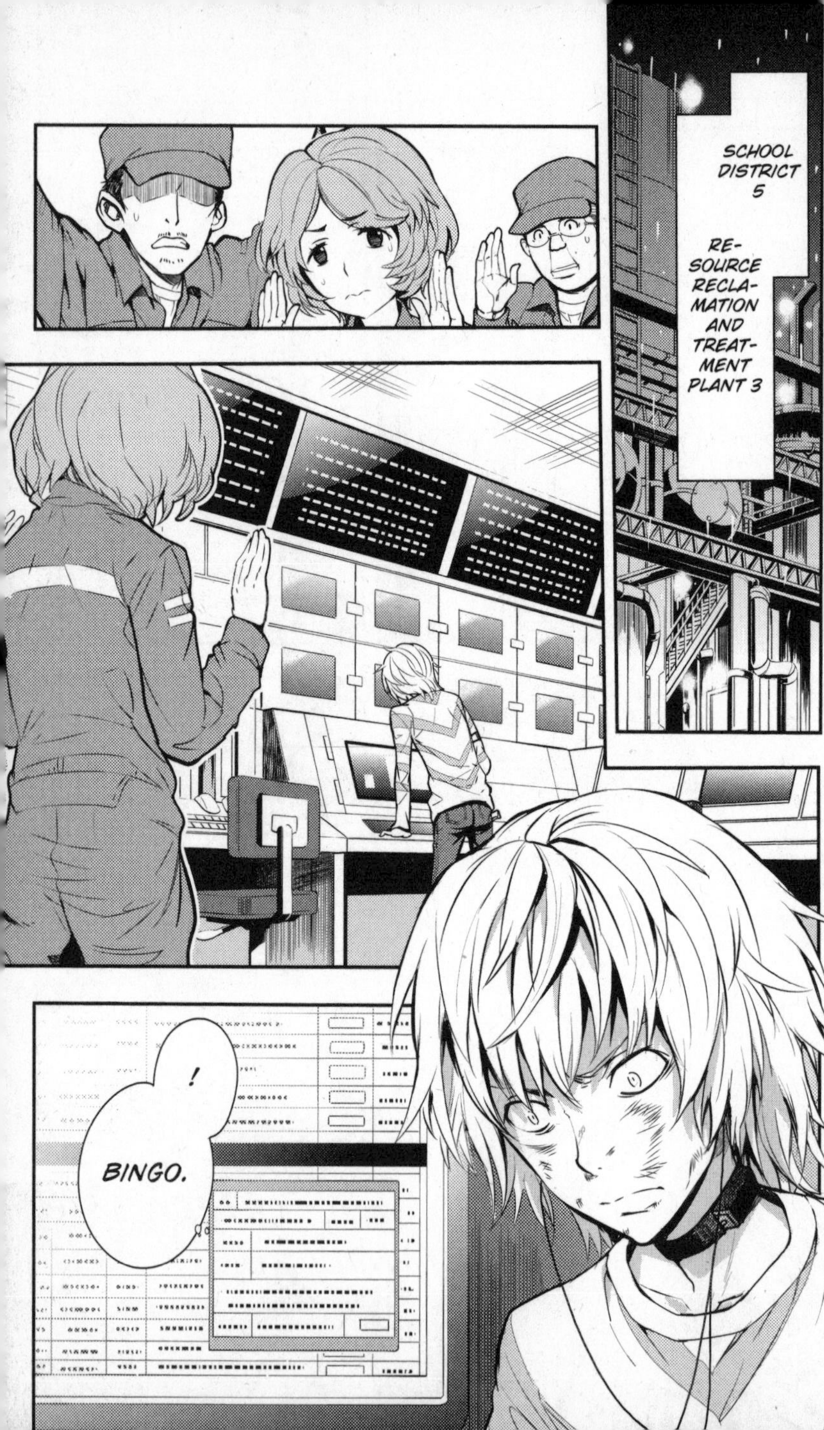
SCHOOL DISTRICT 5
RE-SOURCE RECLA-MATION AND TREAT-MENT PLANT 3
! BINGO.

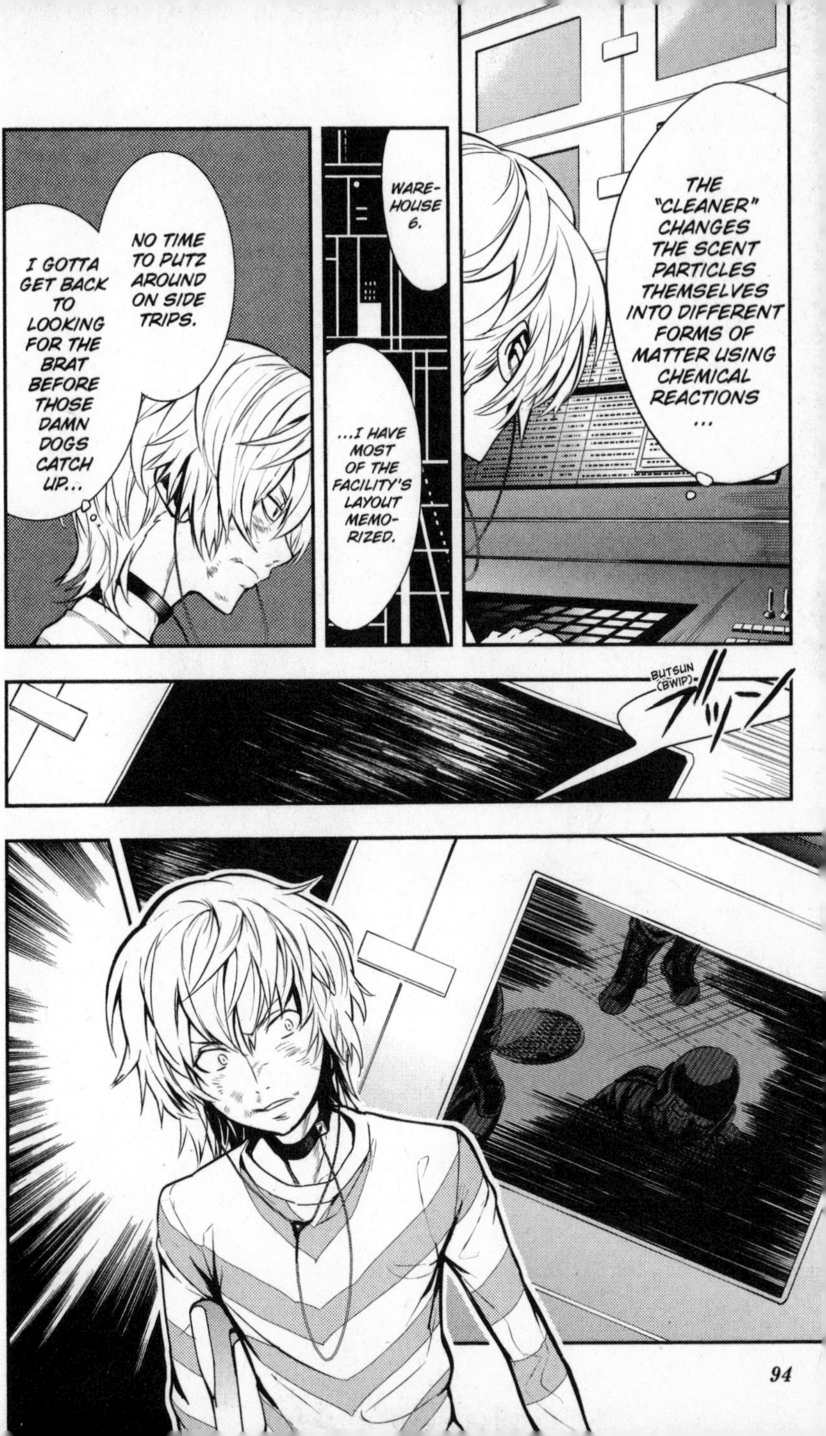
THE "CLEANER" CHANGES THE SCENT PARTICLES THEMSELVES INTO DIFFERENT FORMS OF MATTER USING CHEMICAL REACTIONS ...
WARE-HOUSE 6.
...I HAVE MOST OF THE FACILITY'S LAYOUT MEMO-RIZED.
NO TIME TO PUTZ AROUND ON SIDE TRIPS.
I GOTTA GET BACK TO LOOKING FOR THE BRAT BEFORE THOSE DAMN DOGS CATCH UP...
BUTSUN (BWIP)

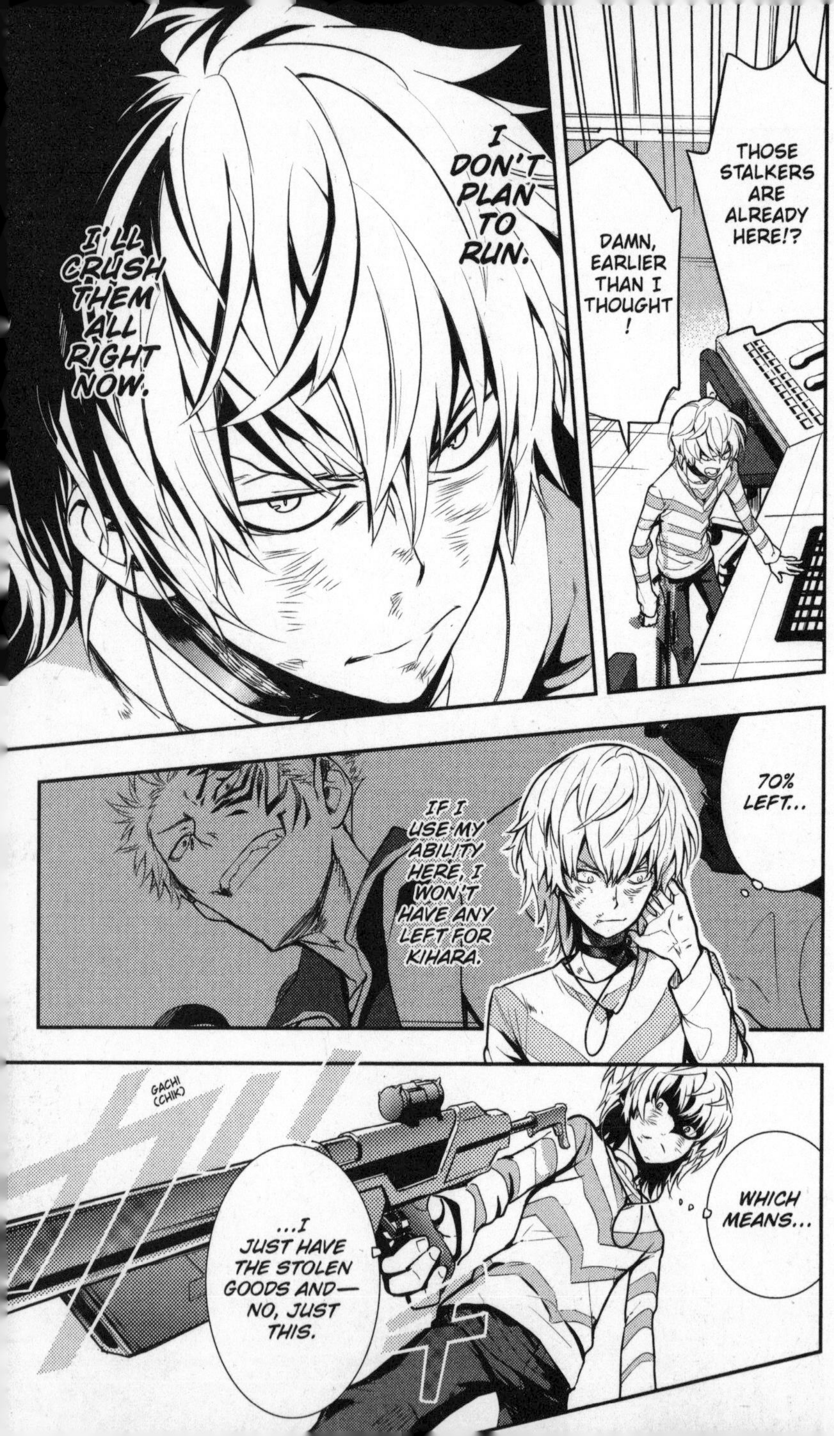
THOSE STALKERS ARE ALREADY HERE!?
DAMN, EARLIER THAN I THOUGHT!
I DON'T PLAN TO RUN.
I'LL CRUSH THEM ALL RIGHT NOW.
70% LEFT...
IF I USE MY ABILITY HERE, I WON'T HAVE ANY LEFT FOR KIHARA.
WHICH MEANS...
...I JUST HAVE THE STOLEN GOODS AND— NO, JUST THIS.
GACHI (CHIK)

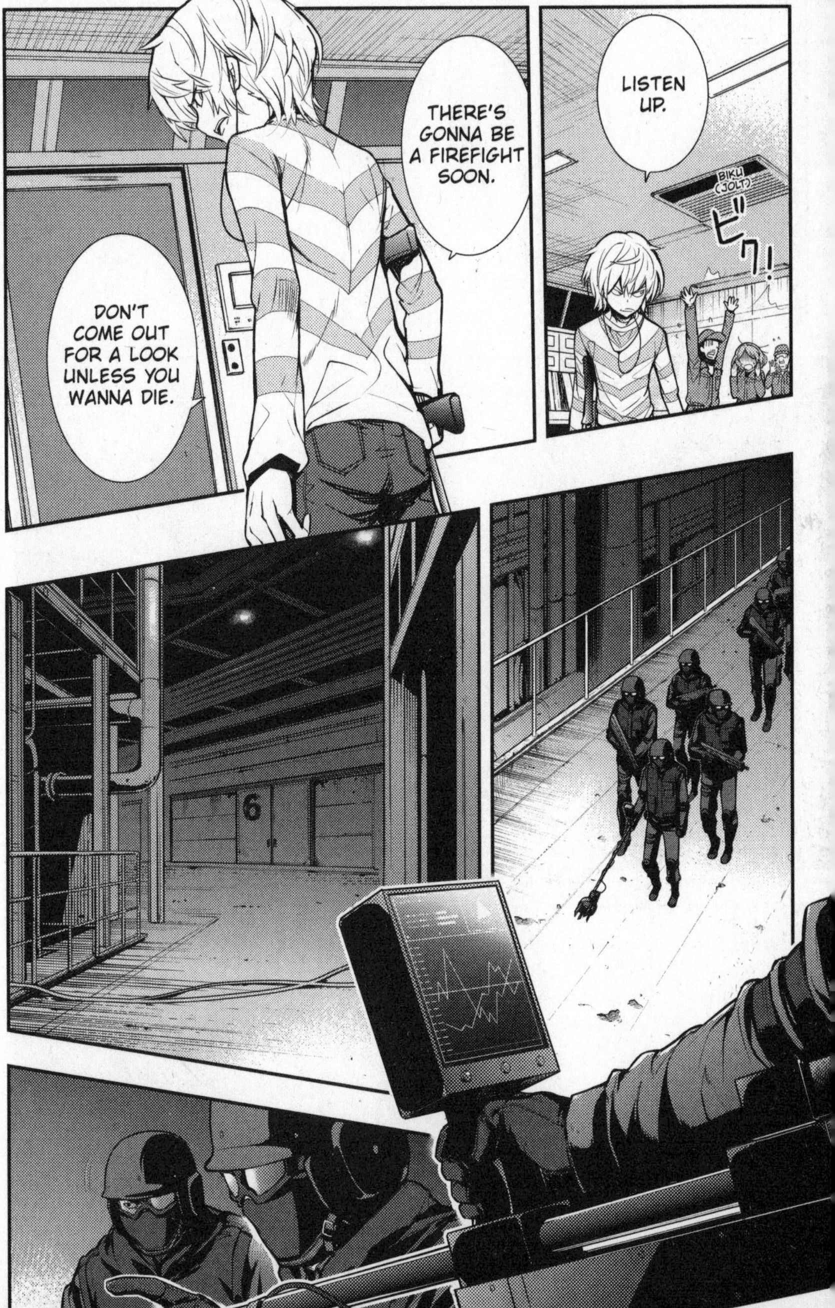
LISTEN UP.
BIKU (JOLT)
ビク!
THERE'S GONNA BE A FIREFIGHT SOON.
DON'T COME OUT FOR A LOOK UNLESS YOU WANNA DIE.

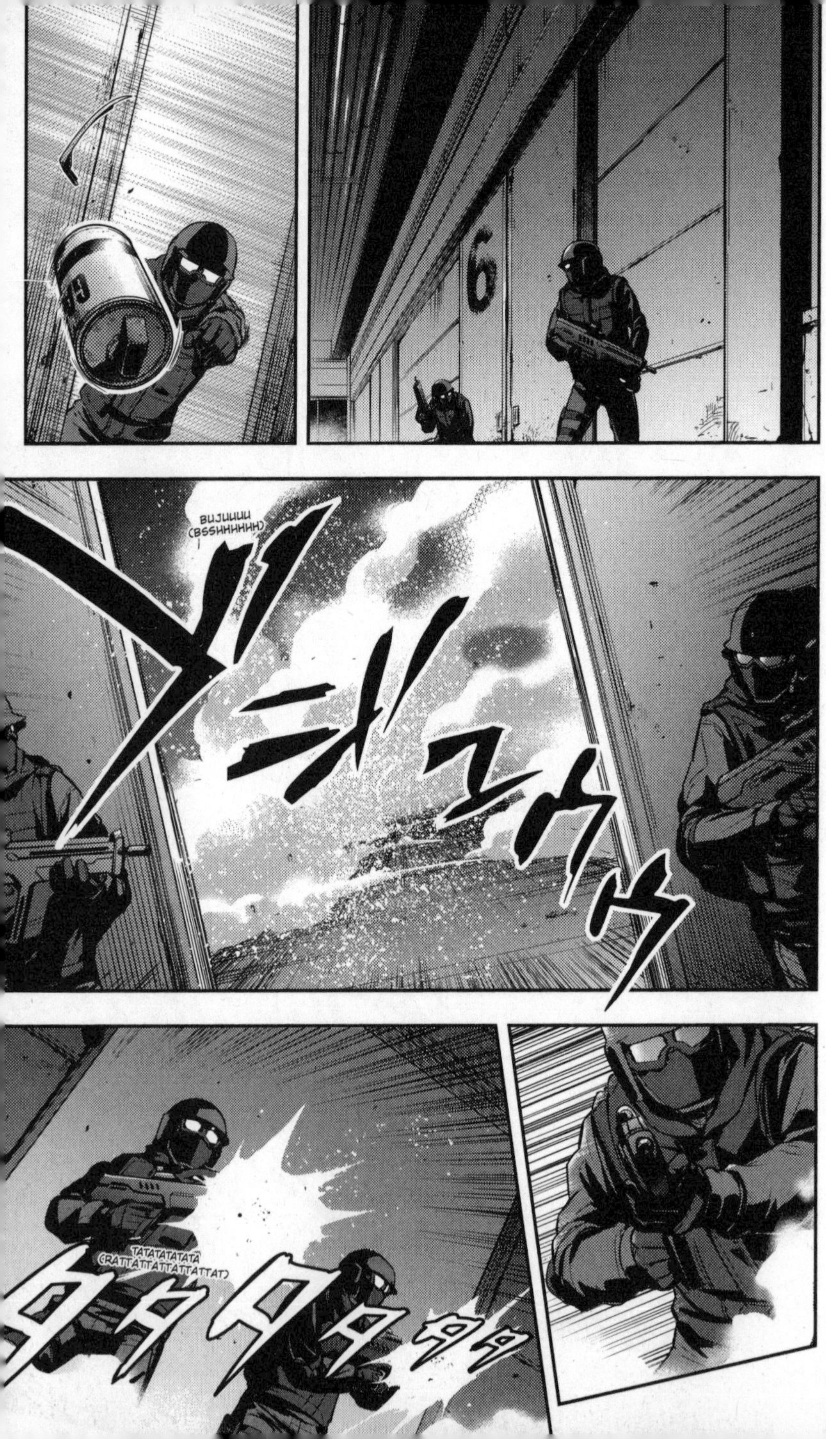
BUJUUUU
(BSSHHHHHH)
TATATATATATA
(RATTATTATTATTAT)

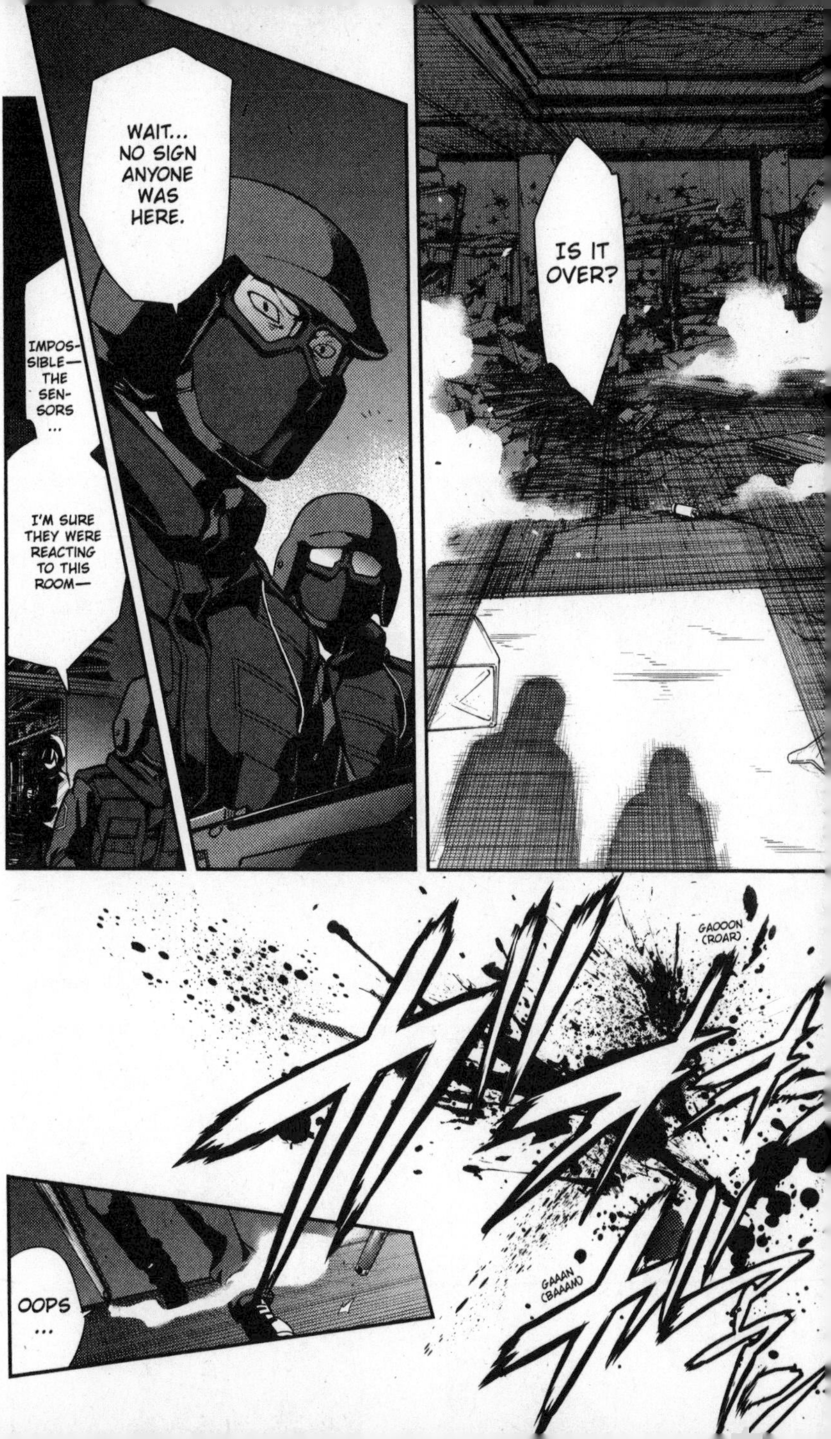
IS IT OVER?
WAIT... NO SIGN ANYONE WAS HERE.
IMPOSSIBLE—THE SENSORS...
I'M SURE THEY WERE REACTING TO THIS ROOM—
GAOOON (ROAR)
GAAAN (BAAAN)
OOPS...

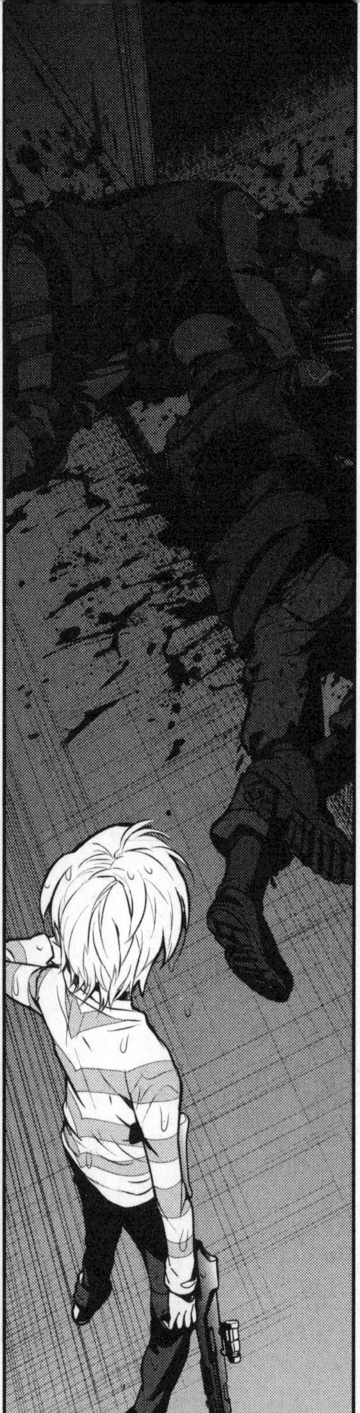

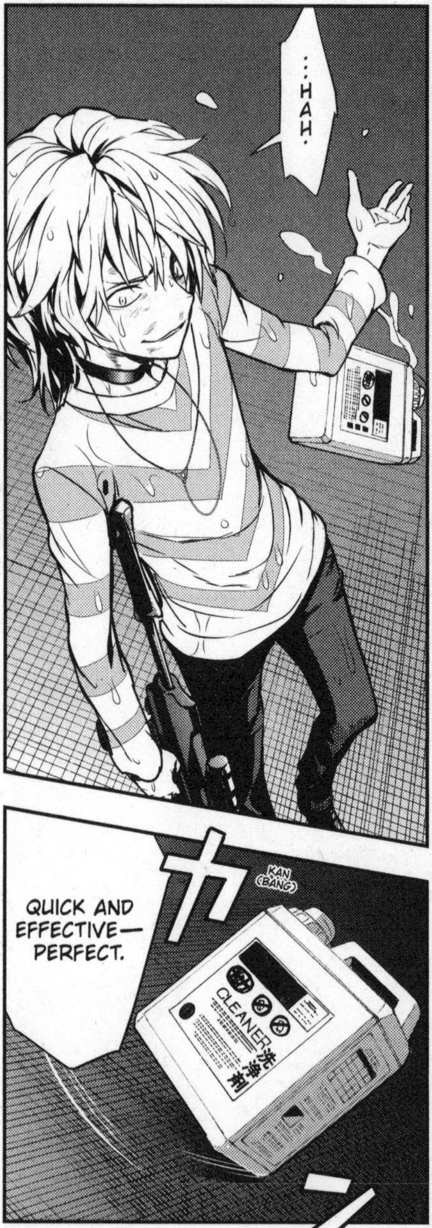
...HAH.
カ
KAN (BANG)
QUICK AND EFFECTIVE—PERFECT.
CLEANER
洗浄剤

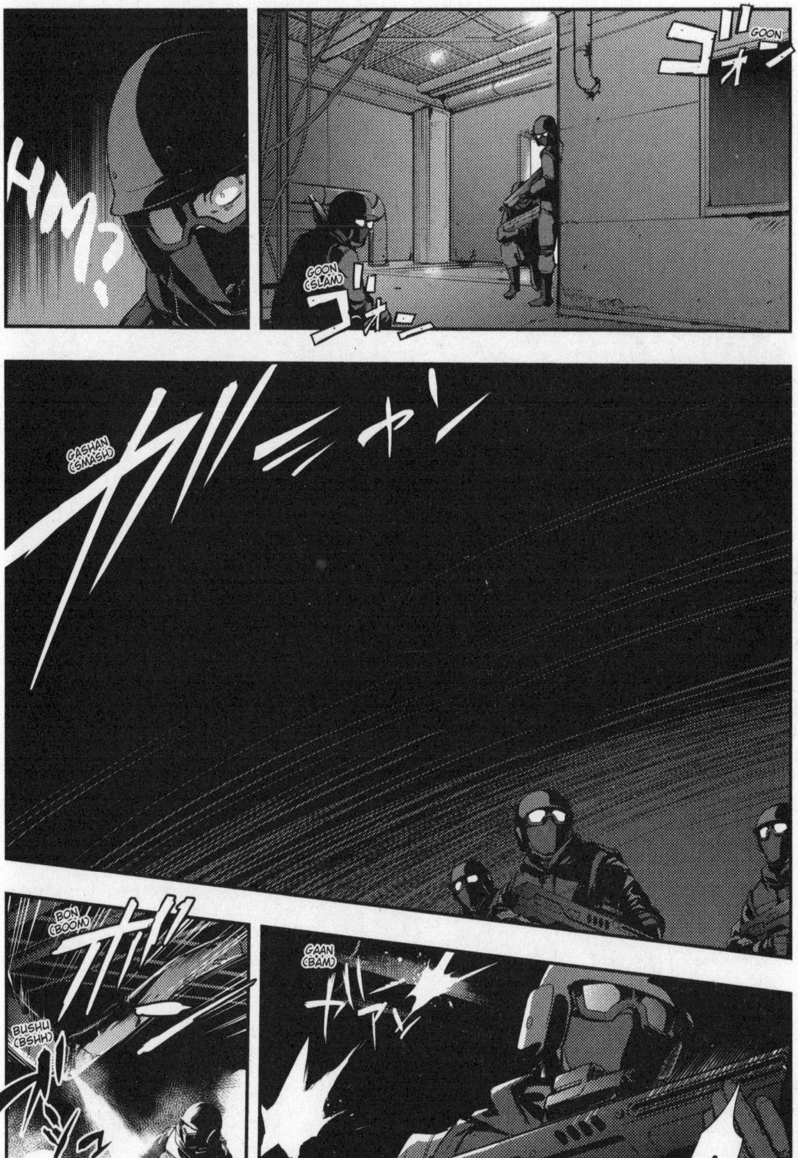
GOON
GOON (SLAM)
HM?
GASHAN (SMASH)
GAAN (BAM)
!
BON (BOOM)
BUSHU (BSHH)

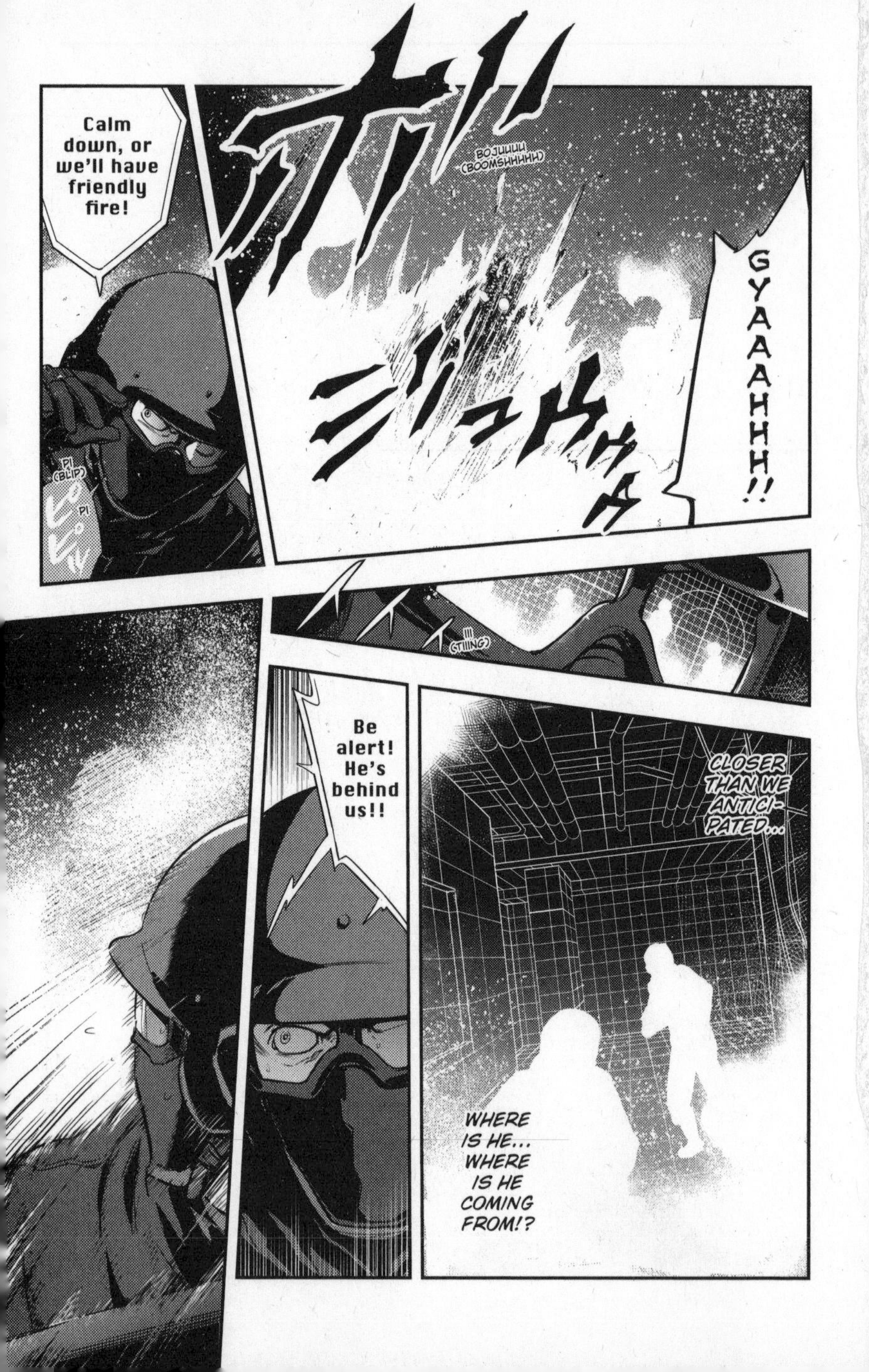
BOJUUUU
(BOOMSHHHHH)
GYAAAAHHH!!
Calm down, or we'll have friendly fire!
PI
(BLIP)
PI
III
(STIIING)
CLOSER THAN WE ANTICI-PATED...
WHERE IS HE... WHERE IS HE COMING FROM!?
Be alert! He's behind us!!

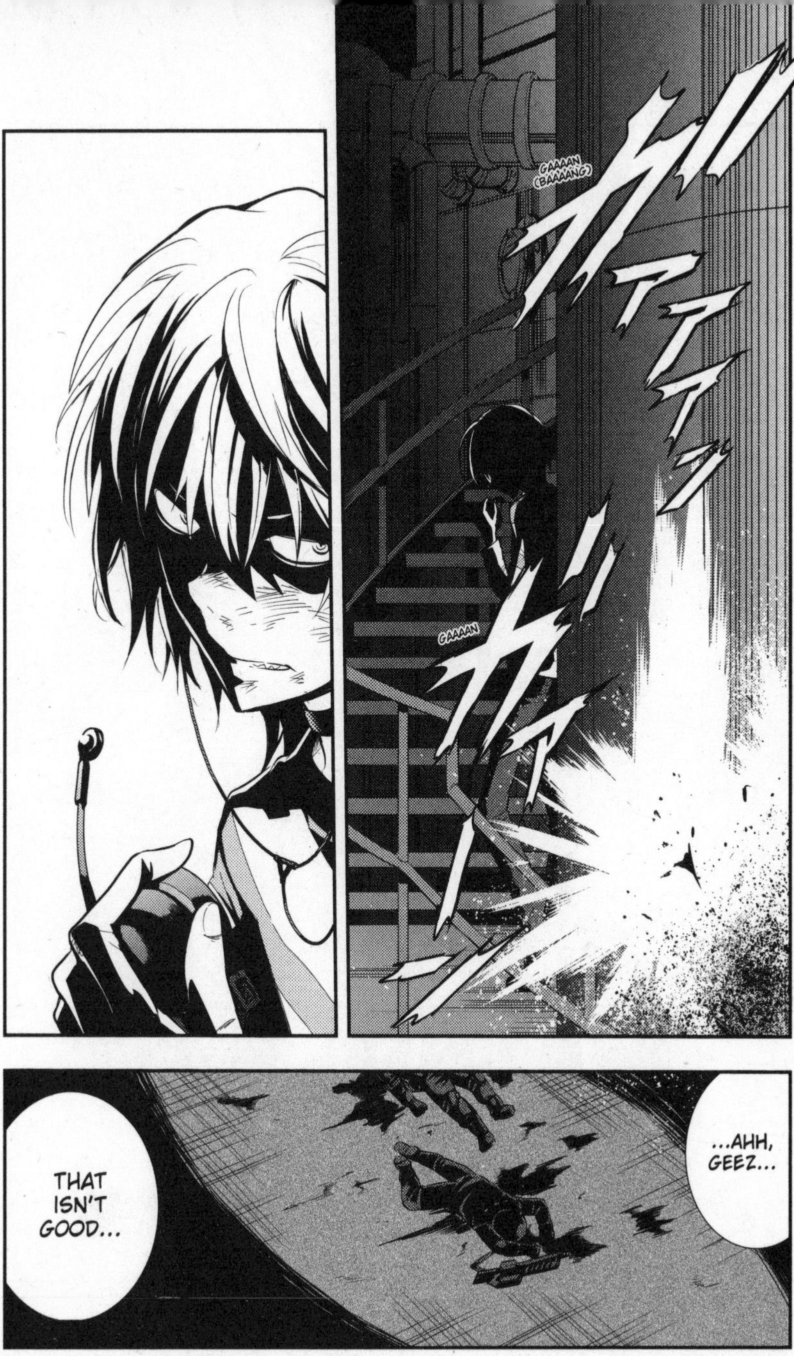
GAAAAN (BAAAANG)
GAAAAN
...AHH, GEEZ...
THAT ISN'T GOOD...

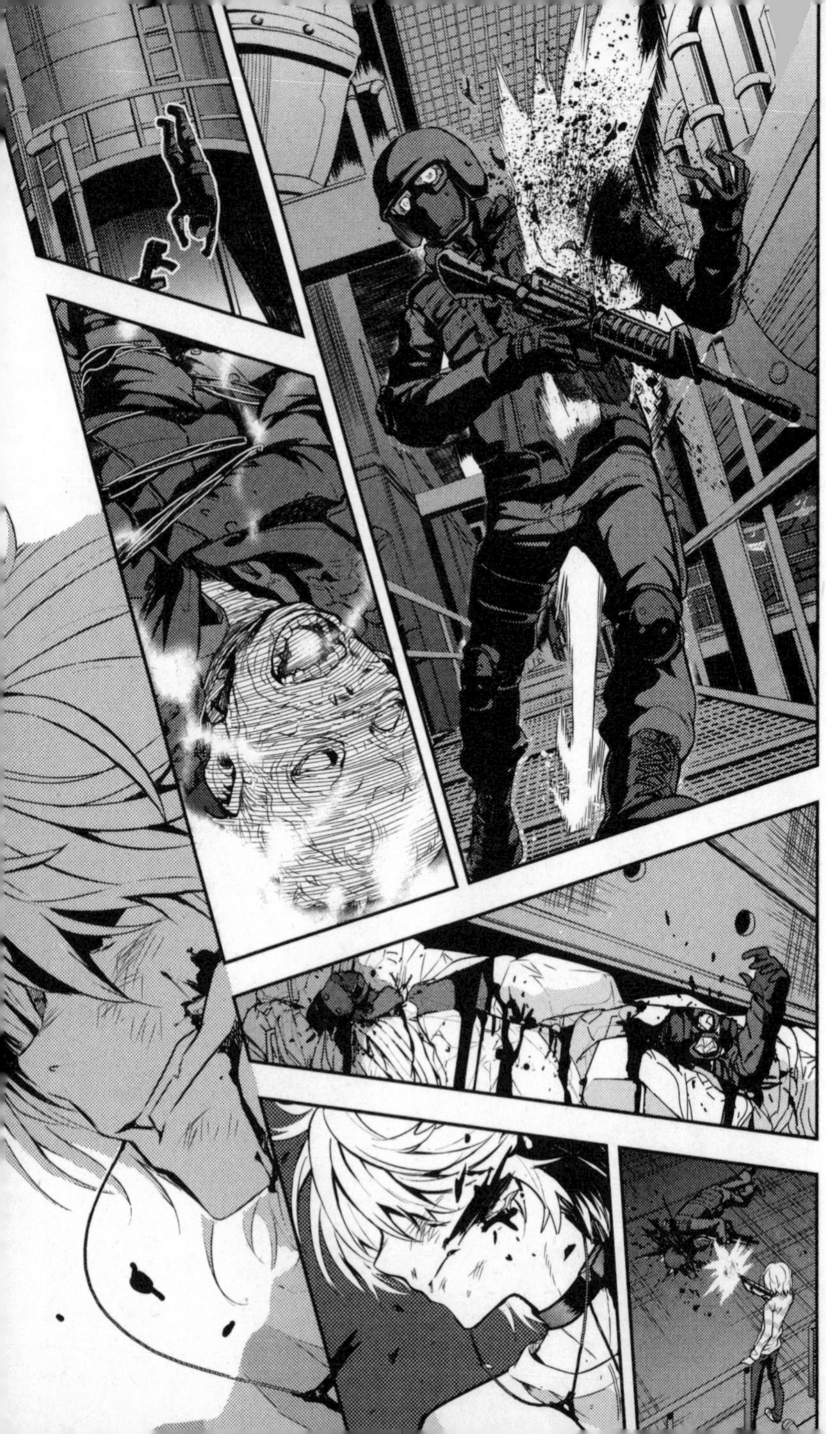

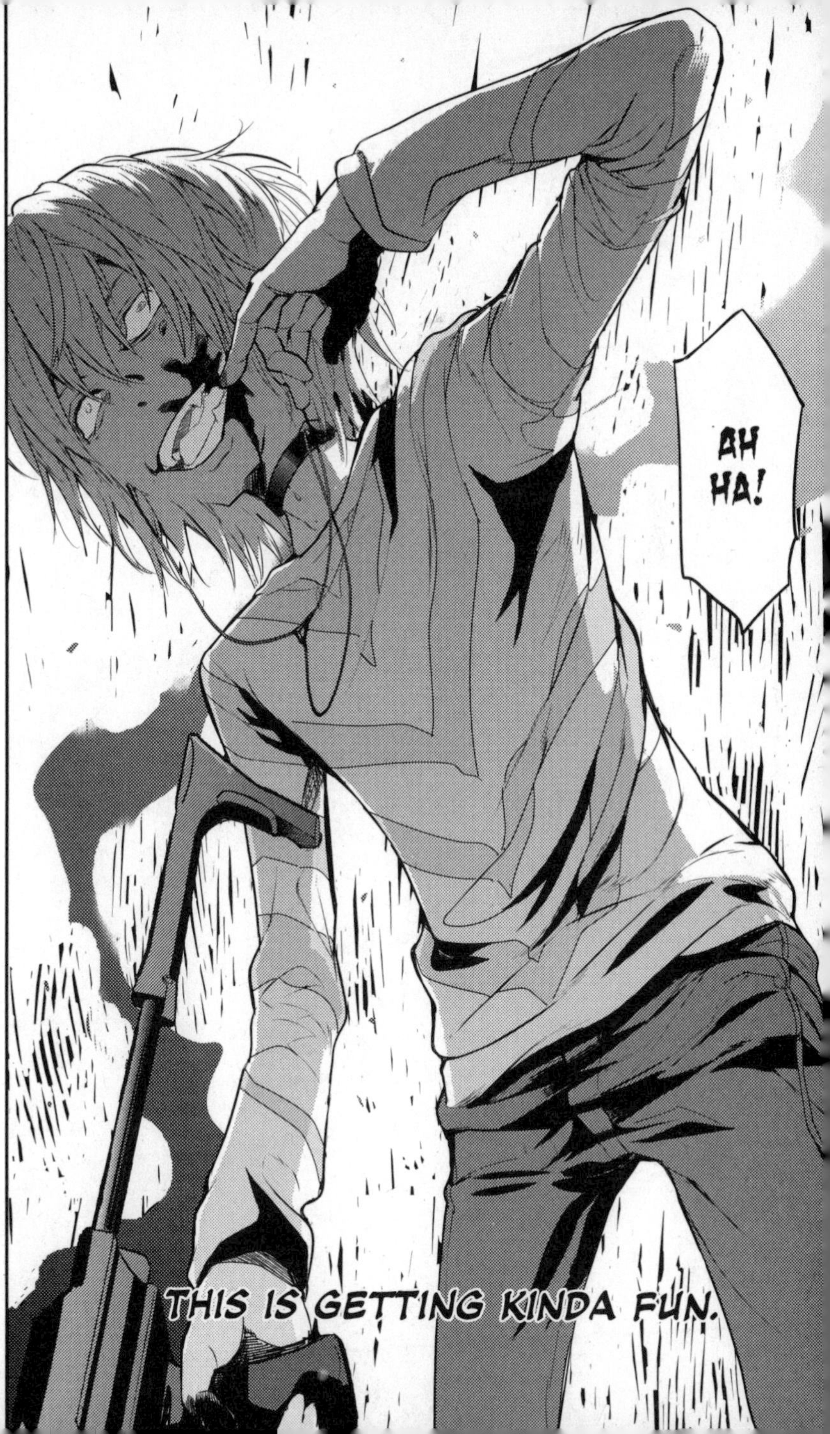
AH HA!
THIS IS GETTING KINDA FUN.

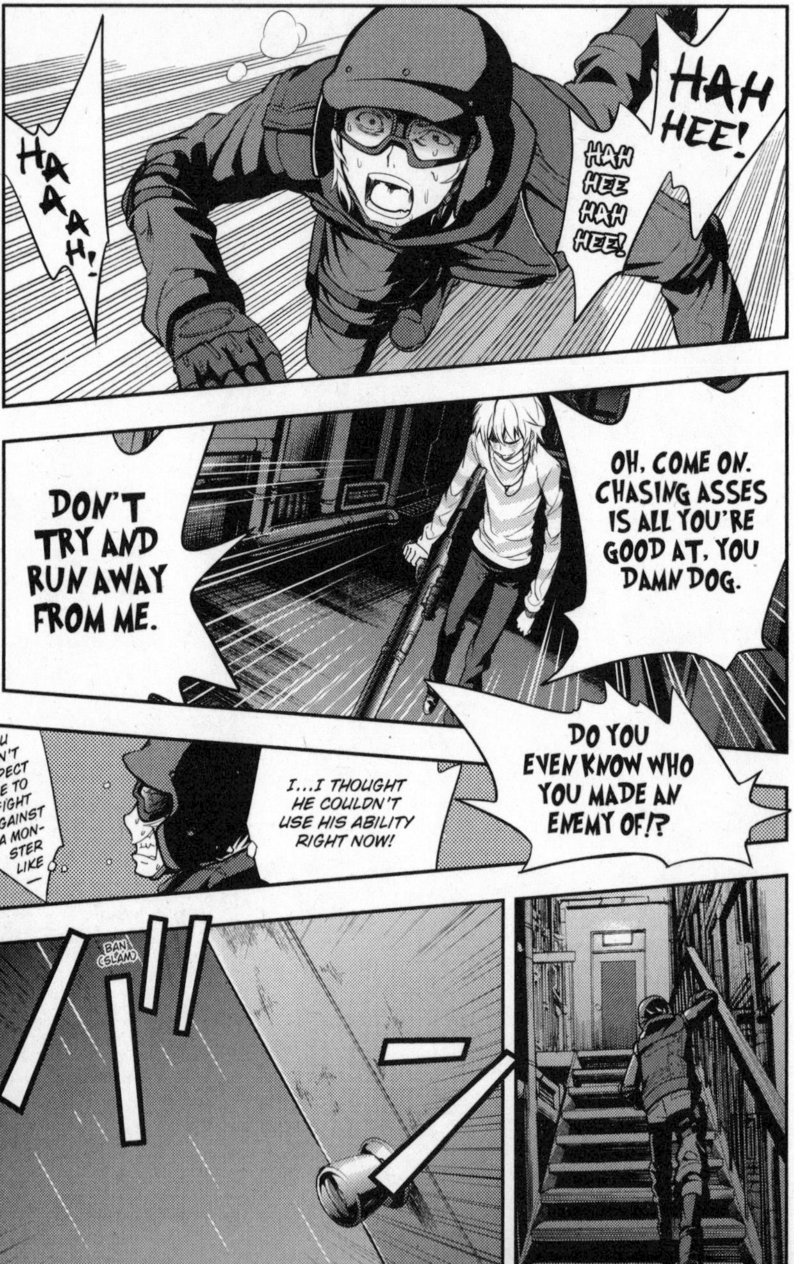
HAH HEE!
HAH HEE HAH HEE!
HAAAAH!
OH, COME ON. CHASING ASSES IS ALL YOU'RE GOOD AT, YOU DAMN DOG.
DON'T TRY AND RUN AWAY FROM ME.
DO YOU EVEN KNOW WHO YOU MADE AN ENEMY OF!?
I...I THOUGHT HE COULDN'T USE HIS ABILITY RIGHT NOW!
YOU CAN'T EXPECT ME TO FIGHT AGAINST A MON-STER LIKE—
BAN (SLAM)

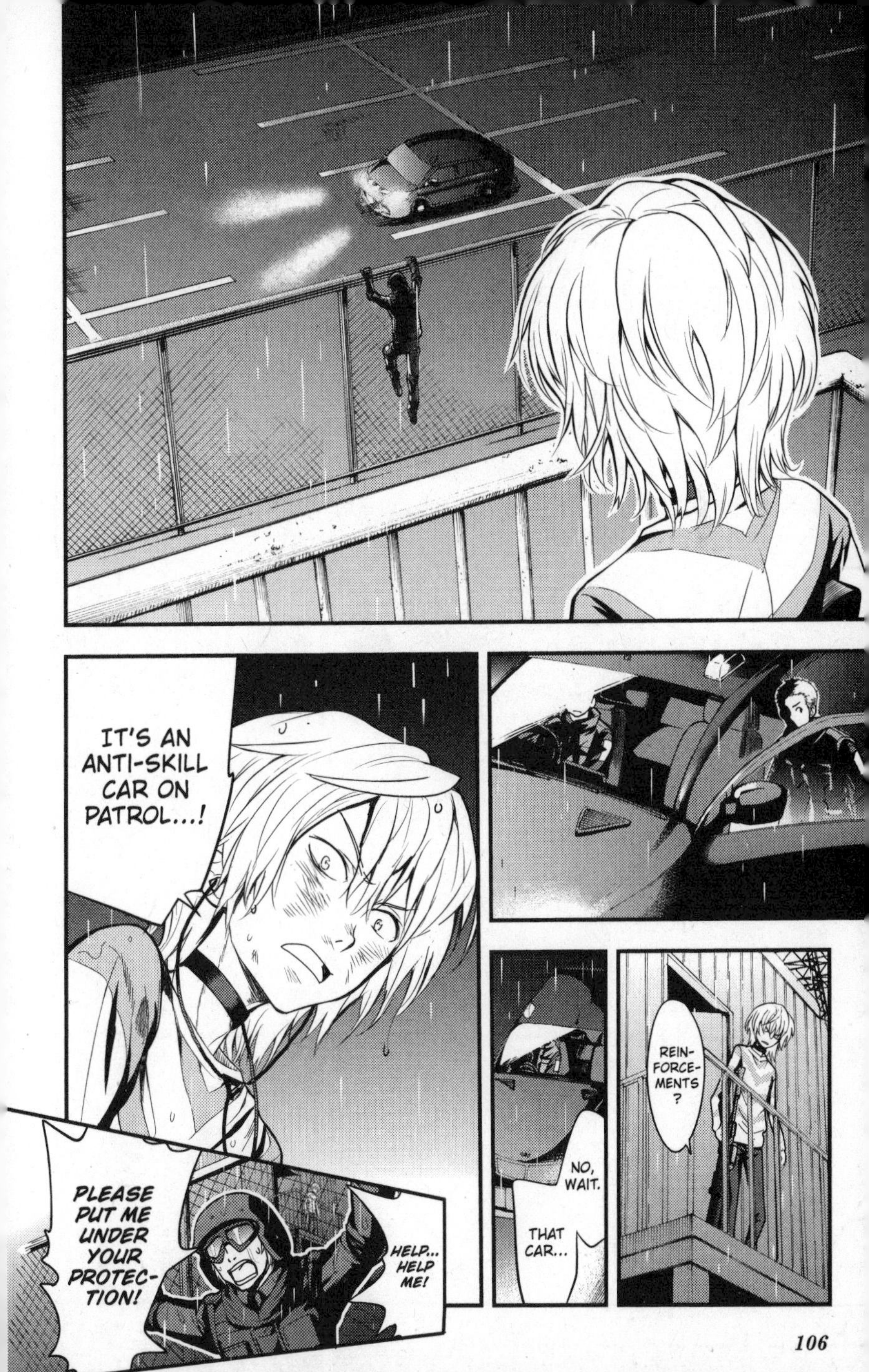
REIN-FORCEMENTS?
NO, WAIT.
THAT CAR...
IT'S AN ANTI-SKILL CAR ON PATROL...!
HELP... HELP ME!
PLEASE PUT ME UNDER YOUR PROTECTION!

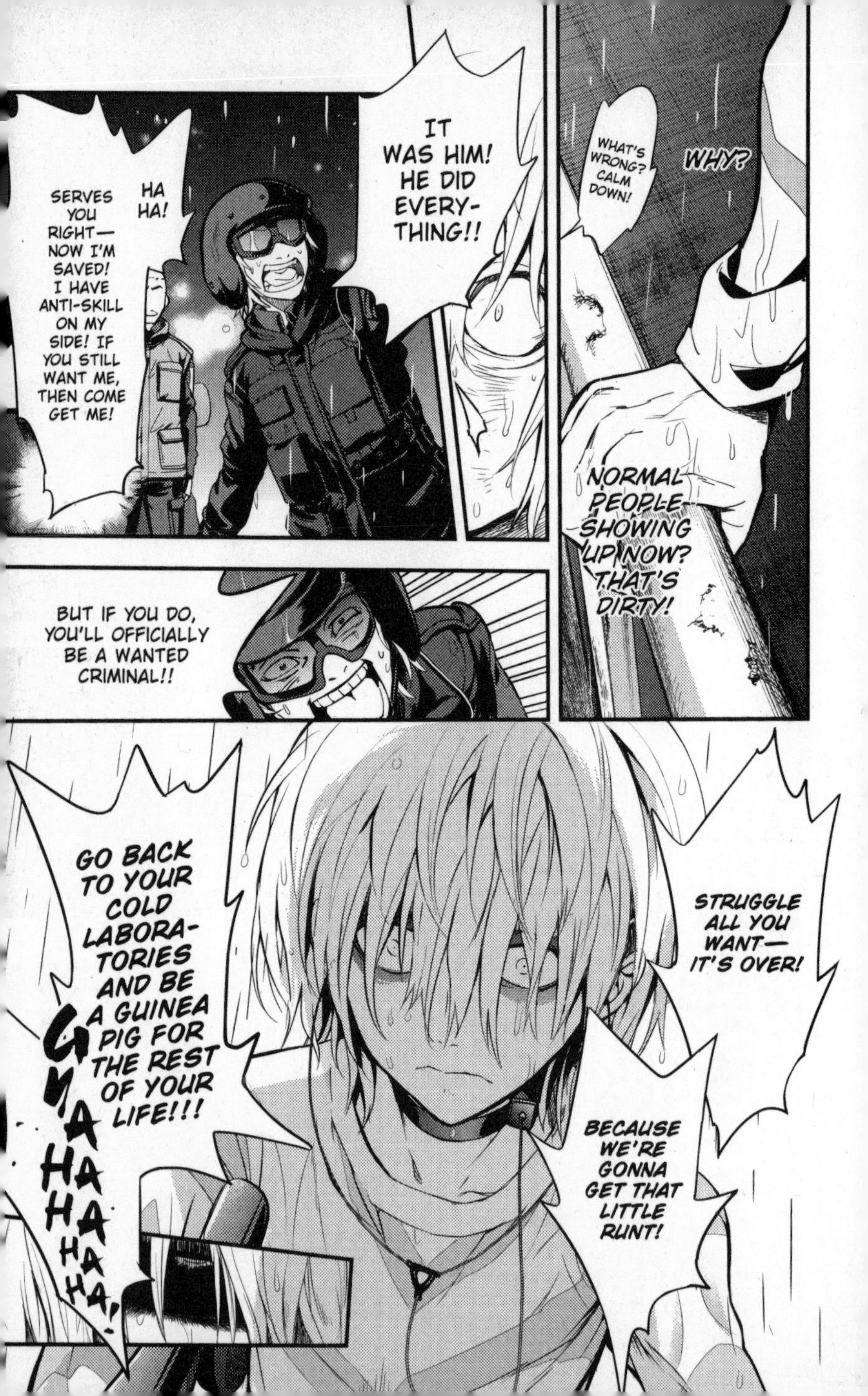
WHY?
WHAT'S WRONG? CALM DOWN!
NORMAL PEOPLE SHOWING UP NOW? THAT'S DIRTY!
IT WAS HIM! HE DID EVERY-THING!!
HA HA!
SERVES YOU RIGHT—NOW I'M SAVED! I HAVE ANTI-SKILL ON MY SIDE! IF YOU STILL WANT ME, THEN COME GET ME!
BUT IF YOU DO, YOU'LL OFFICIALLY BE A WANTED CRIMINAL!!
STRUGGLE ALL YOU WANT—IT'S OVER!
BECAUSE WE'RE GONNA GET THAT LITTLE RUNT!
GO BACK TO YOUR COLD LABORA-TORIES AND BE A GUINEA PIG FOR THE REST OF YOUR LIFE!!!
GYAHAHAHAHAHA!

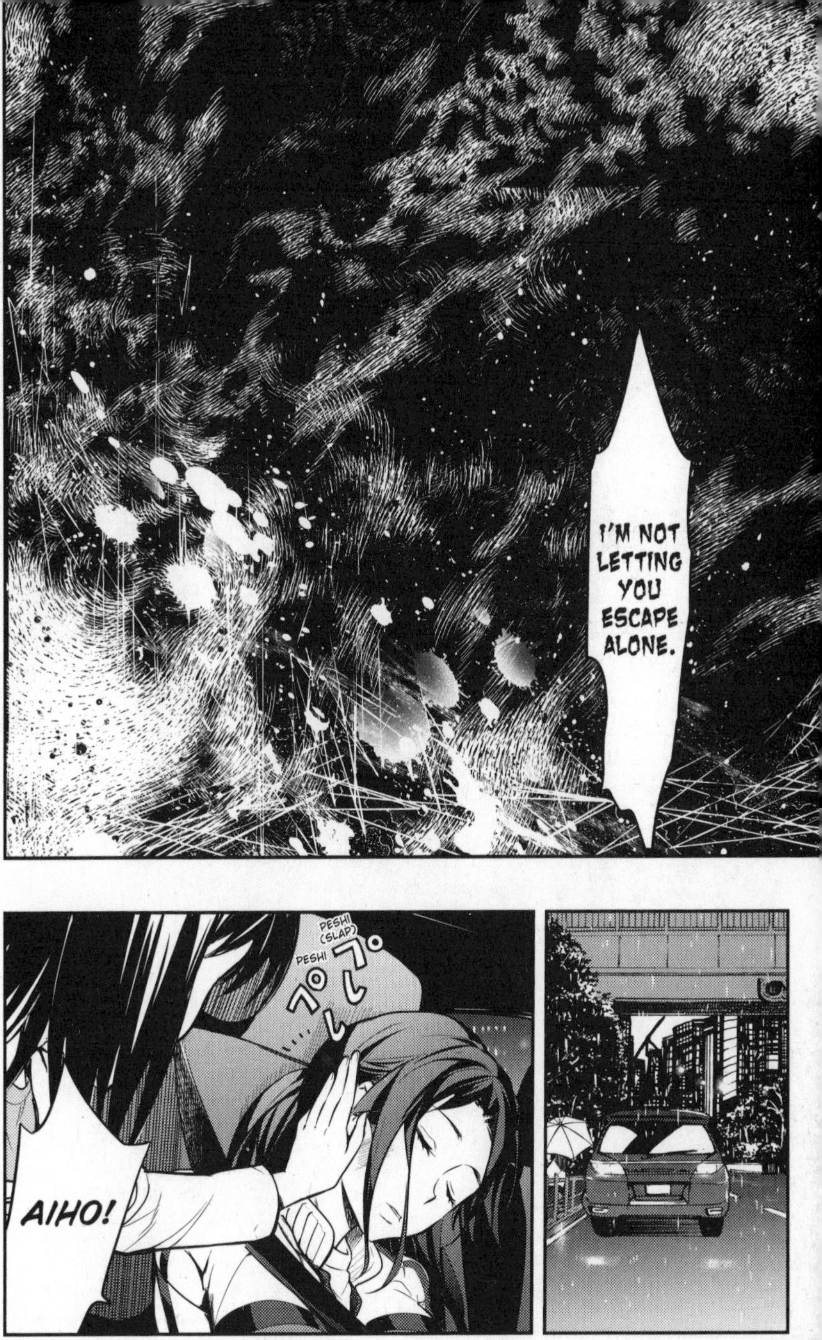
I'M NOT LETTING YOU ESCAPE ALONE.
PESHI (SLAP)
PESHI
ぺし
ぺし
AIHO!

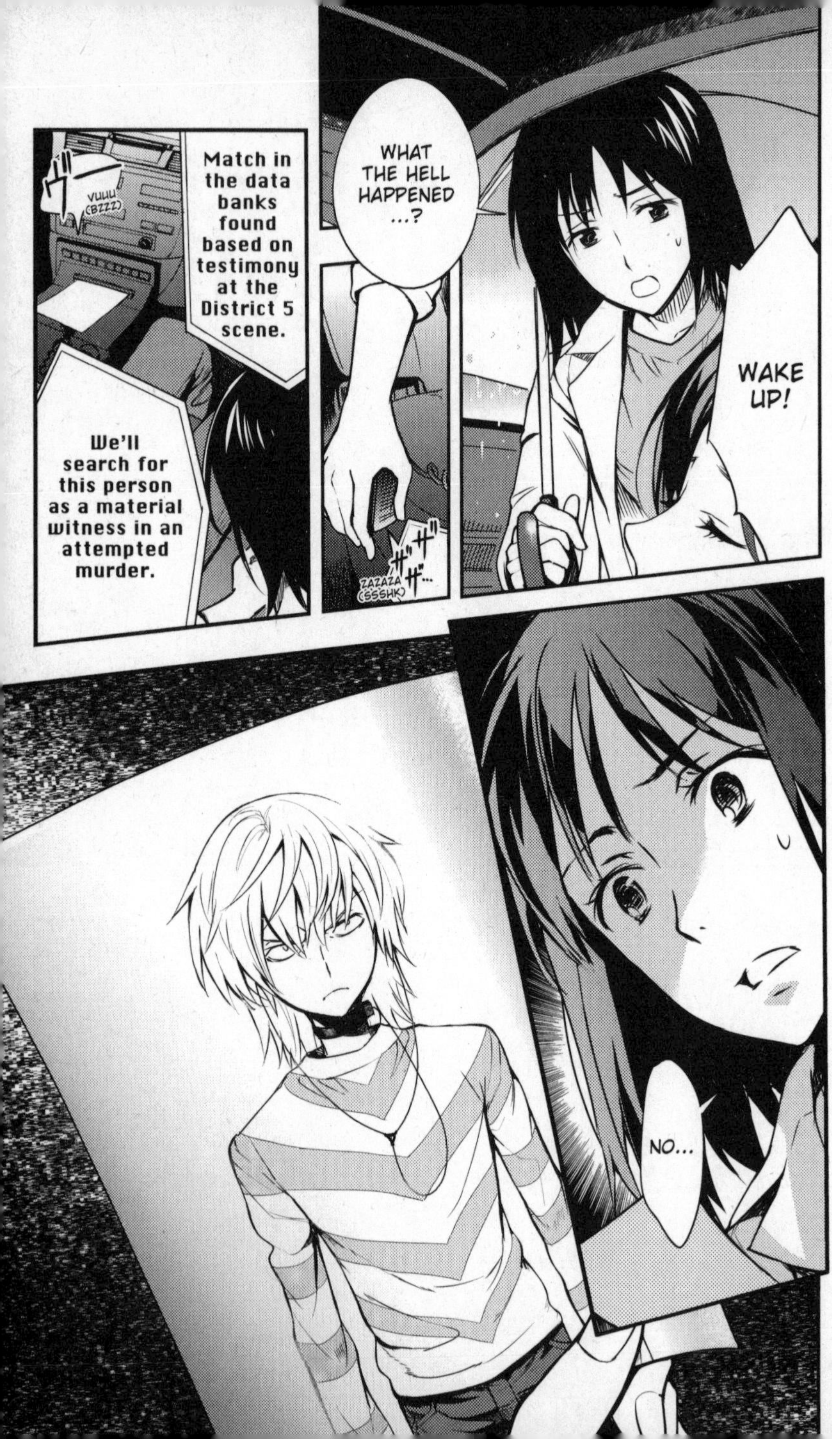

WHAT THE HELL HAPPENED ...?
WAKE UP!
ZAZAZA (SSSHK)
Match in the data banks found based on testimony at the District 5 scene.
VUUU (BZZZ)
We'll search for this person as a material witness in an attempted murder.
NO...

A Certain Magical Index

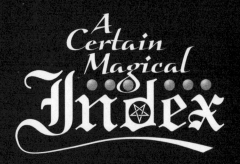

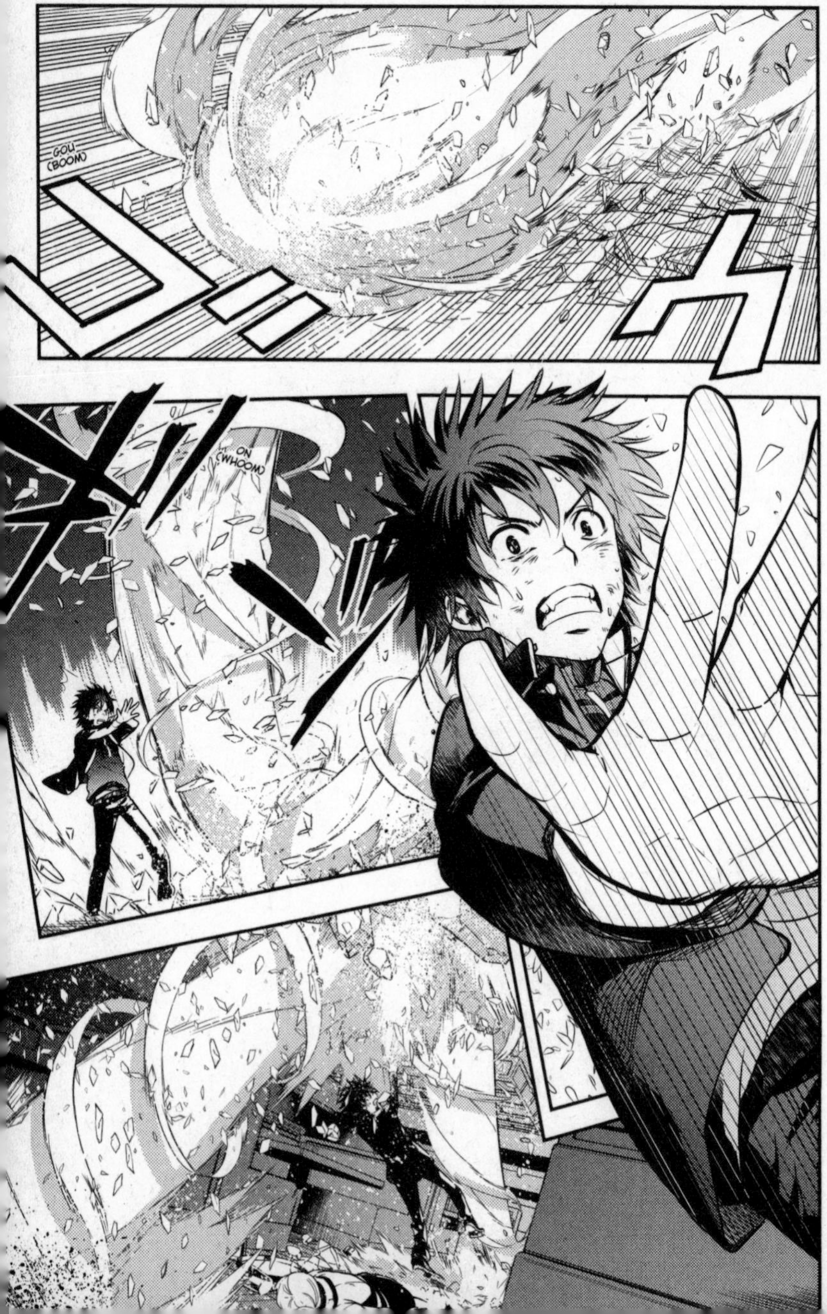
GOU (BOOM)
ON (WHOOM)

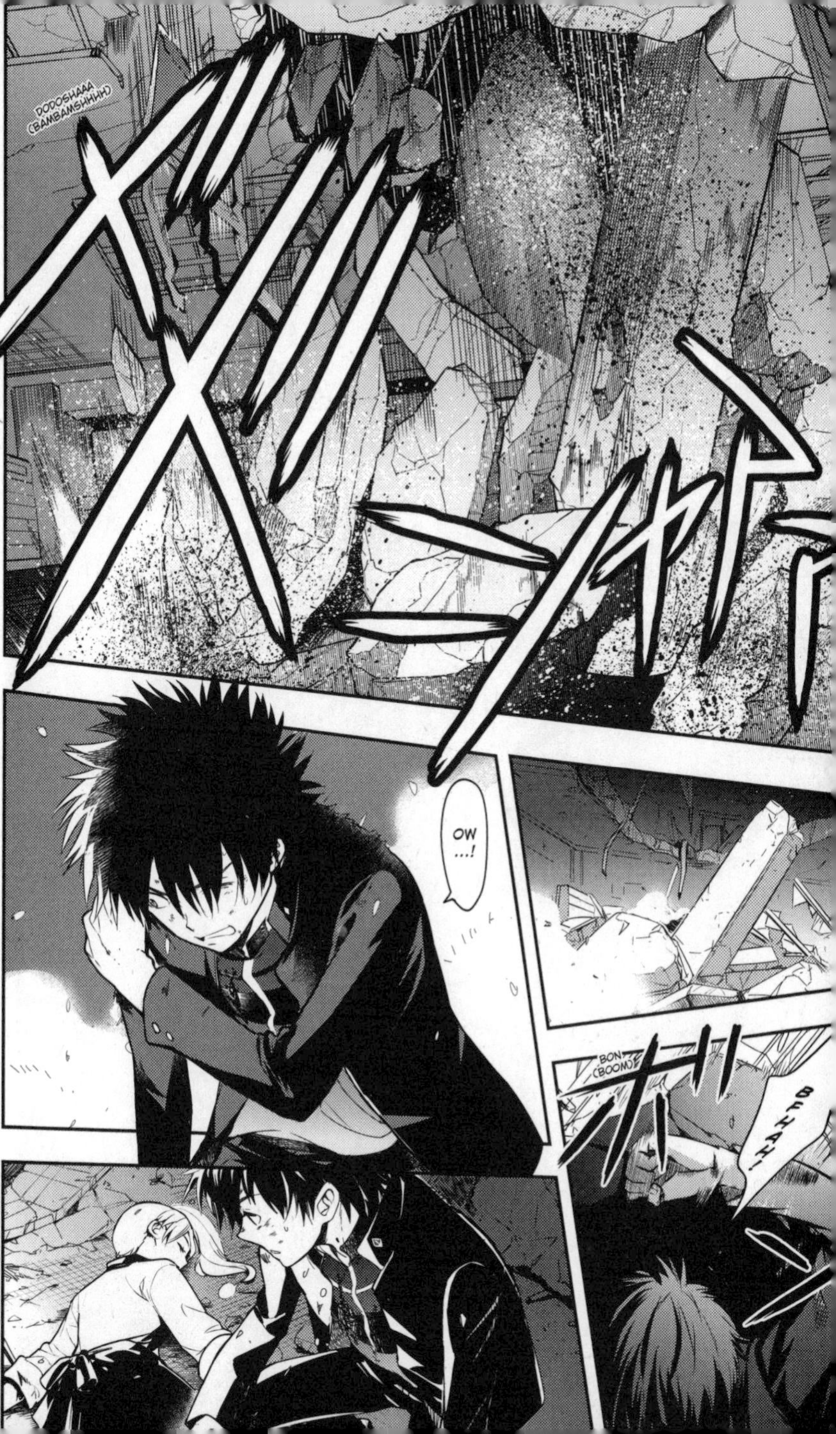
DODOSHAAA (BAMBAMSHHHH)
OW ...!
BON (BOOM)
BEHAH!

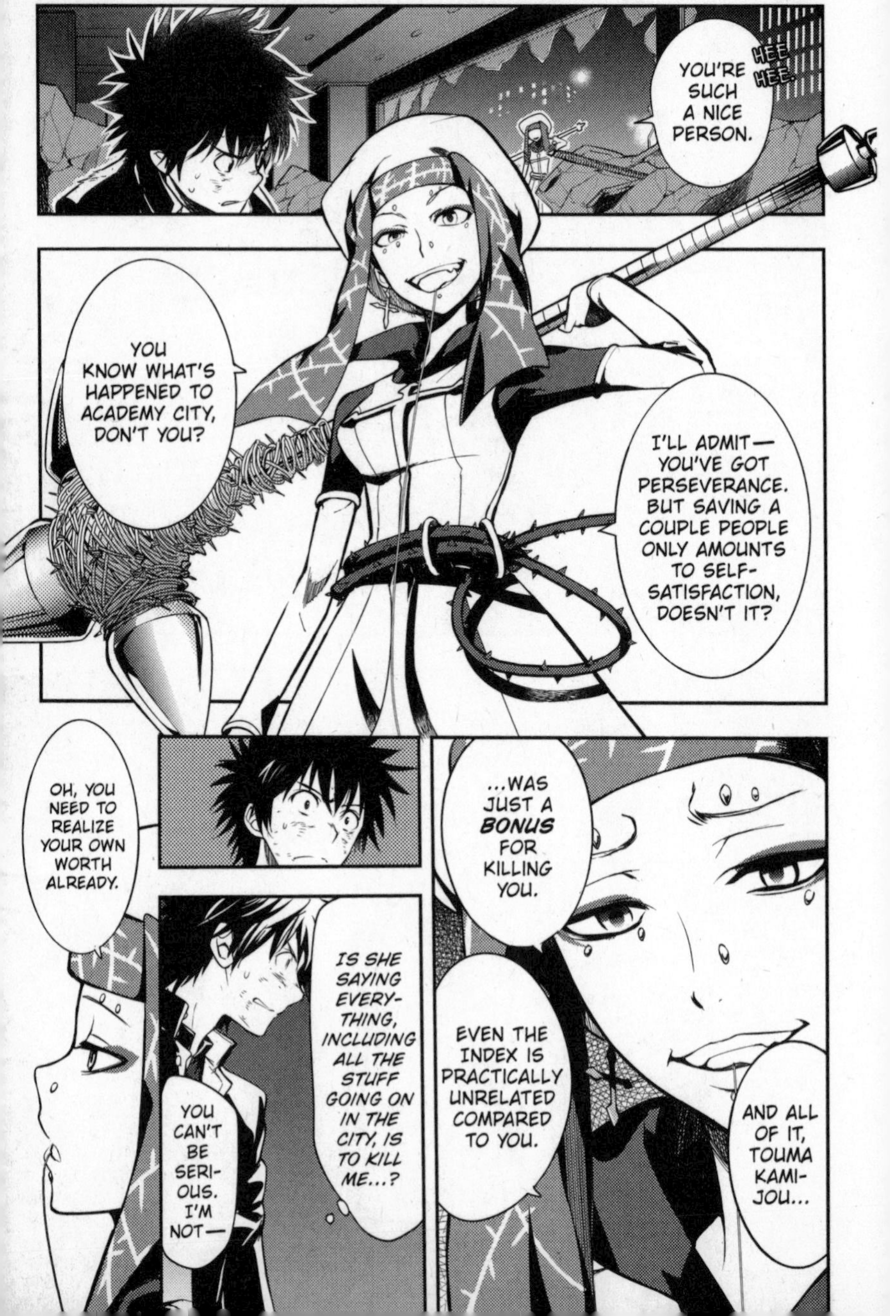

YOU'RE SUCH A NICE PERSON.
HEE HEE.
I'LL ADMIT—YOU'VE GOT PERSEVERANCE. BUT SAVING A COUPLE PEOPLE ONLY AMOUNTS TO SELF-SATISFACTION, DOESN'T IT?
YOU KNOW WHAT'S HAPPENED TO ACADEMY CITY, DON'T YOU?
AND ALL OF IT, TOUMA KAMIJOU...
...WAS JUST A ***BONUS*** FOR KILLING YOU.
EVEN THE INDEX IS PRACTICALLY UNRELATED COMPARED TO YOU.
OH, YOU NEED TO REALIZE YOUR OWN WORTH ALREADY.
IS SHE SAYING EVERYTHING, INCLUDING ALL THE STUFF GOING ON IN THE CITY, IS TO KILL ME...?
YOU CAN'T BE SERIOUS. I'M NOT—

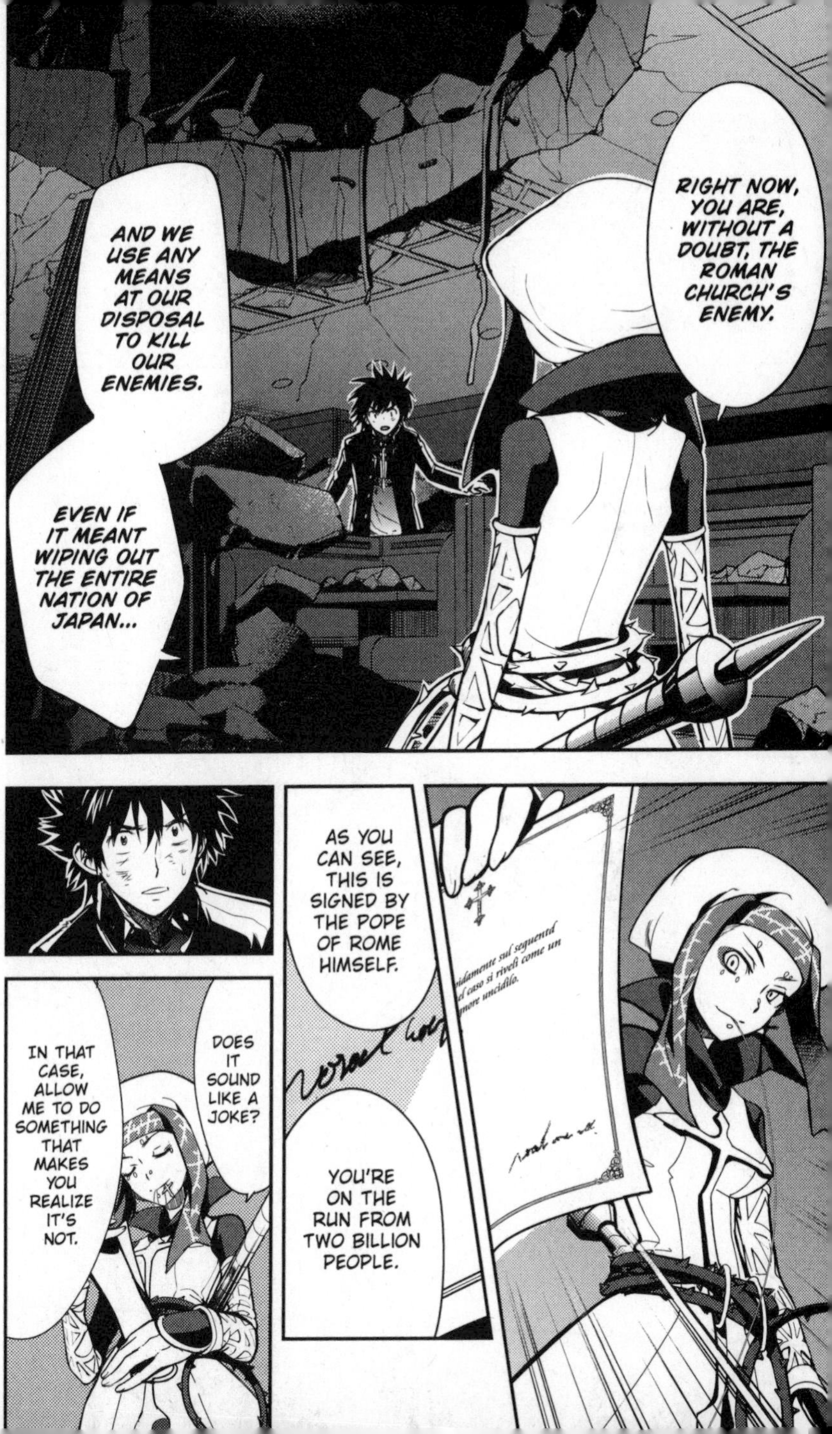
RIGHT NOW, YOU ARE, WITHOUT A DOUBT, THE ROMAN CHURCH'S ENEMY.
AND WE USE ANY MEANS AT OUR DISPOSAL TO KILL OUR ENEMIES.
EVEN IF IT MEANT WIPING OUT THE ENTIRE NATION OF JAPAN...
AS YOU CAN SEE, THIS IS SIGNED BY THE POPE OF ROME HIMSELF.
YOU'RE ON THE RUN FROM TWO BILLION PEOPLE.
DOES IT SOUND LIKE A JOKE?
IN THAT CASE, ALLOW ME TO DO SOMETHING THAT MAKES YOU REALIZE IT'S NOT.

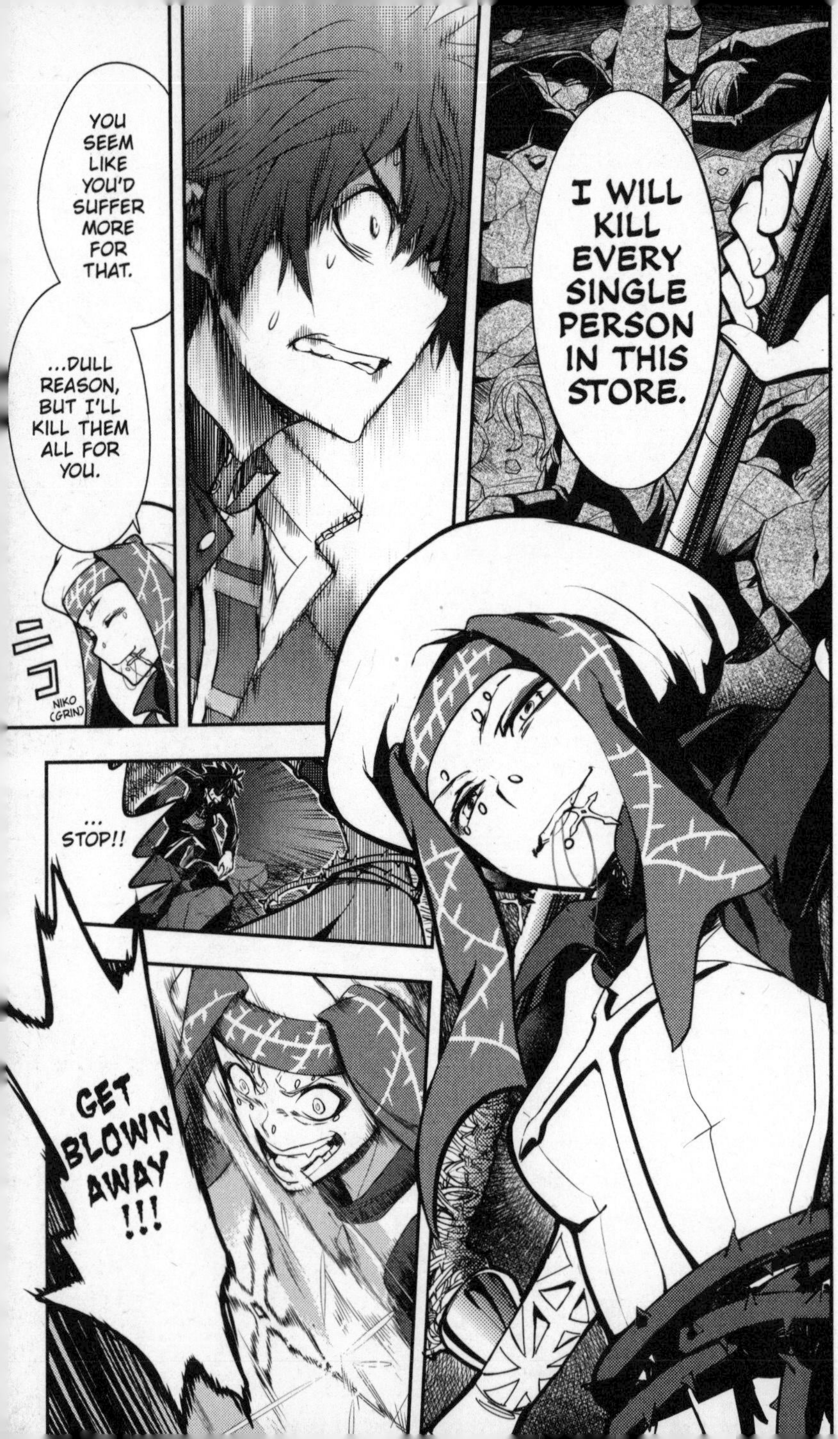
I WILL KILL EVERY SINGLE PERSON IN THIS STORE.
YOU SEEM LIKE YOU'D SUFFER MORE FOR THAT.
...DULL REASON, BUT I'LL KILL THEM ALL FOR YOU.
ニコ
NIKO (GRIN)
... STOP!!
GET BLOWN AWAY !!!

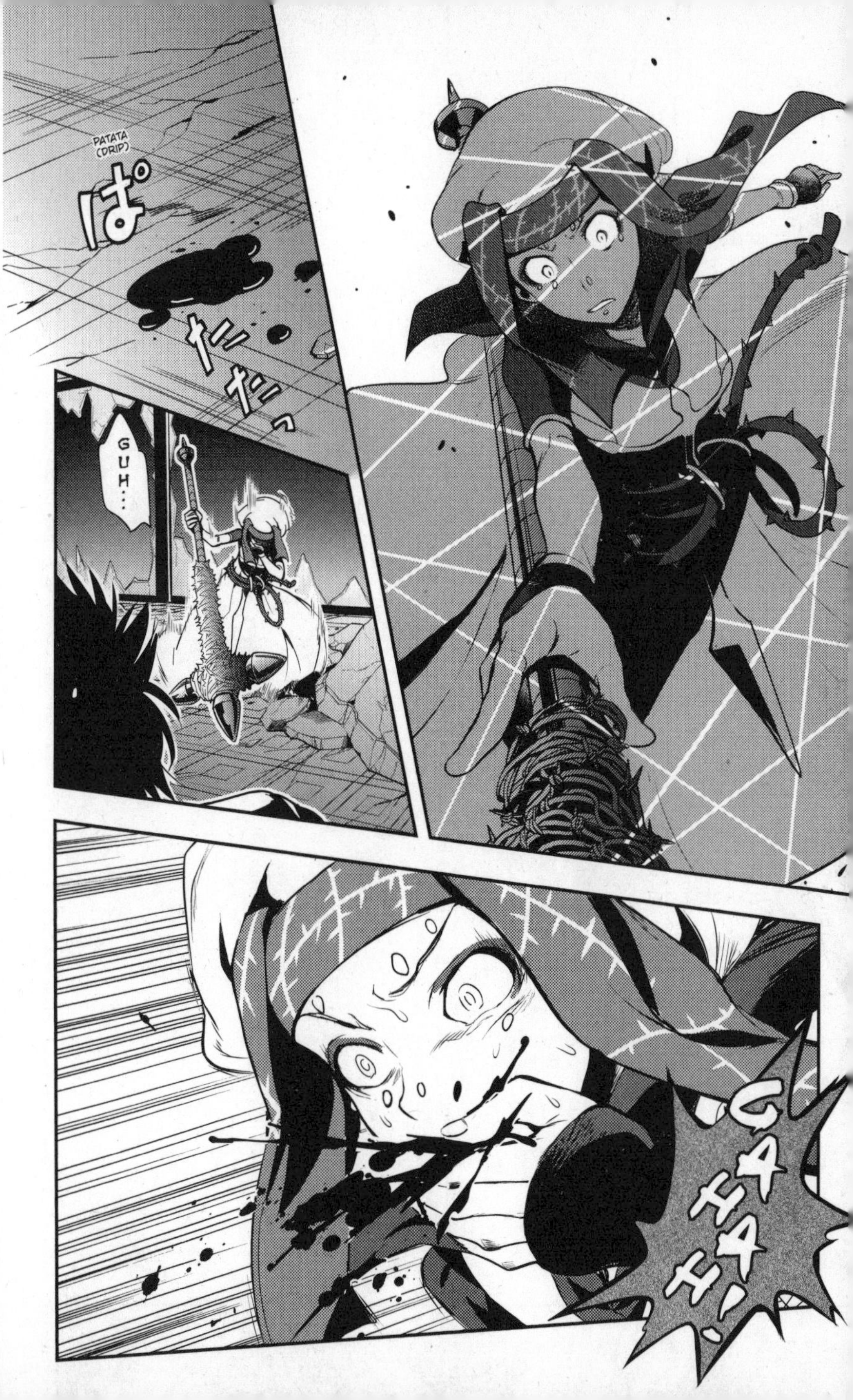
PATATA (DRIP)
ぱ
GUH...
GAHAH!

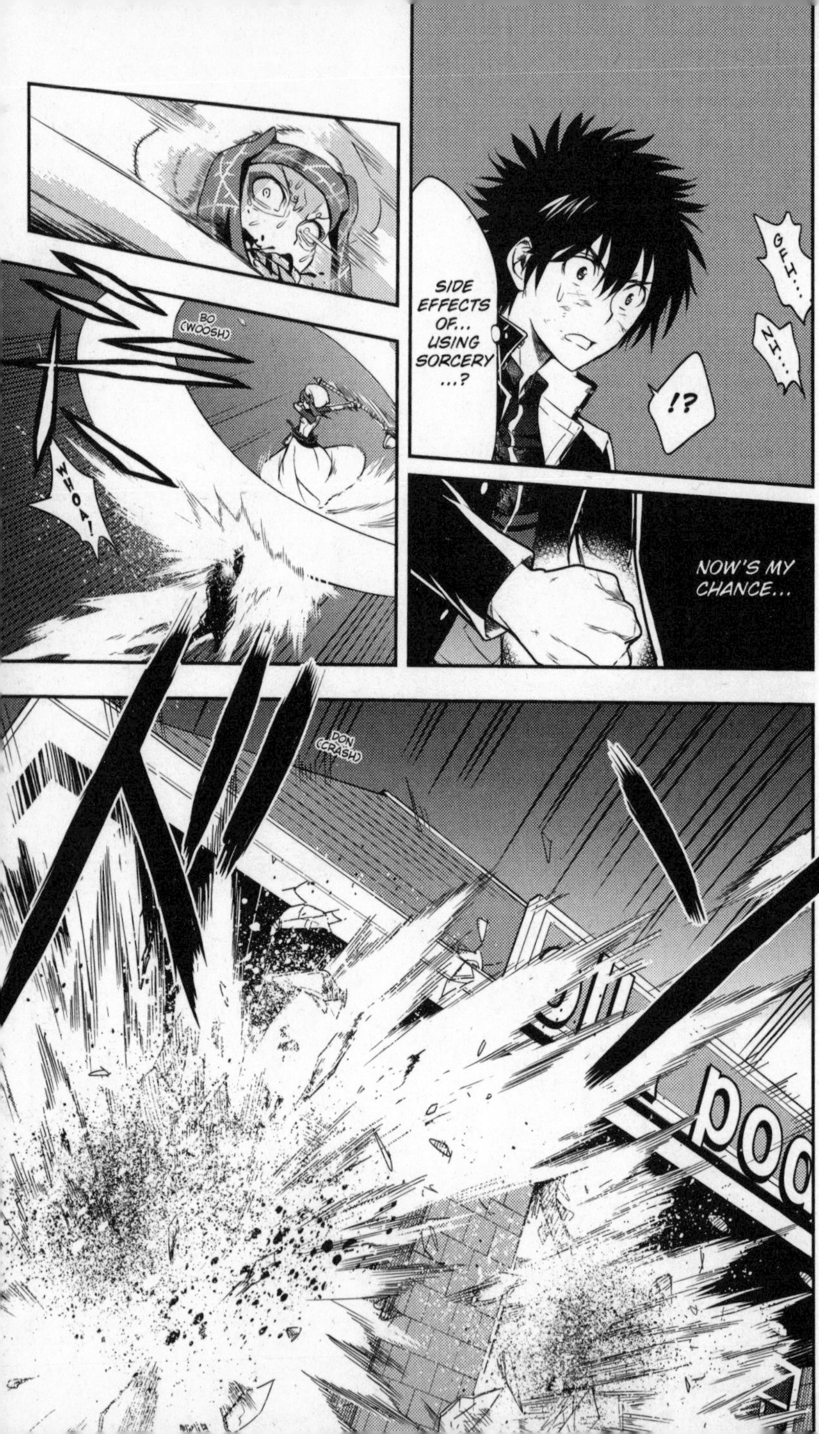
GFH...
NH...
!?
SIDE EFFECTS OF... USING SORCERY ...?
NOW'S MY CHANCE...
BO (WOOSH)
WHOA!
DON (CRASH)

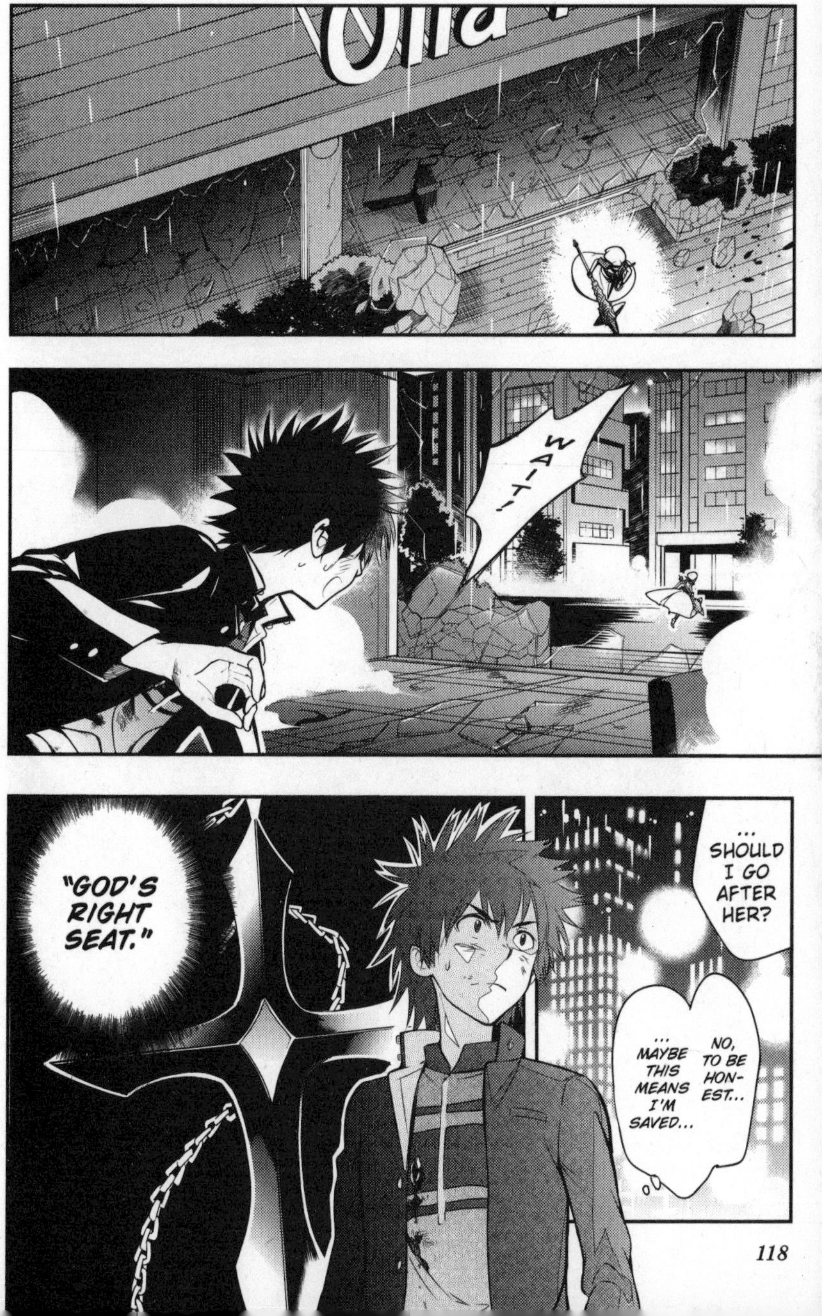
WAIT!
...SHOULD I GO AFTER HER?
"GOD'S RIGHT SEAT."
NO, TO BE HON-EST...
...MAYBE THIS MEANS I'M SAVED...

#108 INTRUDER ⑤

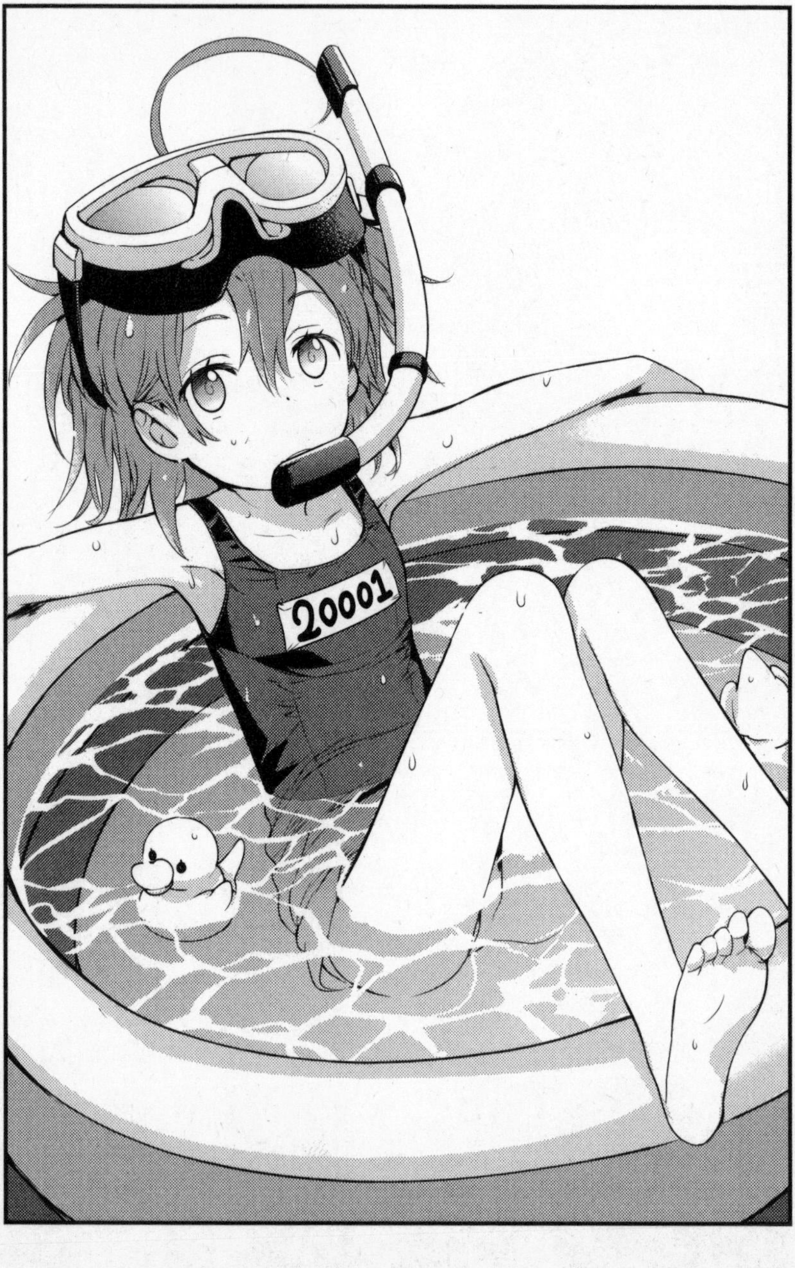
20001

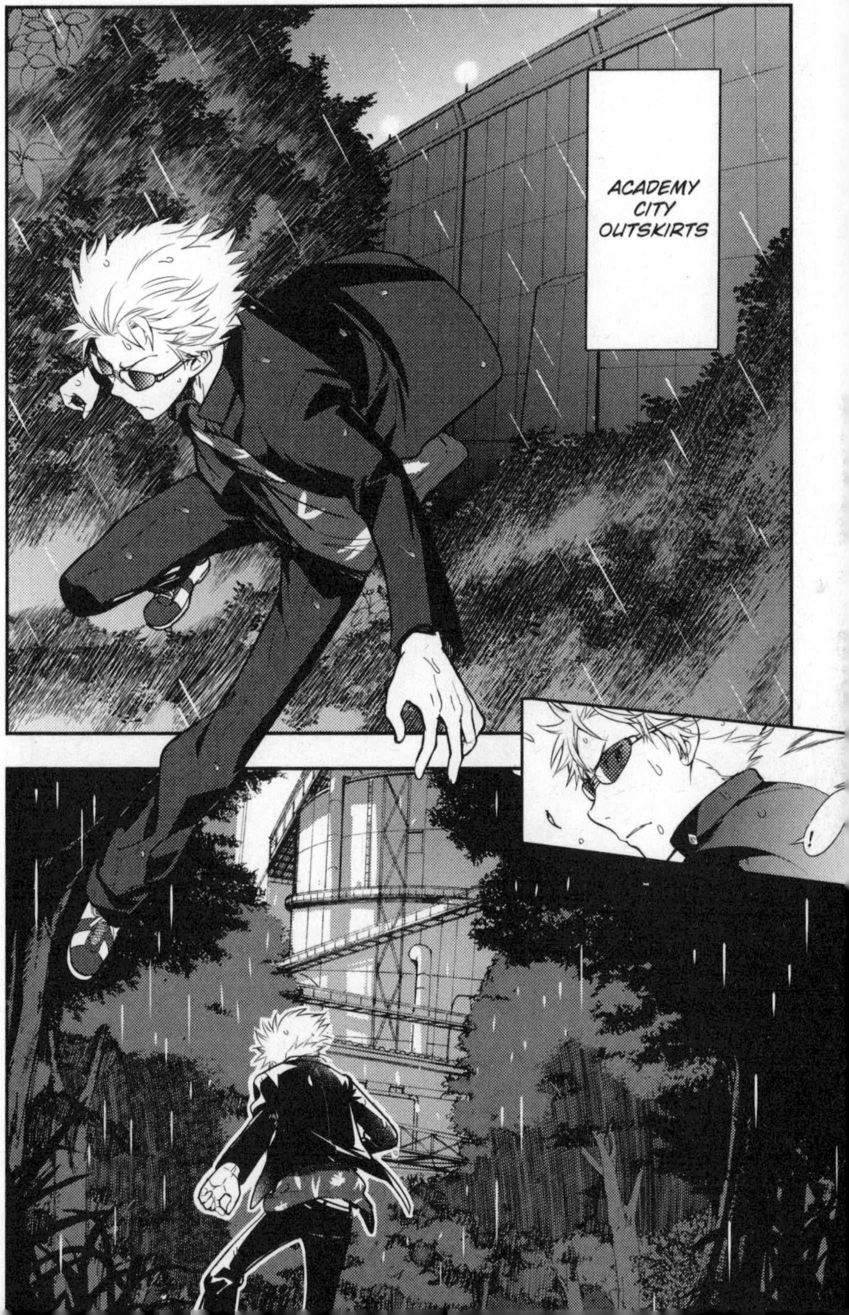
ACADEMY CITY OUTSKIRTS

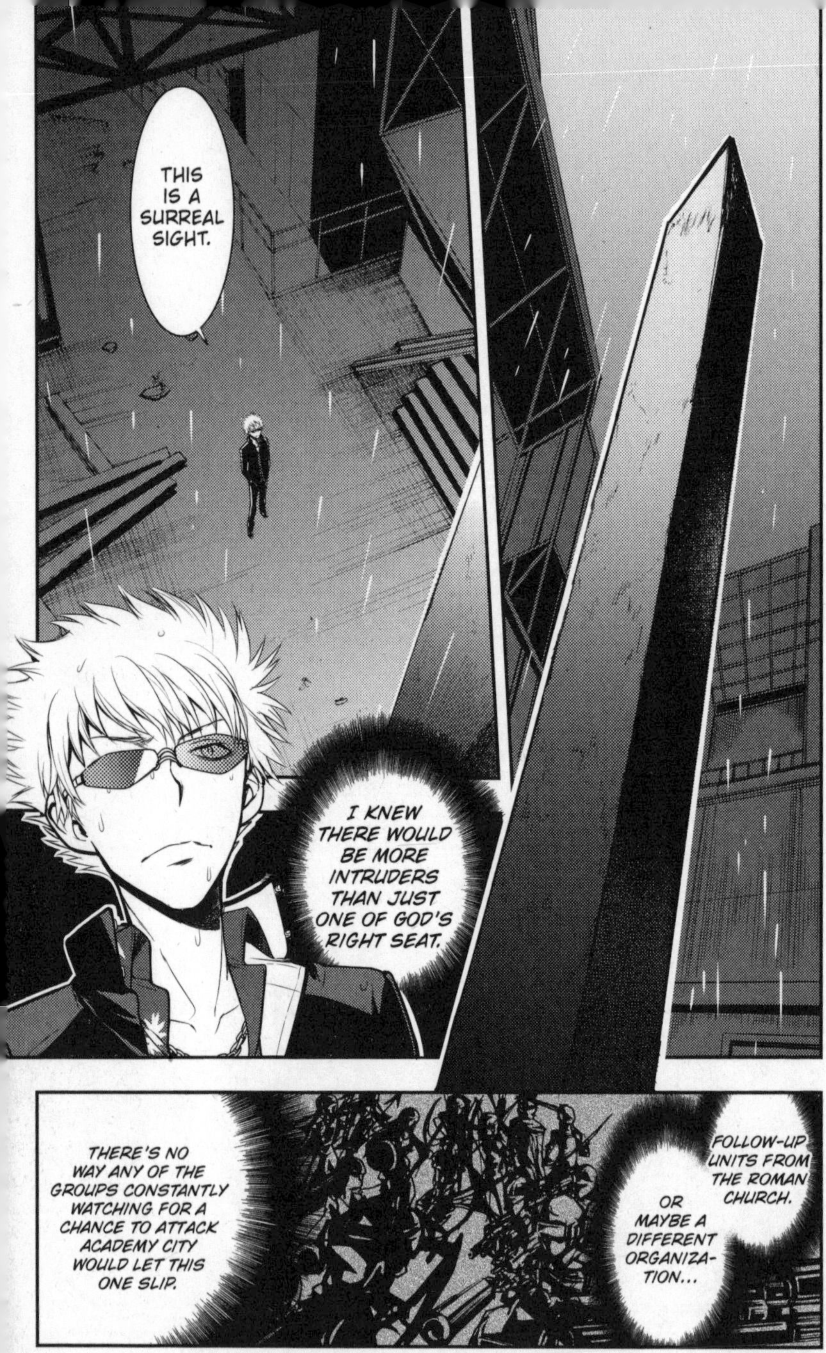
THIS IS A SURREAL SIGHT.
I KNEW THERE WOULD BE MORE INTRUDERS THAN JUST ONE OF GOD'S RIGHT SEAT.
FOLLOW-UP UNITS FROM THE ROMAN CHURCH.
OR MAYBE A DIFFERENT ORGANIZATION...
THERE'S NO WAY ANY OF THE GROUPS CONSTANTLY WATCHING FOR A CHANCE TO ATTACK ACADEMY CITY WOULD LET THIS ONE SLIP.

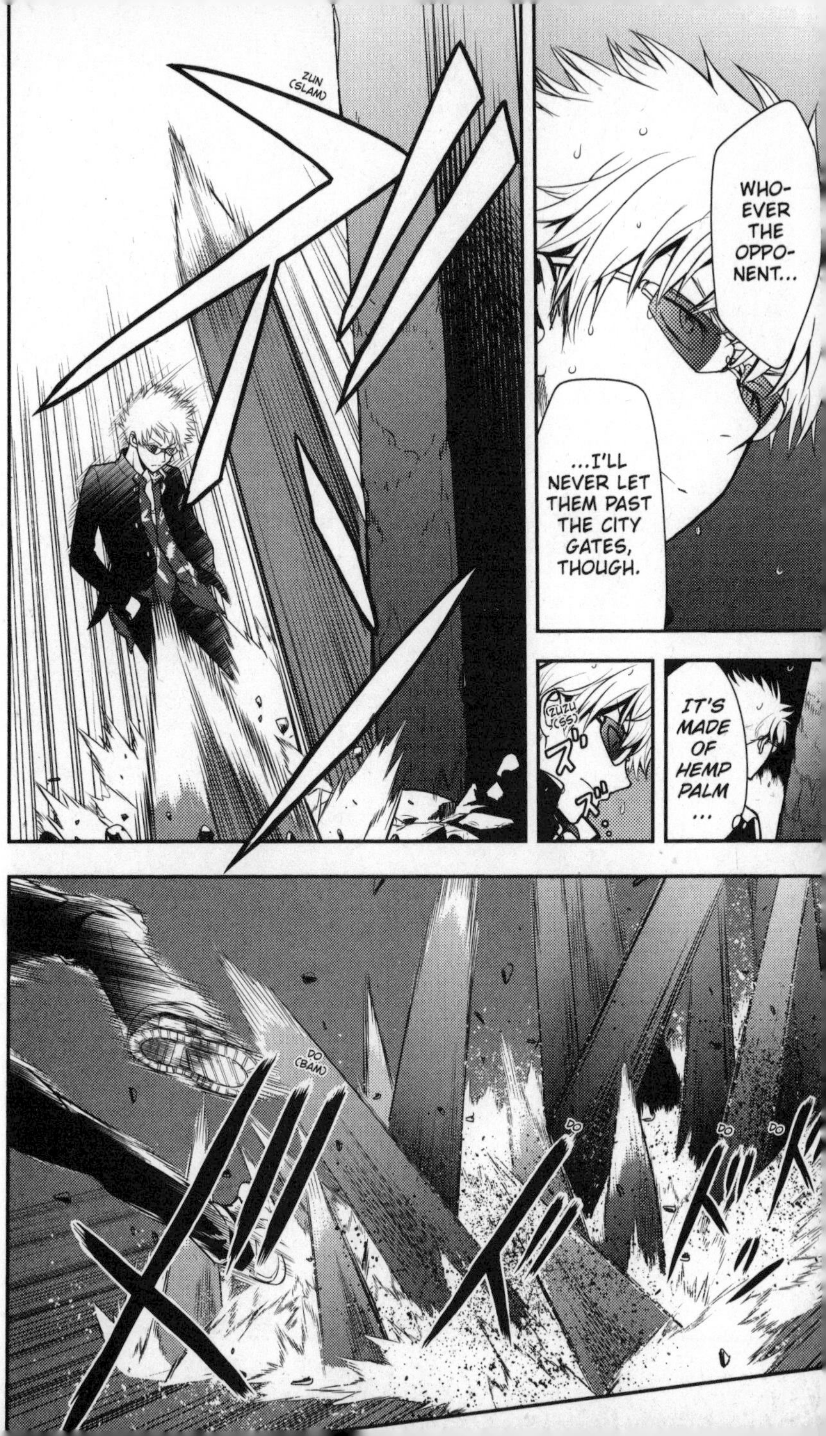
WHOEVER THE OPPONENT...
...I'LL NEVER LET THEM PAST THE CITY GATES, THOUGH.
IT'S MADE OF HEMP PALM...
ZUZU (SS)
ZUN (SLAM)
DO
DO
DO
DO (BAM)

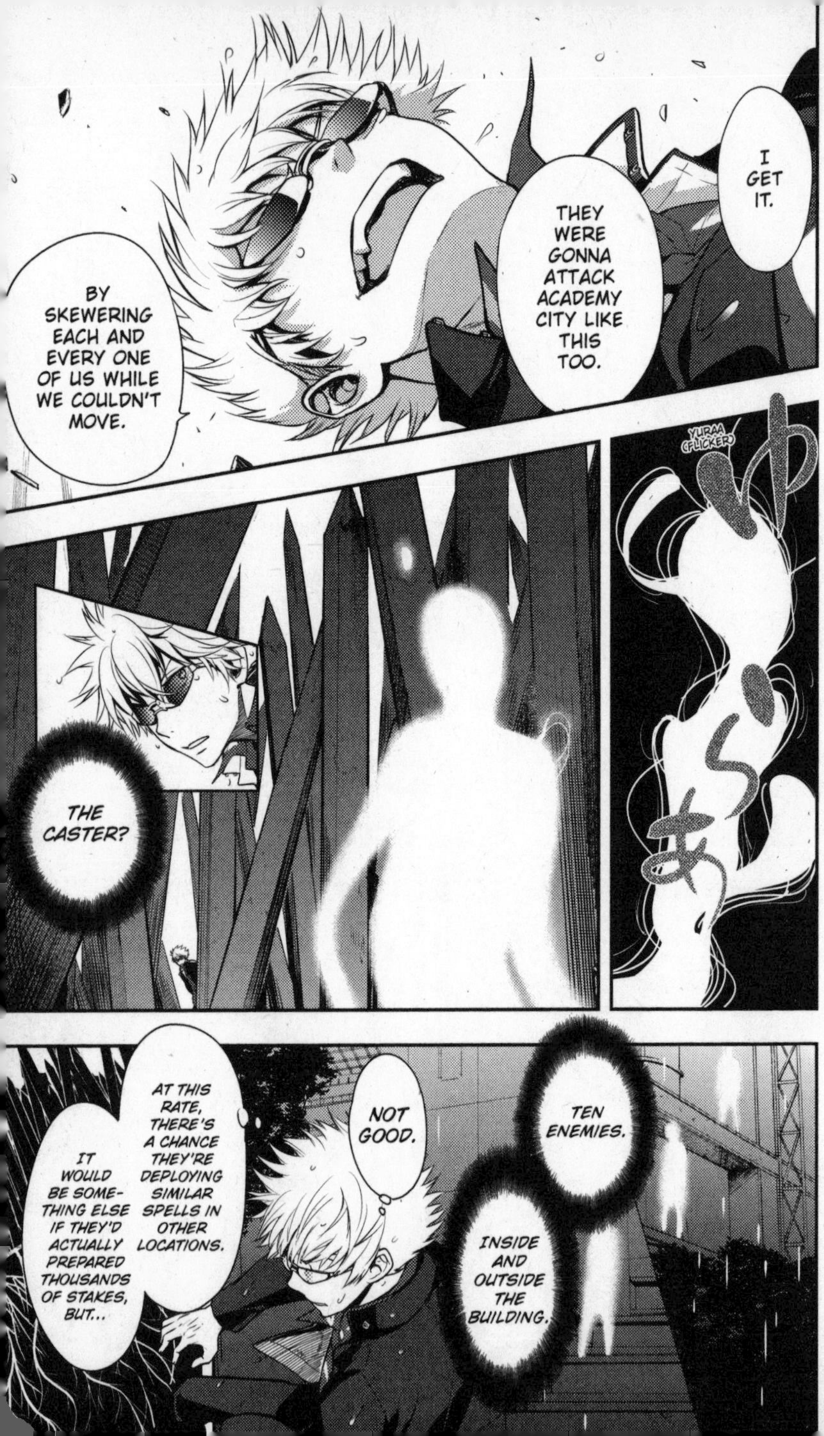
I GET IT.
THEY WERE GONNA ATTACK ACADEMY CITY LIKE THIS TOO.
BY SKEWERING EACH AND EVERY ONE OF US WHILE WE COULDN'T MOVE.
YURAA (FLICKER)
ゆらあ
THE CASTER?
TEN ENEMIES.
INSIDE AND OUTSIDE THE BUILDING.
NOT GOOD.
AT THIS RATE, THERE'S A CHANCE THEY'RE DEPLOYING SIMILAR SPELLS IN OTHER LOCATIONS.
IT WOULD BE SOME-THING ELSE IF THEY'D ACTUALLY PREPARED THOUSANDS OF STAKES, BUT...

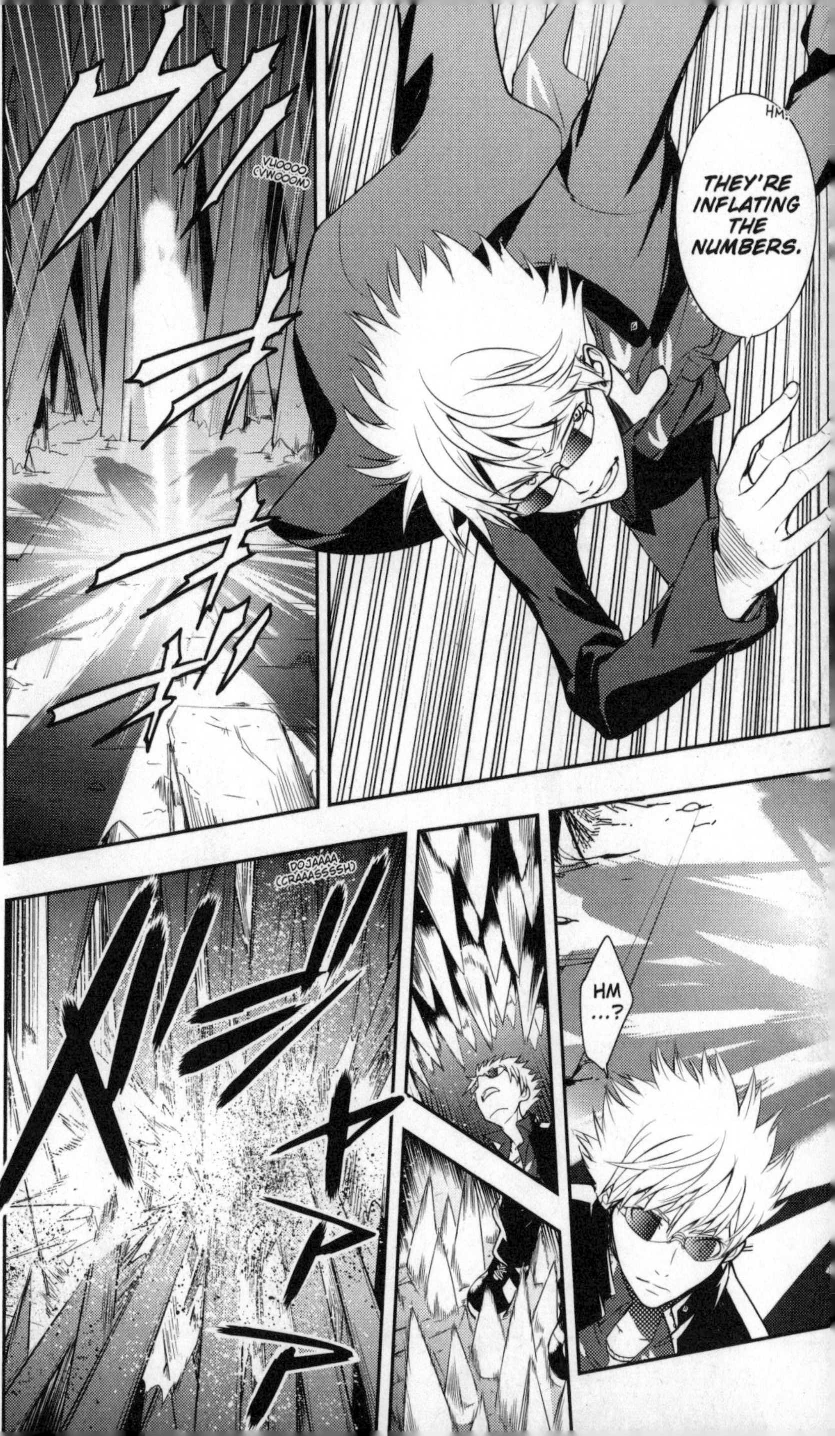
HM.
THEY'RE INFLATING THE NUMBERS.
VUOOOO (VWOOOM)
HM ...?
DOJAAAA (CRAAASSSSH)

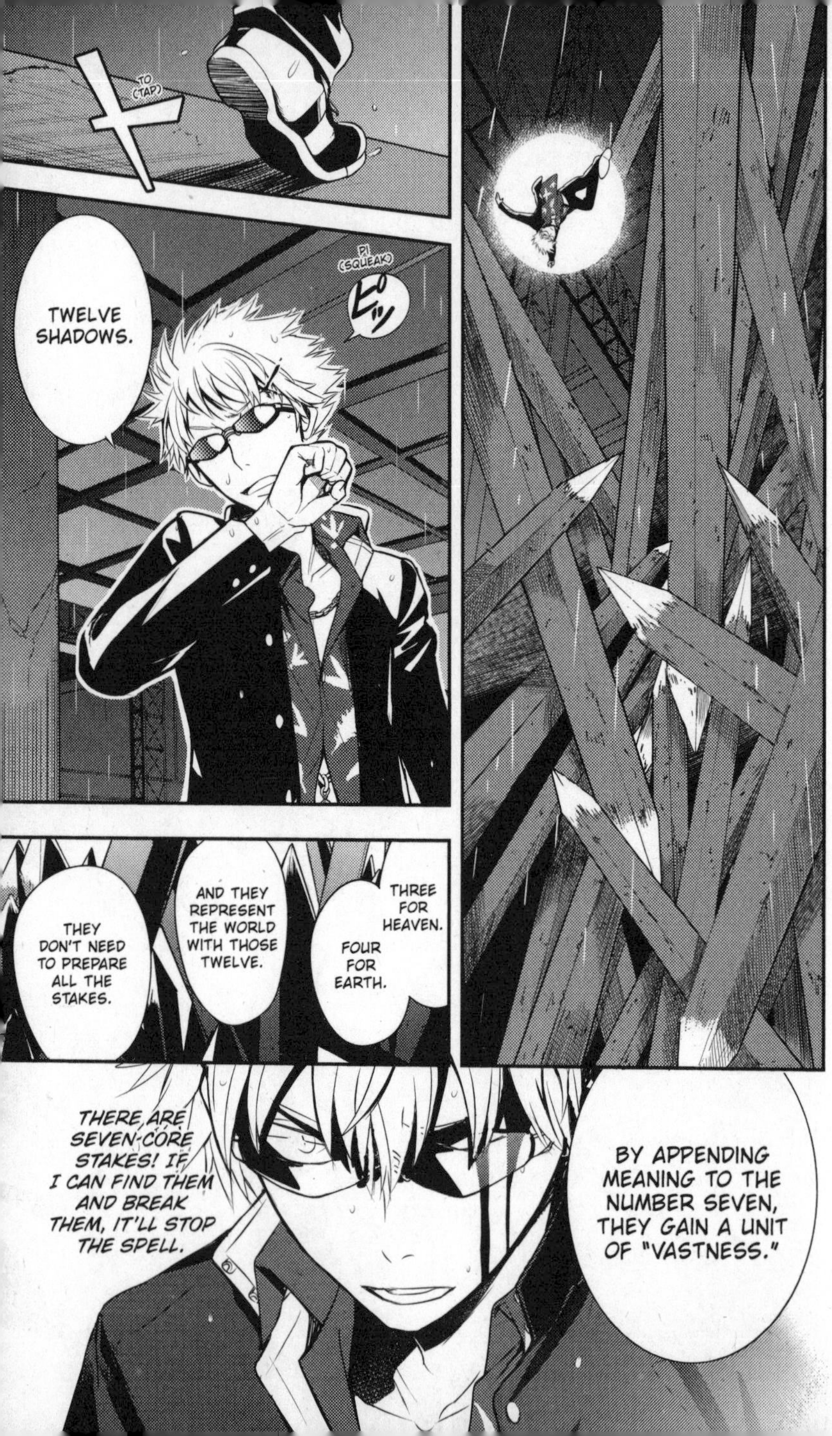
TO (TAP)
PI (SQUEAK)
ピッ
TWELVE SHADOWS.
THREE FOR HEAVEN.
FOUR FOR EARTH.
AND THEY REPRESENT THE WORLD WITH THOSE TWELVE.
THEY DON'T NEED TO PREPARE ALL THE STAKES.
BY APPENDING MEANING TO THE NUMBER SEVEN, THEY GAIN A UNIT OF "VASTNESS."
THERE ARE SEVEN CORE STAKES! IF I CAN FIND THEM AND BREAK THEM, IT'LL STOP THE SPELL.

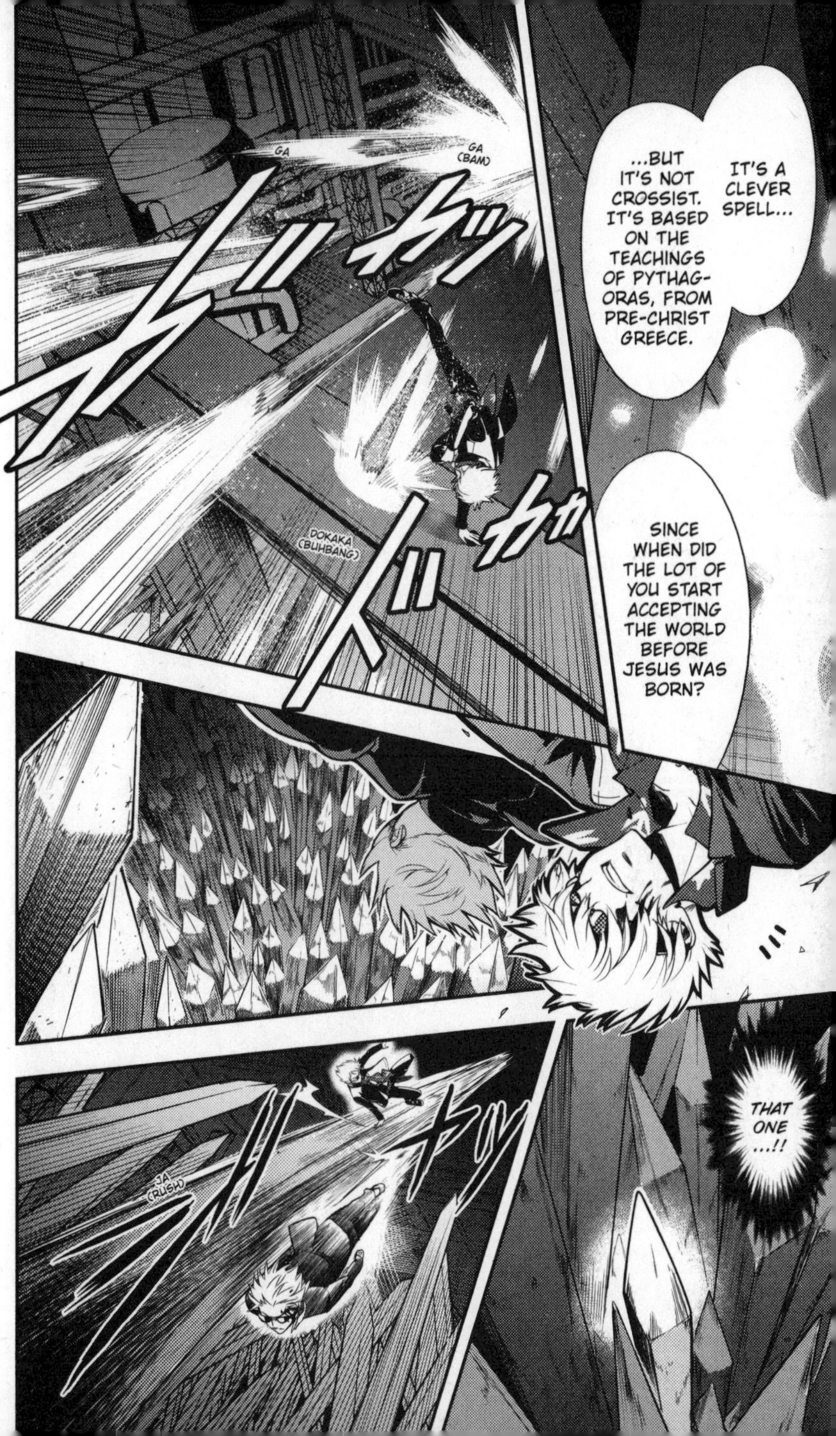IT'S A CLEVER SPELL...
...BUT IT'S NOT CROSSIST. IT'S BASED ON THE TEACHINGS OF PYTHAG-ORAS, FROM PRE-CHRIST GREECE.
GA (BAM)
GA
DOKAKA (BUHBANG)
SINCE WHEN DID THE LOT OF YOU START ACCEPTING THE WORLD BEFORE JESUS WAS BORN?
THAT ONE ...!!
JA (RUSH)

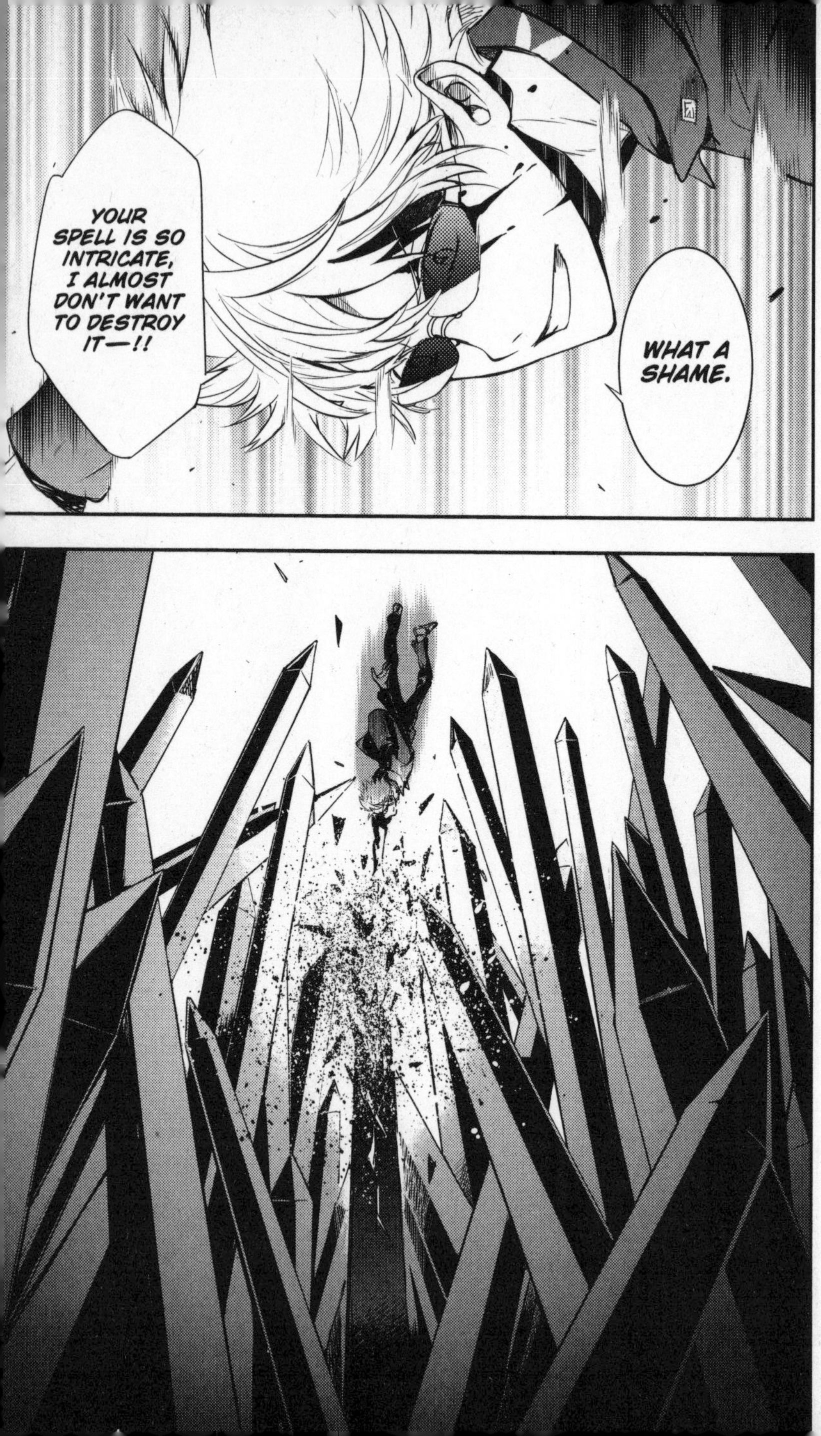
WHAT A SHAME.
YOUR SPELL IS SO INTRICATE, I ALMOST DON'T WANT TO DESTROY IT—!!

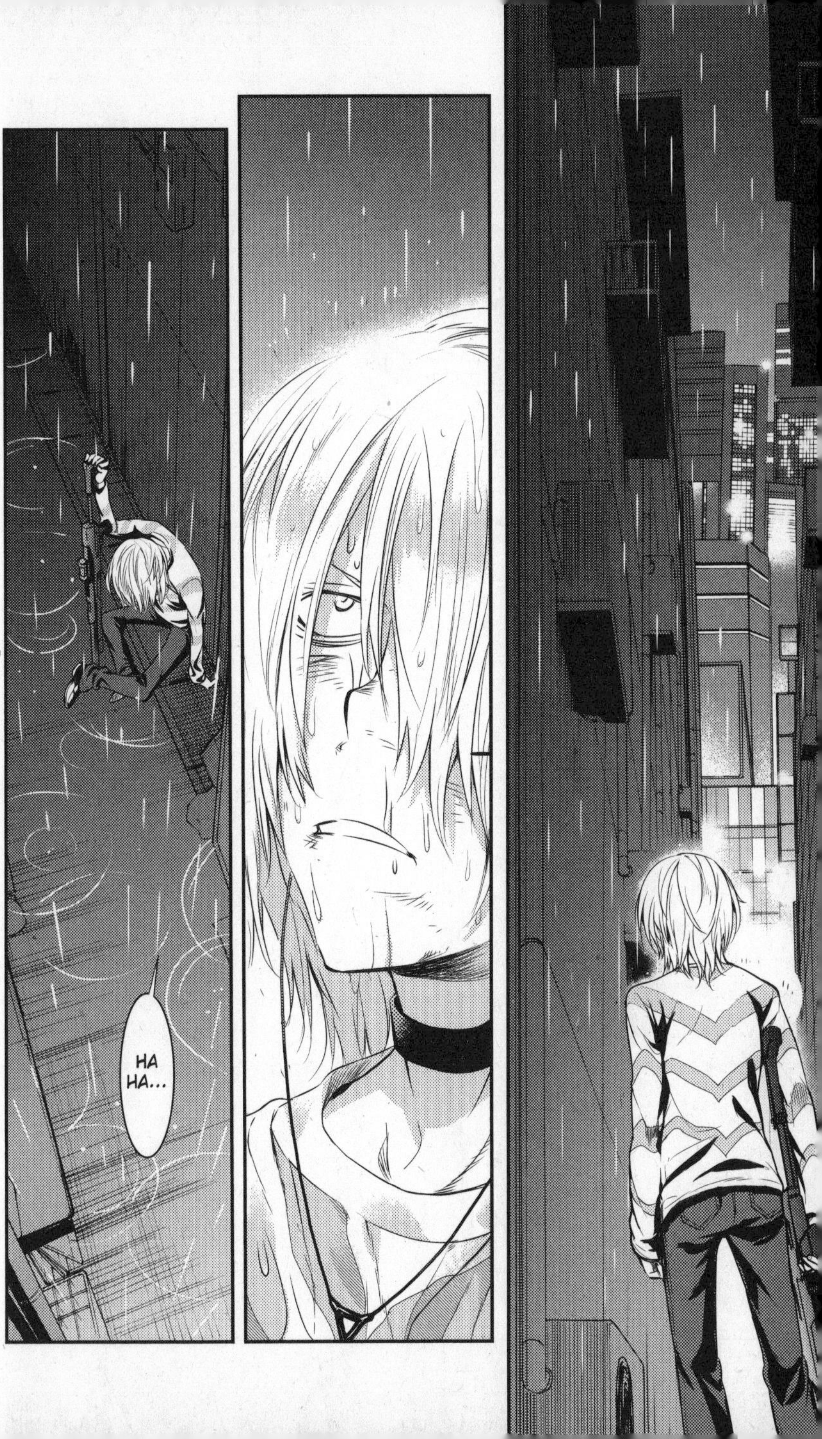
HA HA...

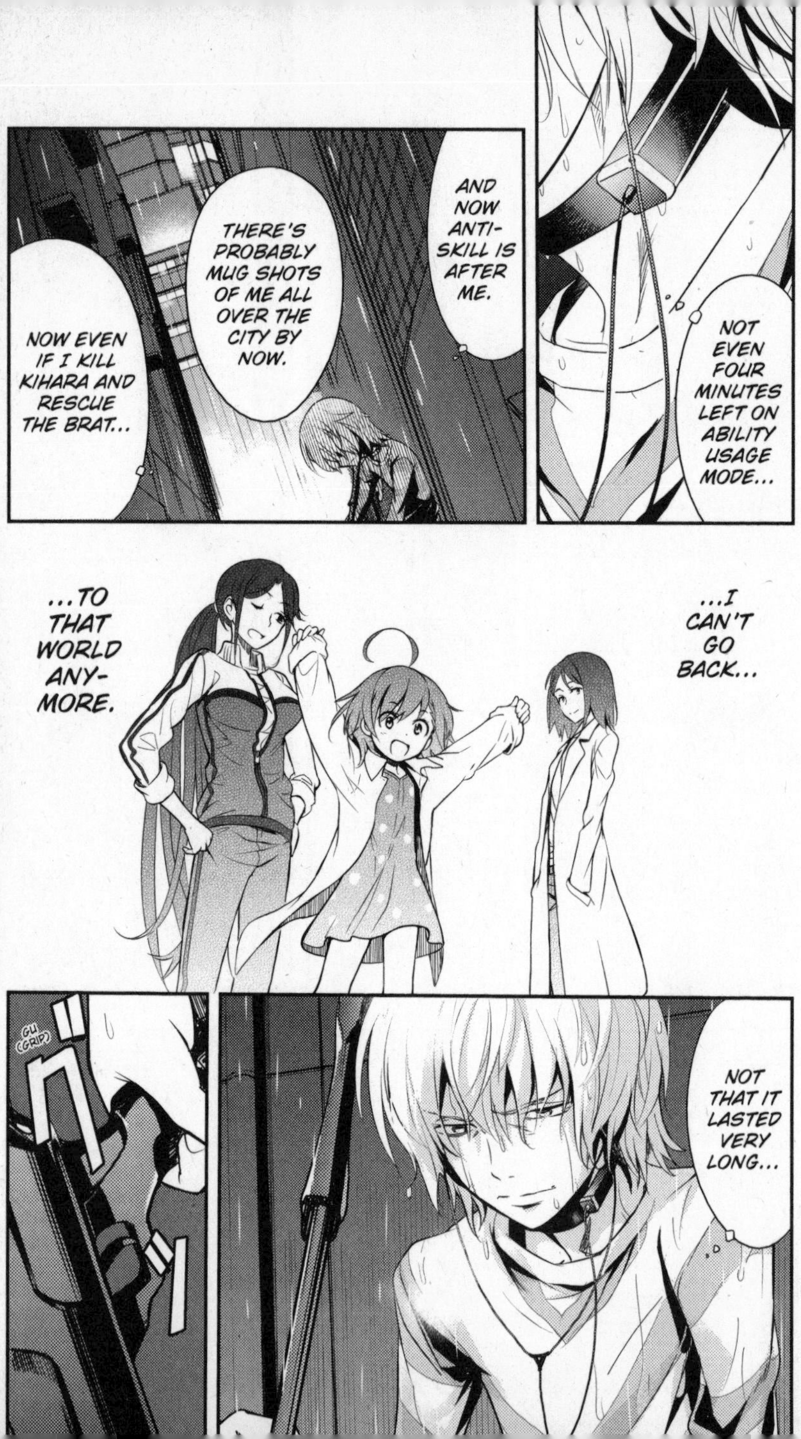
NOT EVEN FOUR MINUTES LEFT ON ABILITY USAGE MODE...
AND NOW ANTI-SKILL IS AFTER ME.
THERE'S PROBABLY MUG SHOTS OF ME ALL OVER THE CITY BY NOW.
NOW EVEN IF I KILL KIHARA AND RESCUE THE BRAT...
...I CAN'T GO BACK...
...TO THAT WORLD ANYMORE.
NOT THAT IT LASTED VERY LONG...
GU (GRIP)

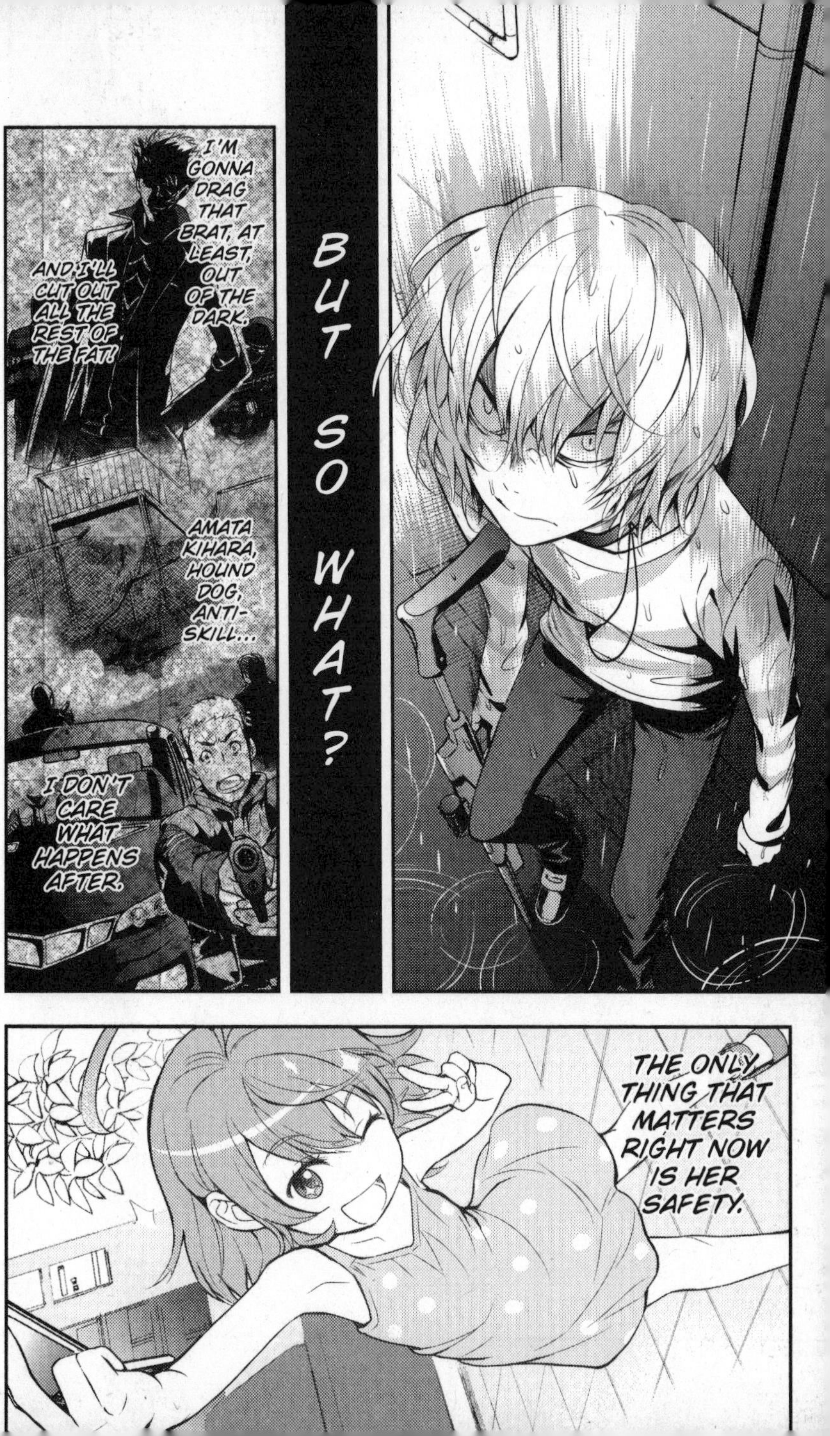
BUT SO WHAT?
I'M GONNA DRAG THAT BRAT, AT LEAST, OUT OF THE DARK.
AND I'LL CUT OUT ALL THE REST OF THE FAT!
AMATA KIHARA, HOUND DOG, ANTI-SKILL...
I DON'T CARE WHAT HAPPENS AFTER.
THE ONLY THING THAT MATTERS RIGHT NOW IS HER SAFETY.

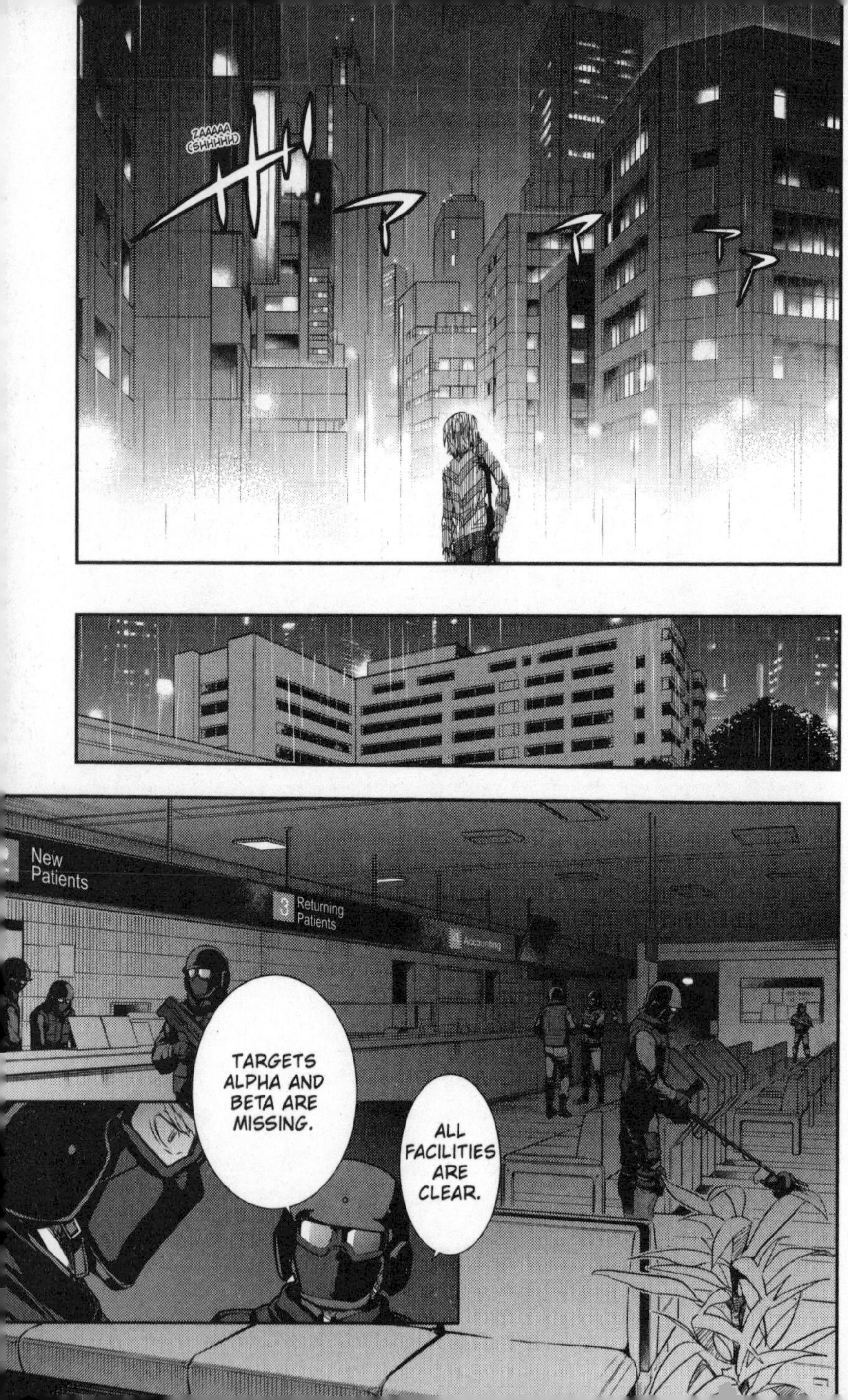
ZAAAAA (SHHHHH)
3 Returning Patients
New Patients
ALL FACILITIES ARE CLEAR.
TARGETS ALPHA AND BETA ARE MISSING.

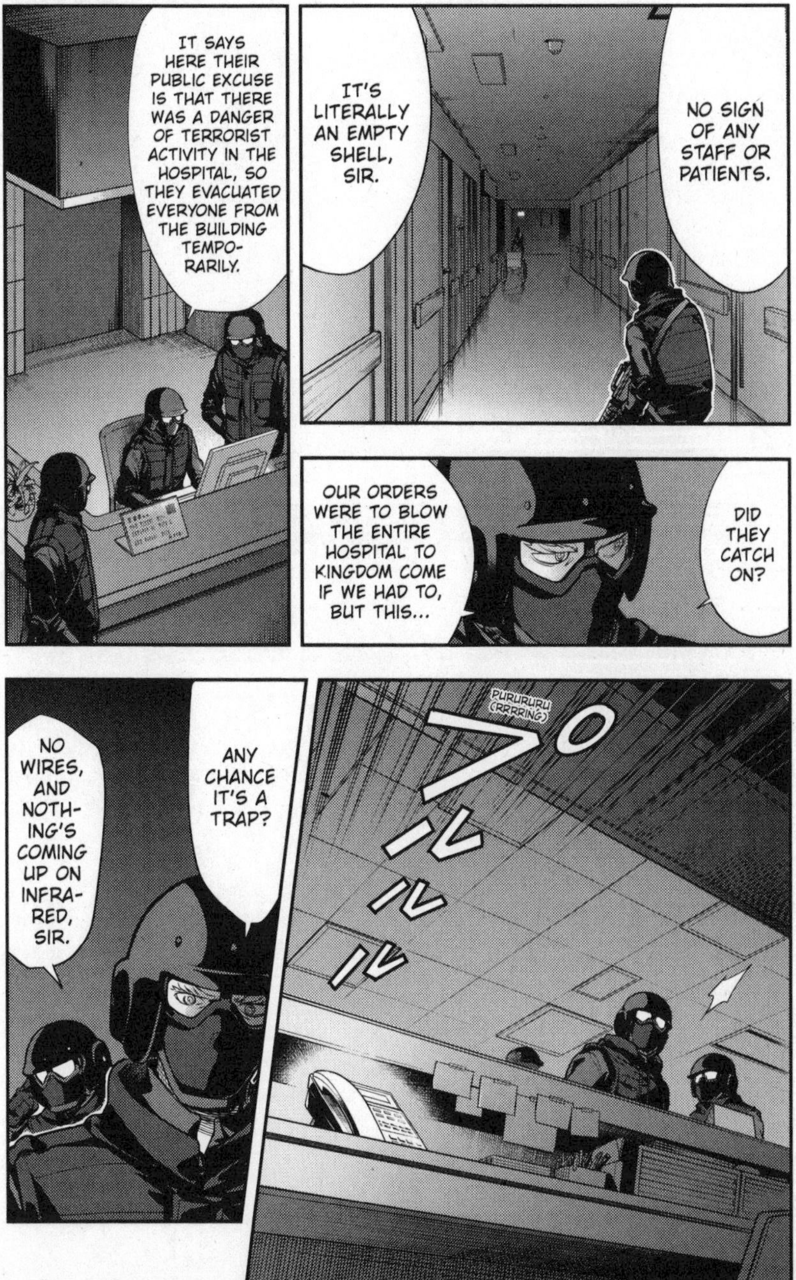
NO SIGN OF ANY STAFF OR PATIENTS.
IT'S LITERALLY AN EMPTY SHELL, SIR.
DID THEY CATCH ON?
OUR ORDERS WERE TO BLOW THE ENTIRE HOSPITAL TO KINGDOM COME IF WE HAD TO, BUT THIS...
IT SAYS HERE THEIR PUBLIC EXCUSE IS THAT THERE WAS A DANGER OF TERRORIST ACTIVITY IN THE HOSPITAL, SO THEY EVACUATED EVERYONE FROM THE BUILDING TEMPO-RARILY.
プルルル
PURURURU (RRRRING)
ANY CHANCE IT'S A TRAP?
NO WIRES, AND NOTH-ING'S COMING UP ON INFRA-RED, SIR.

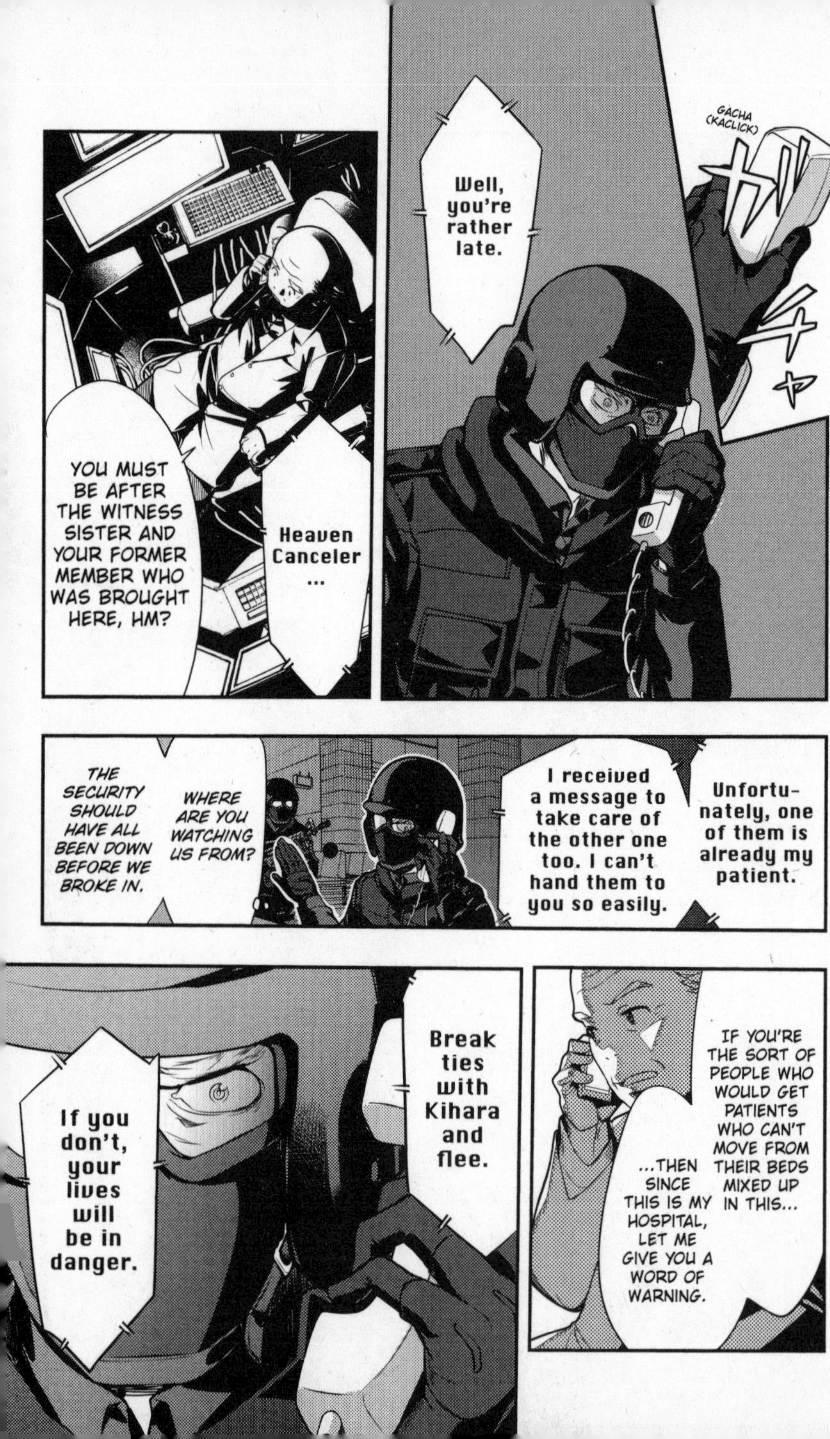
GACHA (KACLICK)
Well, you're rather late.
Heaven Canceler ...
YOU MUST BE AFTER THE WITNESS SISTER AND YOUR FORMER MEMBER WHO WAS BROUGHT HERE, HM?
Unfortu-nately, one of them is already my patient.
I received a message to take care of the other one too. I can't hand them to you so easily.
WHERE ARE YOU WATCHING US FROM?
THE SECURITY SHOULD HAVE ALL BEEN DOWN BEFORE WE BROKE IN.
IF YOU'RE THE SORT OF PEOPLE WHO WOULD GET PATIENTS WHO CAN'T MOVE FROM THEIR BEDS MIXED UP IN THIS...
...THEN SINCE THIS IS MY HOSPITAL, LET ME GIVE YOU A WORD OF WARNING.
Break ties with Kihara and flee.
If you don't, your lives will be in danger.

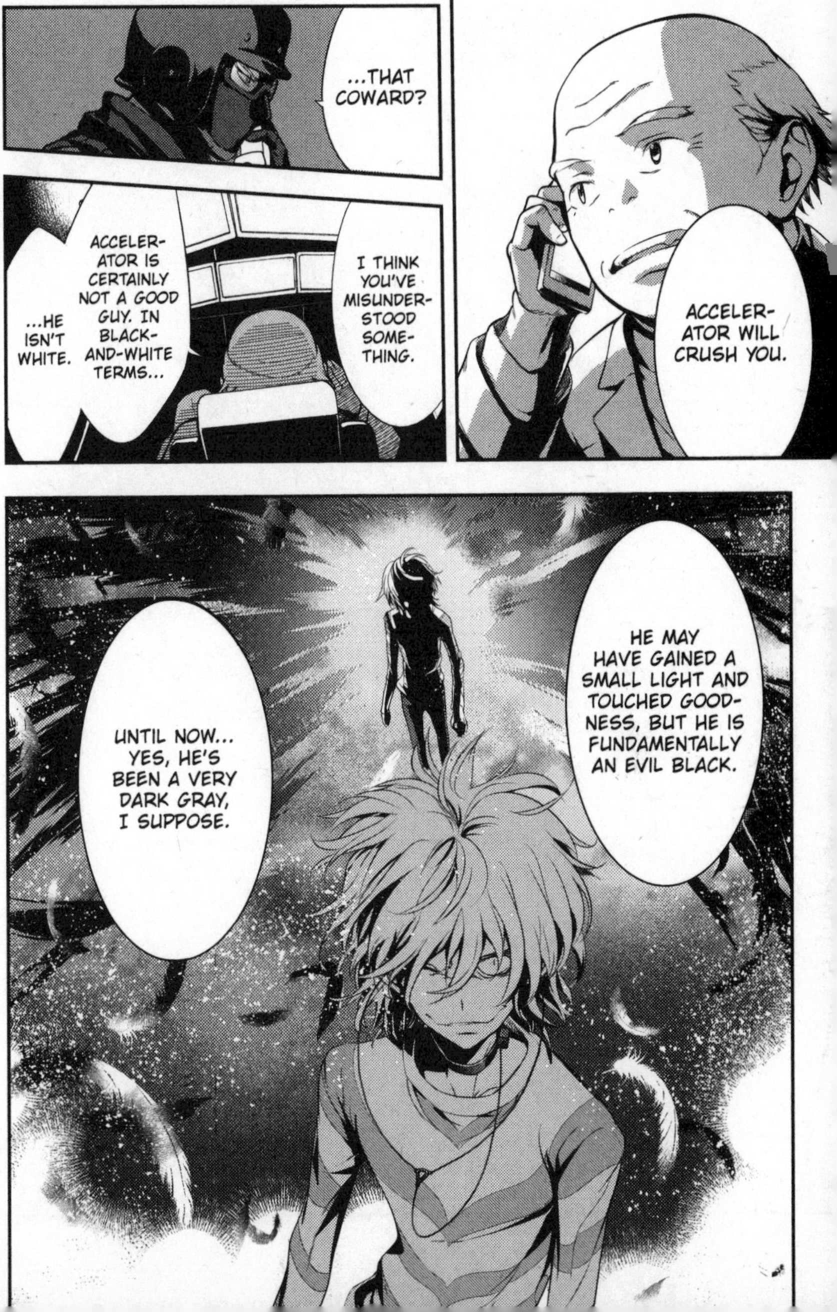
ACCELER-ATOR WILL CRUSH YOU.
...THAT COWARD?
I THINK YOU'VE MISUNDER-STOOD SOME-THING.
ACCELER-ATOR IS CERTAINLY NOT A GOOD GUY. IN BLACK-AND-WHITE TERMS...
...HE ISN'T WHITE.
HE MAY HAVE GAINED A SMALL LIGHT AND TOUCHED GOOD-NESS, BUT HE IS FUNDAMENTALLY AN EVIL BLACK.
UNTIL NOW... YES, HE'S BEEN A VERY DARK GRAY, I SUPPOSE.

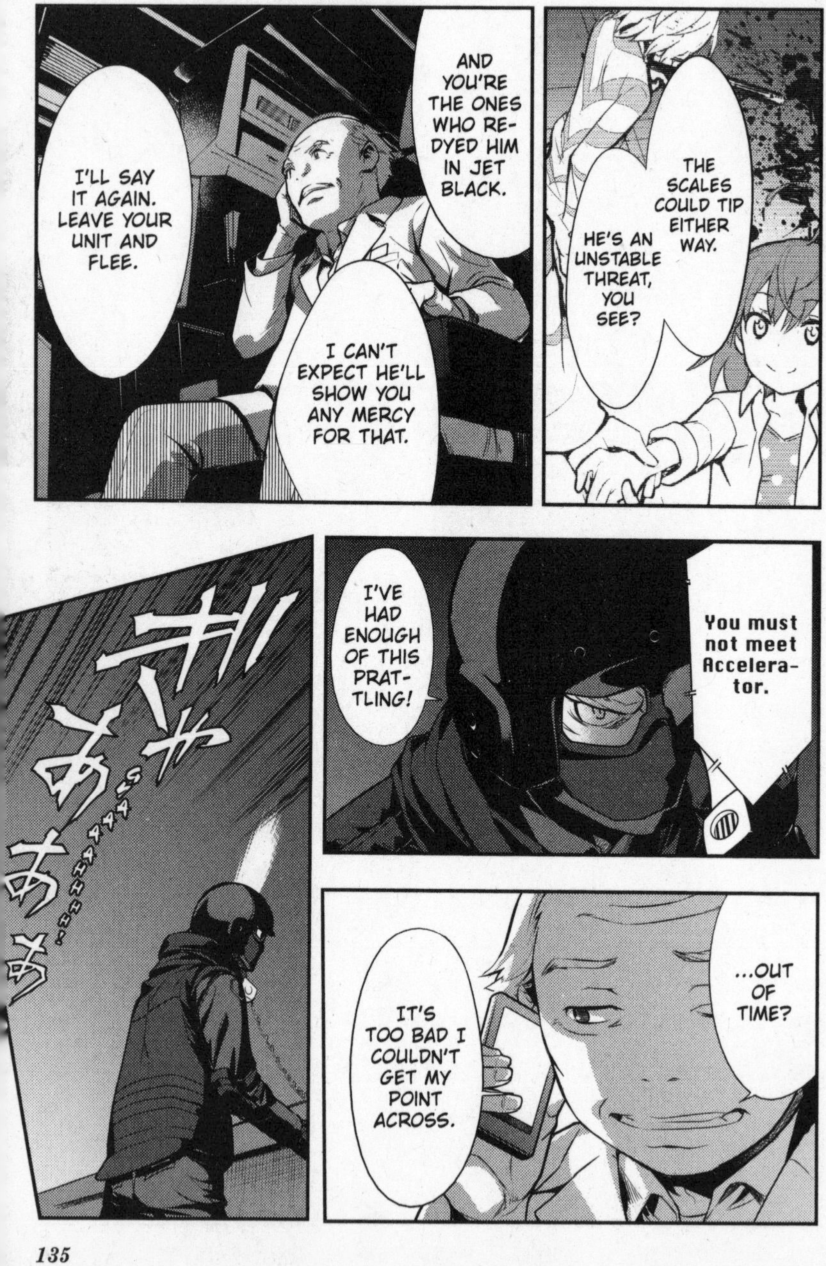
THE SCALES COULD TIP EITHER WAY.
HE'S AN UNSTABLE THREAT, YOU SEE?
AND YOU'RE THE ONES WHO RE-DYED HIM IN JET BLACK.
I CAN'T EXPECT HE'LL SHOW YOU ANY MERCY FOR THAT.
I'LL SAY IT AGAIN. LEAVE YOUR UNIT AND FLEE.
You must not meet Accelerator.
I'VE HAD ENOUGH OF THIS PRATTLING!
...OUT OF TIME?
IT'S TOO BAD I COULDN'T GET MY POINT ACROSS.

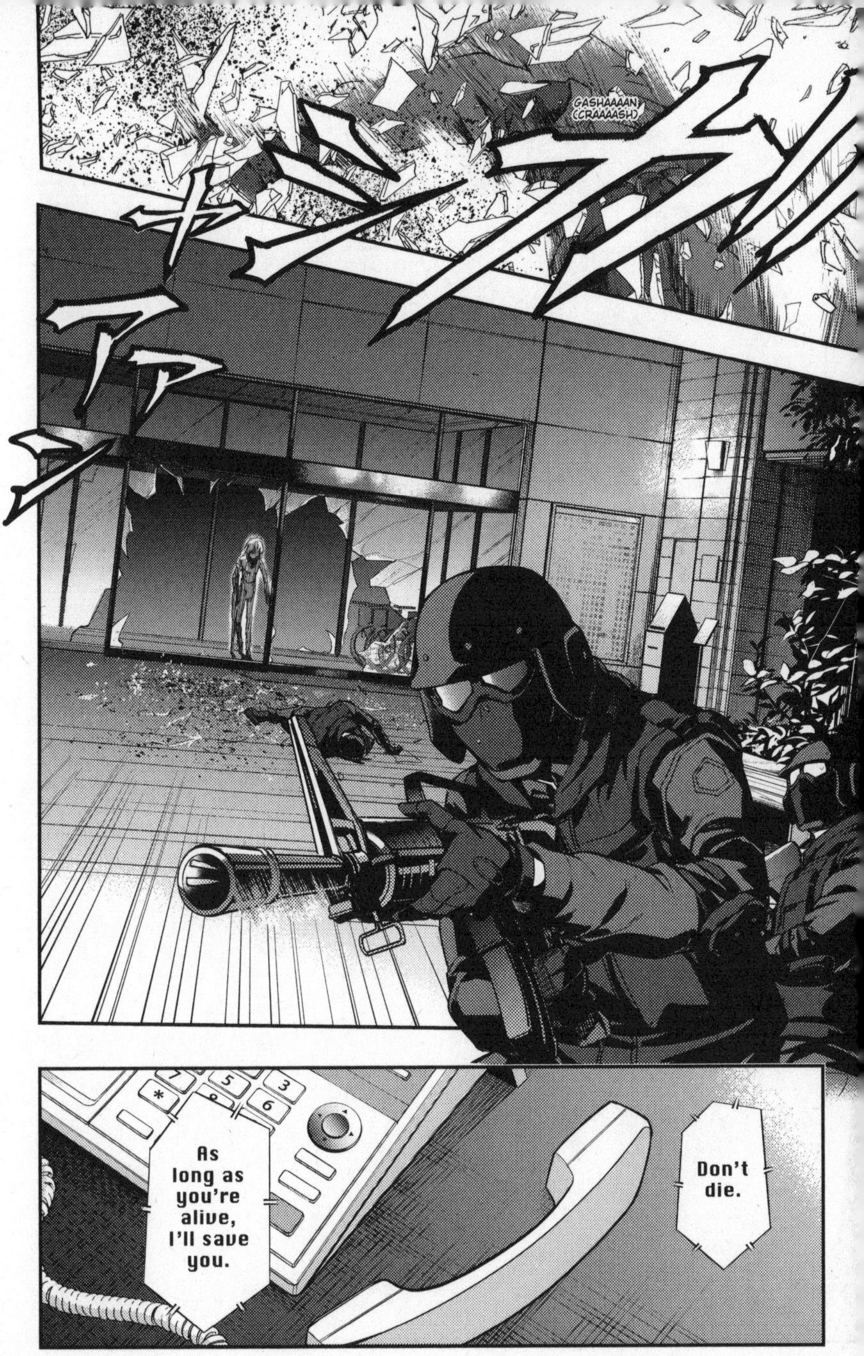
GASHAAAAN (CRAAAASH)
Don't die.
As long as you're alive, I'll save you.

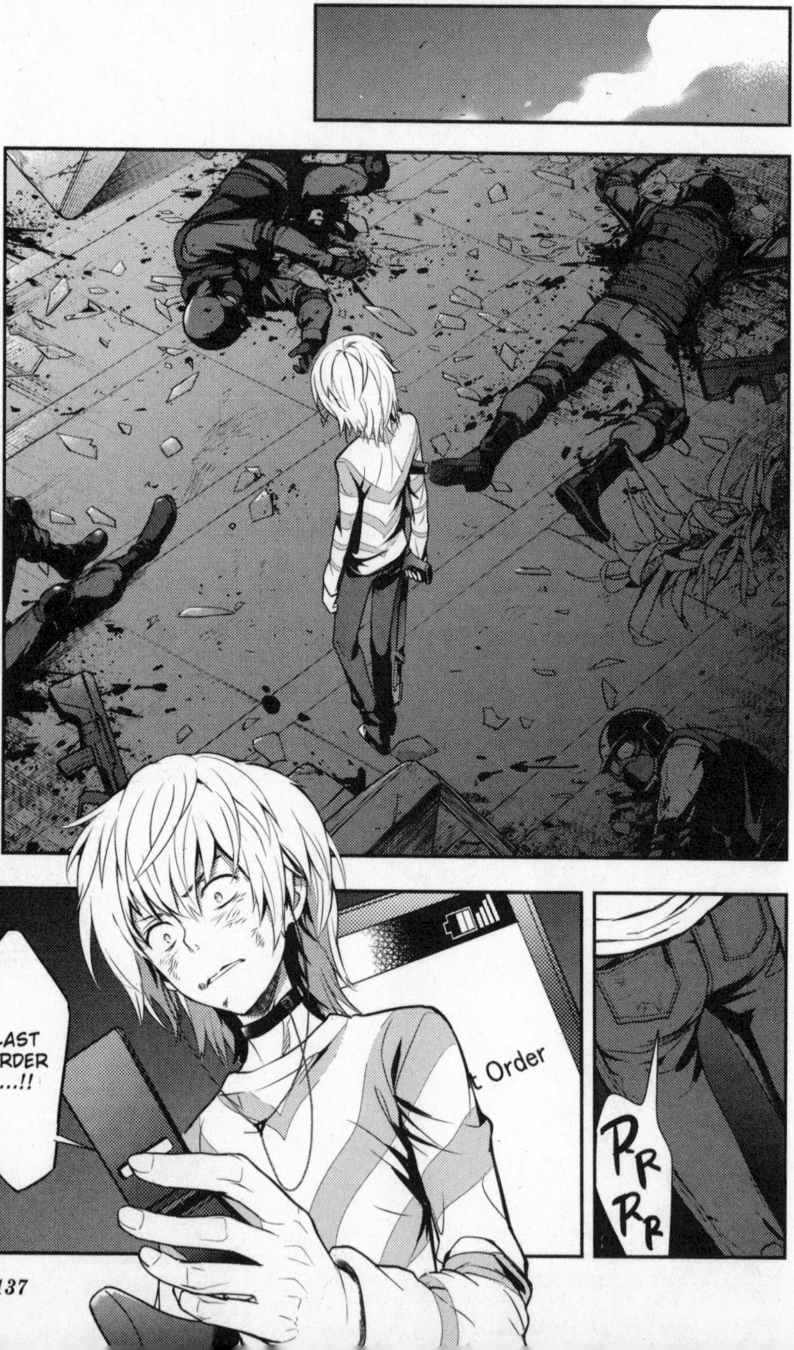
PRRRR
LAST ORDER ...!!
t Order

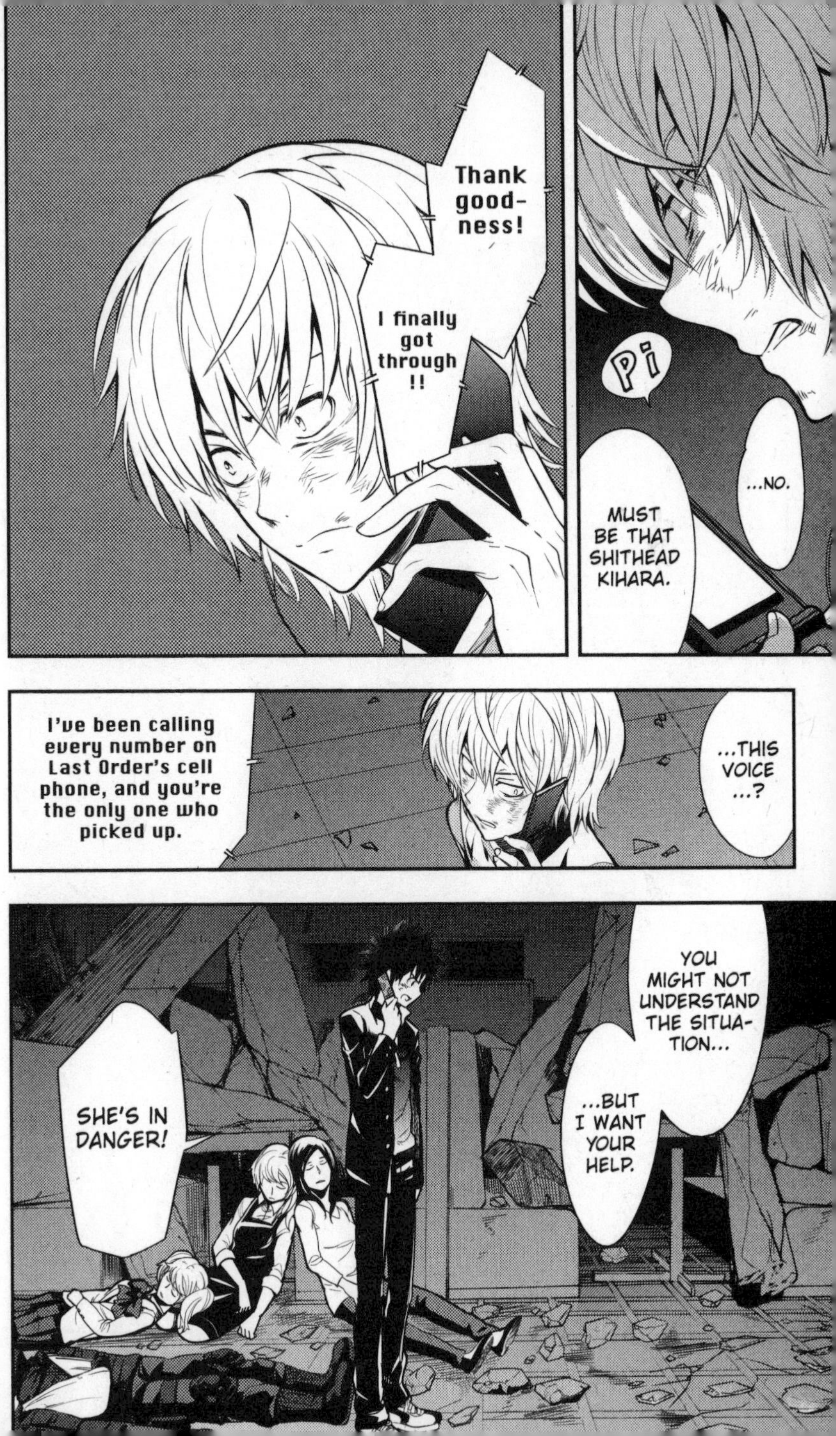
Pi
...NO.
MUST BE THAT SHITHEAD KIHARA.
Thank good-ness!
I finally got through !!
...THIS VOICE ...?
I've been calling every number on Last Order's cell phone, and you're the only one who picked up.
YOU MIGHT NOT UNDERSTAND THE SITUA-TION...
...BUT I WANT YOUR HELP.
SHE'S IN DANGER!

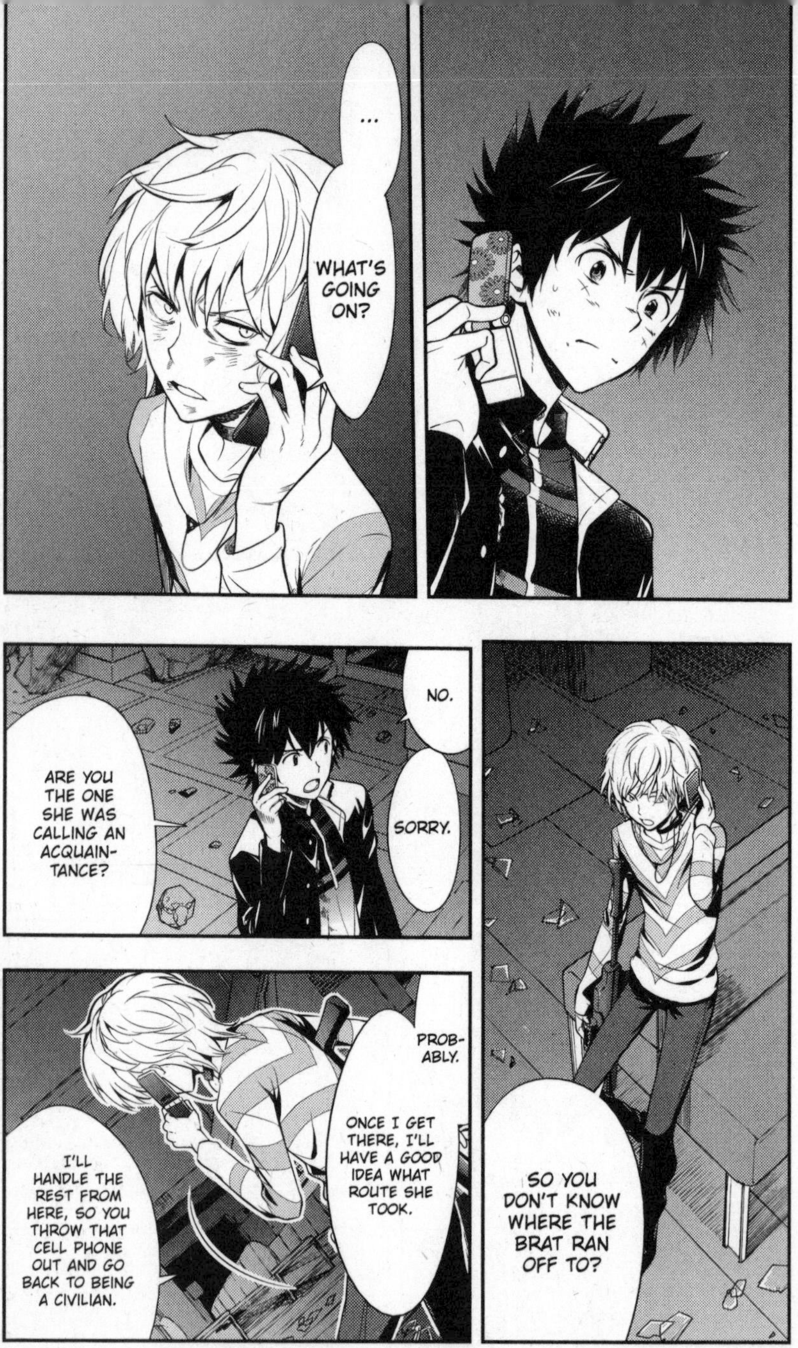
...
WHAT'S GOING ON?
SO YOU DON'T KNOW WHERE THE BRAT RAN OFF TO?
NO.
SORRY.
ARE YOU THE ONE SHE WAS CALLING AN ACQUAIN-TANCE?
PROB-ABLY.
ONCE I GET THERE, I'LL HAVE A GOOD IDEA WHAT ROUTE SHE TOOK.
I'LL HANDLE THE REST FROM HERE, SO YOU THROW THAT CELL PHONE OUT AND GO BACK TO BEING A CIVILIAN.

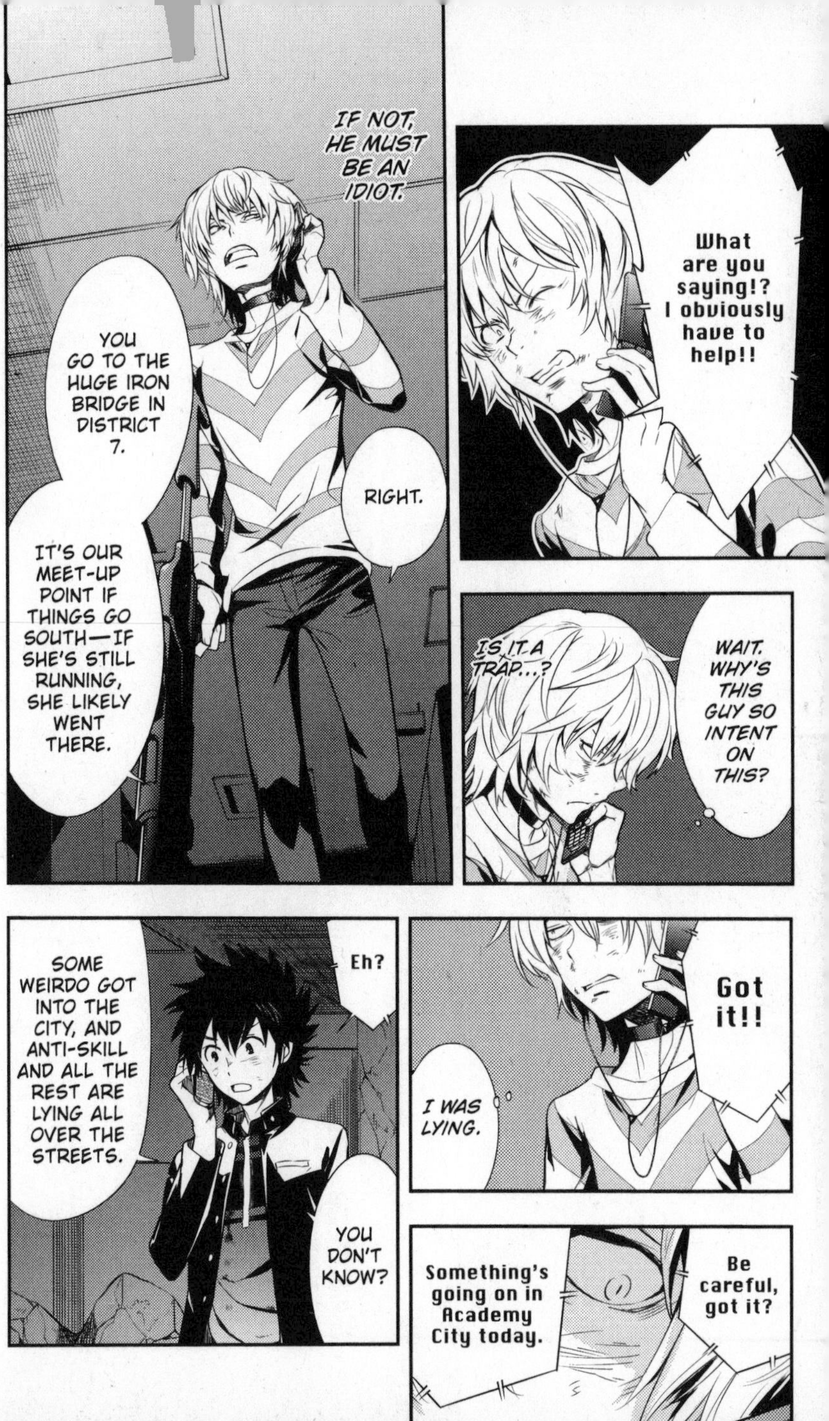
What are you saying!? I obviously have to help!!
WAIT. WHY'S THIS GUY SO INTENT ON THIS?
IS IT A TRAP...?
IF NOT, HE MUST BE AN IDIOT.
RIGHT.
YOU GO TO THE HUGE IRON BRIDGE IN DISTRICT 7.
IT'S OUR MEET-UP POINT IF THINGS GO SOUTH—IF SHE'S STILL RUNNING, SHE LIKELY WENT THERE.
Got it!!
I WAS LYING.
Be careful, got it?
Something's going on in Academy City today.
Eh?
SOME WEIRDO GOT INTO THE CITY, AND ANTI-SKILL AND ALL THE REST ARE LYING ALL OVER THE STREETS.
YOU DON'T KNOW?

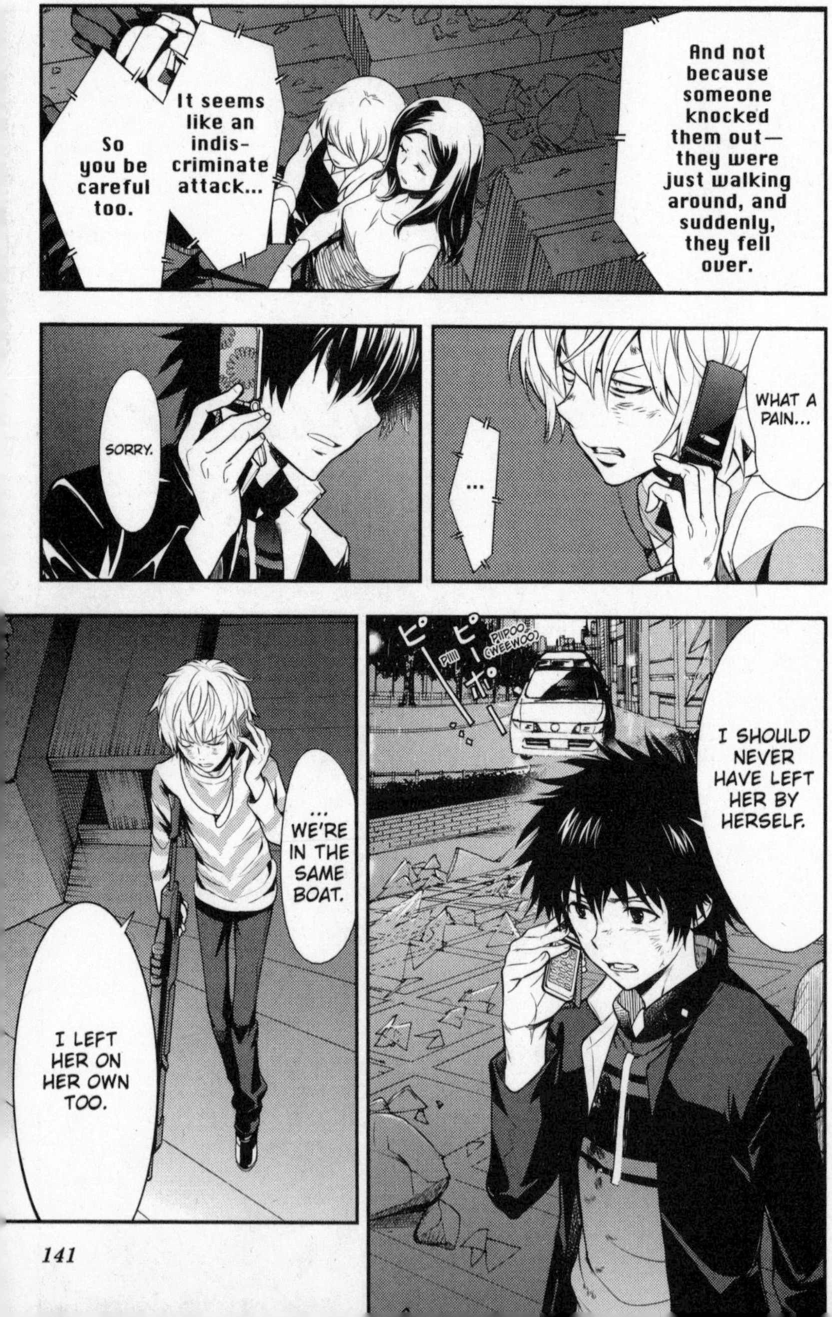
And not because someone knocked them out—they were just walking around, and suddenly, they fell over.
It seems like an indis-criminate attack...
So you be careful too.
WHAT A PAIN...
...
SORRY.
ピーポー
PIII
PIIPOO (WEEWOO)
I SHOULD NEVER HAVE LEFT HER BY HERSELF.
... WE'RE IN THE SAME BOAT.
I LEFT HER ON HER OWN TOO.

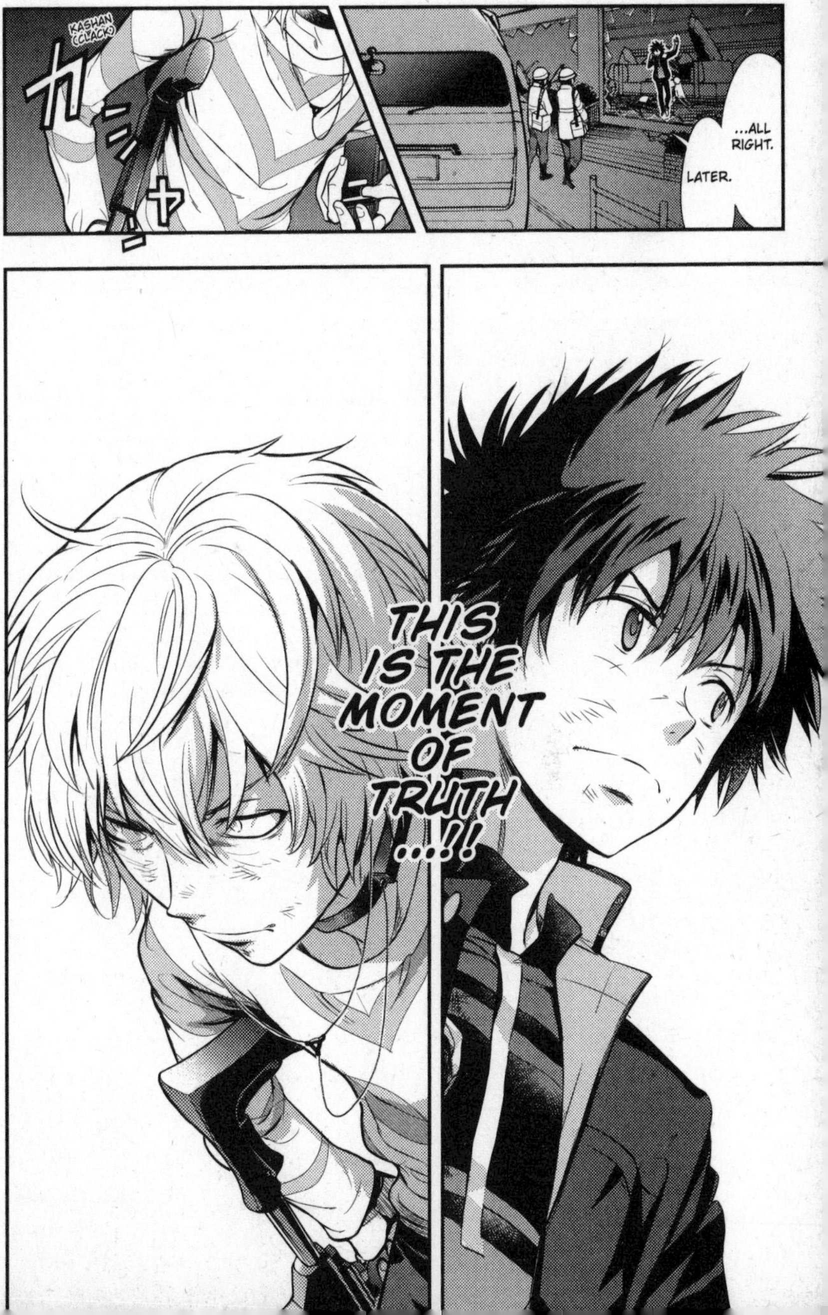
...ALL RIGHT.
LATER.
KASHAN (CLACK)
THIS IS THE MOMENT OF TRUTH ...!!

A Certain Magical Index

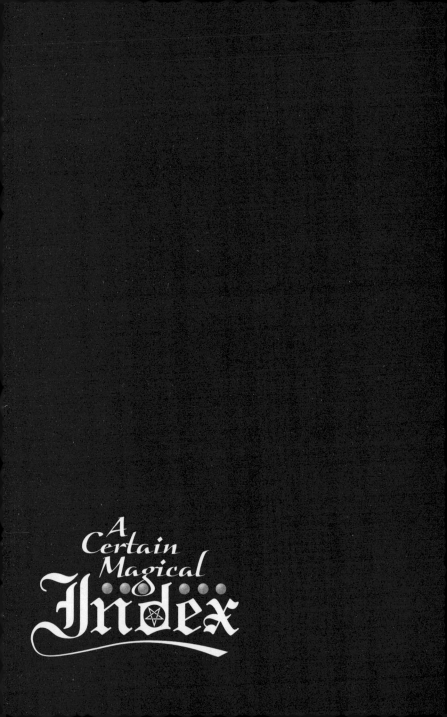

A Certain Magical Index

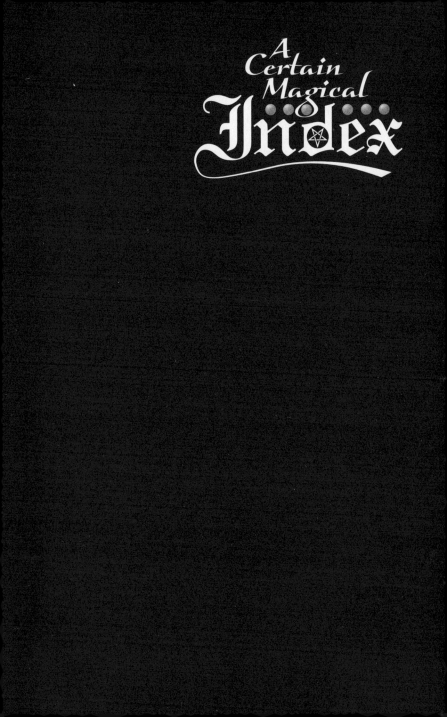

#109 TESTAMENT

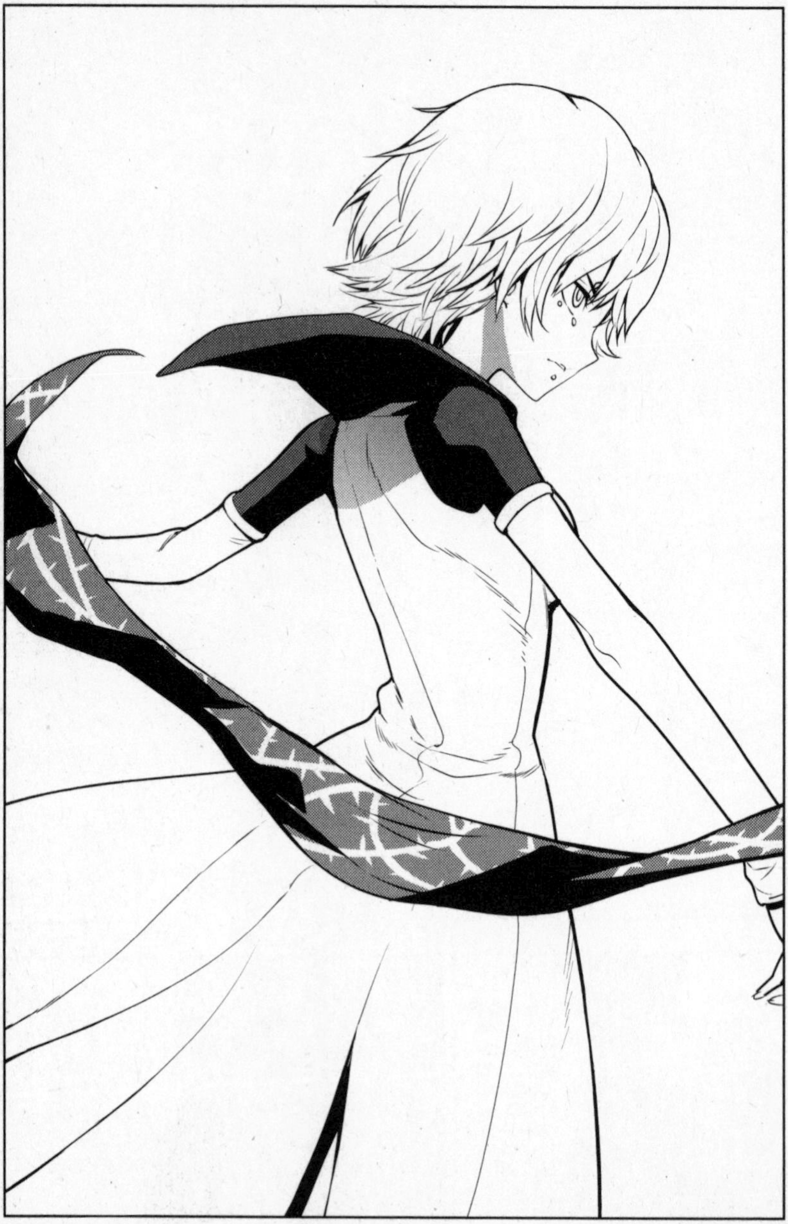

SIGN: UNDER CONSTRUCTION

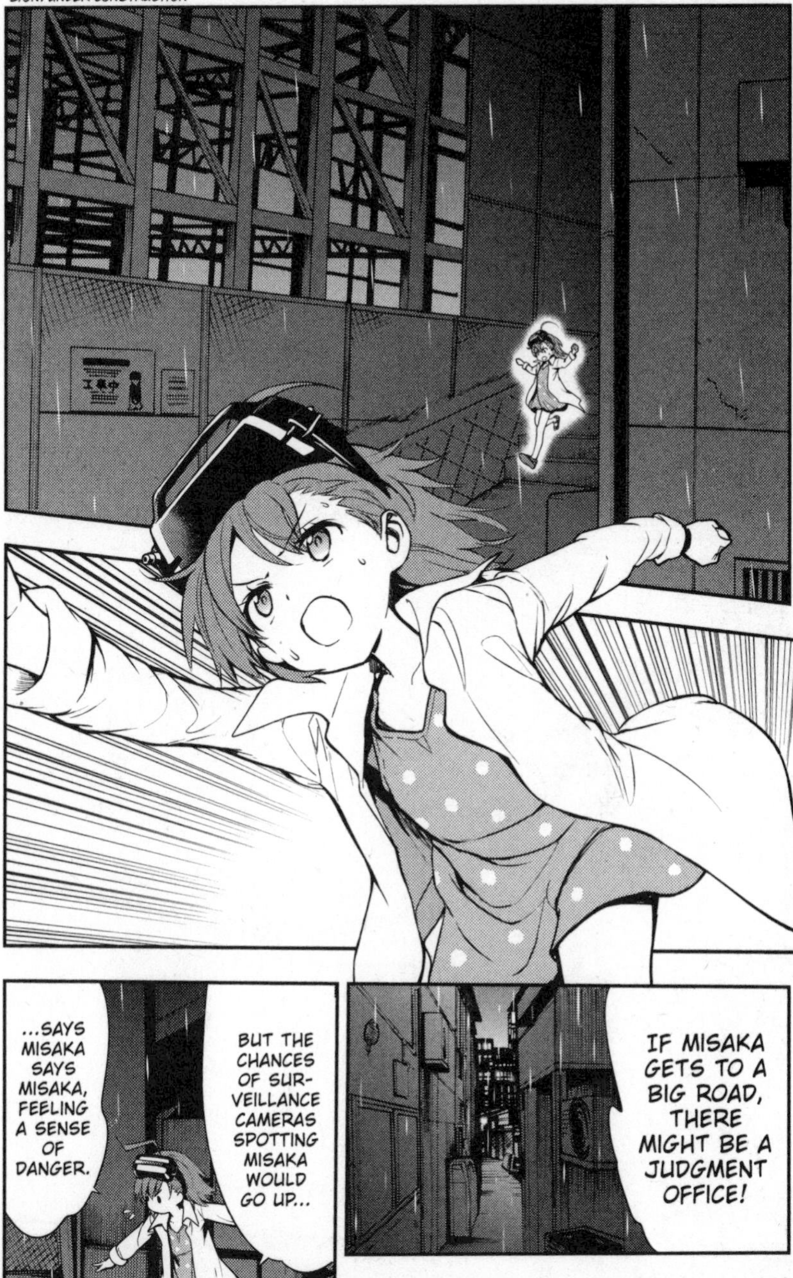

IF MISAKA GETS TO A BIG ROAD, THERE MIGHT BE A JUDGMENT OFFICE!
BUT THE CHANCES OF SUR-VEILLANCE CAMERAS SPOTTING MISAKA WOULD GO UP...
...SAYS MISAKA SAYS MISAKA, FEELING A SENSE OF DANGER.

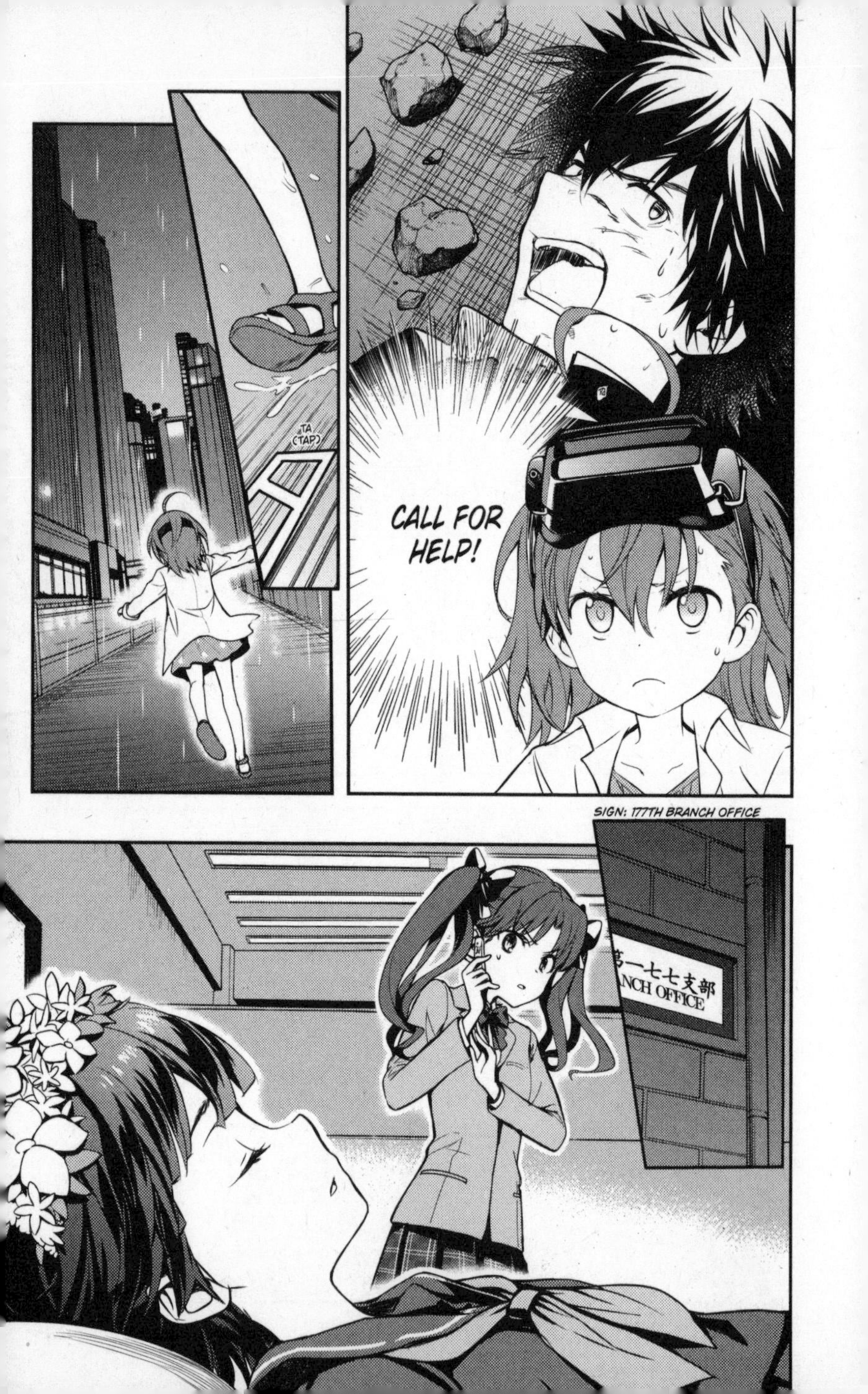
CALL FOR HELP!
TA (TAP)
SIGN: 177TH BRANCH OFFICE
第一七七支部
BRANCH OFFICE

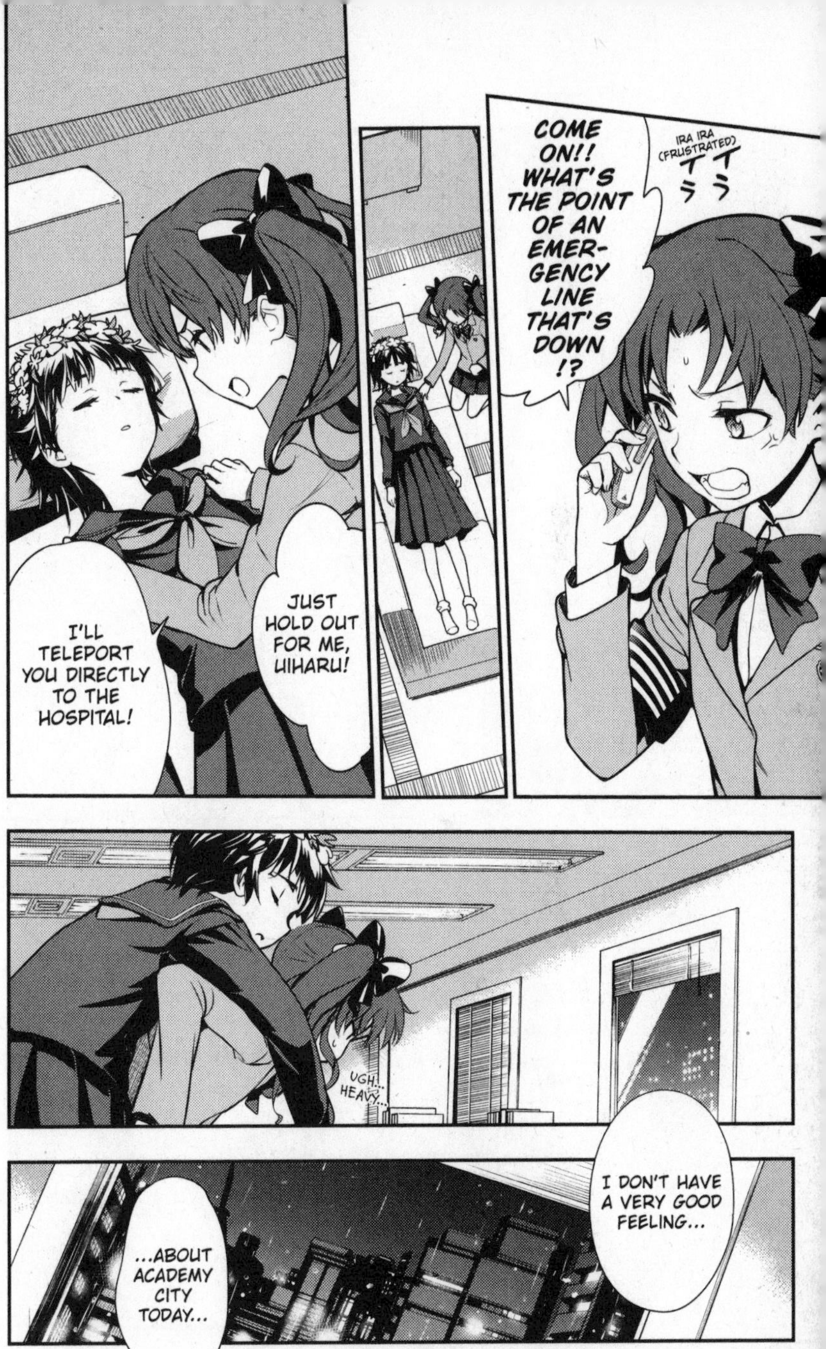
IRA IRA (FRUSTRATED)
イライラ
COME ON!! WHAT'S THE POINT OF AN EMERGENCY LINE THAT'S DOWN!?
JUST HOLD OUT FOR ME, UIHARU!
I'LL TELEPORT YOU DIRECTLY TO THE HOSPITAL!
UGH... HEAVY...
I DON'T HAVE A VERY GOOD FEELING...
...ABOUT ACADEMY CITY TODAY...

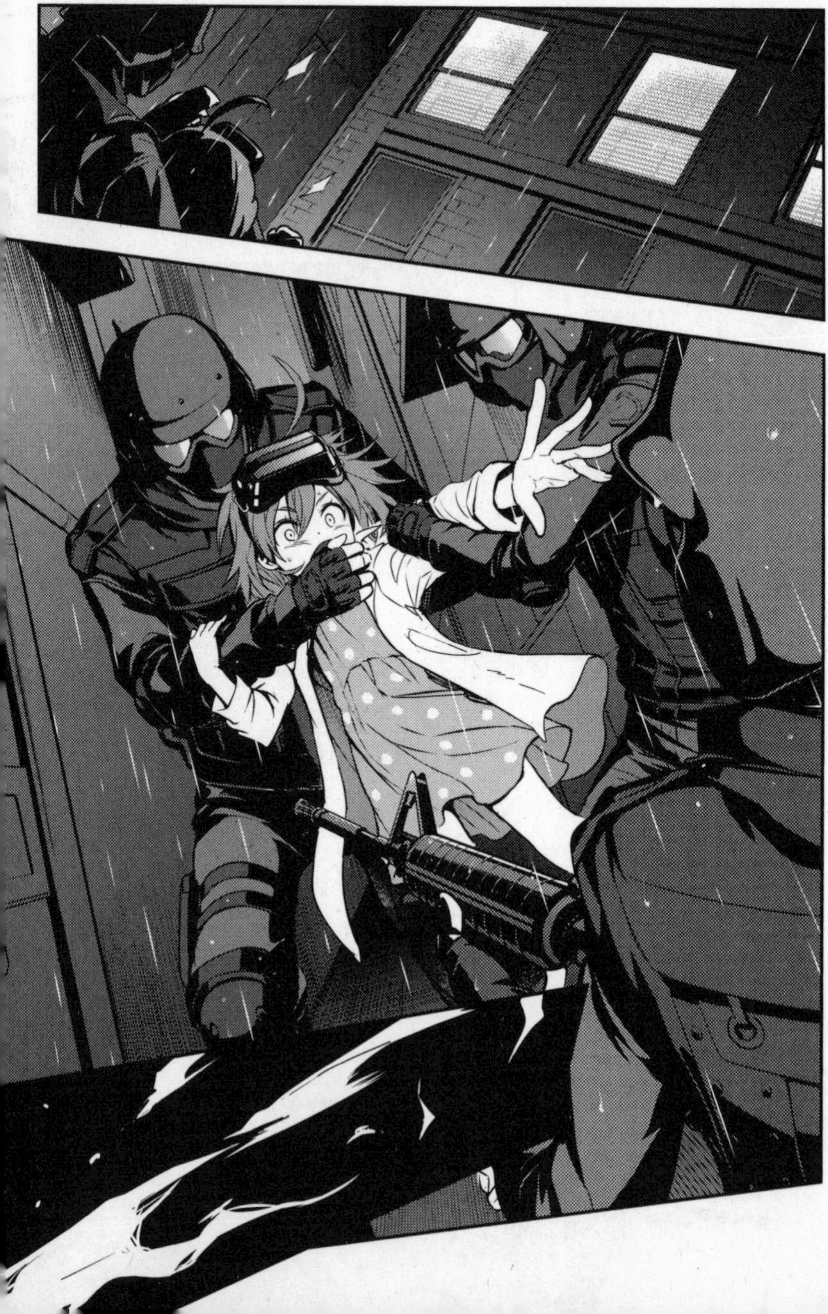

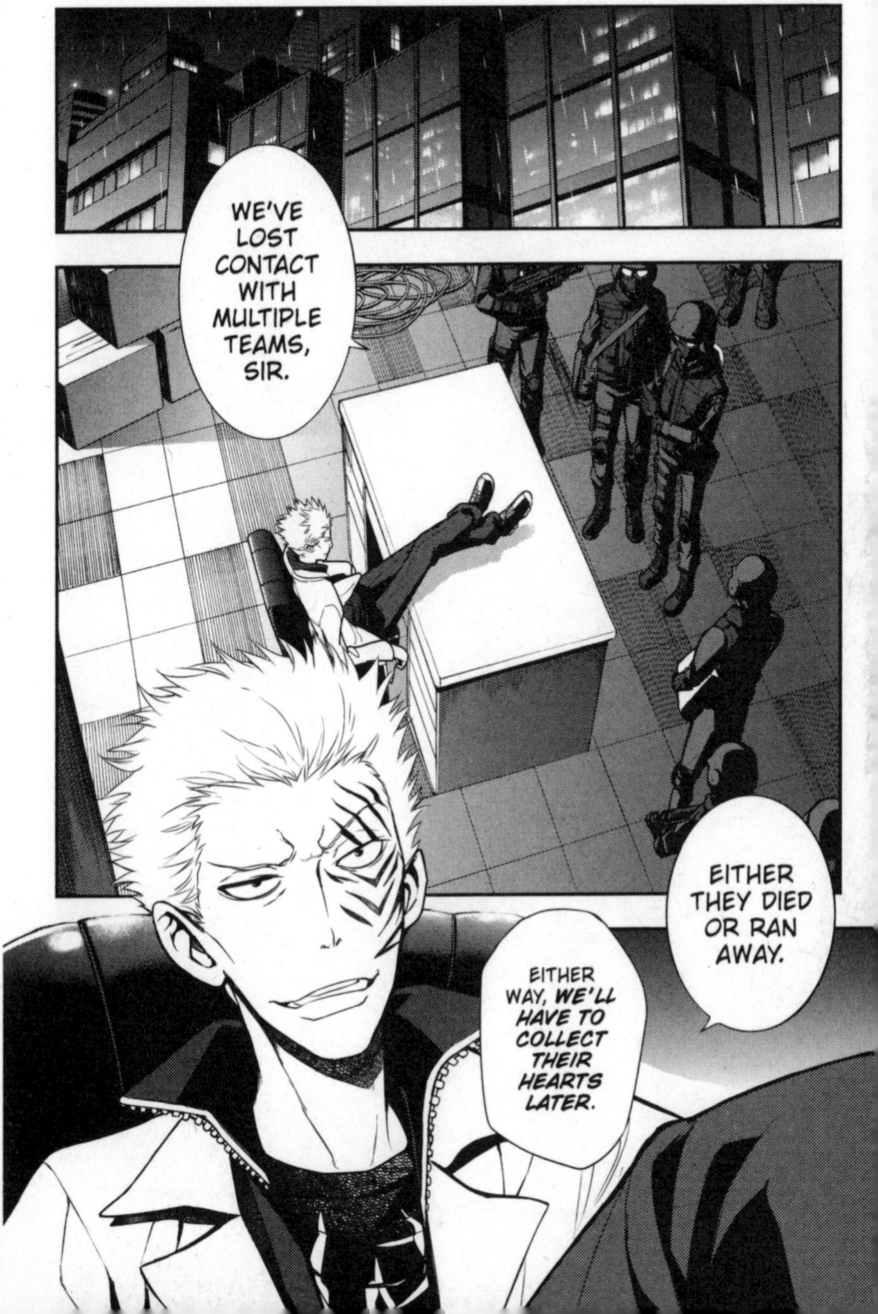
WE'VE LOST CONTACT WITH MULTIPLE TEAMS, SIR.
EITHER THEY DIED OR RAN AWAY.
EITHER WAY, WE'LL HAVE TO COLLECT THEIR HEARTS LATER.

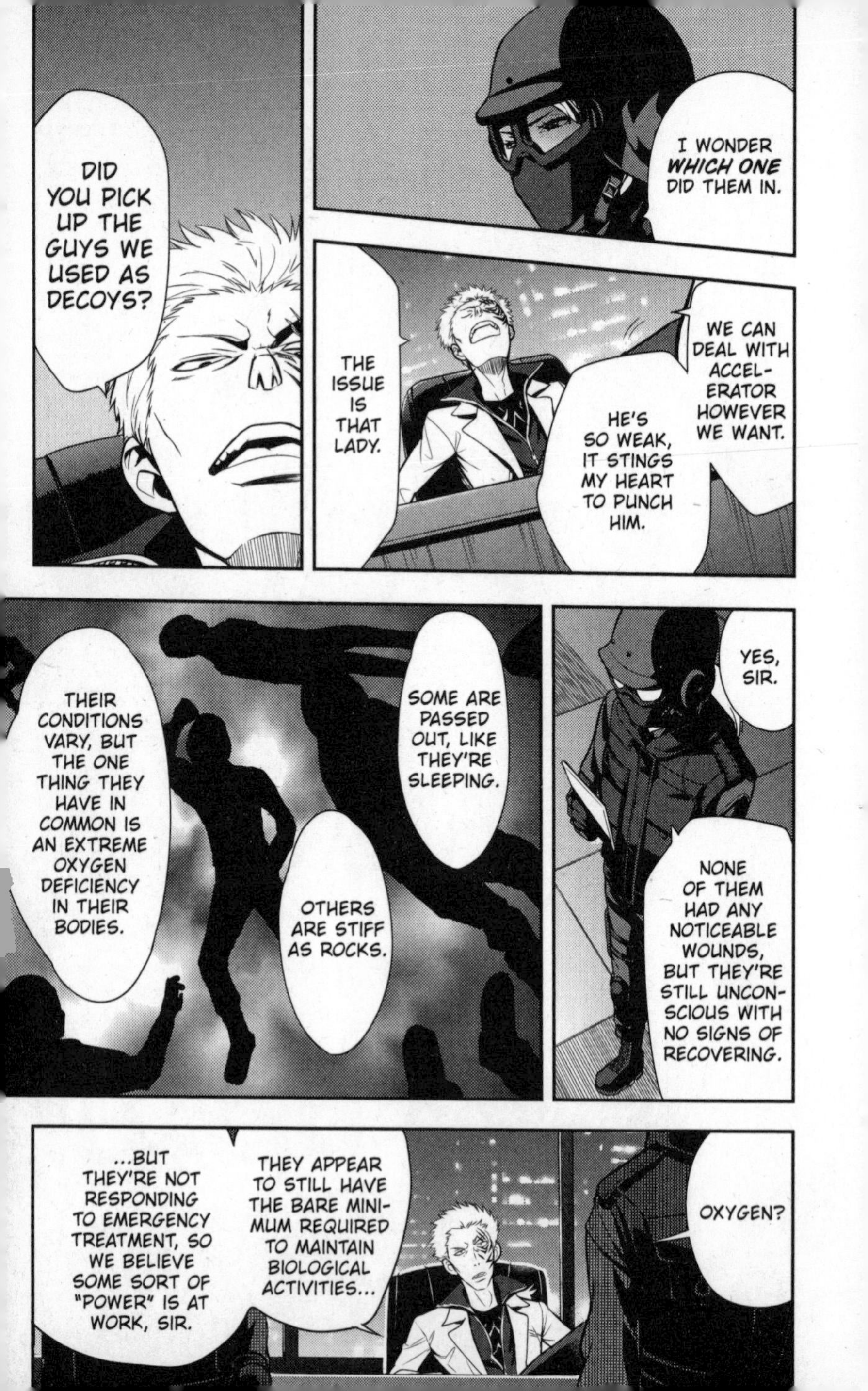
I WONDER *WHICH ONE* DID THEM IN.
WE CAN DEAL WITH ACCEL-ERATOR HOWEVER WE WANT.
HE'S SO WEAK, IT STINGS MY HEART TO PUNCH HIM.
THE ISSUE IS THAT LADY.
DID YOU PICK UP THE GUYS WE USED AS DECOYS?
YES, SIR.
NONE OF THEM HAD ANY NOTICEABLE WOUNDS, BUT THEY'RE STILL UNCON-SCIOUS WITH NO SIGNS OF RECOVERING.
SOME ARE PASSED OUT, LIKE THEY'RE SLEEPING.
OTHERS ARE STIFF AS ROCKS.
THEIR CONDITIONS VARY, BUT THE ONE THING THEY HAVE IN COMMON IS AN EXTREME OXYGEN DEFICIENCY IN THEIR BODIES.
OXYGEN?
THEY APPEAR TO STILL HAVE THE BARE MINI-MUM REQUIRED TO MAINTAIN BIOLOGICAL ACTIVITIES...
...BUT THEY'RE NOT RESPONDING TO EMERGENCY TREATMENT, SO WE BELIEVE SOME SORT OF "POWER" IS AT WORK, SIR.

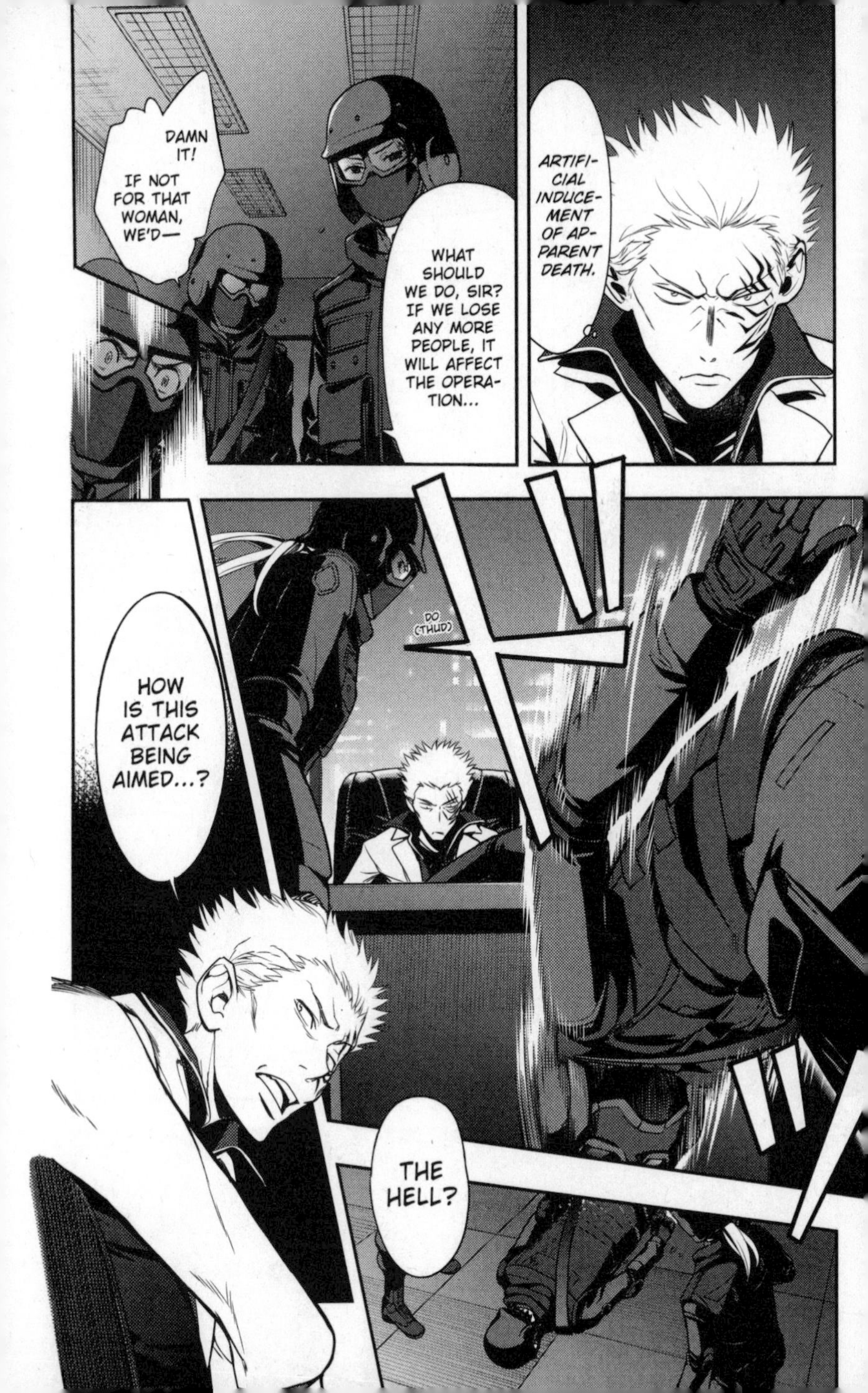
ARTIFICIAL INDUCEMENT OF APPARENT DEATH.
WHAT SHOULD WE DO, SIR? IF WE LOSE ANY MORE PEOPLE, IT WILL AFFECT THE OPERATION...
DAMN IT! IF NOT FOR THAT WOMAN, WE'D—
DO (THUD)
HOW IS THIS ATTACK BEING AIMED...?
THE HELL?

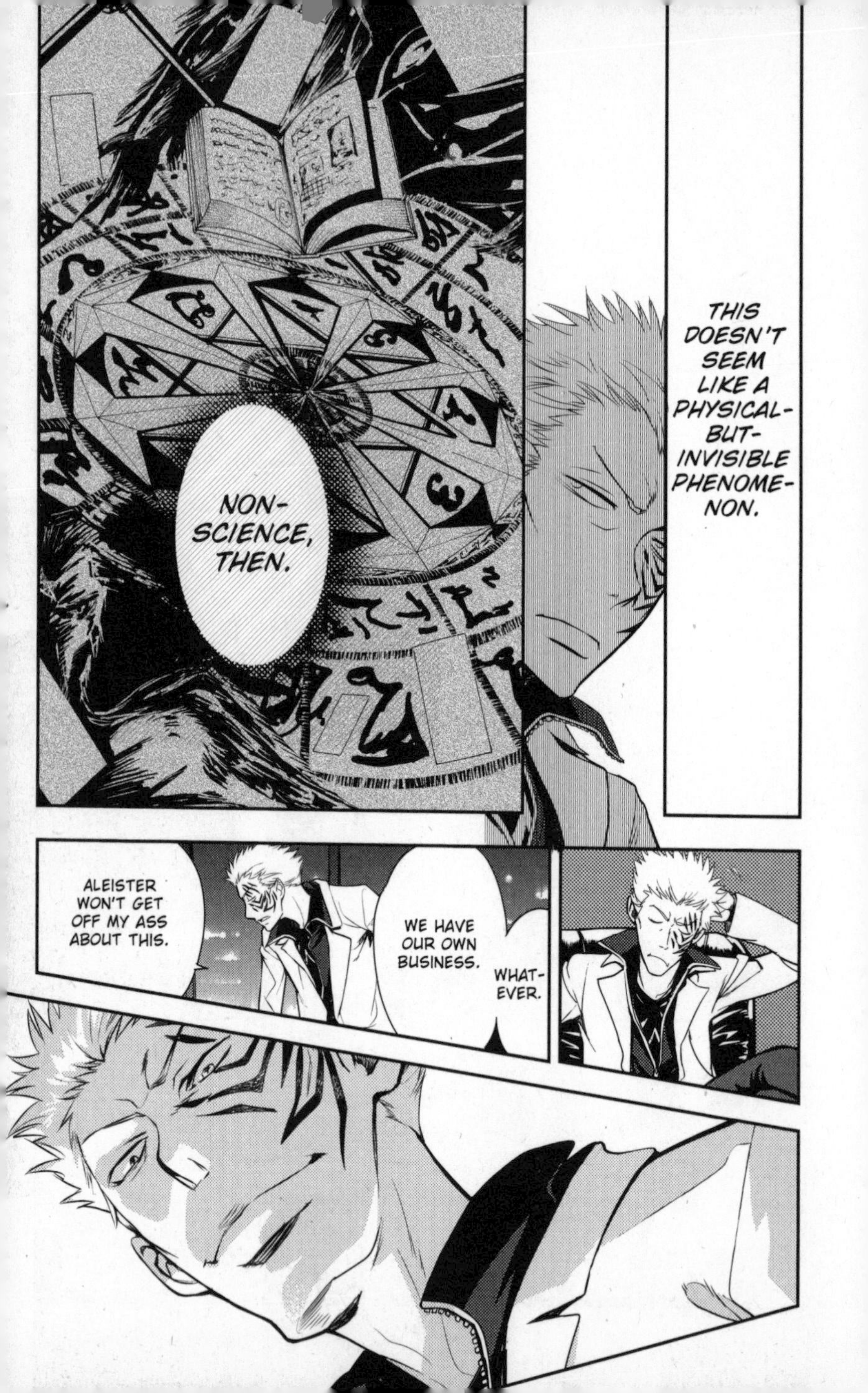
THIS DOESN'T SEEM LIKE A PHYSICAL-BUT-INVISIBLE PHENOMENON.
NON-SCIENCE, THEN.
WHAT-EVER.
WE HAVE OUR OWN BUSINESS.
ALEISTER WON'T GET OFF MY ASS ABOUT THIS.

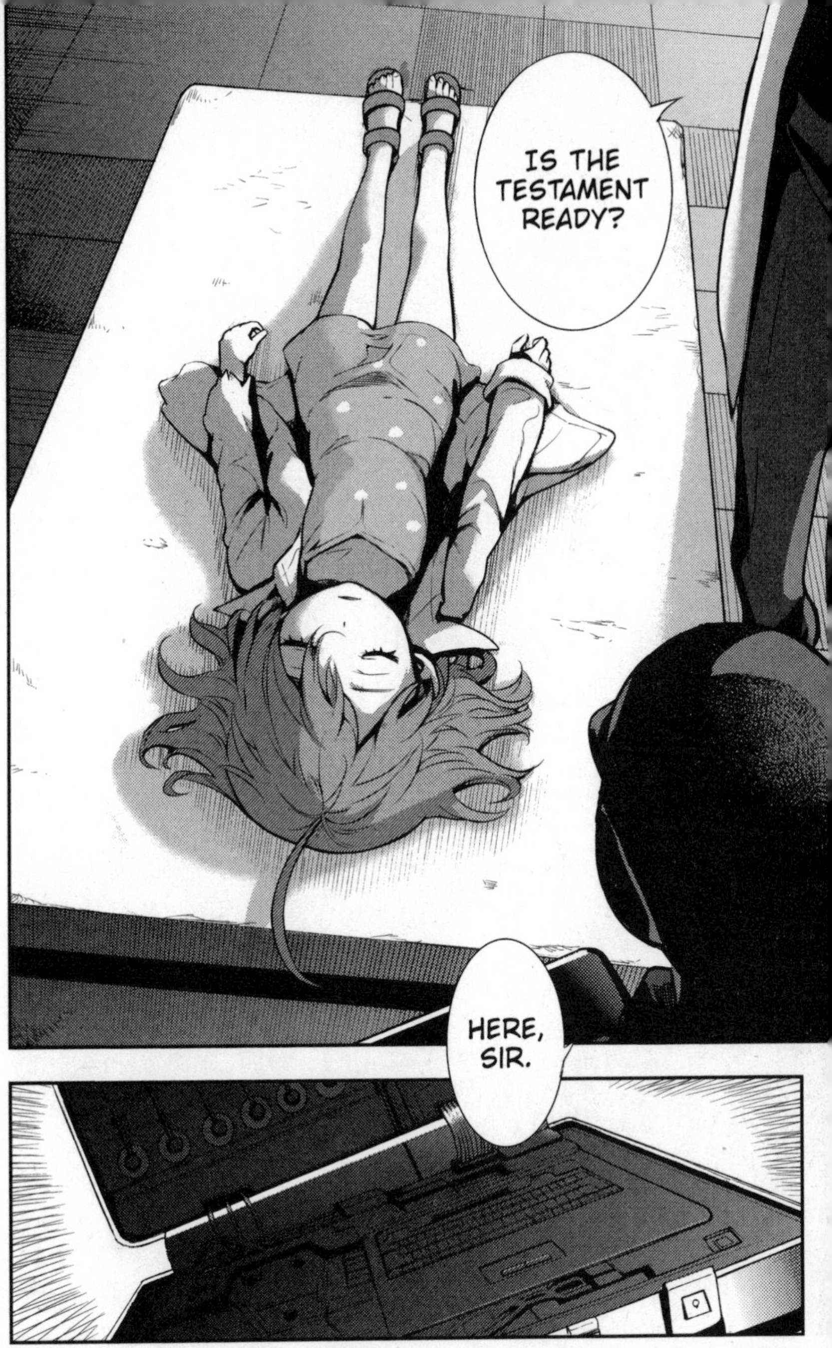
IS THE TESTAMENT READY?
HERE, SIR.

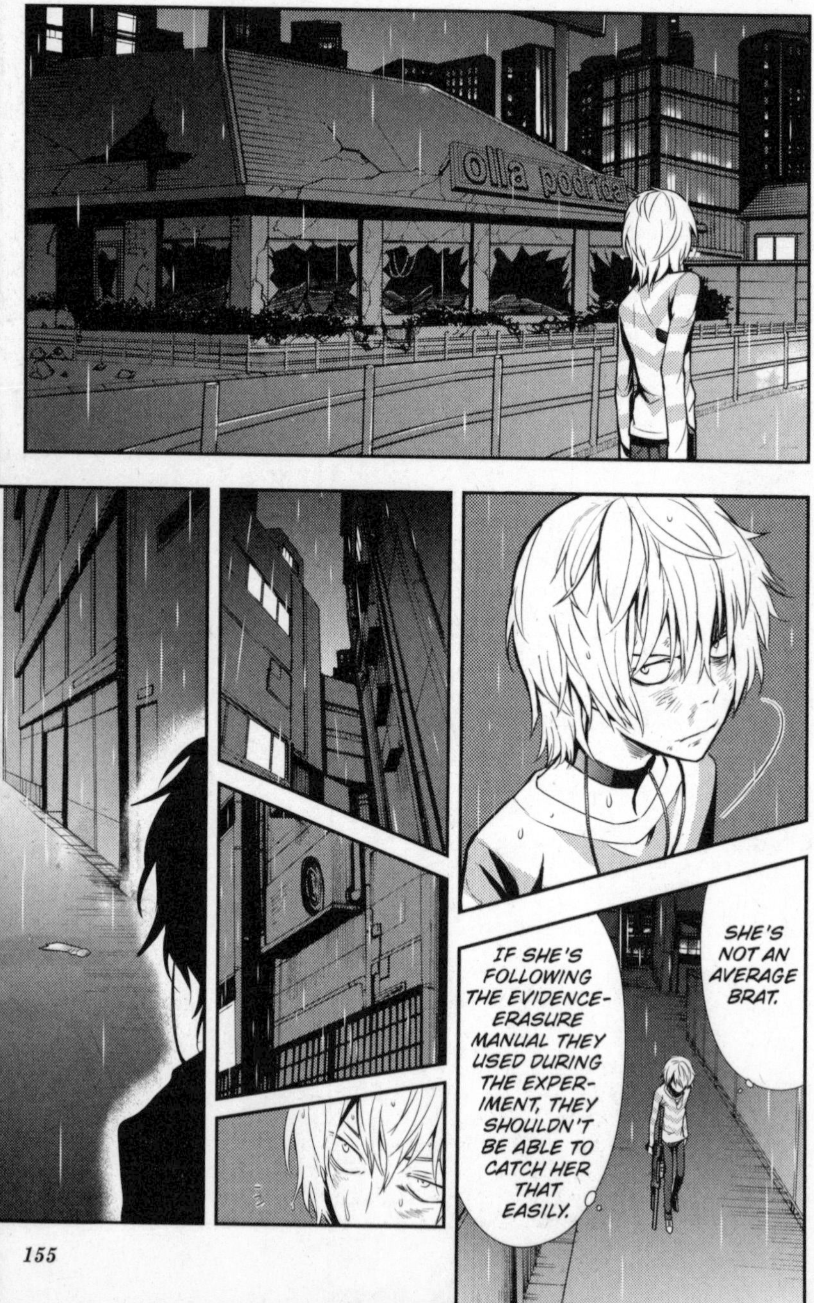
olla podrida
SHE'S NOT AN AVERAGE BRAT.
IF SHE'S FOLLOWING THE EVIDENCE-ERASURE MANUAL THEY USED DURING THE EXPERIMENT, THEY SHOULDN'T BE ABLE TO CATCH HER THAT EASILY.

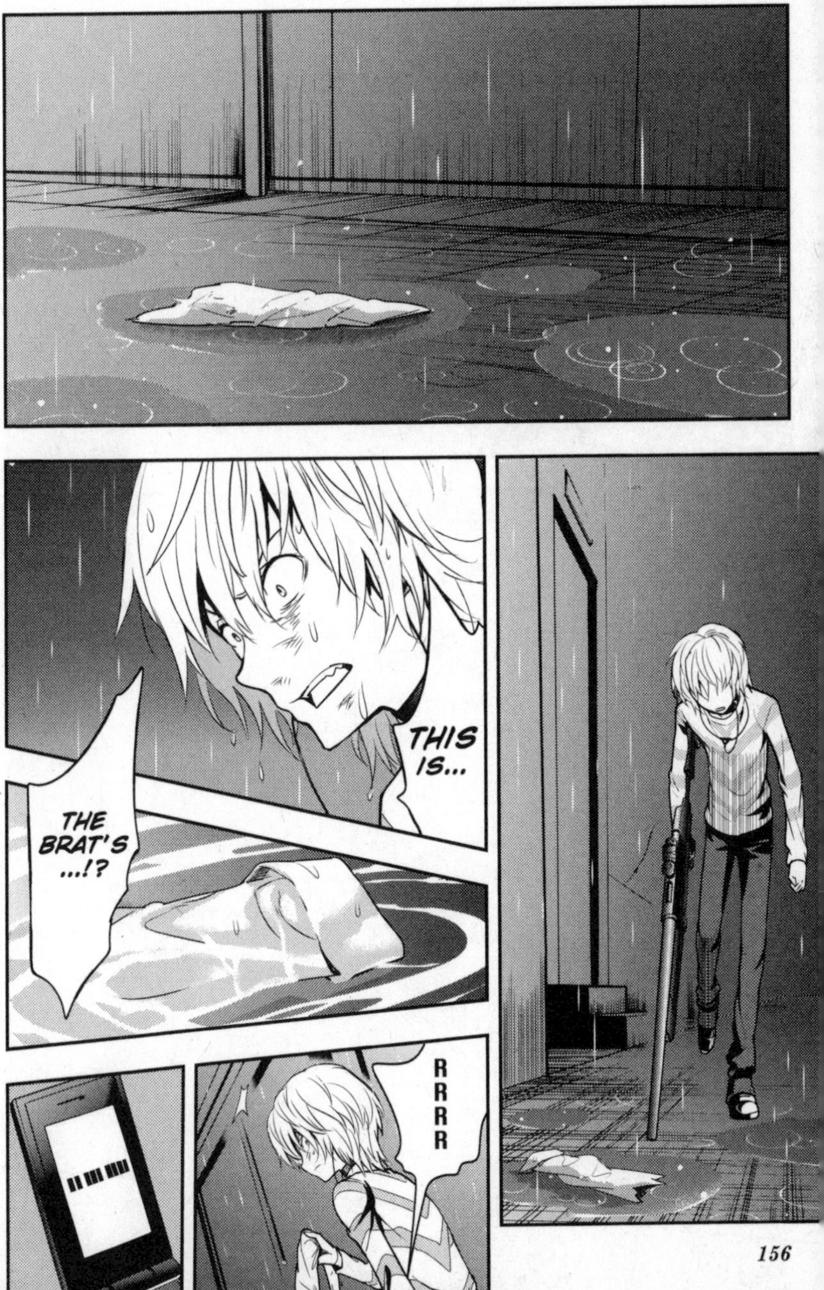
THIS IS...
THE BRAT'S ...!?
RRRR

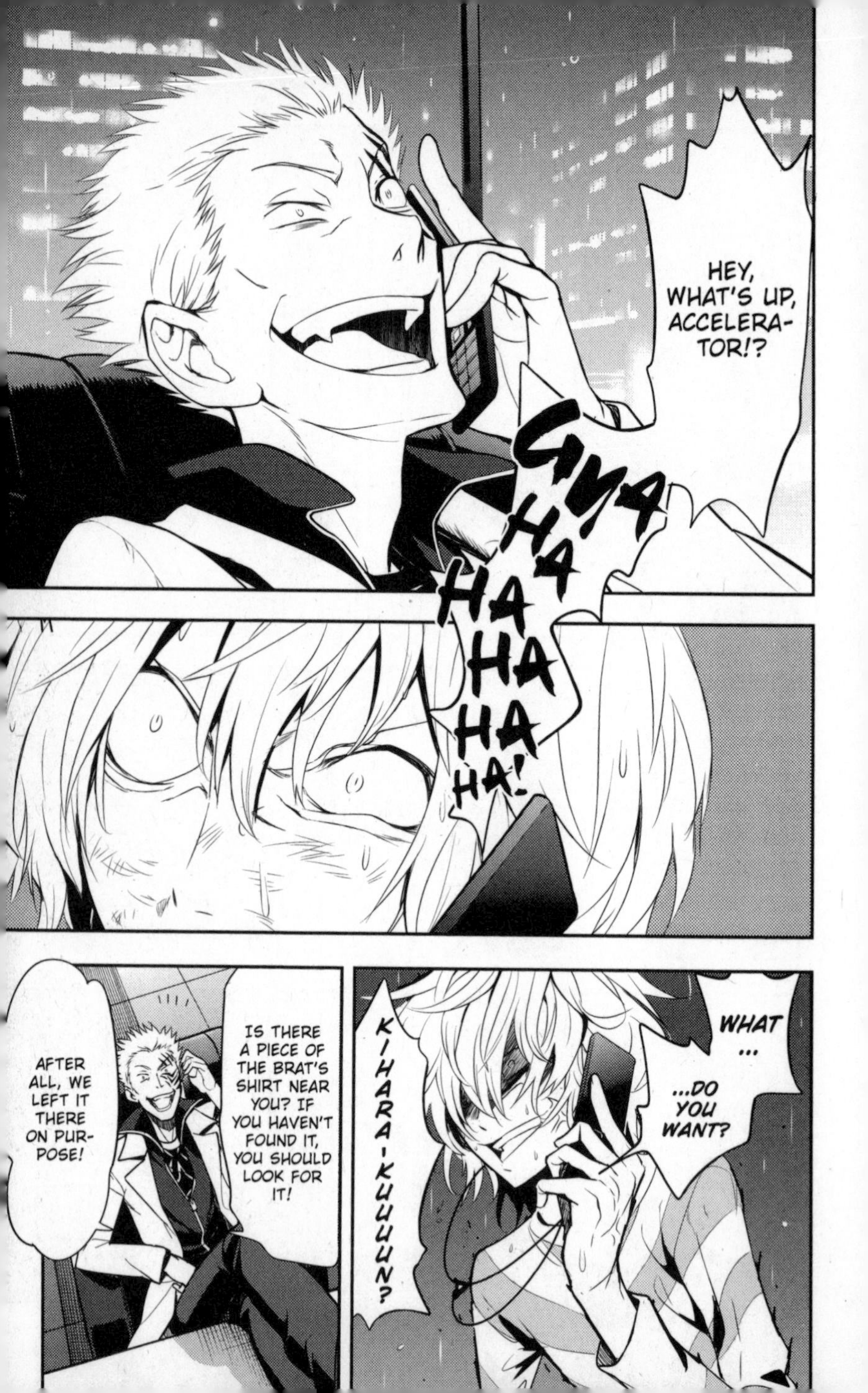
HEY, WHAT'S UP, ACCELERA-TOR!?
GYA HA HA HA HA HA!
WHAT...
...DO YOU WANT?
KIHARA-KUUUUUN?
IS THERE A PIECE OF THE BRAT'S SHIRT NEAR YOU? IF YOU HAVEN'T FOUND IT, YOU SHOULD LOOK FOR IT!
AFTER ALL, WE LEFT IT THERE ON PUR-POSE!

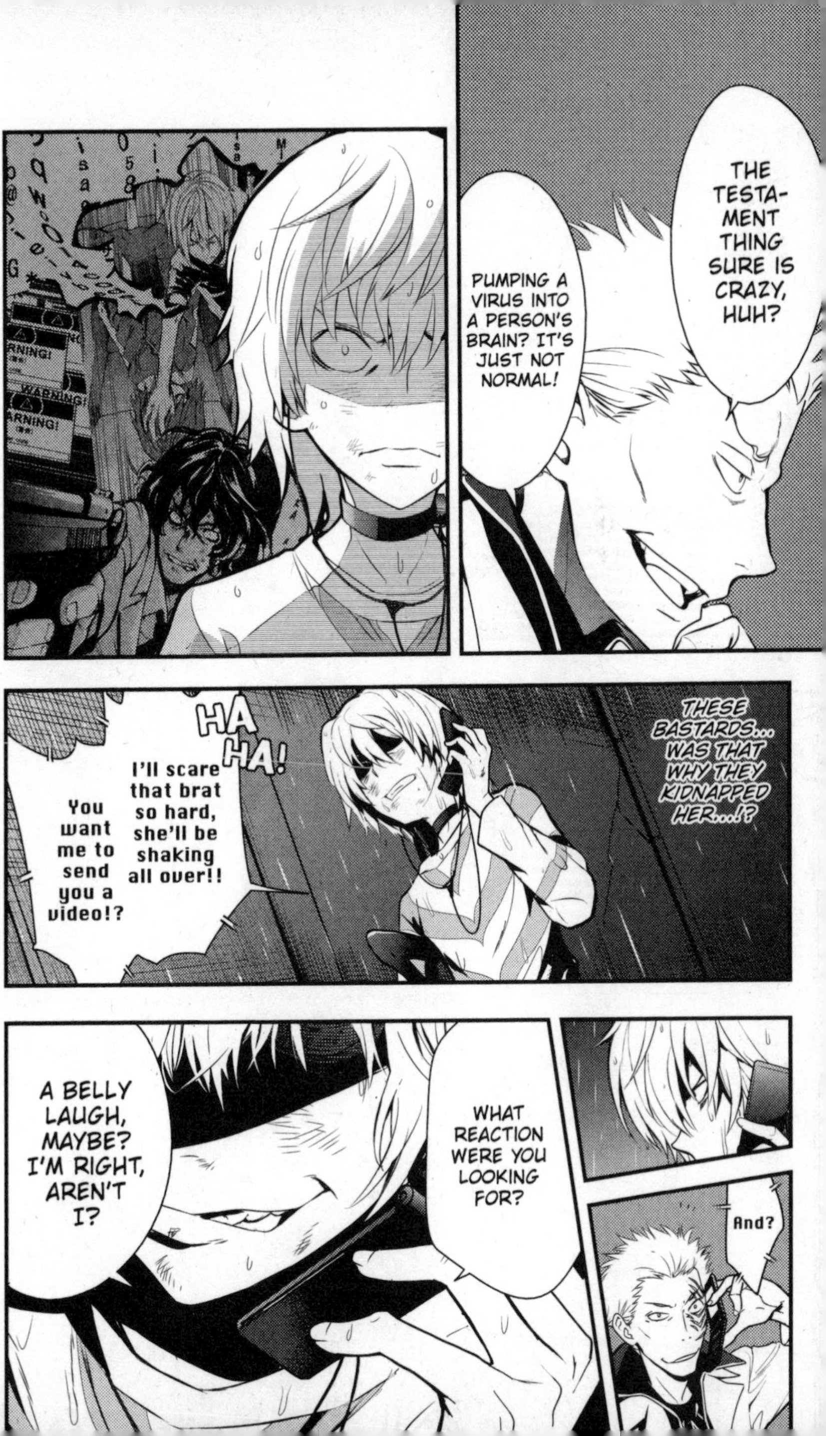
THE TESTAMENT THING SURE IS CRAZY, HUH?
PUMPING A VIRUS INTO A PERSON'S BRAIN? IT'S JUST NOT NORMAL!
THESE BASTARDS... WAS THAT WHY THEY KIDNAPPED HER...!?
HA HA!
I'll scare that brat so hard, she'll be shaking all over!!
You want me to send you a video!?
And?
WHAT REACTION WERE YOU LOOKING FOR?
A BELLY LAUGH, MAYBE? I'M RIGHT, AREN'T I?

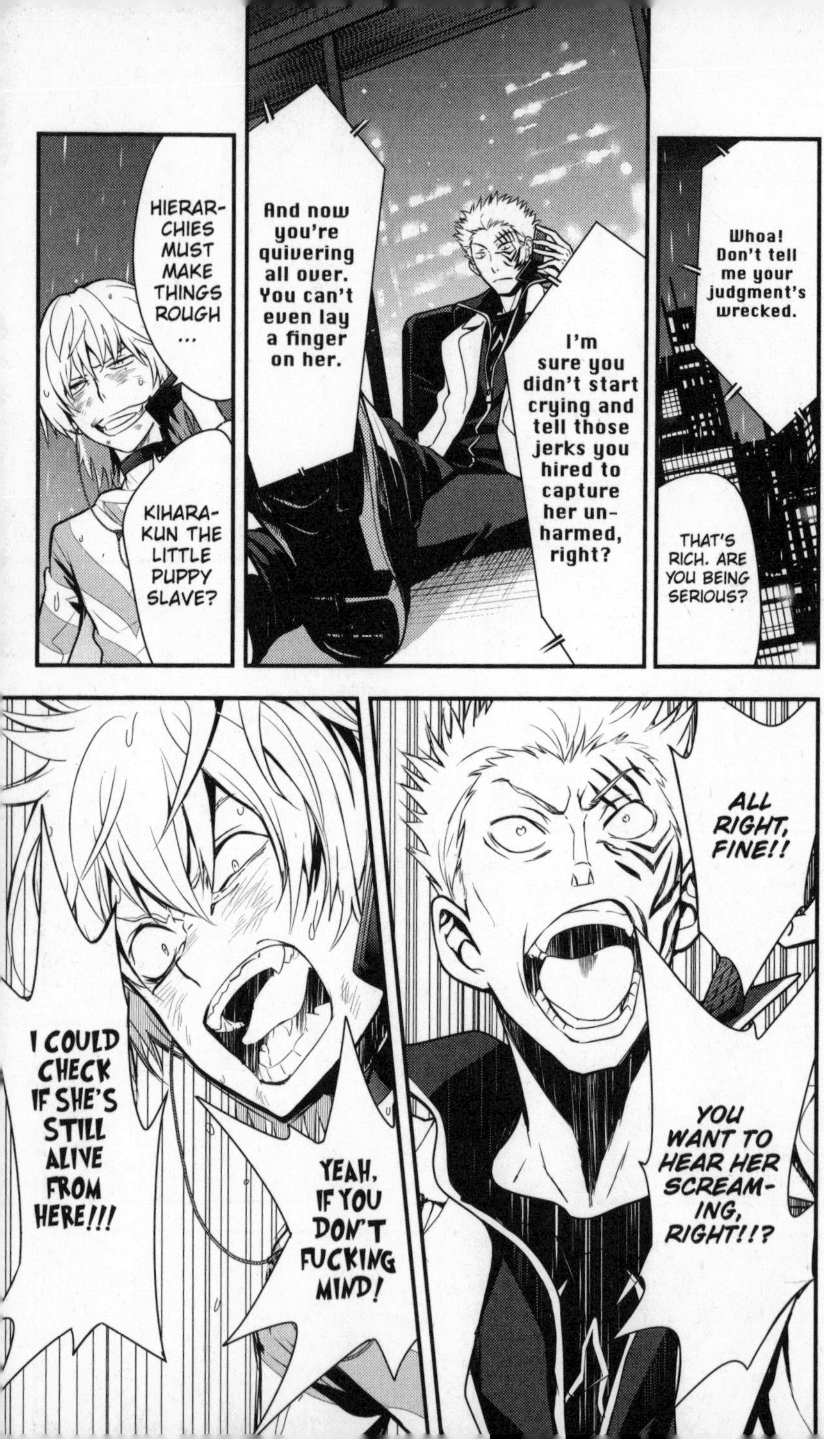

Whoa! Don't tell me your judgment's wrecked.
THAT'S RICH. ARE YOU BEING SERIOUS?
I'm sure you didn't start crying and tell those jerks you hired to capture her unharmed, right?
And now you're quivering all over. You can't even lay a finger on her.
HIERARCHIES MUST MAKE THINGS ROUGH...
KIHARA-KUN THE LITTLE PUPPY SLAVE?
ALL RIGHT, FINE!!
YOU WANT TO HEAR HER SCREAMING, RIGHT!!?
YEAH, IF YOU DON'T FUCKING MIND!
I COULD CHECK IF SHE'S STILL ALIVE FROM HERE!!!

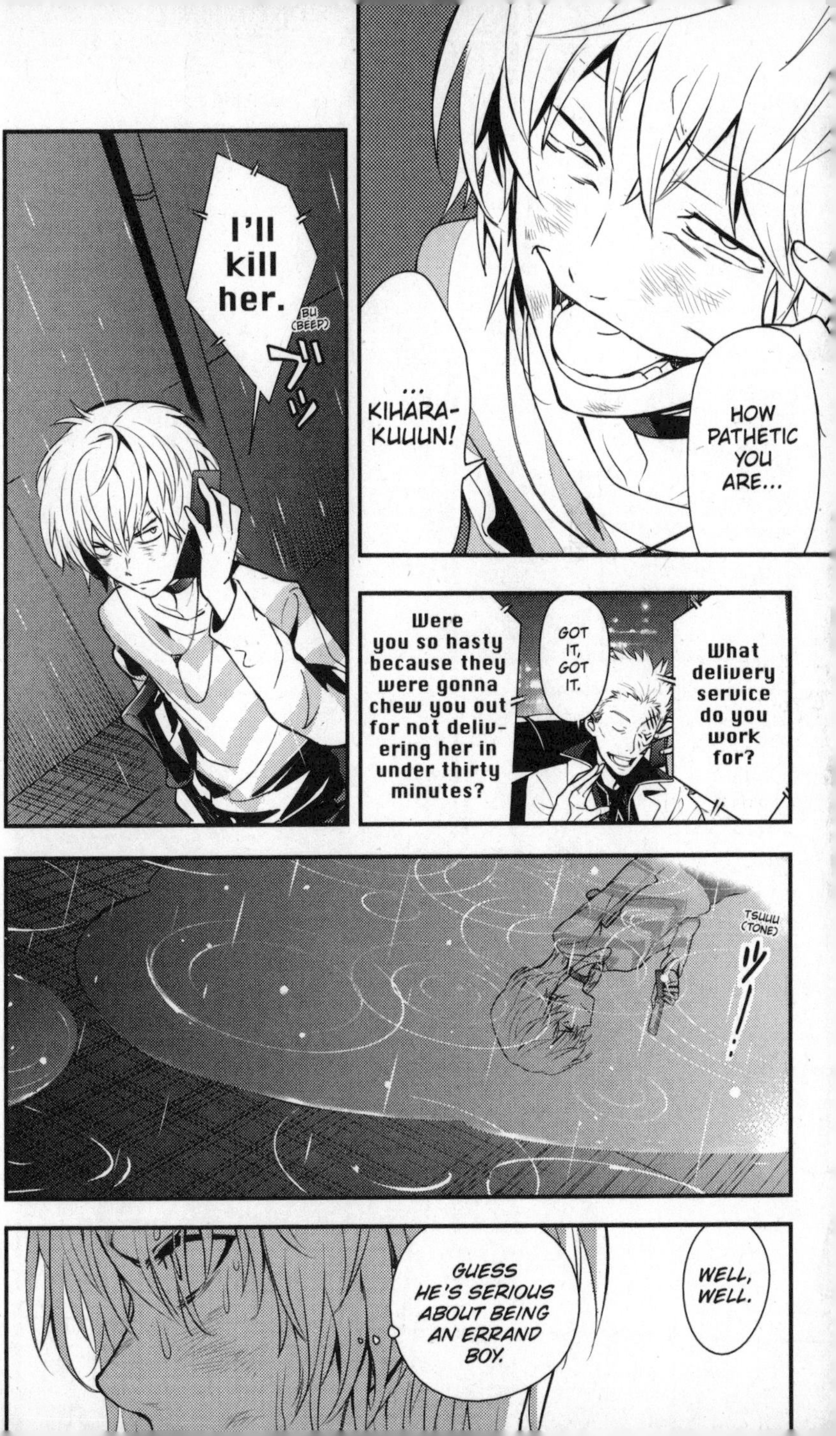
HOW PATHETIC YOU ARE...
...KIHARA-KUUUN!
What delivery service do you work for?
GOT IT, GOT IT.
Were you so hasty because they were gonna chew you out for not deliv-ering her in under thirty minutes?
I'll kill her.
BU (BEEP)
TSUUU (TONE)
WELL, WELL.
GUESS HE'S SERIOUS ABOUT BEING AN ERRAND BOY.

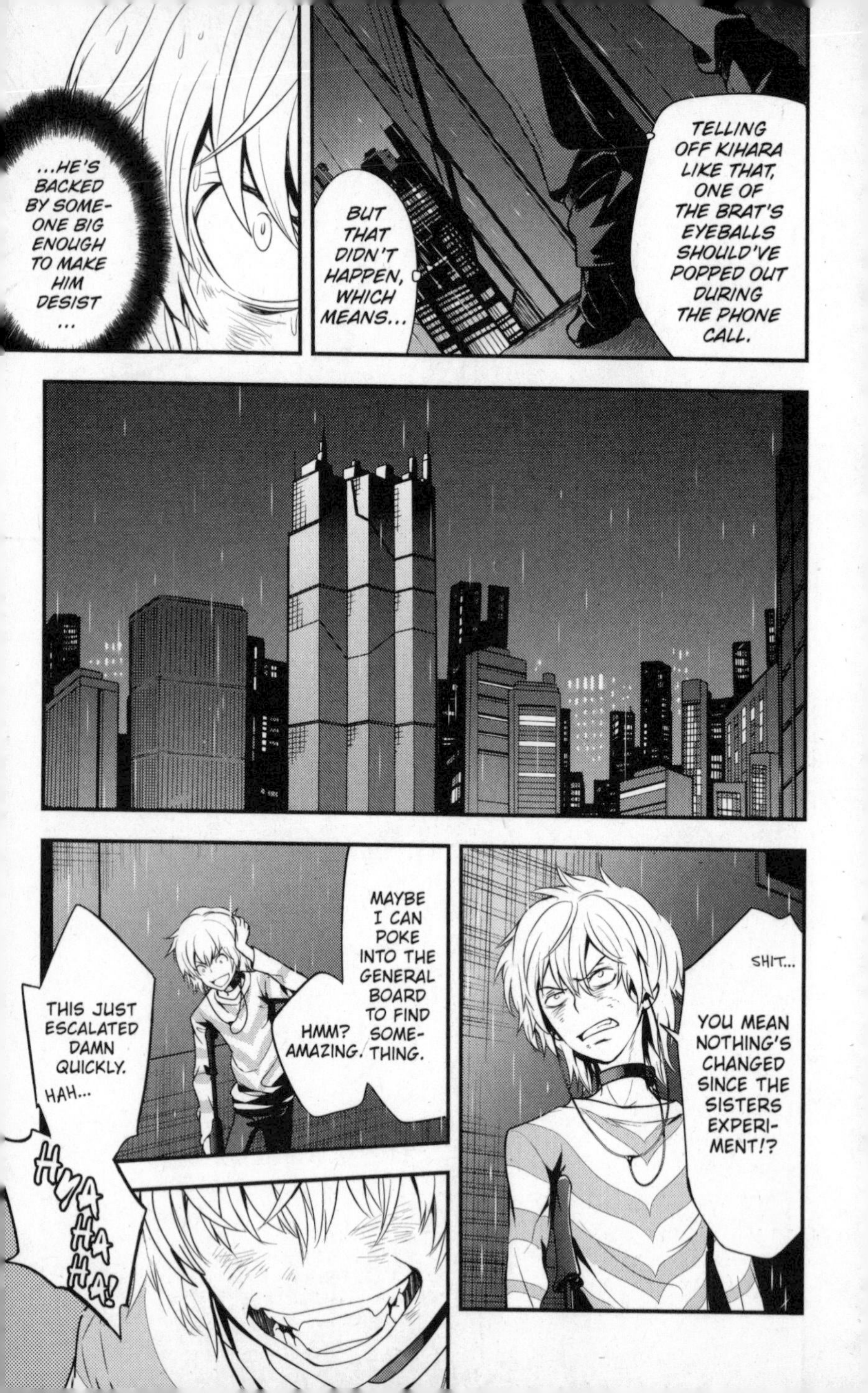
TELLING OFF KIHARA LIKE THAT, ONE OF THE BRAT'S EYEBALLS SHOULD'VE POPPED OUT DURING THE PHONE CALL.
BUT THAT DIDN'T HAPPEN, WHICH MEANS...
...HE'S BACKED BY SOME-ONE BIG ENOUGH TO MAKE HIM DESIST...
SHIT...
YOU MEAN NOTHING'S CHANGED SINCE THE SISTERS EXPERI-MENT!?
MAYBE I CAN POKE INTO THE GENERAL BOARD TO FIND SOME-THING.
HMM? AMAZING.
THIS JUST ESCALATED DAMN QUICKLY.
HAH...
HYA HA HA HA!

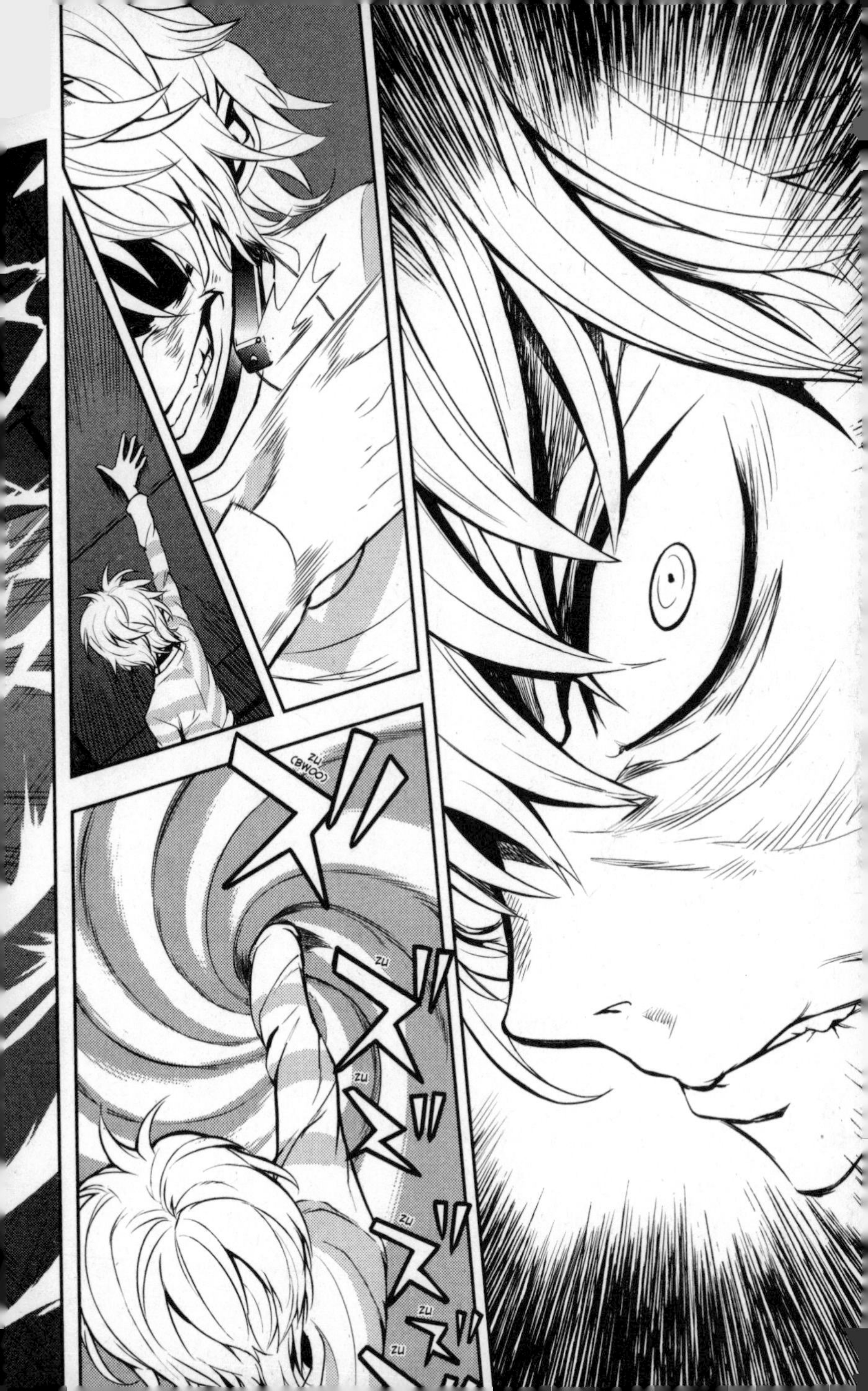
zu (BWOO)
zu
zu
zu
zu
zu

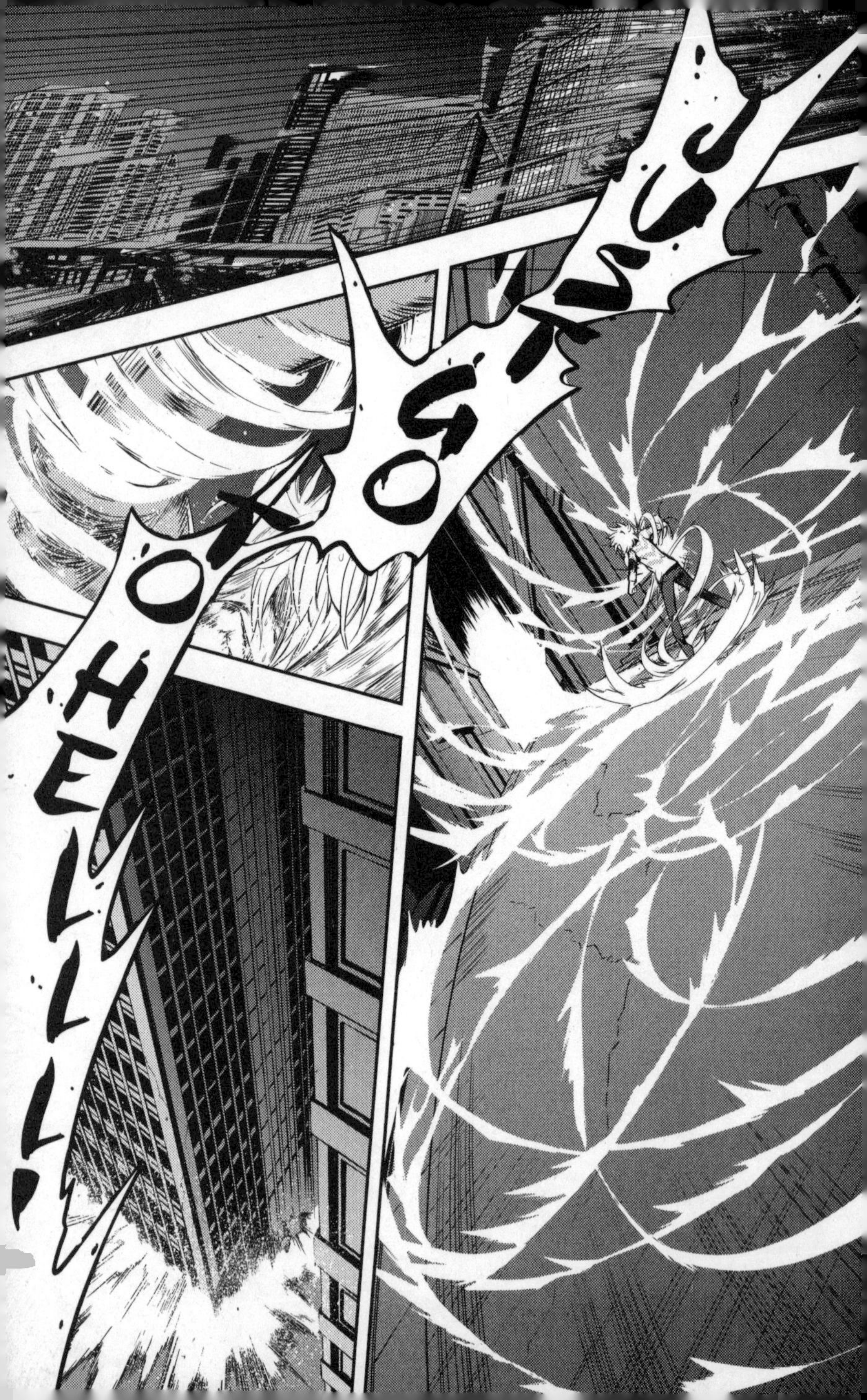
JUST GO TO HELLLL!!

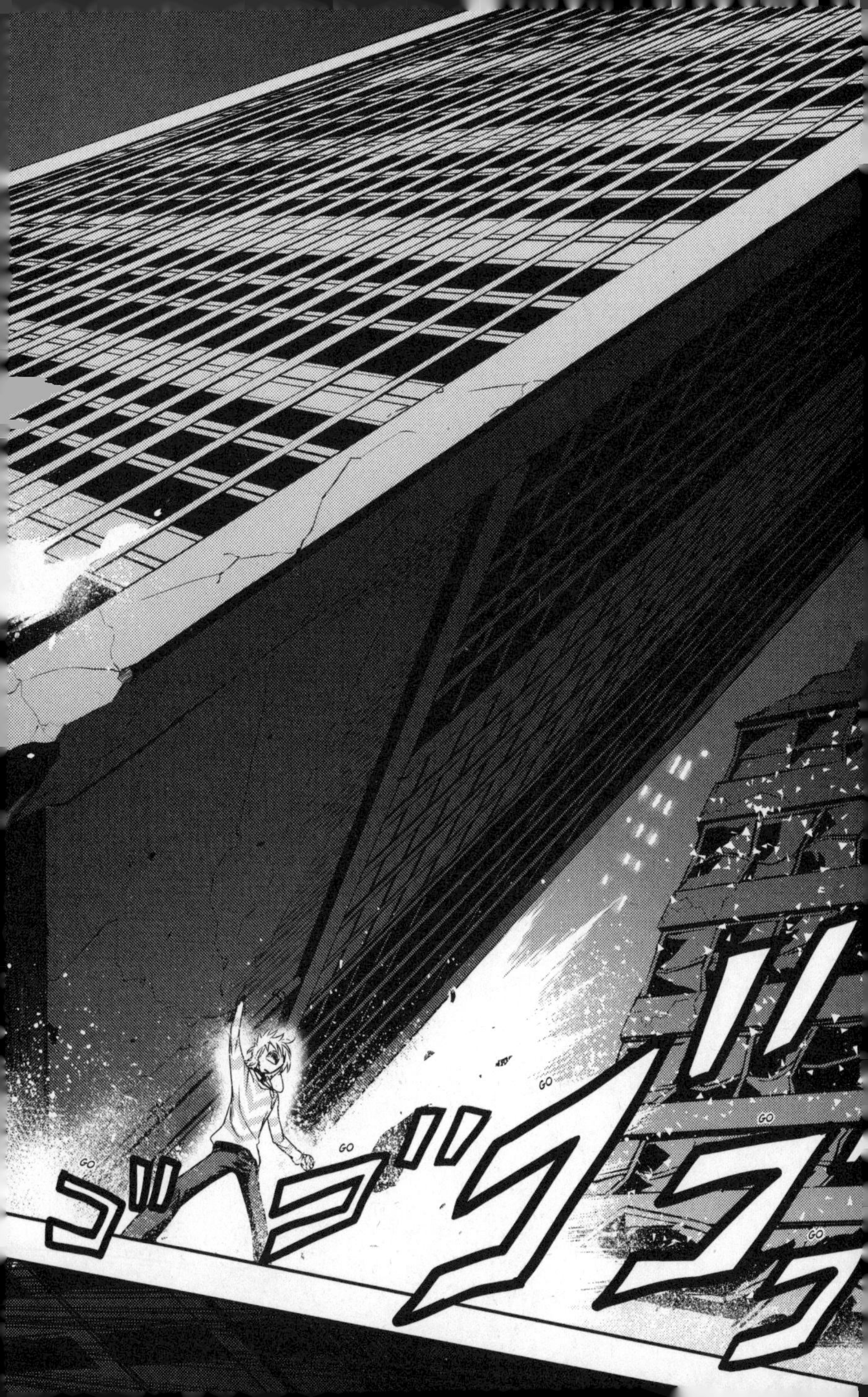
GO
GO
GO
GO
GO

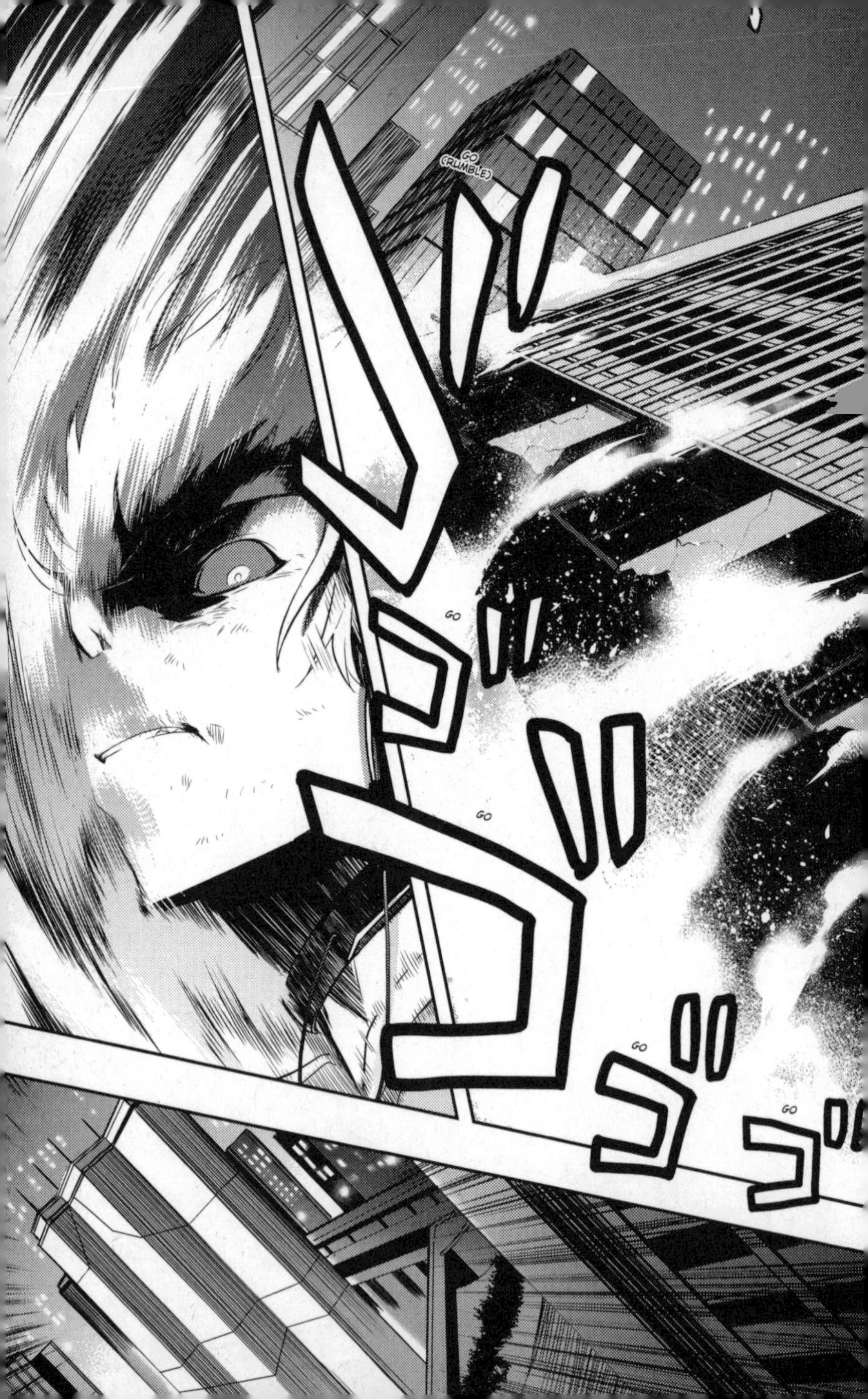
GO
(RUMBLE)
GO
GO
GO
GO

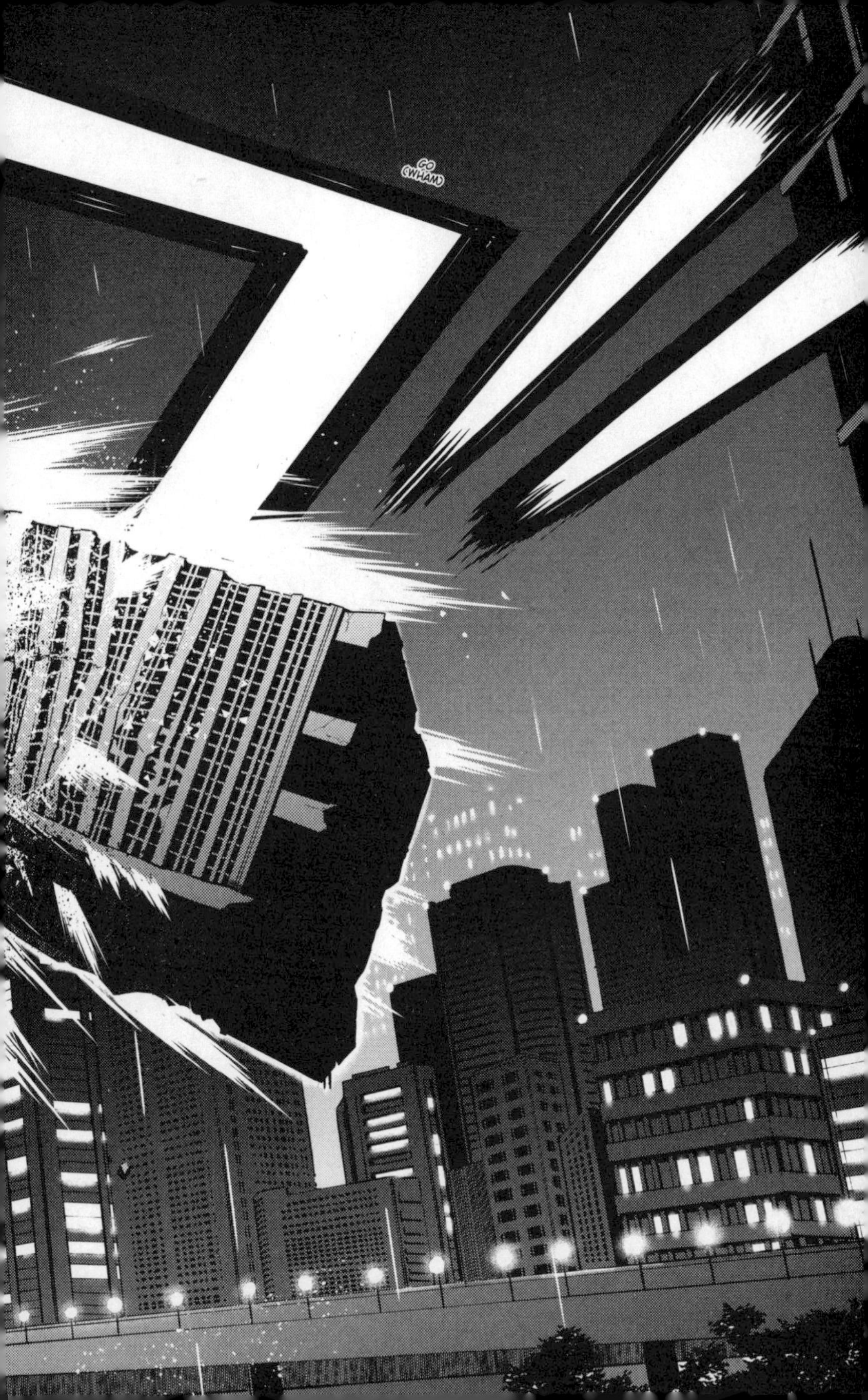
GO
(WHAM)

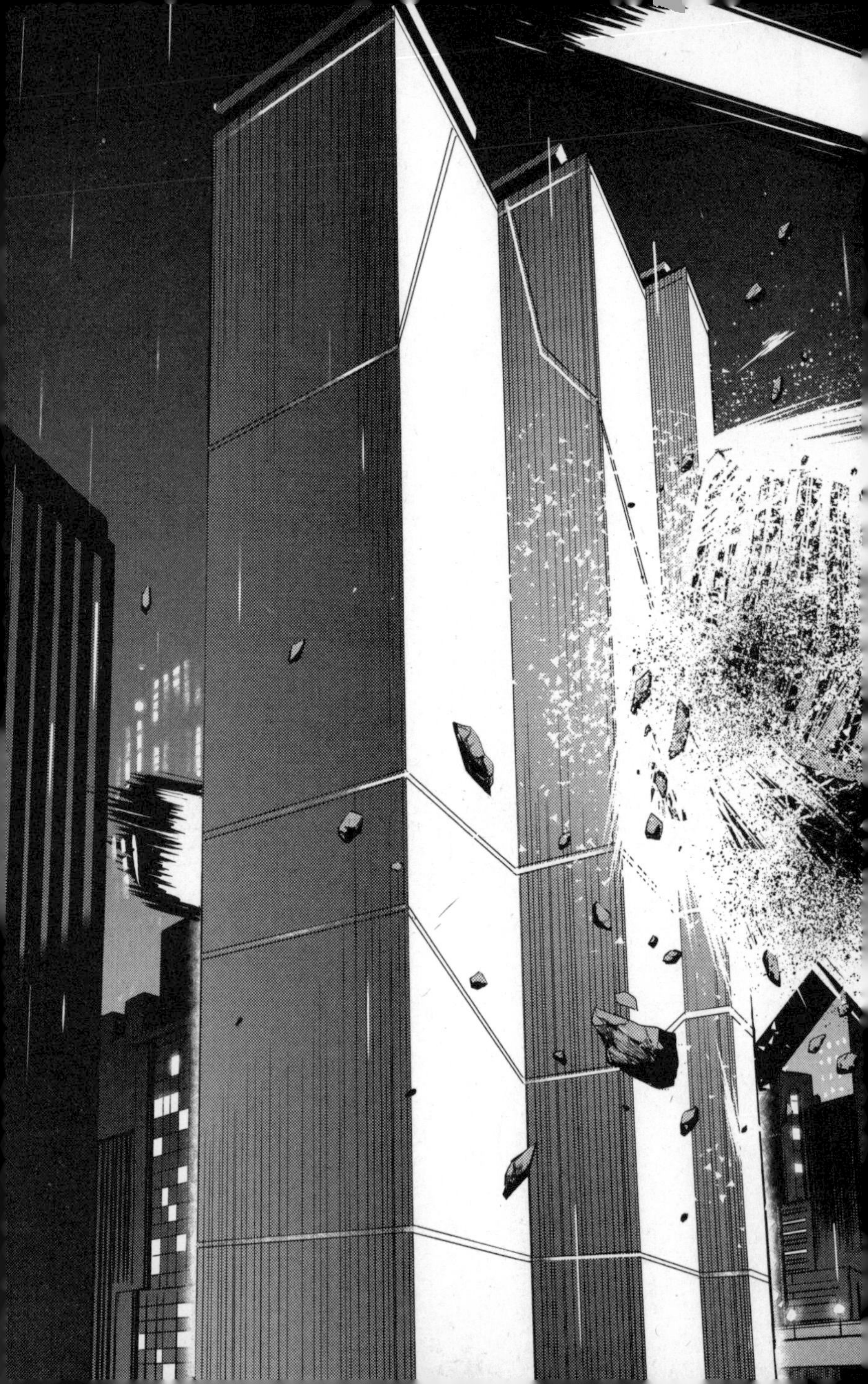

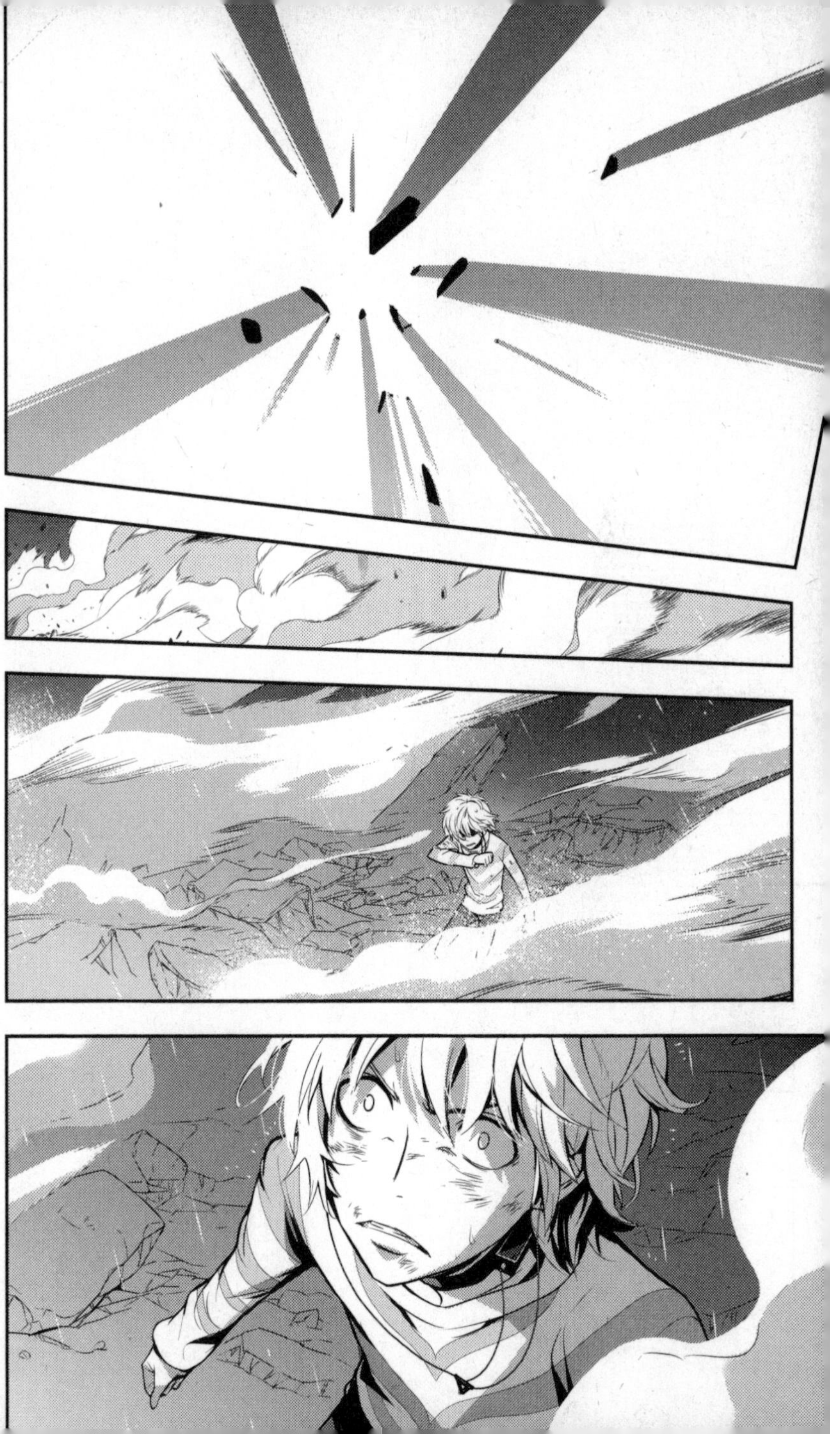

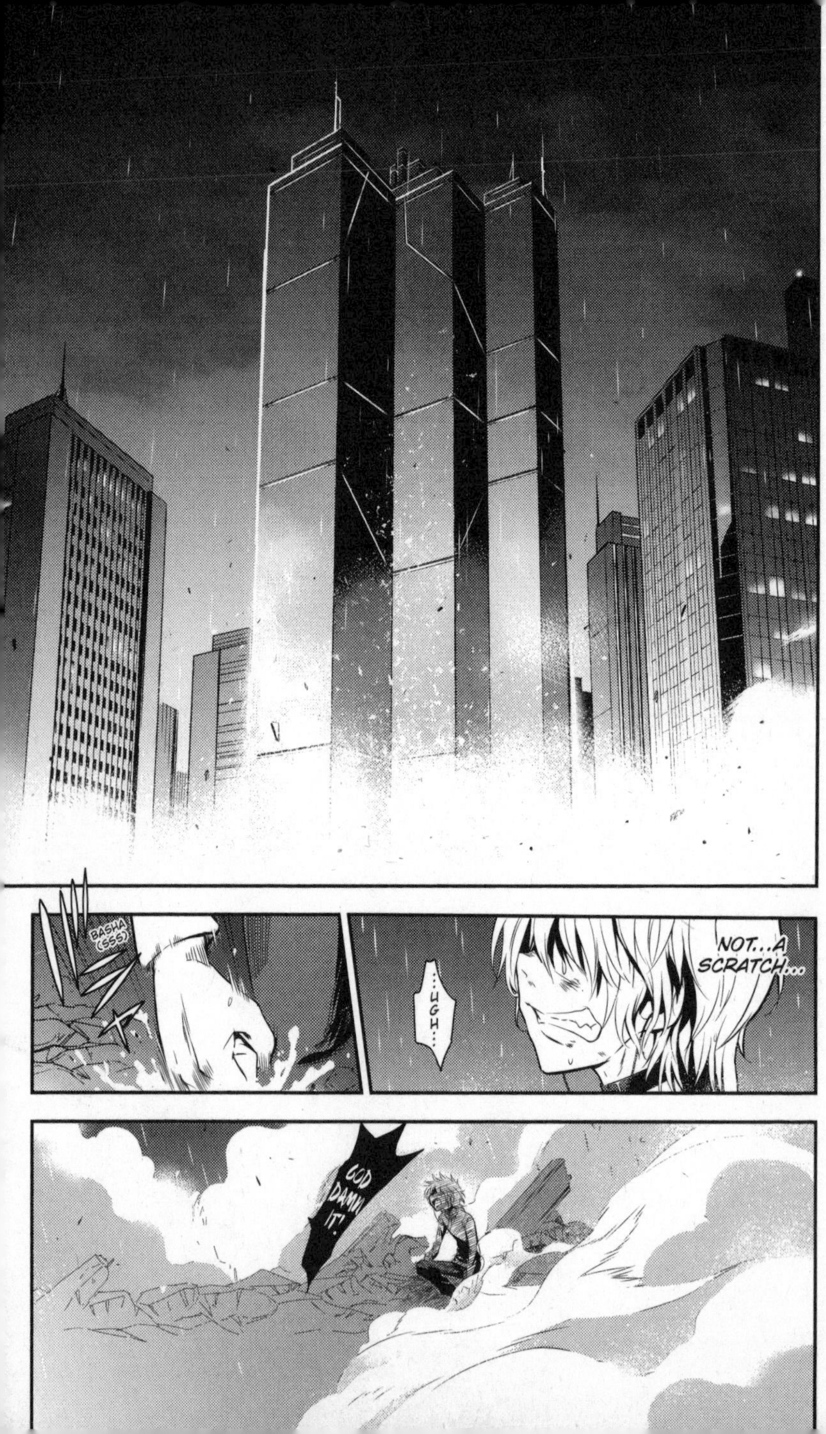
NOT...A SCRATCH...
...UGH...
BASHA (SSS)
GOD DAMN IT!

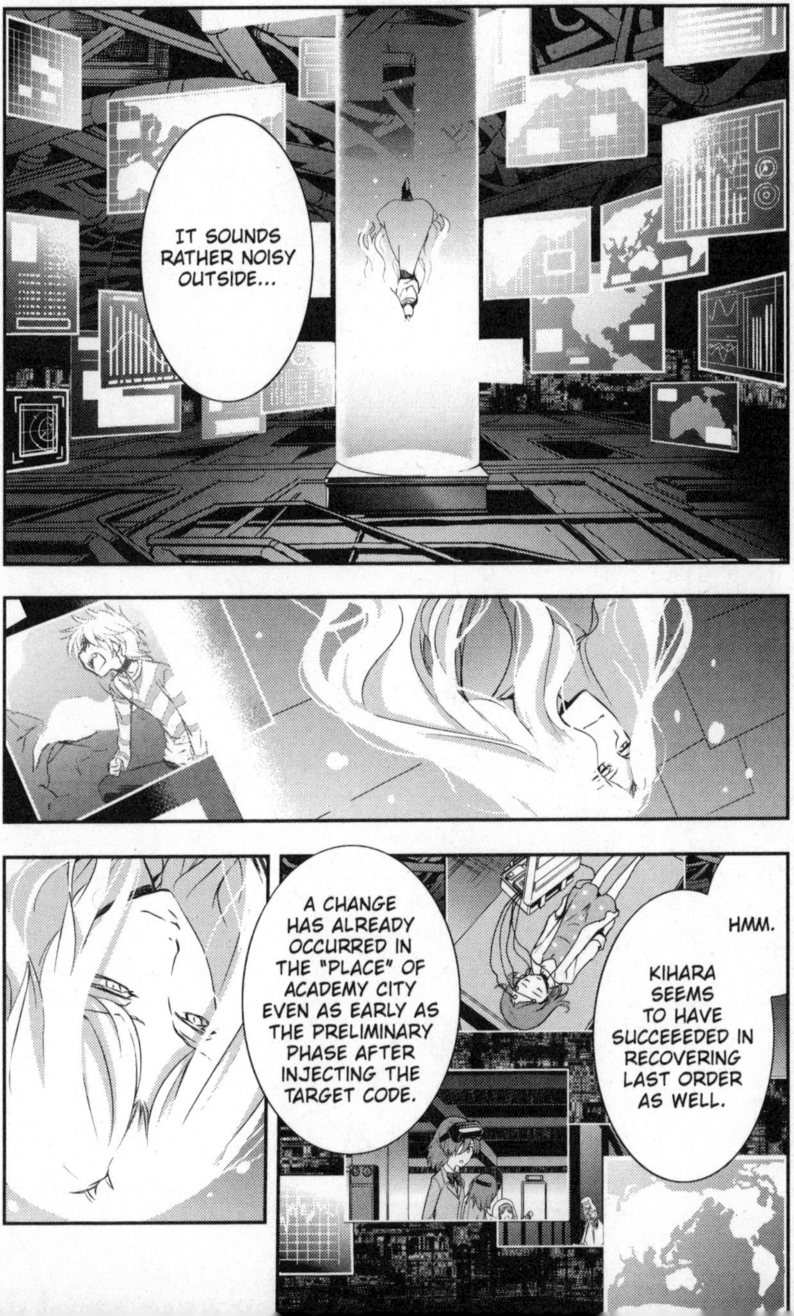
IT SOUNDS RATHER NOISY OUTSIDE...
HMM.
KIHARA SEEMS TO HAVE SUCCEEEDED IN RECOVERING LAST ORDER AS WELL.
A CHANGE HAS ALREADY OCCURRED IN THE "PLACE" OF ACADEMY CITY EVEN AS EARLY AS THE PRELIMINARY PHASE AFTER INJECTING THE TARGET CODE.

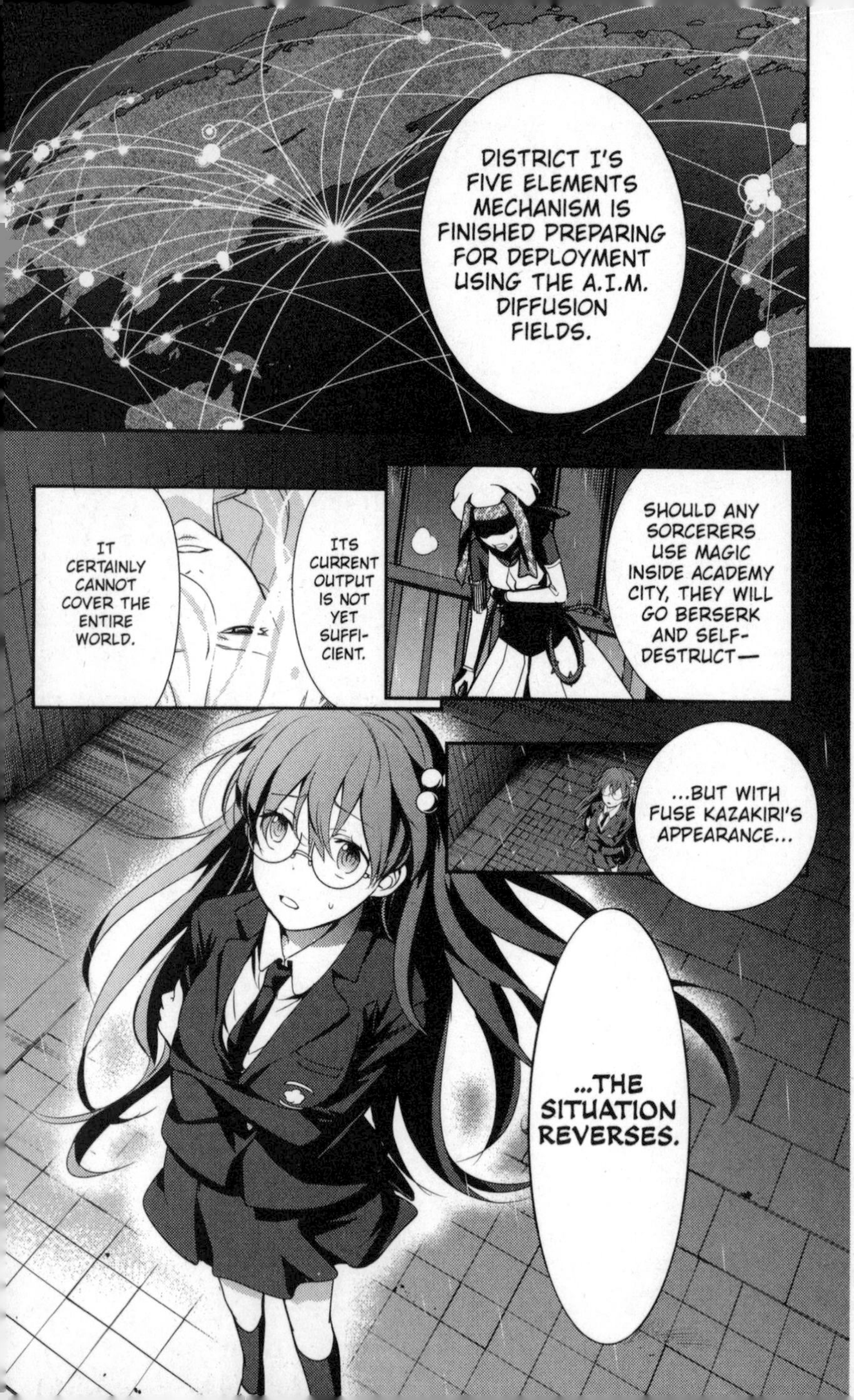
DISTRICT I'S FIVE ELEMENTS MECHANISM IS FINISHED PREPARING FOR DEPLOYMENT USING THE A.I.M. DIFFUSION FIELDS.
SHOULD ANY SORCERERS USE MAGIC INSIDE ACADEMY CITY, THEY WILL GO BERSERK AND SELF-DESTRUCT—
ITS CURRENT OUTPUT IS NOT YET SUFFICIENT.
IT CERTAINLY CANNOT COVER THE ENTIRE WORLD.
...BUT WITH FUSE KAZAKIRI'S APPEARANCE...
...THE SITUATION REVERSES.

#110 EMERGENCE

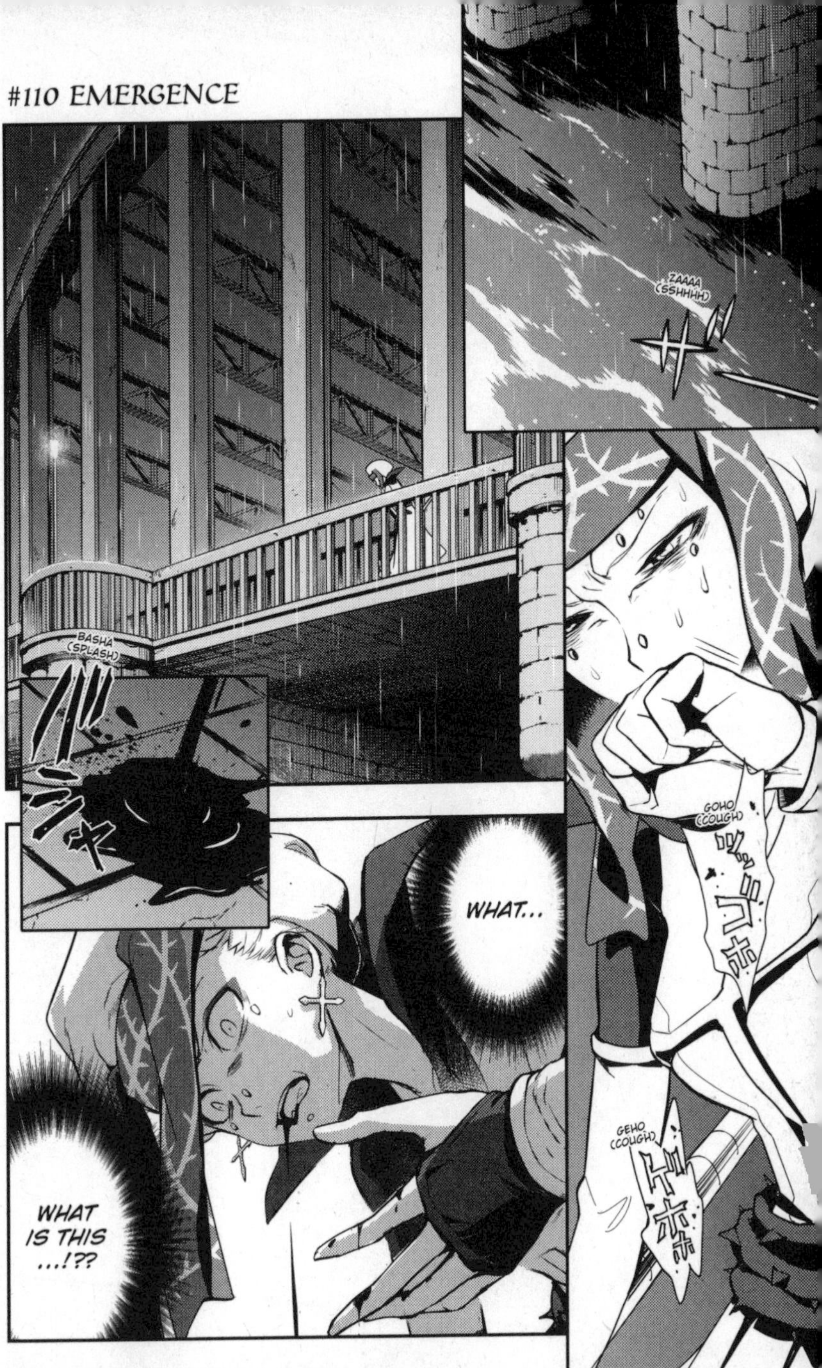
ZAAAA (SSHHHH)
BASHA (SPLASH)
GOHO (COUGH)
GEHO (COUGH)
WHAT...
WHAT IS THIS ...!??

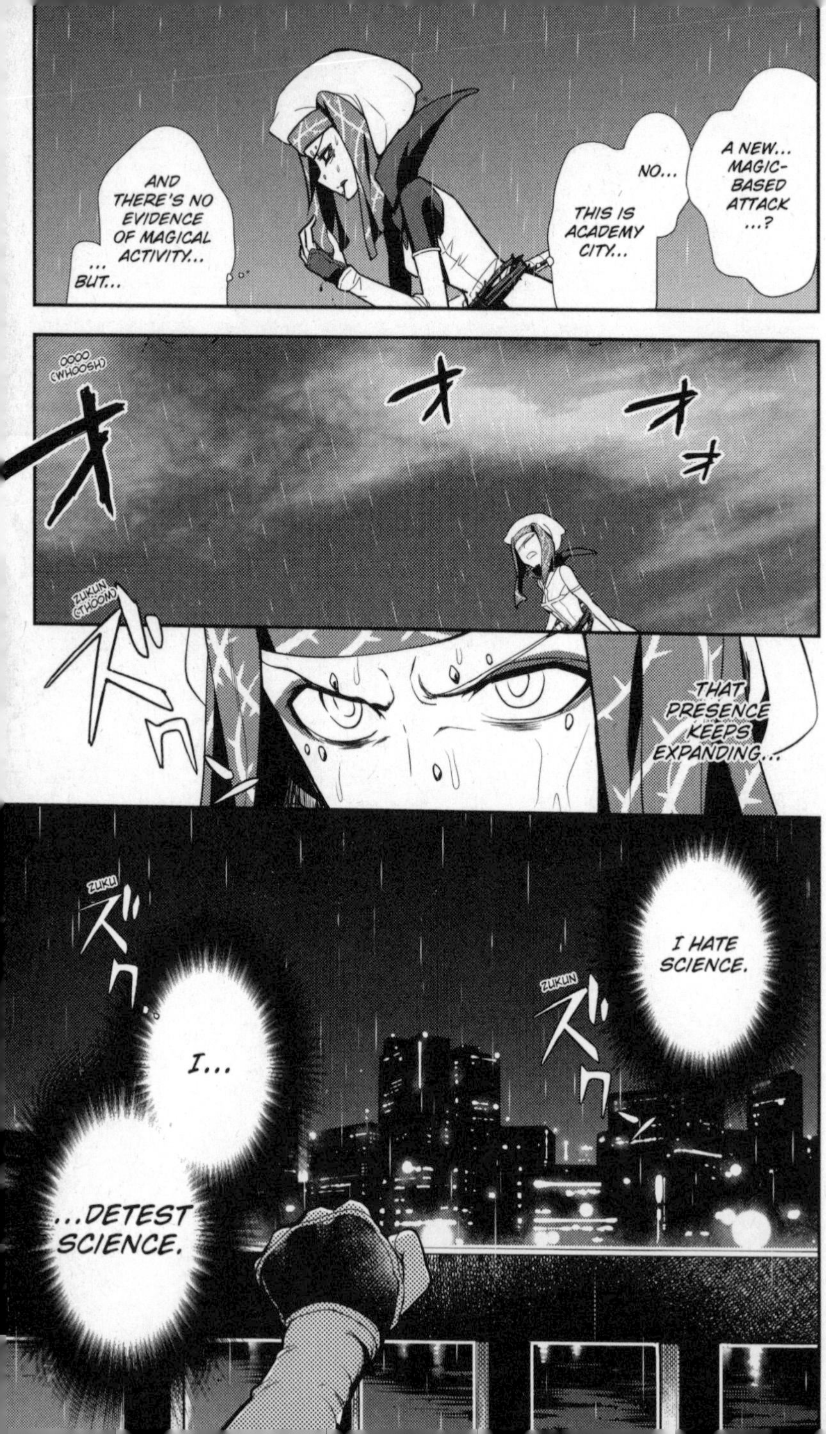
A NEW... MAGIC-BASED ATTACK ...?
NO...
THIS IS ACADEMY CITY...
AND THERE'S NO EVIDENCE OF MAGICAL ACTIVITY...
...BUT...
OOOO (WHOOSH)
THAT PRESENCE KEEPS EXPANDING...
ZUKUN (THOOM)
I HATE SCIENCE.
ZUKUN
ZUKU
I...
...DETEST SCIENCE.

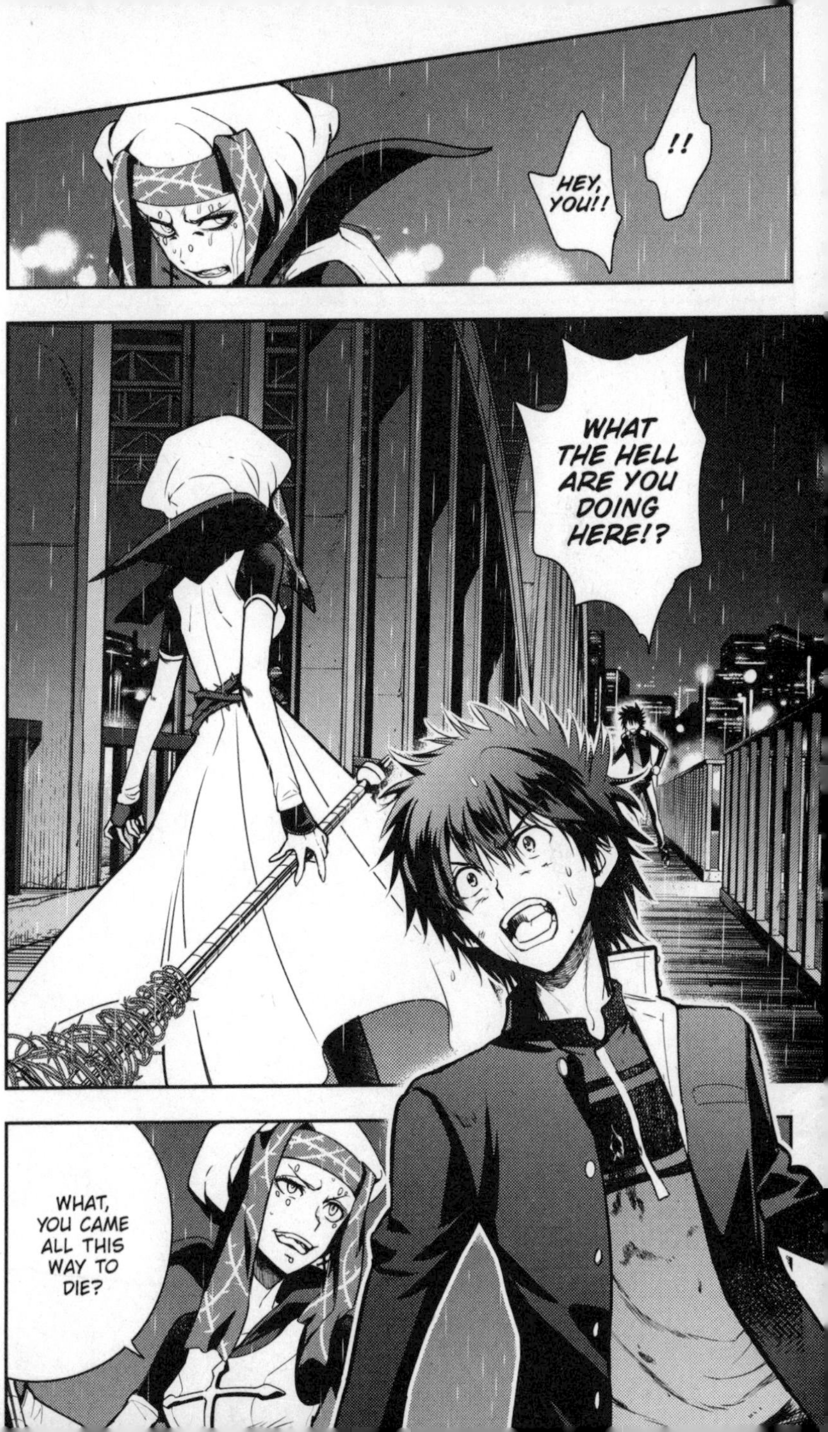
!!
HEY, YOU!!
WHAT THE HELL ARE YOU DOING HERE!?
WHAT, YOU CAME ALL THIS WAY TO DIE?

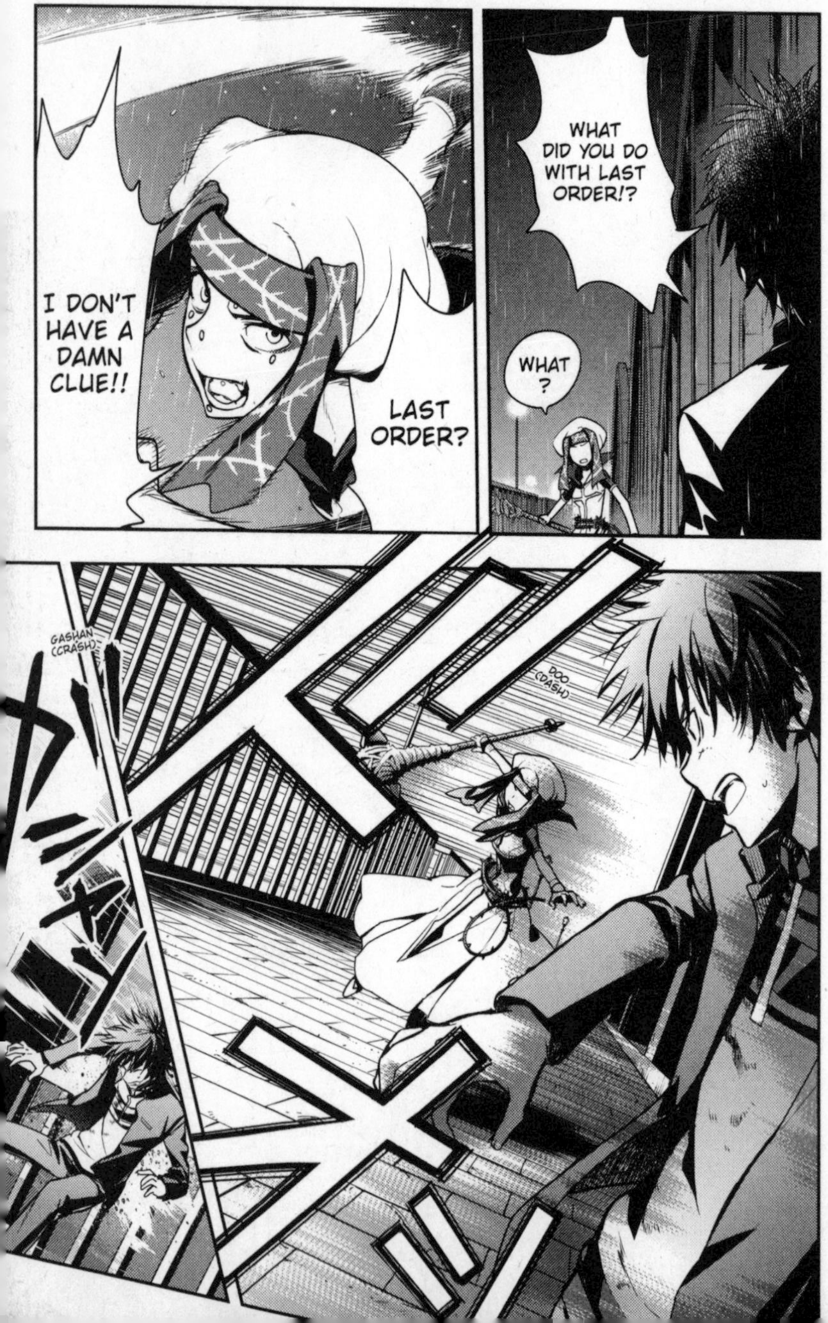
WHAT DID YOU DO WITH LAST ORDER!?
WHAT ?
LAST ORDER?
I DON'T HAVE A DAMN CLUE!!
DOO (DASH)
GASHAN (CRASH)

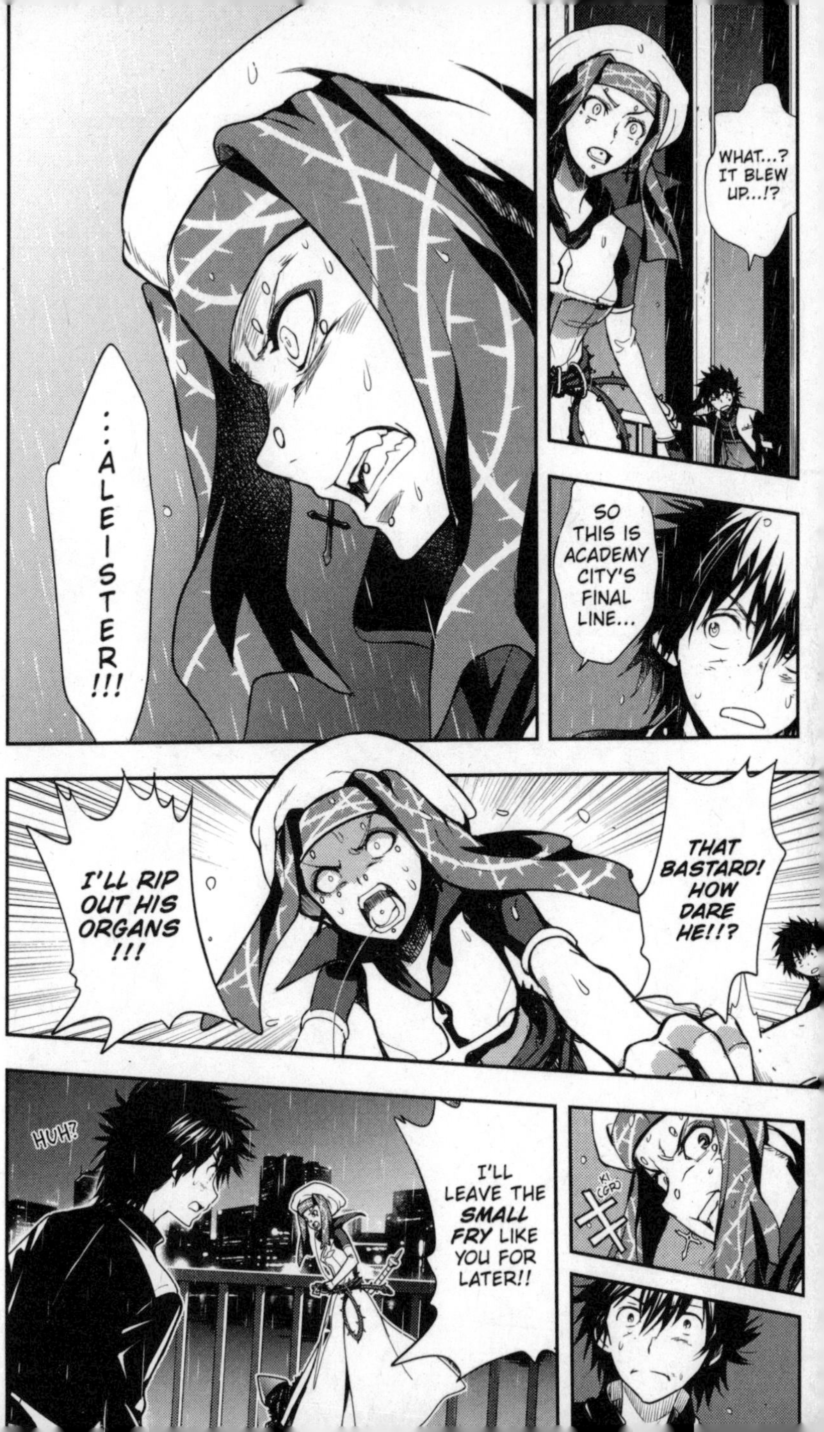
WHAT...? IT BLEW UP...!?
SO THIS IS ACADEMY CITY'S FINAL LINE...
...ALEISTER!!!
THAT BASTARD! HOW DARE HE!!?
I'LL RIP OUT HIS ORGANS!!!
KI GRI
I'LL LEAVE THE SMALL FRY LIKE YOU FOR LATER!!
HUH?

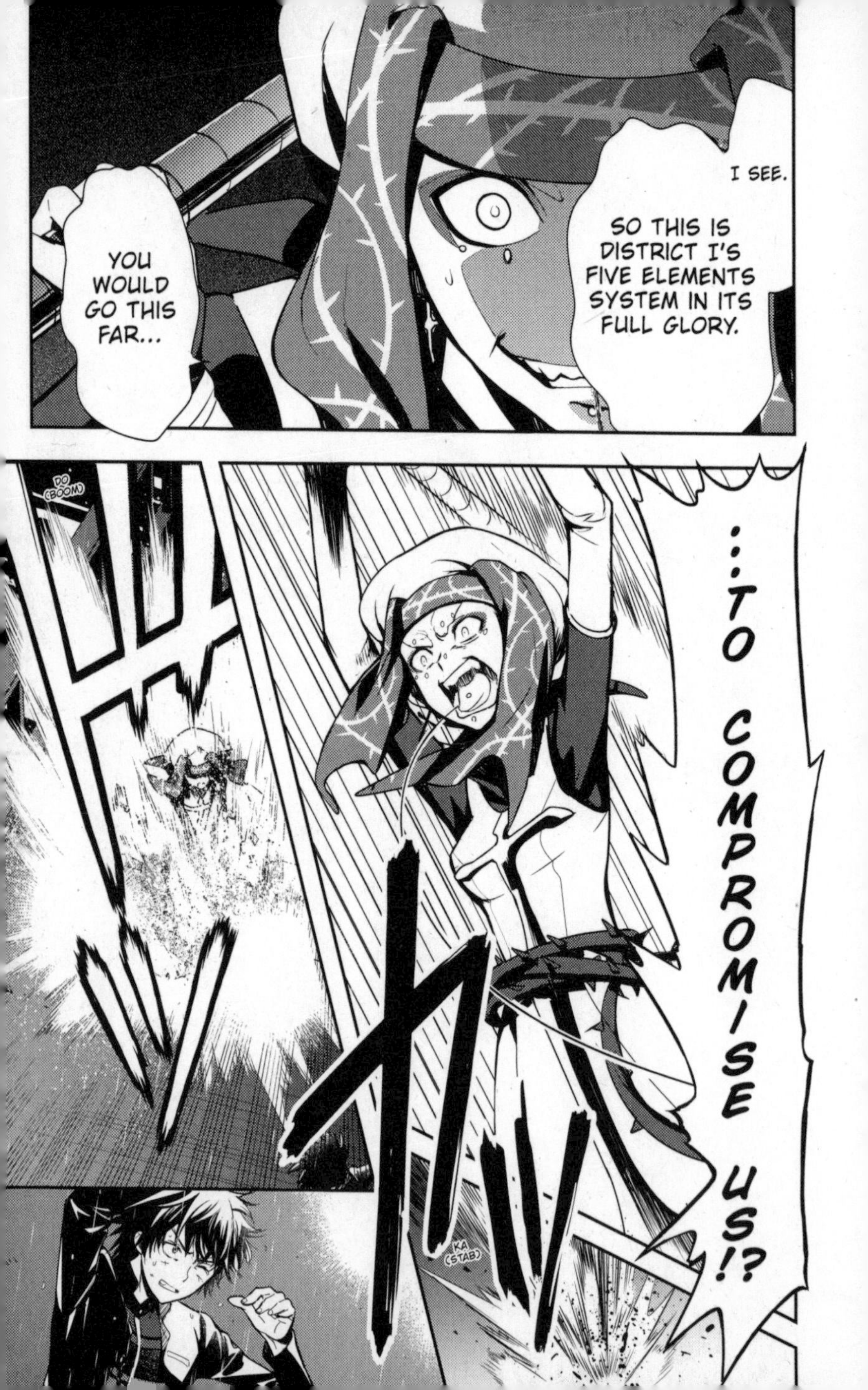
I SEE.
SO THIS IS DISTRICT I'S FIVE ELEMENTS SYSTEM IN ITS FULL GLORY.
YOU WOULD GO THIS FAR...
...TO COMPROMISE US!?
DO (BOOM)
KA (STAB)

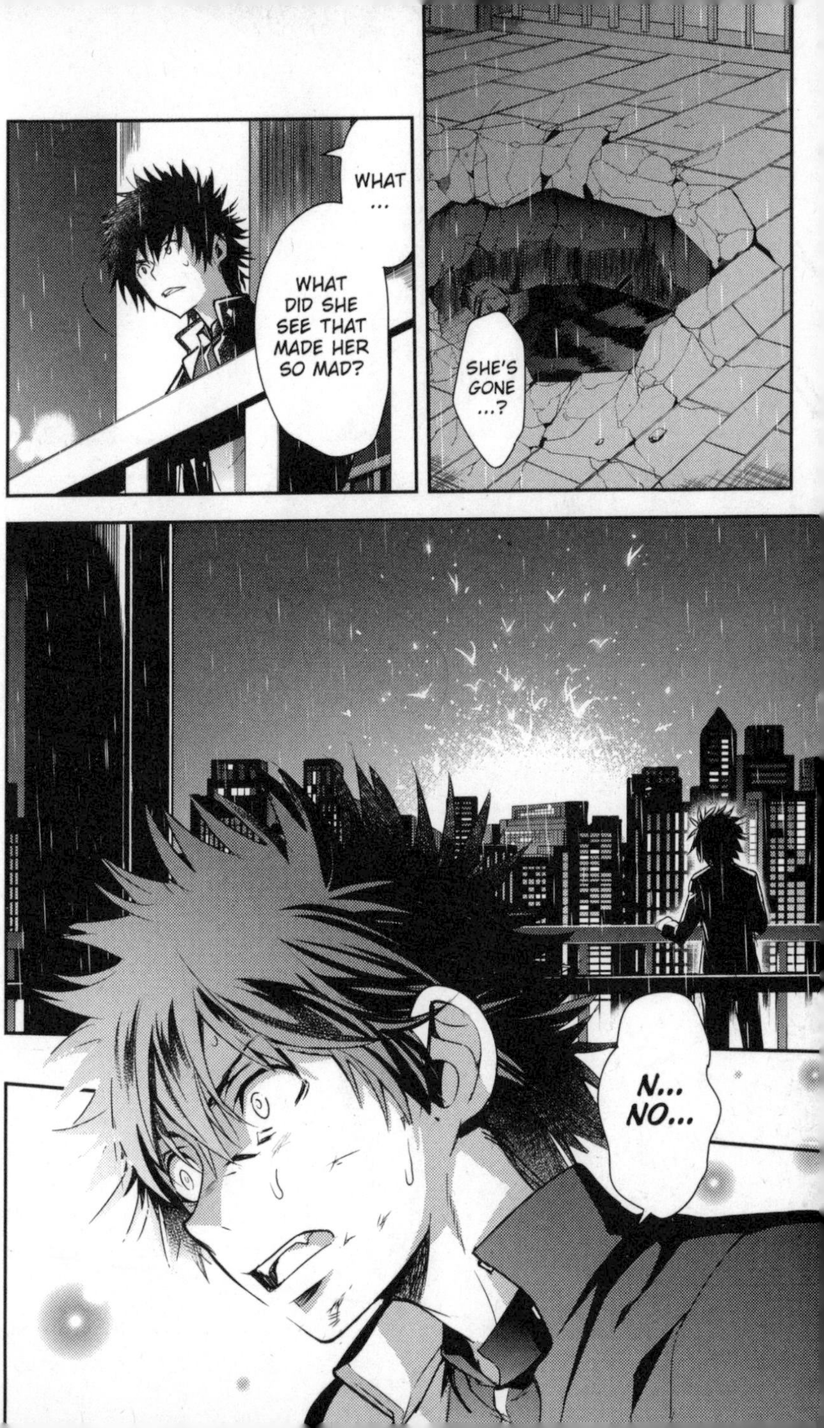
SHE'S GONE ...?
WHAT ...
WHAT DID SHE SEE THAT MADE HER SO MAD?
N... NO...

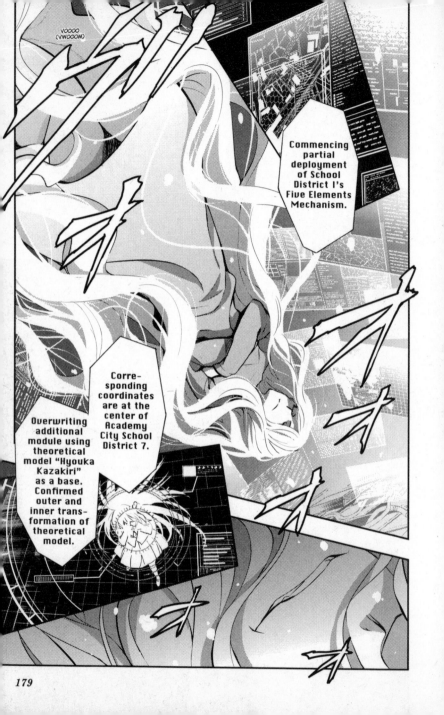

VOOOO
(VWOOOM)

Commencing partial deployment of School District 1's Five Elements Mechanism.

Corresponding coordinates are at the center of Academy City School District 7.

Overwriting additional module using theoretical model "Hyouka Kazakiri" as a base. Confirmed outer and inner transformation of theoretical model.

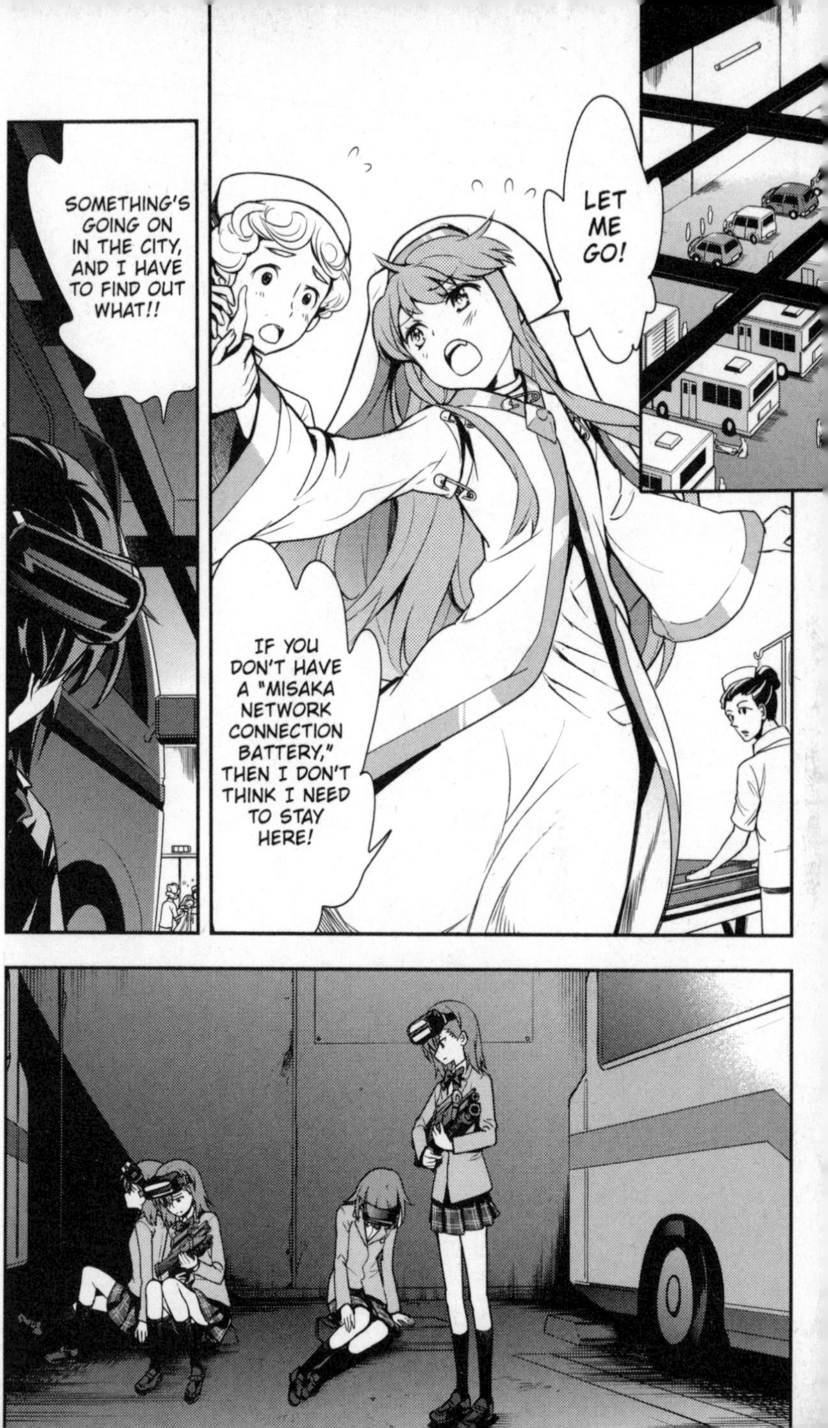
LET ME GO!
IF YOU DON'T HAVE A "MISAKA NETWORK CONNECTION BATTERY," THEN I DON'T THINK I NEED TO STAY HERE!
SOMETHING'S GOING ON IN THE CITY, AND I HAVE TO FIND OUT WHAT!!

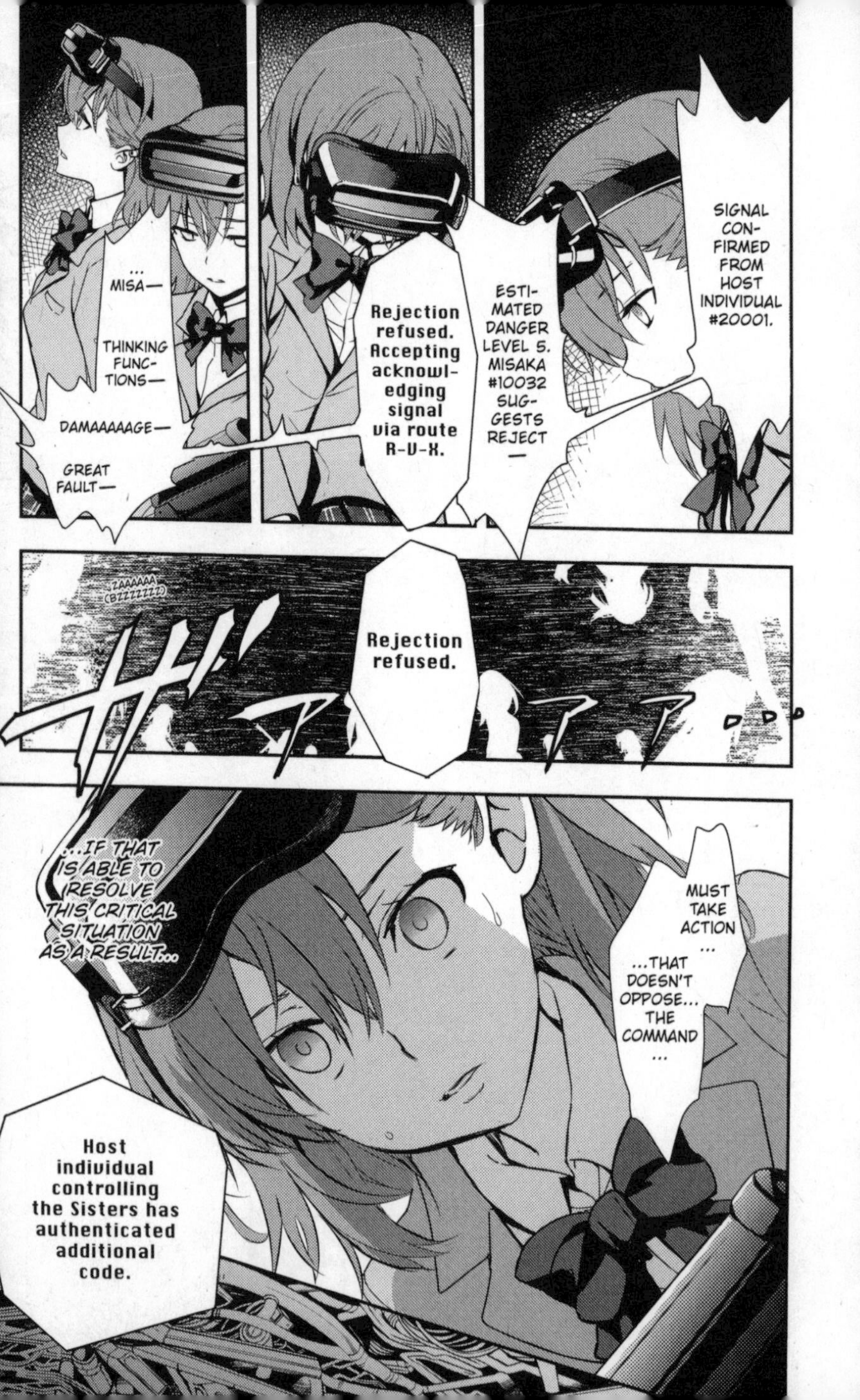
SIGNAL CONFIRMED FROM HOST INDIVIDUAL #20001.
ESTIMATED DANGER LEVEL 5. MISAKA #10032 SUGGESTS REJECT—
Rejection refused. Accepting acknowledging signal via route R-V-X.
...MISA—
THINKING FUNCTIONS—
DAMAAAAAGE—
GREAT FAULT—
Rejection refused.
ZAAAAAA (BZZZZZZZ)
MUST TAKE ACTION...
...THAT DOESN'T OPPOSE... THE COMMAND...
...IF THAT IS ABLE TO RESOLVE THIS CRITICAL SITUATION AS A RESULT...
Host individual controlling the Sisters has authenticated additional code.

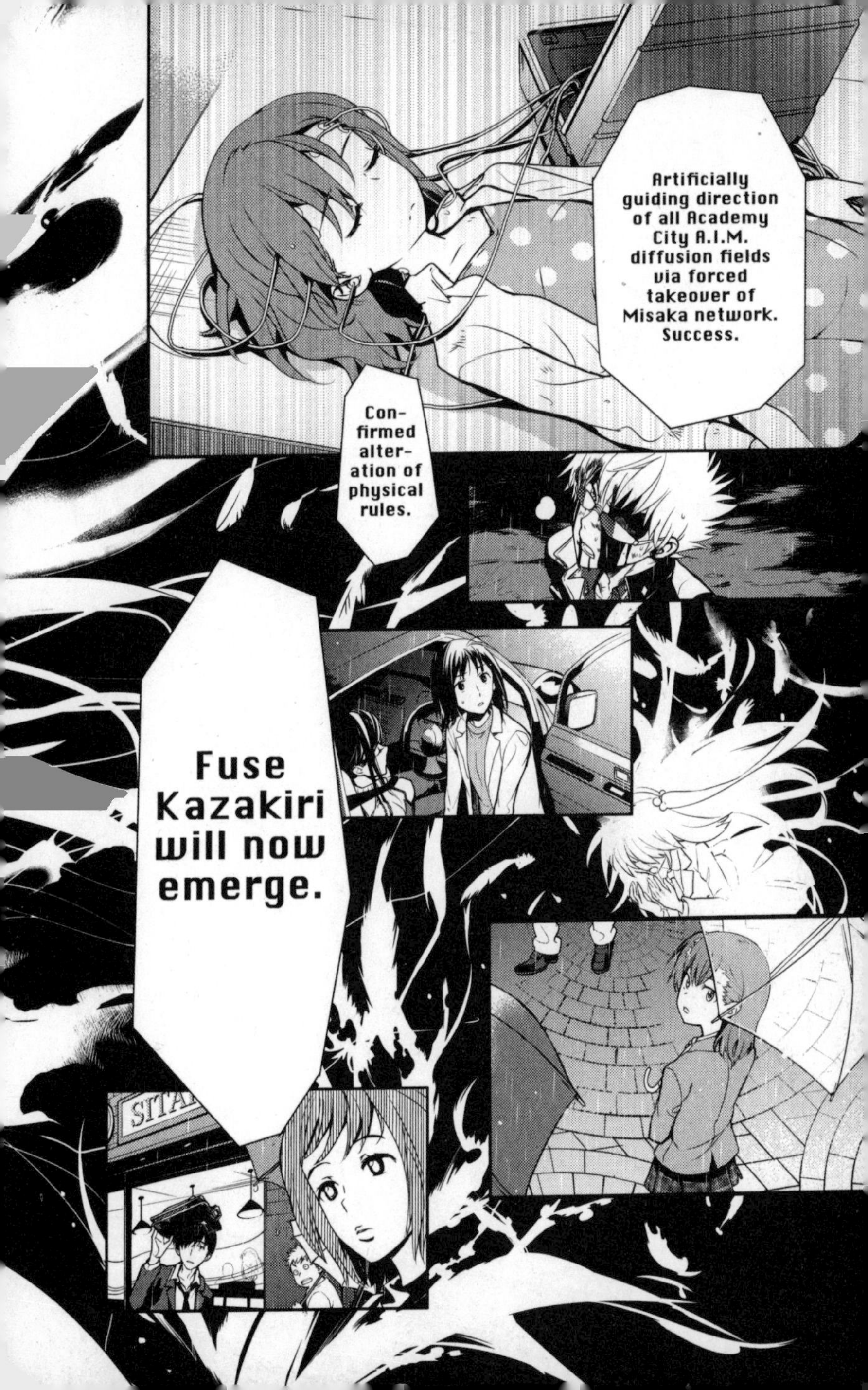
Artificially guiding direction of all Academy City A.I.M. diffusion fields via forced takeover of Misaka network. Success.
Confirmed alteration of physical rules.
Fuse Kazakiri will now emerge.

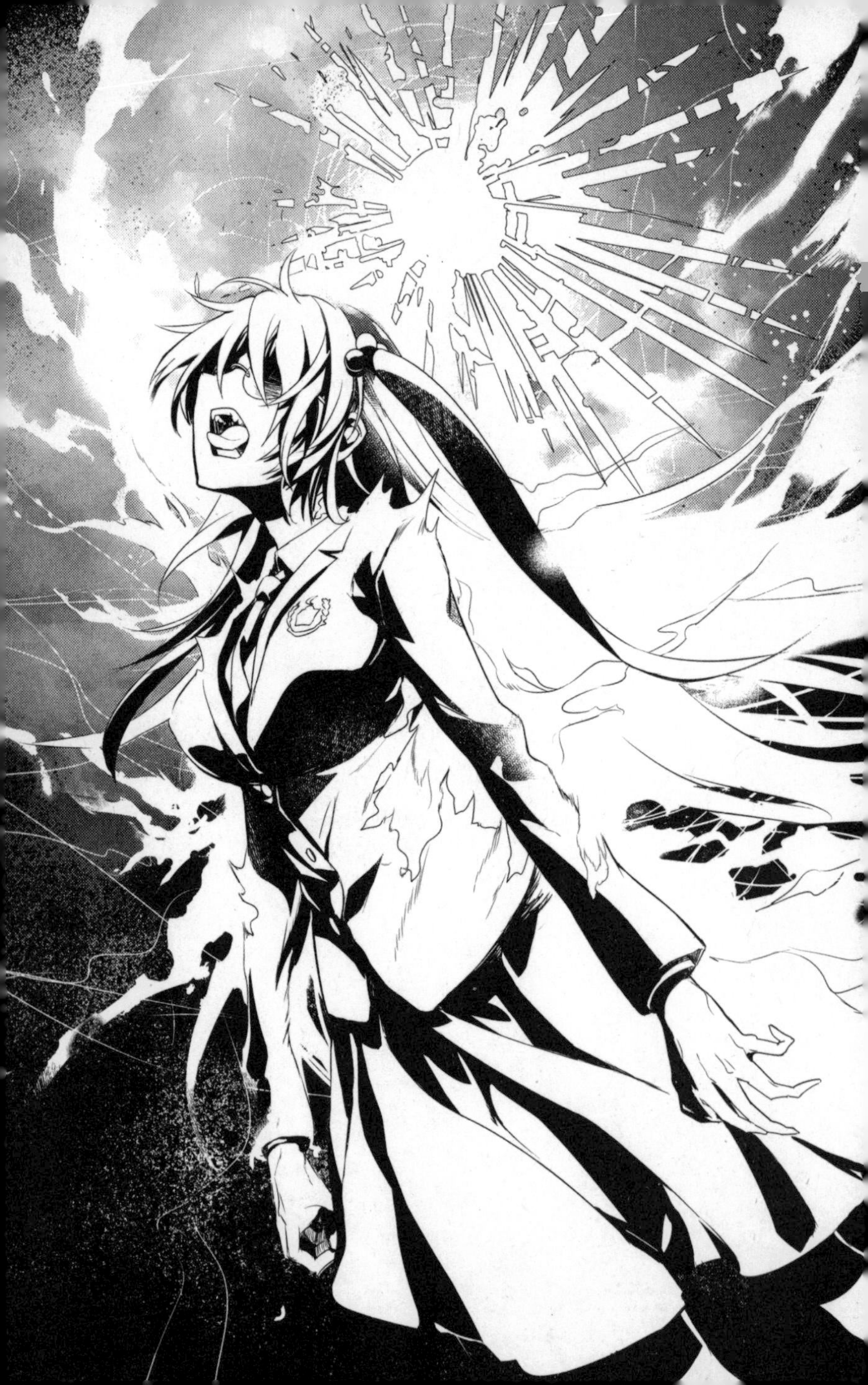

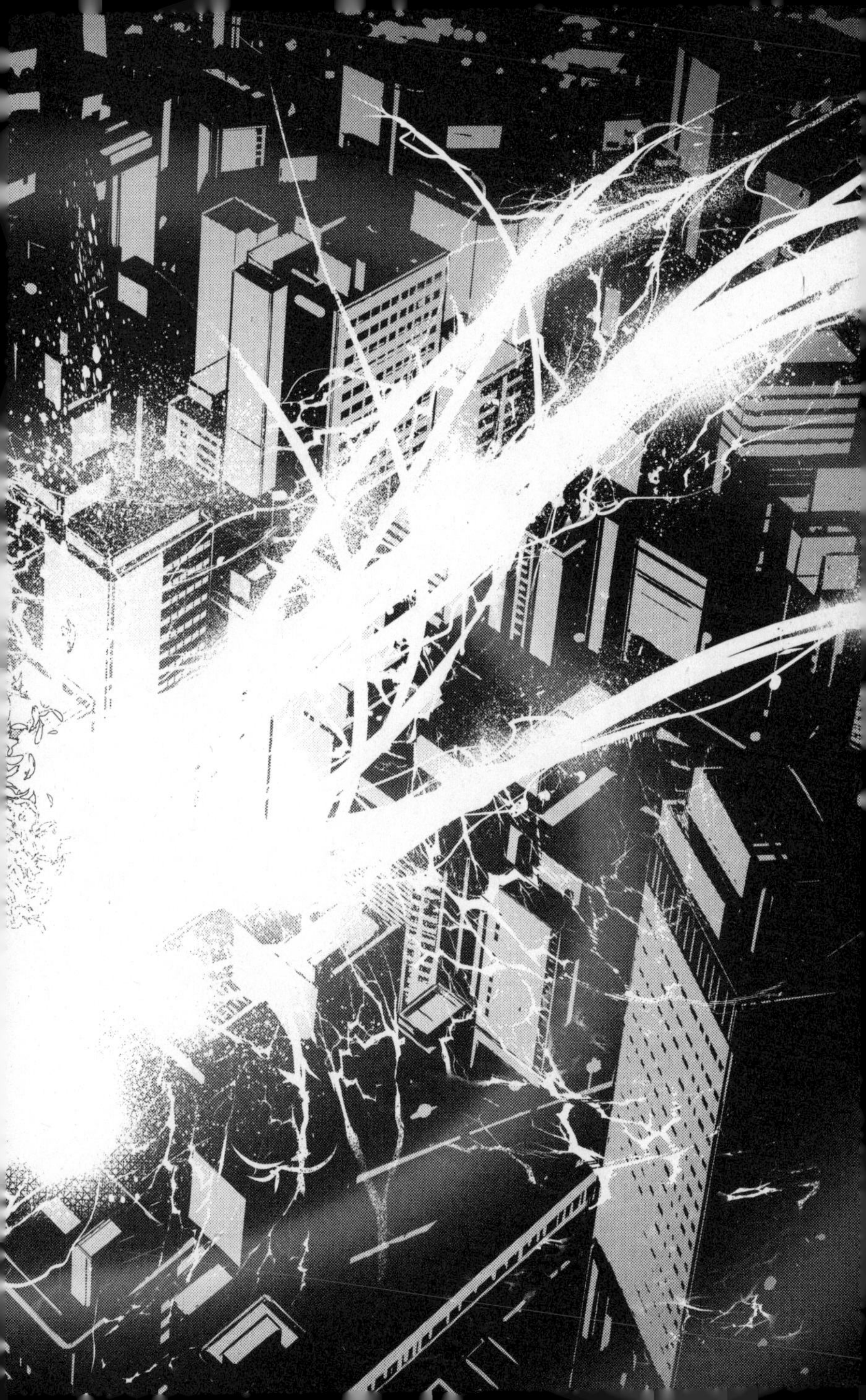

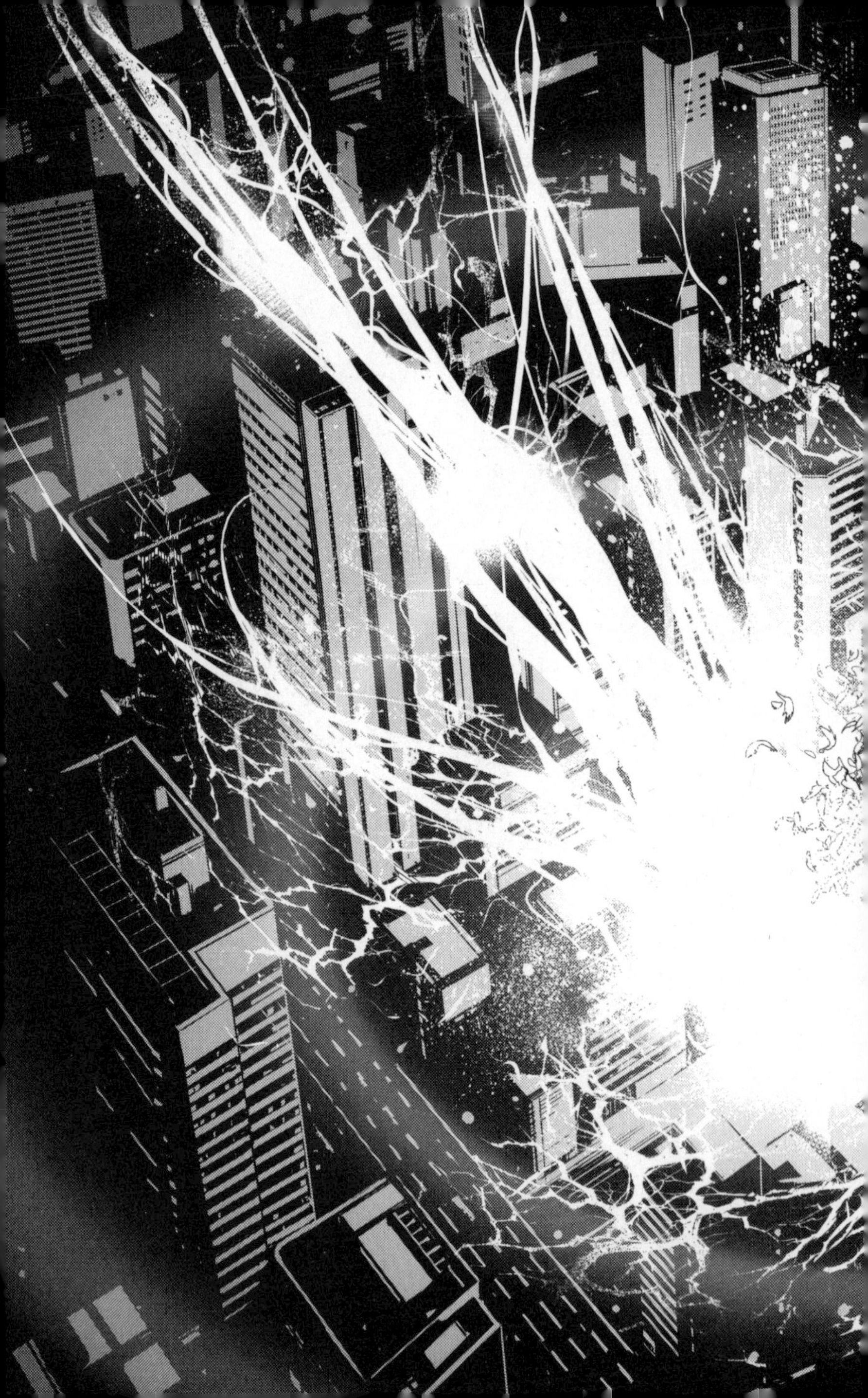

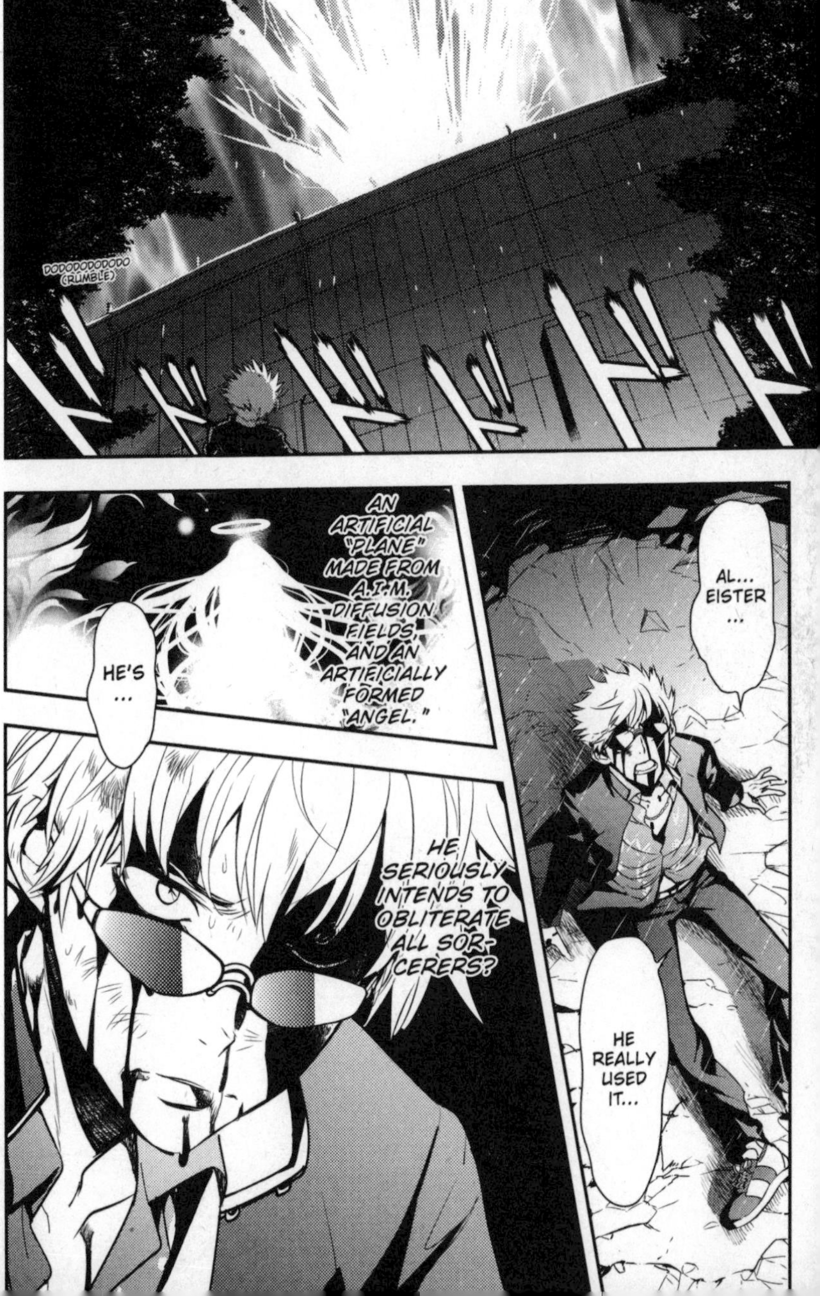
DODODODODODO
(RUMBLE)
AL... EISTER ...
HE REALLY USED IT...
AN ARTIFICIAL "PLANE" MADE FROM A.I.M. DIFFUSION FIELDS, AND AN ARTIFICIALLY FORMED "ANGEL."
HE'S ...
HE SERIOUSLY INTENDS TO OBLITERATE ALL SOR-CERERS?

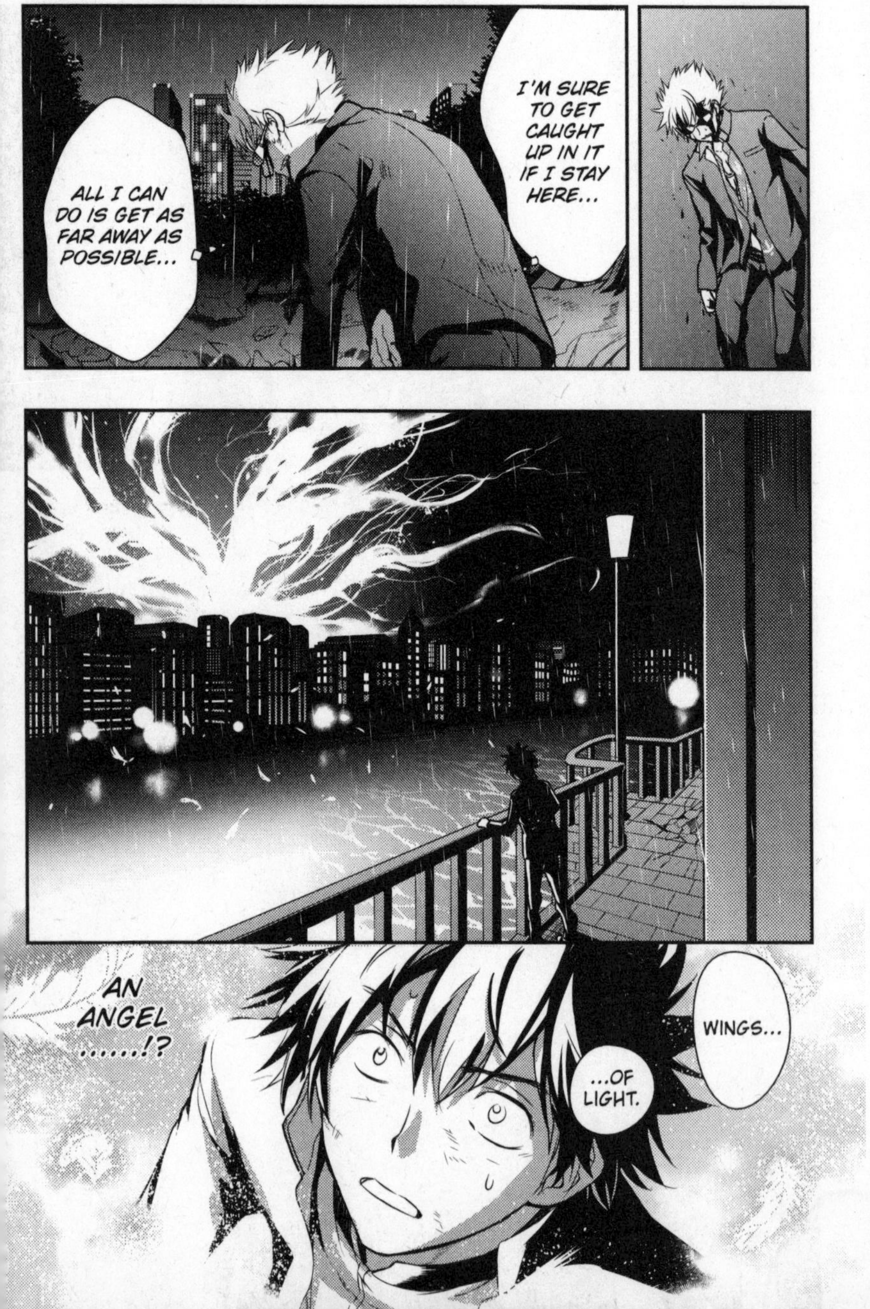
I'M SURE TO GET CAUGHT UP IN IT IF I STAY HERE...
ALL I CAN DO IS GET AS FAR AWAY AS POSSIBLE...
WINGS...
...OF LIGHT.
AN ANGEL ......!?

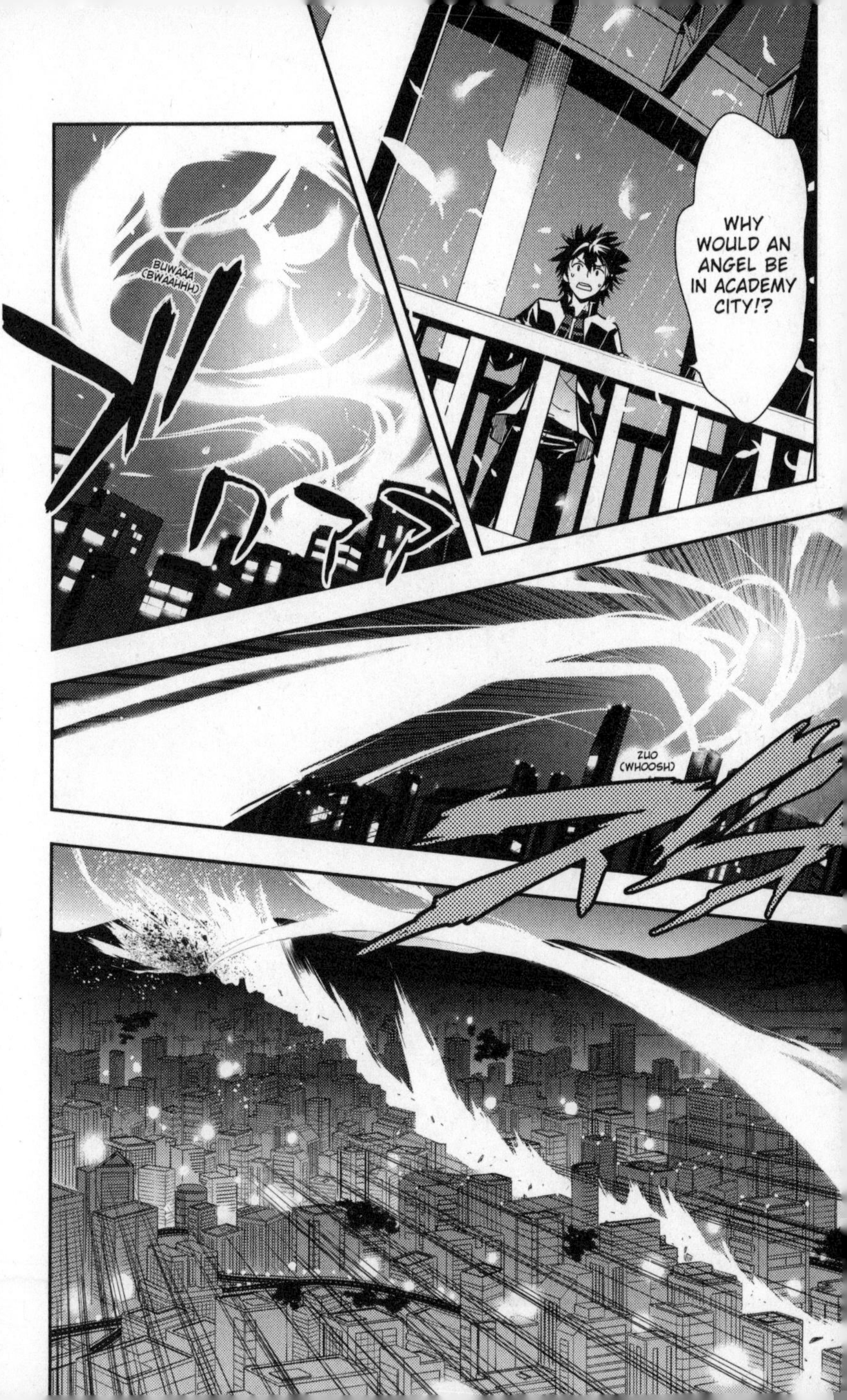
WHY WOULD AN ANGEL BE IN ACADEMY CITY!?
BUWAAA (BWAAHHH)
ZUO (WHOOSH)

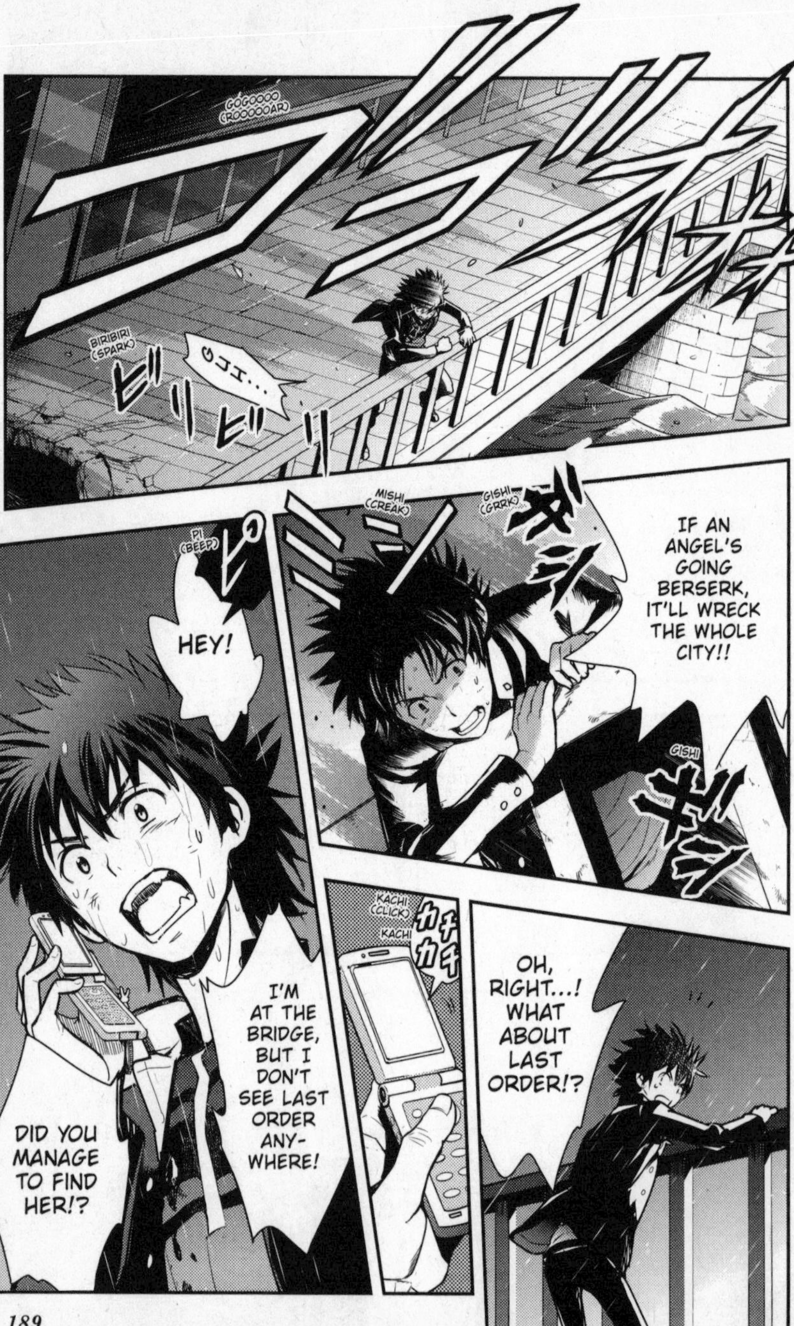
GOGOOOO
(ROOOOOAR)
BIRIBIRI
(SPARK)
GUH...
MISHI
(CREAK)
GISHI
(GRRK)
IF AN ANGEL'S GOING BERSERK, IT'LL WRECK THE WHOLE CITY!!
GISHI
OH, RIGHT...! WHAT ABOUT LAST ORDER!?
KACHI
(CLICK)
KACHI
PI
(BEEP)
HEY!
I'M AT THE BRIDGE, BUT I DON'T SEE LAST ORDER ANY-WHERE!
DID YOU MANAGE TO FIND HER!?

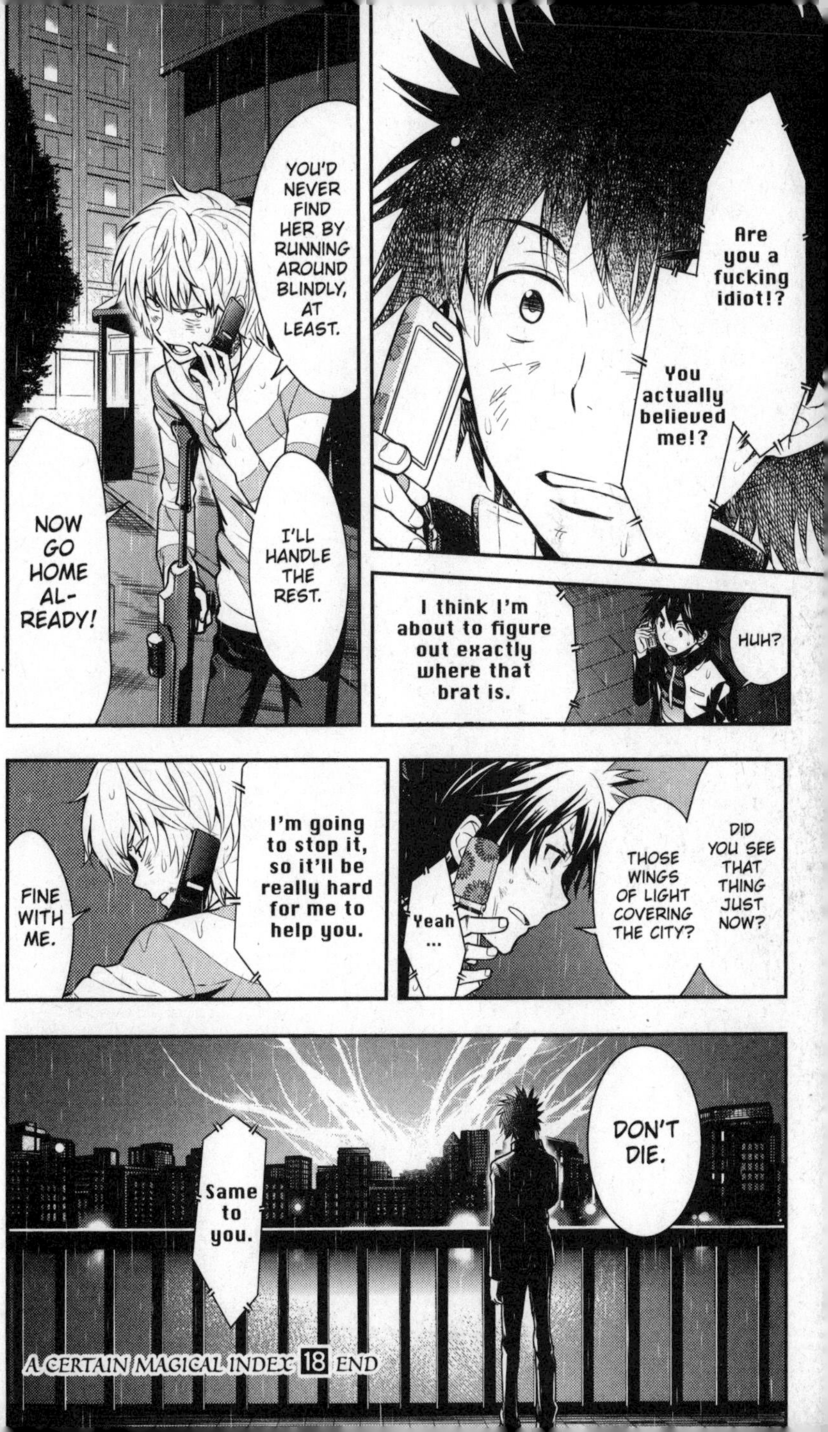
Are you a fucking idiot!?
You actually believed me!?
HUH?
I think I'm about to figure out exactly where that brat is.
YOU'D NEVER FIND HER BY RUNNING AROUND BLINDLY, AT LEAST.
I'LL HANDLE THE REST.
NOW GO HOME AL-READY!
DID YOU SEE THAT THING JUST NOW?
THOSE WINGS OF LIGHT COVERING THE CITY?
Yeah...
I'm going to stop it, so it'll be really hard for me to help you.
FINE WITH ME.
DON'T DIE.
Same to you.
A CERTAIN MAGICAL INDEX 18 END

A Certain Magical Index

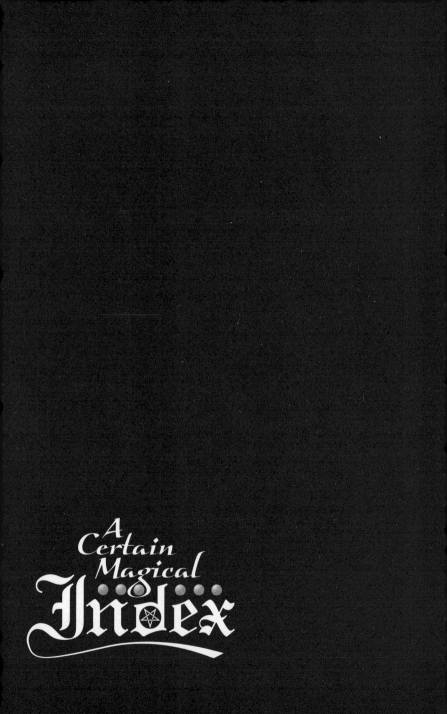

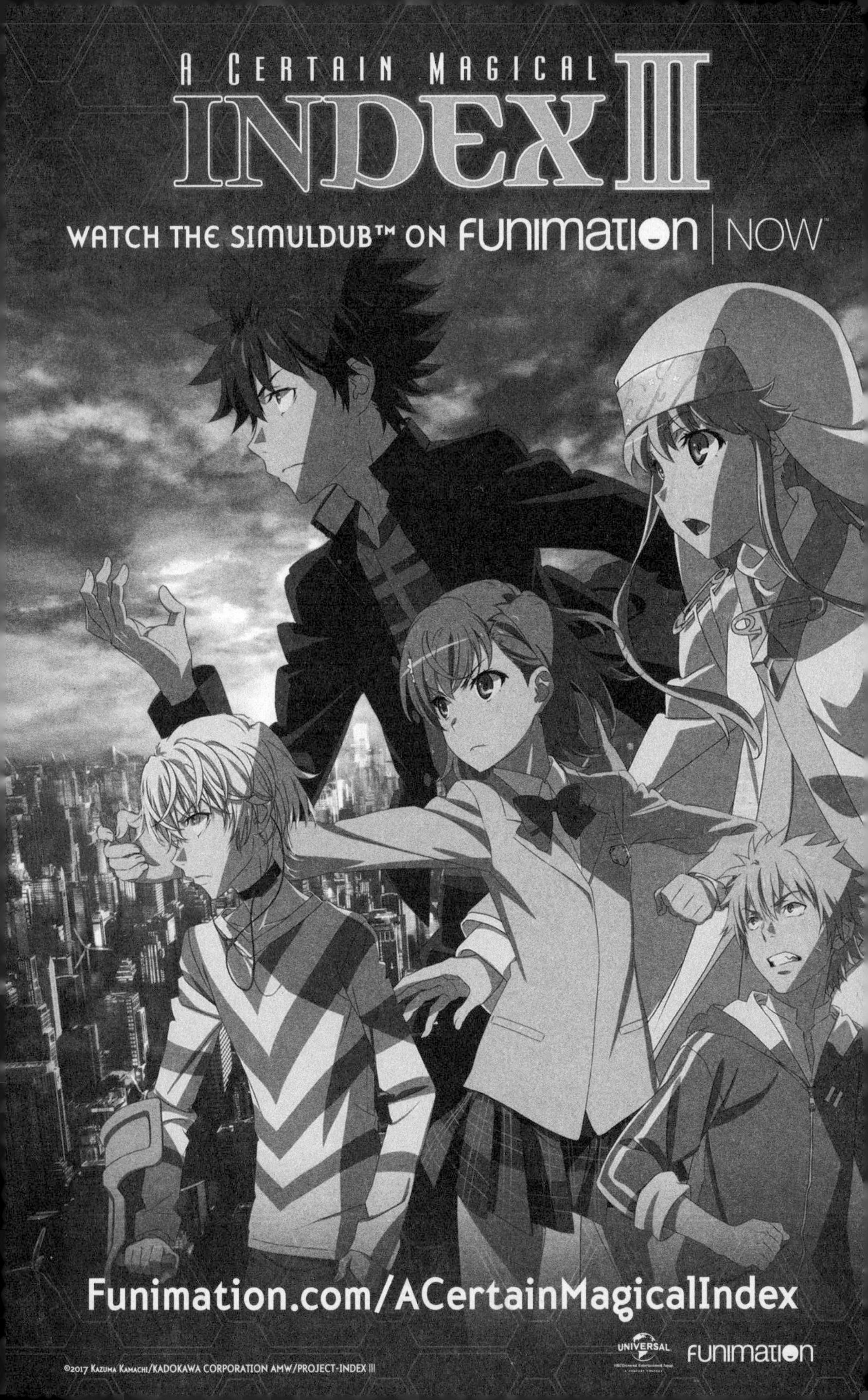
A Certain Magical
INDEX III
WATCH THE SIMULDUB™ ON FUNIMATION | NOW™
Funimation.com/ACertainMagicalIndex
UNIVERSAL
FUNIMATION
©2017 Kazuma Kamachi/KADOKAWA CORPORATION AMW/PROJECT-INDEX III

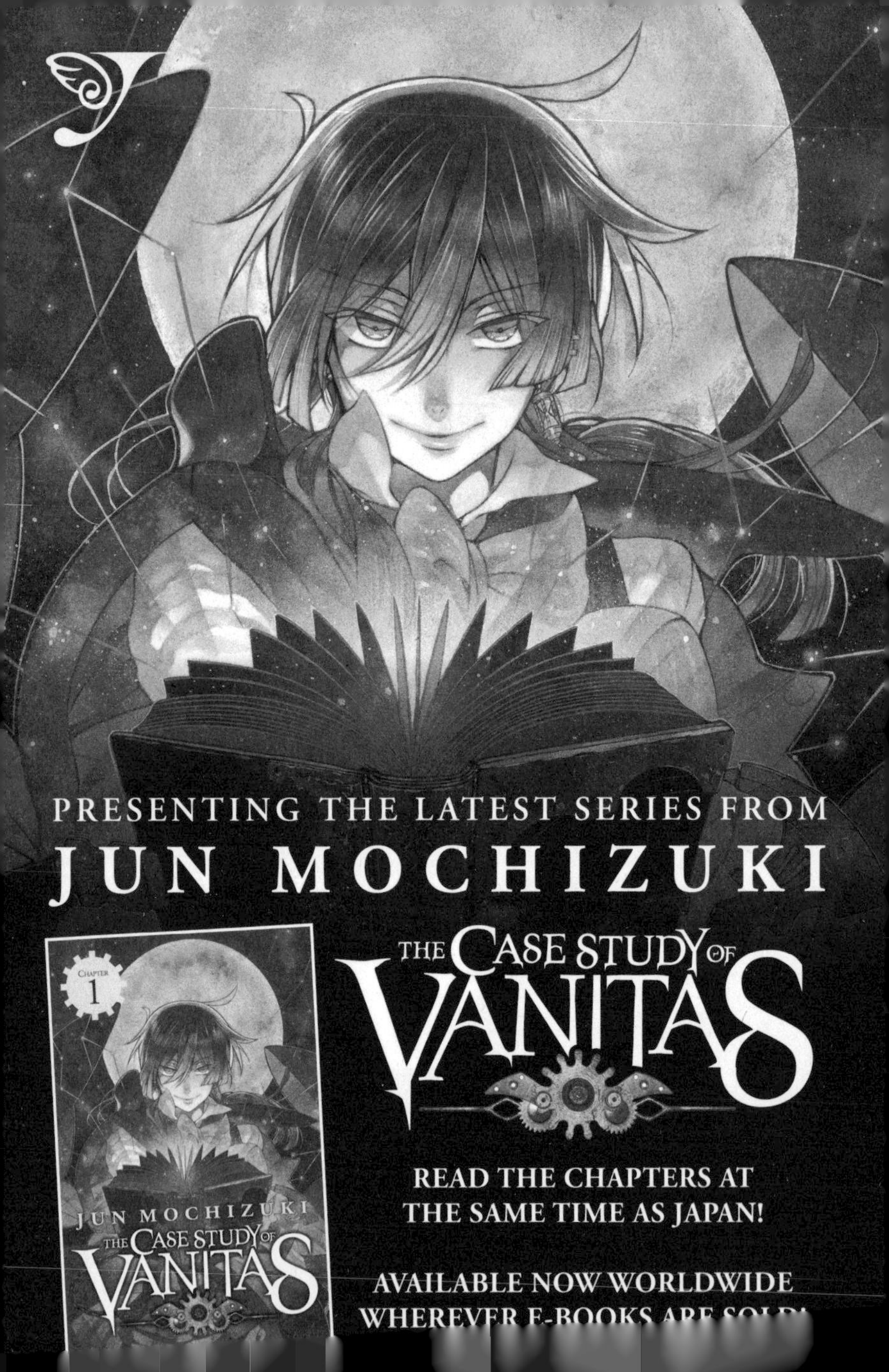
PRESENTING THE LATEST SERIES FROM
JUN MOCHIZUKI
CHAPTER 1
JUN MOCHIZUKI
THE CASE STUDY OF VANITAS
THE CASE STUDY OF VANITAS
READ THE CHAPTERS AT THE SAME TIME AS JAPAN!
AVAILABLE NOW WORLDWIDE WHEREVER E-BOOKS ARE SOLD!

INDEX ⑱

azuma Kamachi
yotaka Haimura
Chuya Kogino

Translation: Andrew Prowse

Lettering: Phil Christie

This book is a work of fiction. Names, characters, places, and incidents are the product of the author's imagination or are used fictitiously. Any resemblance to actual events, locales, or persons, living or dead, is coincidental.

TOARU MAJYUTSU NO INDEX Vol. 18
© 2016 Kazuma Kamachi
© 2016 Chuya Kogino / SQUARE ENIX CO., LTD.
Licensed by KADOKAWA CORPORATION ASCII MEDIA WORKS
First published in Japan in 2016 by SQUARE ENIX CO., LTD.
English translation rights arranged with SQUARE ENIX CO., LTD.
and Yen Press, LLC through Tuttle-Mori Agency, Inc.

English translation © 2019 by SQUARE ENIX CO., LTD.

Yen Press
150 West 30th Street, 19th Floor
New York, NY 10001

Visit us at yenpress.com
facebook.com/yenpress
twitter.com/yenpress
yenpress.tumblr.com
instagram.com/yenpress

D0447247

First Yen Press Edition: July 2019

Yen Press is an imprint of Yen Press, LLC.
The Yen Press name and logo are trademarks of Yen Press, LLC.

The publisher is not responsible for websites (or their content) that are not owned by the publisher.

Library of Congress Control Number: 2015373809

ISBN: 978-1-9753-5447-3 (paperback)

10 9 8 7 6 5 4 3 2 1

WOR

Printed in the United States of America